Starting Your Subchapter "S" Corporation

Starting Your Subchapter "S" Corporation

How to Build a Business the Right Way

Second Edition

Arnold S. Goldstein, Ph.D.

Robert L. Davidson, III

JOHN WILEY & SONS, INC.

New York · Chichester · Brisbane · Toronto · Singapore

This publication is designed to provide accurate and
authoritative information in regard to the subject
matter covered. It is sold with the understanding that
the publisher is not engaged in rendering legal, accounting,
or other professional service. If legal advice or other
expert assistance is required, the services of a competent
professional person should be sought. *From a Declaration
of Principles jointly adopted by a Committee of the
American Bar Association and a Committee of Publishers.*

Library of Congress Cataloging-in-Publication Data:

Goldstein, Arnold S.
  Starting your subchapter "S" corporation : how to build a business
the right way / by Arnold S. Goldstein and Robert L. Davidson III.—
2nd ed.
      p.   cm.
  Includes index.
  ISBN 0-471-57203-9 (cloth : alk. paper). —ISBN 0-471-57204-7
(pbk. : alk. paper)
  1. Subchapter S corporations—Taxation.   I. Davidson, Robert L.,
III. II. Title.
KF6491.G65 1992
346.73'066—dc20
[347.30666]   92-7752

Printed in the United States of America

10 9 8 7 6 5 4 3 2 1

PREFACE

Tens of thousands of businesses have elected to take advantage of the "S Corporation," sometimes known as the "S-Chapter Corporation" or "Subchapter S Corporation." The S Corporation became particularly popular with the passage of the 1986 Tax Reform Act where, for the first time, the individual tax rate was lower than the corporation tax rate. But, as you will see as you read and study this book, there are other advantages to be gained through S Corporation organization, not the least of which are lowest possible taxes coupled with the limited liability (the "corporate veil") of a regular corporation. This second edition is in response to the enthusiastic reception for the first edition and the need to stay abreast of recent changes in the tax law.

If your business is presently operated as a regular corporation, you will find all the needed information to quickly and conveniently convert it to an S Corporation. Conversely if you are planning to start a new business or presently operate an existing business under a proprietorship or partnership form of organization, this guide will help you set up an S Corporation by guiding you through the process of forming a regular corporation, which is a first step towards an S Corporation.

While the S Corporation offers many tax benefits there are also several disadvantages to an S Corporation; therefore, you should carefully review the pros and cons before deciding to become an S Corporation. Further, not all corporations can qualify for S Corporation status. For these reasons you should have your situation carefully analyzed by a qualified accountant or tax attorney if there is any question whether an S Corporation can best serve your needs.

Within this guide you will find both the information you need to determine how an S Corporation functions and what you must do to properly administer it and take advantage of its several significant benefits. You will also find forms you need to convert your present corporations to an S Corporation, to maintain your corporate records in full legal compliance, and to protect yourself, your corporation, and other shareholders with essential agreements.

This book will also answer your critical questions and many more in a clear, straightforward manner.

Setting up your own S Corporation is not as difficult as you might imagine. You will discover that as you read these pages and gain the knowledge you need.

Delray Beach, Florida
Princeton, New Jersey
July 1992

ARNOLD S. GOLDSTEIN, PH.D.
ROBERT L. DAVIDSON, III

ABOUT THE AUTHORS

Dr. Arnold S. Goldstein is president of the Florida consulting firm of The Garrett Group. He is a popular writer on management topics. His prior books include *The Complete Guide to Buying and Selling a Business* and *Starting on a Shoestring* (both published by John Wiley & Sons).

Dr. Goldstein holds the degrees of Bachelor of Science, Master of Business Administration, Doctor of Jurisprudence, Master of Laws, and Doctor of Philosophy, and is a member of the Massachusetts and Federal Bars and numerous professional and civic organizations.

Robert L. Davidson, III, is an attorney and publications consultant in Princeton, New Jersey, where he specializes in author-publisher contracts and small business law.

He is author, co-author, editor, and co-editor of nine books, the most recent of which is *Contracting Your Services* (John Wiley & Sons).

Mr. Davidson holds the degrees of Bachelor and Master of Science in Chemical Engineering, and the law degree of Juris Doctor. He is a member of the New Jersey and Federal Bars and numerous professional and honor societies.

CONTENTS

1 CHOOSING THE FORM OF ORGANIZATION

OVERVIEW

Most people when starting a business consider the various types of business organization available to them. An individual venturing into business has the choice of operating his or her business as a sole proprietorship or corporation. If two or more people are going into business together they also have a choice—a partnership or corporation form of organization.

Whether to incorporate or to conduct a business in some other form—a sole proprietorship or a partnership—involves many considerations. If you are currently doing business you will have the demands on your time of running a business that often prevents you from taking time out to carefully consider your options, assess your situation, and plan. Even if you are not yet in business, but are planning to start a new enterprise, do not rush into business without first carefully considering the best form of organization. Many factors go into the decision of selecting the best structure of a business enterprise. Some of the more important factors in determining what type of business entity you should use include:

1. Liability and personal exposure.
2. Costs including filing fees.
3. Management structure and whether it needs to be centralized or dispersed.
4. The available methods of raising capital.
5. The ability to attract and keep key personnel through various fringe benefits or participations such as stock options.
6. Tax considerations.

1

The three basic forms of business entity—individual or sole proprietorship, partnership, and corporation—each offer their own unique advantages and disadvantages.

SOLE PROPRIETORSHIPS

A sole proprietorship is a business that is owned by an individual who is solely responsible for all aspects of the business. The owner is personally responsible for all debts of the business even in excess of the amount invested.

When an individual forms a business and operates it in his or her own name (or a trade name), that person runs the risk of having all of his or her personal assets exposed to creditors of the business. So, for example, if an employee accidentally injures a customer or some other person, the owner of the business stands liable for the injury. Even if there is insurance coverage, the possibility always exists that liability may exceed the coverage provided by the policy.

Other drawbacks exist. If the sole proprietor becomes ill or dies, the business he or she has developed immediately loses much of its value. Moreover, the business terminates with the death of the proprietor. This will create added problems in disposing of the business.

The advantages of a sole proprietorship include:

1. Low start up costs since legal and filing fees are at a minimum. However, many states and cities require at least a filing with the county clerk, especially if a fictitious business name is adopted.

2. Greatest freedom from regulation.

3. Owner is in direct control.

4. Minimum working capital requirements.

5. Tax advantages to owners of small businesses.

6. All profits inure to the owner.

The disadvantages include:

1. Unlimited liability. The proprietor is responsible for the full amount of business debts no matter how incurred, which means that his or her personal property may be taken to cover debts of the business.

2. Unstable business life, since the sole owner's death or illness would terminate the business.

3. Difficulty in raising capital and in obtaining long-term financing.

PARTNERSHIPS

A partnership is a legal entity that is jointly owned by two or more individuals (although in some cases partners may also be corporations or other entities). As in the sole proprietorship, the owners are personally liable for all debts of the firm unless a special type of partnership, the limited partnership, is set up. Limited partnerships are very complex legal structures, and still must have at least one partner who has unlimited liability. Even partnership agreements for regular partnerships can be quite complex.

The partnership shares many of the benefits and drawbacks of the sole proprietorship. Each partner is personally liable for all of the business debts. The partnership relation comes to an end whenever any partner decides he or she no longer wants to be part of the business or if a partner dies.

Other drawbacks include the difficulty of obtaining new partners, particularly if they do not share profits on an equal basis.

As in the case of the sole proprietorship, the partnership is not a taxable entity. Its profits, gains, losses, and credits "pass through" to its partners.

The advantages of a partnership include:

1. Ease of formation (although more complicated than the sole proprietorship).

2. Low start up costs, especially since there usually are fewer filing fees and franchise taxes.

3. Limited outside regulation, unless the type of business itself is one that is in a regulated industry.

4. Broader management base than a sole proprietorship and a more flexible management structure than the corporation.

5. Possible tax advantages, since it avoids the double taxation of corporations, and because income can be taxed at personal income rates. Naturally, the personal income situations of the partners could also make this a disadvantage.

6. Additional sources of capital, and leverage by adding limited and special partners.

7. Each partner can bind all of the copartners, and, in the absence of restrictions in the partnership agreement, may terminate the partnership.

8. The duration of the entity can be limited to a stated time, or can continue indefinitely by amendment.

The disadvantages of a partnership include:

1. Unlimited liability of at least one partner and, except in limited partnership situations, all the partners have unlimited liability. The personal assets of each of the general partners are available to satisfy partnership debts.

2. The life of a partnership is unstable since changing partners by adding new ones or by death or departure of partners causes the partnership to terminate.

3. Obtaining large sums of capital is relatively difficult as the financing cannot be obtained from the public through a stock offering.

4. The acts of just one partner, even unauthorized acts in many cases, bind all the partners.

5. An individual partnership interest cannot be easily sold or disposed.

6. Most tax supported fringe benefits like pension and profit-sharing arrangements available only to corporations are unavailable to partnerships.

CORPORATIONS

A corporation is a business that is formed and authorized by law to act as a single entity, although it is constituted and owned by one or more persons. It is legally endowed with rights and responsibilities and has a life of its own independent of the owners and operators. It has been defined by the U.S. Supreme Court as "an artificial being, invisible, intangible, and existing only in contemplation of the law."

The most significant feature of a corporation is its ability to shield its shareholders from personal liability. The shareholder is not liable for the debts of the business. Except in cases of fraud, the shareholders maximum risk is the amount of money he or she invests in it.

Second, the corporate form of organization also makes it easier to attract additional investors.

Third, the corporation has perpetual life. The death or disability of a shareholder has no effect on the continued existence of the corporation.

The advantages of a corporation include:

1. Limited liability, that is, the owners are liable for debts and obligations of the corporation only to the extent of their investment in the corporation, with the exception that they can be personally liable for certain types of taxes such as payroll taxes that have been withheld from the employees paychecks but not paid over to the Internal Revenue Service (IRS), as well as state sales taxes. If the business fails or loses a lawsuit, the general creditors cannot attach the owners homes, cars, and other personal property.

2. Capital can be raised more easily than in other forms of ownership. This does not mean, however, that a new corporation can easily sell stock. In the first place, the sale of stock is highly regulated by both federal and state governments and obtaining bank loans for a fledgling business may

be no easier for a new corporation than for a partnership or proprietorship.

3. Ownership is more easily transferable and this includes transferring shares to family members as gifts or otherwise, as well as selling your interest to some other person; however, in many small corporations it is advisable to put restrictions on the transfer of shares, especially if the persons owning and working in the business must be able to work closely together. This is generally done in the form of a stockholders' agreement.

4. Since the corporation is an independent legal entity it has a life of its own or continuous existence. It does not cease just because one of the owners dies or wishes to retire.

5. There is centralized management that usually rests with the board of directors and is exercised by the officers.

6. As a legal entity it can enter into contracts and sue and be sued, and the consent and signature of the owners is not necessary.

7. Corporations have a built-in impetus to increase the capital by reinvesting it, since salaries are normally set at the beginning of the year. In addition, surplus earnings can be set aside for a future date, although there are federal tax penalties if these surpluses exceed certain amounts.

8. Many companies offer discounts to corporations, an indication that they favor corporate accounts.

9. Retirement funds such as Keogh, defined-contribution plans, money-purchase plans, and other profit-sharing, pension, and stock option plans offer greater benefits to corporations.

The disadvantages of a corporation include:

1. It is subject to more governmental regulations than partnerships and sole proprietorships.

2. It may be a more expensive and complex form of business to organize.

3. Recordkeeping requirements can be very extensive.

4. Operating across state lines can be complicated because of the need of corporations to "qualify to do business" in states where they are not incorporated. This is explained in greater detail later.

5. Ending the corporate existence, and in many cases even changing some of the structure if it requires an amendment to the certificate of incorporation, can be more complicated and costly than for partnerships and proprietorships.

There is one more drawback to a regular corporation (commonly referred to as a C Corporation): The corporation is a person for tax purposes. This means that if it has a profit it must pay a tax on the profits whether the profits were retained by the corporation or distributed to stockholders as dividends.

However, if the corporation had a loss, the loss does not work to the benefit of the shareholders. At most the loss can be saved and applied against corporate profits in future years. Yet if the corporation has a profit distributed to shareholders as dividends, they are taxed a second time as dividends to the shareholders who receive the dividends.

That, of course, is the one traditional drawback of a corporation—the double taxation on profits and dividends. And it is for that reason that so many businesspeople have selected proprietorships or partnerships despite their serious disadvantages of unlimited liability.

But with the passage of the Tax Reform Act of 1986 and lowered corporate tax rates, many more people are discovering the very best form of organization is the S Corporation because only this form of organization offers the many advantages of a corporation with the favorable tax treatment afforded the proprietorship or partnership.

2 | WHY AN S CORPORATION?

OVERVIEW

The S Corporation combines what is generally considered the best of all possible worlds: it provides the limitations on liability associated with incorporation and the "pass through" taxation of a partnership or proprietorship (i.e., single, not double taxation).

An S Corporation is a corporation that, for most tax purposes, is treated as if it is a partnership or proprietorship. That means it is not a tax-paying entity. Instead, the S Corporation is viewed only as a financial conduit. Its income, deductions, credits, and losses are passed through to its shareholders who pay whatever tax is due. If, at the end of the year, your S Corporation earns a profit, it does not pay any taxes on that profit. Instead, the profit is recognized as your income and you pay the tax.

On the other hand, if you formed a regular corporation, the profits of that business would be taxed *twice*. First, the corporation would pay a corporate tax on the profit, then when that after-tax profit is distributed to you as a shareholder, you would pay a hefty income tax on it as dividend income. That is what is meant when referring to the *double taxation* imposed on corporate profits.

Those benefits become significantly more important with Congress' enactment of the Tax Reform Act of 1986, which added a vital new incentive for considering S incorporation. Prior to that date, the maximum tax rate for individuals was 50 percent—4 percent higher than the 46 percent corporation tax rate.

Under the 1986 Tax Reform Act, however, a reverse situation exists. The maximum tax rates for individuals is *6 percent lower* for individuals (28 percent) than for corporations (34 percent). That means that if you form a regular corporation and it has a profit, the profit will be taxed at a maximum rate of 34 percent; whatever is left can be distributed to you as a dividend and can be taxed again at the maximum individual rate of 28 percent. Had you formed an S Corporation, that profit would have been taxed only once, and then at the lower, individual rates.

With this overview of the major benefits of an S Corporation, we can summarize them as:

1. No double taxation.
2. Personal deductions of corporate losses.
3. Lower tax rates.
4. Tax savings on sale of corporate assets.

SINGLE TAXATION AND LOWER TAX RATES

To see how much an S Corporation can actually save in taxes let's use some actual numbers.

Assume your business operates as a regular corporation and earns an annual profit of $100,000, which will be taxed at a flat rate of 34 percent. Based on current tax rates, your corporate and personal taxes on the $100,000 would be $44,323. We calculate that by first deducting $22,250 for corporate taxes. This leaves the corporation with $77,750 to distribute to you as dividend income. If you and your spouse file jointly, your tax on the $77,750 is $22,073. This means that between you and the corporation you spent approximately 45 cents on every dollar for taxes!

Now let's assume you formed an S Corporation. That $100,000 in corporate profits would be taxed only once—to you. We do not have to deduct a corporate tax because as an S Corporation there is no corporate tax (federal). Therefore you would pay a personal tax of $28,293 on the $100,000 leaving you approximately $16,000 more after all tax payments. Of course, the actual tax savings will vary based on the amount of profits earned by your corporation and your personal tax situation. However, the combination of one tax instead of two coupled with lower personal tax rate ensures lower taxes if you choose an S Corporation form of organization.

Tax Note:
Remember: With an S Corporation you are taxed on corporate earnings whether you take the earnings as dividends or retain the earnings in the corporation. With a regular C Corporation you do not personally pay taxes on corporate earnings unless first paid to you as dividends. Therefore, the actual tax savings in a given year will depend on the portion of earnings distributed as dividends.

PERSONAL DEDUCTIONS OF CORPORATE LOSSES

Losses accrued by a regular corporation are worthless to the stockholders as a tax-saving device.

A tax advantage available to shareholders of the S Corporation because of the profit or loss pass-through provisions is the ability to carryforward or carryback losses generated by the S Corporation. These losses can apply against the shareholder's positive income from other sources. For example, if your S Corporation lost $25,000 last year (and you had at least $25,000 invested in the business) you can use the $25,000 as a deduction on your personal return. If you had other income and you are in the 28 percent tax bracket, the corporation's $25,000 loss would mean a personal tax savings of approximately $7,000 to you.

Of course, if the corporation has several stockholders, each can take a percentage of the loss allocated to their percentile ownership.

TAX SAVINGS ON THE SALE OF CORPORATE ASSETS

Just as a regular corporation creates a double tax or earned income, so too does it create a double tax situation when the business sells assets that have appreciated.

For example, assume you've been operating a regular corporation for several years and that you've decided to sell the business. If the corporation has assets that have appreciated, under the 1986 Tax Reform Act the appreciated gain on that asset is fully taxable to the corporation. After the corporation pays that tax and remits the remaining balance to you as a stockholder, you'll pay a second tax on any gain you've received. The concept is almost the same as the double taxation on profits discussed above.

If, however, you formed an S Corporation, only one tax would be paid—the tax at the shareholder's level. If the corporation you are about to form will have assets that will appreciate in value, then you have an important added reason for forming an S Corporation.

Tax Tip:
If you have a regular corporation, obviously you should consider converting to an S Corporation. If you do and the corporation has appreciable assets, then the 1986 Tax Reform Act provides that any appreciation that occurred before the switch may be subject to double taxation; appreciation that occurs after the switch will be taxed only once. Therefore, you should obtain an independent appraisal of the asset at the time you elect S Corporation status.

CAN YOU BENEFIT FROM AN S CORPORATION?

Virtually every type of business operation can benefit by being operated by an S Corporation. Perhaps the only situations where an S Corporation may not be advisable involve businesses that expect to retain rather than distribute profits. Because it is treated as if it is a partnership, an S Corporation must report that its shareholders have earned profits even if it does not distribute those profits. For example, if your S Corporation earns $50,000 in profits and you decide to invest that money in new equipment, your personal return must show the $50,000 of profits as income to you. But even in this situation, the fact that individual tax rates are lower than corporate rates may justify a decision in favor of the S Corporation.

Situations that clearly can benefit from the S Corporation option include:

1. Service industries with modest equipment or capital asset requirements.
2. Fully developed businesses that will not require additional capital investments.
3. Enterprises that will invest in real estate, equipment, or other property that will rapidly appreciate in value.
4. Start-up ventures that are expected to operate at a loss for the first year or two.

Tax Warning:

Most deductions and expenses allowed as deductions for regular corporations are also available to S Corporations. However, there is one exception: deductions based on medical reimbursement or health insurance plans are not available to S Corporations (see Chapter 8 on fringe benefits). Still, the other benefits available when the S Corporation option is selected will, usually, far outweigh this drawback. A list of what the IRS will and will not allow as S Corporation deductions is given in Chapter 9.

WHEN TO BE TAXED AS A REGULAR CORPORATION

S Corporation status is one tax strategy of many available to small businessowners. Like other tax-saving techniques it is not recommended in all cases. You should elect to be taxed as a regular corporation when:

1. Your enterprise becomes profitable, and you want to build up earnings to expand your business.

    If you choose to be taxed as a regular corporation, your earnings will be subject only to corporate rates, which are taxed at lower rates than individual income tax when income is below $75,000. The first $50,000 of corporate profits, for example, is taxed at a 15 percent rate; the next $25,000 is taxed at a 25 percent rate. On the other hand, joint filers are taxed at 15 percent for the first $29,750 of income (and lower for other taxpayers) and at a rate of 28 percent for all income above that level. Not until a corporation's profits go over $75,000 does its rate jump to 34 percent. Therefore, it may be wise to remain a C Corporation until net income exceeds $75,000 when the shift to an S Corporation will likely be more beneficial.

2. You've owned a profitable service business for several years, and rather than drain earnings from the company, you now want to accumulate them in the corporation and diversify. As above, regular corporate rates may leave more cash for reinvestment. Of course, it may be possible to pull sufficient income out of a C Corporation as salary to avoid double taxation.

3. You formed your S Corporation several years ago as a tax shelter. The shelter's earnings have risen while annual depreciation deductions have diminished. The "shelter" is now poised to become very profitable, throwing profits into your high-bracket personal tax return. The solution: give up S Corporation status and let the profits be taxed at corporate rates. Again, this only is advisable if the corporation will return profits and the annual profits do not exceed $75,000.

4. If there is considerable passive losses, such as through real estate investment, these passive loss generators should be taken out of the S Corporation and owned by a C Corporation or held personally or through some other entity.

A FINAL WORD

How and when you can use an S Corporation will depend upon several factors:

1. The type of business you own.
2. Its profitability.
3. Your personal tax bracket.
4. The types of assets used by your business.
5. Growth prospects.
6. State law and its recognition of the S Corporation status.
7. Other factors.

If you *can* use it, an S Corporation may save you a substantial amount of tax each year . . . and *help you build more wealth!*

However, consult your tax advisor before you act. He or she may point out other factors that apply in your particular case, or perhaps a tax trap you're nearing.

But don't delay. With the tax savings an S Corporation offers, you may be able to move much more quickly into the financial future you deserve.

3 | INCORPORATING YOUR BUSINESS

OVERVIEW

Once you have decided that an S Corporation is the form of organization you wish to utilize for a business, you must first organize a valid corporation under state law. These laws vary from state to state and also vary in complexity. However, with planning most people can easily create a corporation without a lawyer, thus, saving hundreds of dollars in legal fees.

WHERE TO INCORPORATE

The first question is to decide the state within which to organize the corporation. There are 50 states and the District of Columbia to choose from. You may have heard of the great advantages of incorporating in the state of Delaware, and it is true that a great percentage of the publicly held corporations in this country are incorporated there. There are reasons for this, many of which are no longer valid for public corporations, and most of which never made much sense for a small corporation. As a matter of fact, many of these large Delaware corporations started out in other states and only when they grew in size to become large national corporations, did they move their "corporate entity" to Delaware. Delaware's Division of Incorporations will send out a list of these advantages to incorporating in that state to anyone who requests them:

1. The fees payable to the State of Delaware are based upon the number of shares of authorized capital stock, with the no par shares fee one-half the par shares fee.

2. The franchise tax compares favorably with that of any other state.

3. Shares of stock owned by persons outside Delaware are not subject to taxation.

4. Shares of stock that are part of the estate of a nonresident decedent are exempt from the state Inheritance Tax Law.

5. The policy of Delaware courts has always been to construe the Corporation Law liberally, to interpret any ambiguities or uncertainties in the wording of the statutes so as to reach a reasonable and fair construction. This causes the careful investor to have confidence in the security of the investment.

6. The corporation service companies throughout the nation consider the Delaware Corporation Law among the most attractive for organization purposes and the state of Delaware a valuable jurisdiction in which to organize new companies.

7. Directors have greater statutory protection from liability.

Although the above advantages are important, it does not follow that Delaware should be the location of your corporation. There are many reasons for incorporating elsewhere. First, of course, is that most corporations will be established to operate a business that is located somewhere else in the country and that will not likely ever open a branch in Delaware. If your business is, for example, going to be a retail store in New York City, it would be more advisable to set up a New York corporation. If you were to set up a Delaware corporation, and operate a store in New York City, you would still have to qualify "to do business" in the state of New York that would then require filing an application to do business as a foreign corporation, paying franchise taxes as a foreign corporation in New York, and annual reporting and paying of taxes in New York as well as Delaware. The advantages of Delaware incorporation would have to be very great indeed to overcome the burden for most small businesses of being subject to regulation by two states. Needless to say, incorporating in the state where you are located usually makes the greatest sense. Of course, if the corporation is sufficiently large to benefit from Delaware incorporation, it will likely require the services of an attorney whose advice on the state of incorporation should always be carefully considered.

Make your decision on what state to incorporate in on the important factors: First, as we have already mentioned, where your actual physical facilities are can be the most important factor. Second, the costs of incorporating in that state, and if you incorporate in a state other than the one in which you are going to be located, what it will cost to become authorized to do business in the state where you are located. These costs include fees to check and reserve the name you want to use for your corporation, the cost of filing incorporation papers, and whether there is a one time organizational fee or franchise tax. (This is often based upon the number of shares you will have authorized for the corporation to issue.) If you need to be authorized to do business in another state, the filing fees, name reservation fees, and initial franchise fees should be determined and considered. In addition to the initial costs, you must determine what the annual fees are. For example, is there an annual report to file with the Secretary of State and what is the filing fee? Is there an annual franchise tax? Is there a state or local income tax, and how is it determined? Not all states provide the same type of tax treatment for state taxation as the IRS does for federal taxation. (A list of those states that provide S Corporation tax procedures can be found in Appendix 3.) While these cost factors may be considered, the issues of convenience and taxes are probably more critical factors in selecting the state of incorporation.

Further considerations include whether the laws covering corporations in your state of choice are beneficial to the corporation. For example, some states require three incorporators and three directors. If you plan to have a corporation that only one person is going to own or control it might be that your state might require you to have more board members than you want. The discussion in this book about what goes in the certificate of incorporation will cover many of these items that vary from state to state. Before you make the final decision on the location of your corporation, you should obtain a copy of the corporation statutes and read them for obstacles. These statutes can be found in public libraries, law libraries and, in many instances, the Secretary of State's office will make them available for free or for a small charge. A publication entitled *Martindale-Hubbell Law Directory*, which can also be found in public and law libraries, contains summaries of the laws of all 50 states.

Once you have decided what state to incorporate in, a great deal of information about how to set up that corporation free or for minimal fees can be obtained from the appropriate Secretary of State. A listing of the addresses and telephone numbers of persons to contact in the various states is contained in Appendix 3.

SELECTION OF THE CORPORATION'S NAME

The first step in organizing your corporation is to select a corporate name and then check to see if the state in which you are going to incorporate will allow you to use the name.

Other than your own originality, the only obstacle will be the state statutes that prohibit certain words. Not all states have the same prohibitions, so you should check your particular state. Many prohibited names are used in the name of organizations or corporations, but by and large they are in fields in which special licensing or regulation is required. Often corporations in these fields must be organized pursuant to statutes regulating that particular field, and it is not advisable to attempt to set up such a corporation without the assistance of a lawyer. Many states allow you to reserve a corporate name for a specified period of time prior to actual incorporation.

The fee for such reservation is usually modest, and protects your choice in names until the incorporation process is completed.

In considering the name, you should also check what must be included. All states require that a corporate name include an indication that there is limited liability so that people dealing with the organization know that if it fails, they cannot collect their debts from the owners personally.

The next question will be whether the name you want is already being used by someone else. Even similar names can cause problems, and most states will not allow a name that is the same or "deceptively similar" to a name already on record in the state. Therefore, XYZ Corp. may be a problem, for example, even if you are going to be a restaurant and the already existing XYZ, Inc. is a bakery. However, even changing one word in the name may solve the problem. Therefore, XYZ Bakery, Inc. or XYZ Foods, Inc. may be allowed if XYZ, Inc. is refused.

THE REGISTERED AGENT

States generally require that a corporation incorporated there must maintain a registered agent in the state in order to receive communications and to be available to receive summons in lawsuits and other service. Generally, this agent may be the office of the corporation itself, so if you are physically in the state of incorporation, the corporation itself, or an officer thereof, may be the registered agent.

If you incorporate in a state where you do not actually have an office, you need to have an agent there, and there are many organizations in the business of representing corporations for an annual fee, which are easily located in law directories. Even if you do incorporate in the state where you live and where your operating headquarters is located, you may be required to register as a "foreign" corporation in those other states where you will be doing business. Again, you will need registered agents located in those other states.

FORMING THE CORPORATION

You are now at the stage of readiness of prepare and file a certificate of incorporation (in many states it is titled "Article of Incorporation"). Many states will supply you with a blank form or with a model form that must be re-typed. There are even complete corporate kits and books available to set up a corporation. *How To Form Your Own Corporation Without A Lawyer* (Enterprise Publishing, 725 Market Street, Wilmington, Delaware 19807) and *The J.K. Lasser Corporation Form-File* (Simon & Schuster, 1230 Avenue of the Americas, New York, New York 10020) are two recommended.

Among the items of information that may be required in a certificate of incorporation are the following:

1. Name of the corporation.

2. Fiscal year.

3. Purposes of the corporation.

4. Aggregate number of shares authorized for issuance, the par value of shares, and the classes of shares if more than one class.

5. Preferences, limitations, and relative rights of shares.

6. Amount of beginning capital.

7. Any provisions regarding shareholders preemptive rights.

8. Any lawful provisions limiting statutory corporate powers.

9. Address of initial registered office and name of person as registered agent at that address.

10. Number of directors constituting initial board of directors.

11. Name and address of each of the initial directors.

12. Name and address of each incorporator.

Of course, not all of these items may be required in the certificate in any particular state, and many of them will not apply or be appropriate in your case. The only way to be sure what is required is to check the state statute, including any updates or recent changes in the state incorporation law.

Once your certificate of incorporation has been drafted and signed it should be mailed or delivered to the Secretary of State's office or other state office as is proper along with the required fees. Generally you will be notified by return mail that the certificate has been accepted and filed. Your evidence of filing is generally a receipt from the state. You may also request from the state a copy of the certificate of incorporation with their certificate of filing and the official date the corporate life began. The fee for this is usually based on the number of pages in the certificate and will be only a few dollars. You may also request a certified copy attesting to the corporate existence as it may come in handy for future transactions.

Help is available in setting up a new corporation. Of course, you can use an attorney to prepare your corporate documents, but, it will be less expensive to use a commercial incorporation service. You may find them listed under LEGAL FORMS in your telephone company Yellow Pages, or you can contact one of the following firms that provide incorporation services for all states. Any of these firms can help you by providing a corporate kit (share certificates, forms for minutes, seal, and related materials), as well as reserving a name and registering your corporation.

All-State Legal Supply Co.
One Commerce Drive, Cranford, NJ 07106
Telephone: (800) 222–0510; (908) 272–0800; (609) 921–0104

The Company Corporation
725 Market Street, Wilmington, DE 19801
Telephone: (302) 575–0400

Graham-Pierce Legal Printers
1607 West Highway 50, PO Box 1866, Fairview Heights, IL 62208
Telephone: (800) 851–3899; (618) 632–5600

Julius Blumberg, Inc.
62 White Street, New York, NY 10013
Telephone: (800) 221–2972; (212) 431–5000

DISSOLVING YOUR CORPORATION

At some point in time you may want to dissolve your corporation. This will certainly be true when you sell the business assets.

A corporation may be dissolved by:

1. Expiration of the period specified in the corporate charter (Certificate of Incorporation) if any expiration date is stated.

2. A surrender of the charter. When the shareholders of a corporation, by requisite vote, surrender the corporate charter to the state, and is formally accepted by the state.

3. Filing of a Certificate of Dissolution with the Secretary of State of the state of incorporation.

4. Consolidation. When a corporation "A," unites with another corporation "B," to form a third but entirely separate corporation "C," corporations A and B cease to exist and are said to have been dissolved "by consolidation." The new corporation C, assumes all the assets and property rights, privileges as well as the liabilities, of former corporations A and B.

5. Merger. When a corporation "A," merges into another corporation "B," only one of the two (corporation "A") is dissolved "by merger." But corporation "B" survives. The surviving corporation (corporation B in this example) absorbs all the assets and property rights, privileges, and often the liabilities of the absorbed corporation, but continues its own separate corporate existence thereafter.

6. Provisions specified in the corporate charter—such as the death of a principal. This provision is rare, however, as corporations have a perpetual life independent of its principals.

7. Action by the Attorney General. The state (and only the state) can sue to terminate the existence of a corporation. And if satisfied that the state has proven its case (e.g., when the court finds a corporation has not filed

required taxes or documents or that it has abused or neglected to use its powers), the court may revoke the corporate charter.

8. Directors' or shareholders' petition. The board of directors (or a majority thereof) may be empowered by statute to petition for the dissolution of a corporation upon the occurrence of certain events; for example, when the assets of the corporation are not sufficient to discharge its liabilities. The stockholders of a majority of all outstanding shares entitled to vote on the issue may also be empowered by statute to make such petition to the court on similar grounds.

9. Shareholders' petition under deadlock statutes. A typical so-called "dead-lock statute" commonly provides: "Unless otherwise provided in the certificate of incorporation, the holders of one-half of all outstanding shares of a corporation entitled to vote in an election of directors may present a petition for dissolution on one or more of the following grounds:

    (a) That the directors are so divided respecting the management of the corporation's affairs that the votes required for action by the board cannot be obtained.

    (b) That the shareholders are so divided that the votes required for the election of directors cannot be obtained.

    (c) That there is internal dissension and two or more factions of shareholders are so divided that dissolution would be beneficial to the shareholders."

The dissolution of a corporation carries with it important tax and liability questions and, therefore, dissolution should be undertaken only after consultation with an attorney and accountant.

Also bear in mind that a dissolution of the corporation is not the same as revocation of S Corporation status. As you will see in Chapter 4, your corporation remains in existence under a switch from S to C status. On the other hand, dissolution of the corporation creates the status of proprietorship or partnership if there are two or more owners.

CHECKLIST

Steps in the Incorporation Process

1. Decide whether to incorporate.

2. Decide where to incorporate.

3. Select a corporate name.

4. Select a registered agent, if necessary.

5. Draft certificate of incorporation.

6. Sign certificate of incorporation and file with Secretary of State with appropriate filing fees.

7. Hold incorporator's initial meeting to elect directors and transact first business.

8. Hold organizational meeting of initial Board of Directors.

9. Select corporate seal, stock certificates, issue shares, elect officers, and open bank accounts.

10. Apply for all Employer Identification Number (EIN).

11. Choose a fiscal year.

12. File a "doing business as" certificate, if necessary.

13. Apply for authorization to do business in other states, if necessary.

14. Obtain necessary state and local licenses and/or permits.

15. *Elect S Corporation status, if desired.*

4 | QUALIFYING YOUR S CORPORATION

OVERVIEW

Any corporation that satisfies the eligibility rules of an S Corporation or "Small Business Corporation" can benefit from its advantageous tax benefits.

The basic requirements are:

- There must be a corporation.
- The corporation must have no more than 35 shareholders.
- Each shareholder must be a natural person or an estate.
- The corporation may have only one class of stock, although there are limited exceptions to this requirement.
- The corporation must be a "Small Business Corporation."

CORPORATE EXISTENCE

In order to qualify as an S Corporation, the business seeking to qualify must be a corporation. If your existing or proposed business operates or will operate as a sole proprietorship or partnership, it must first be converted to a corporation. Only domestic corporations chartered within one of the states or U.S. possessions will qualify.

Frequently, a new business will incorporate and immediately thereafter file for S Corporation election.

35 OR FEWER SHAREHOLDERS

The IRS limits to 35 the number of shareholders an S Corporation may have. In calculating whether a corporation has more than 35 shareholders, follow the following guidelines.

• Husbands and wives are considered as one person, even if they own their stock in their separate names. For example, if Mr. Jones owns twenty shares of S Corporation in his name only and Mrs. Jones owns 30 shares in her name only, they will be viewed as one shareholder for S Corporation purposes. Similarly, jointly held stock (e.g., shares owned by John Jones and Mary Jones as joint tenants or tenants in common) is viewed as being owned by one shareholder.

• Shares held in a qualified trust by a trustee or custodian for beneficiaries are usually considered as being owned by the beneficiary not the custodian or trustee. For example, if a parent holds shares as trustee or custodian for each of the parent's three children, there are three shareholders for S Corporation purposes, not one. Therefore, it is important to verify the number of beneficiaries in a trust acquiring shares.

In the event shares of an S Corporation become owned by 36 or more shareholders, the business will lose its S Corporation status. It will thereafter be treated as a regular C Corporation and will be subject to double taxation.

SHAREHOLDER QUALIFICATIONS

Any individual who is either a citizen or resident of the United States, as well as estates and certain trusts, may be a shareholder in an S Corporation.

Shareholders who do not fit into one of those categories are not qualified to be S Corporation shareholders, and if they obtain shares, the business will lose its S Corporation status.

Since an individual must be a natural person, both partnerships and corporations are disqualified from owning shares in an S Corporation. Therefore, an S Corporation cannot be a subsidiary of another corporation. The individual must be either a citizen or resident of the United States, and an alien visiting this country does not qualify as a shareholder. Further, if shares are jointly held, by spouses, for example, and one spouse is a nonresident alien, the corporation has a disqualified shareholder and S Corporation status will be denied. Only residence in the United States qualifies an alien for shareholder status in an S Corporation. Residence in a territory or a possession is not sufficient.

As to estates, a business will not lose its S Corporation status if a qualified shareholder dies and his or her shares pass to the decedent's estate. However, time limits can be imposed and an estate may become disqualified if the estate remains open an inordinate amount of time. This should be reviewed with counsel for the estate and counsel for the corporation.

Similarly, the estate of a bankrupt may also be a shareholder in an S Corporation. If an individual shareholder files for bankruptcy, his or her assets, including his or her shares in the corporation, are placed in the bankrupt's estate and is qualified to be a shareholder in an S Corporation. However, under both a decedent's estate and bankrupt estate, the shares must not be passed on to individuals or parties otherwise unqualified to be a stockholder in an S Corporation.

The matter is more complex when it comes to trusts. Although certain trusts may qualify to become shareholders in an S Corporation, the applicable rules are complex and highly detailed. In the event that a shareholder in an S Corporation intends to establish a trust that includes the corporation shares, qualified legal counsel should be obtained.

Because a corporation can easily lose its S Corporation status if a shareholder transfers shares to an unqualified recipient, all shareholders should enter into an agreement to protect the corporation (and other shareholders) from an involuntary termination. (Such an agreement is at the end of Chapter 13.) Further, trusts and estates expected to become transferees of S Corporation shares should be first approved by counsel for the corporation.

ONE CLASS OF STOCK

An S Corporation may have only one class of stock issued and outstanding.

Even if the corporation is authorized to issue more than one share of stock (i.e., common and preferred shares), it continues to qualify for S status as long as only one class is issued.

The fact that shares may have different voting rights (i.e., voting and nonvoting common stock) do not constitute different classes provided they are treated equally in all other respects with regard to dividends and liquidation.

To determine whether a corporation has more than one class of stock, ask whether every shareholder is entitled to receive the same (1) dividend at the same time as every other shareholder, and (2) amount for each share he or she holds and at the same time as every other shareholder in the event of liquidation. If all economic rights are the same, then the shares will be considered the same class.

Tax Warning:
Loans to the corporation may, under certain circumstances, be viewed as creating a second class of stock, which then disqualifies the S Corporation status.
The test is whether the loan has the characteristics of an "arms-length" loan

bearing conventional lending terms. More lenient terms may be viewed as an equity investment creating the interpretation of a second class of stock.

In order to be considered a loan, a shareholder loan must:

1. Be in writing.
2. Require the corporation to pay interest at fixed times (e.g., monthly, quarterly, or annually) and set a rate of interest that does not depend on the corporation profits, the corporation discretion, or similar factors.
3. Oblige the corporation to repay the entire principal amount of the loan by a certain date.
4. Not allow the loan to be convertible to stock at either the borrower's or lender's option.
5. Require the corporation to make payments in accordance with the terms of the note.

As suggested above, the safe harbor rules do not present any real problem for a shareholder who seeks to lend money to an S Corporation. The loan terms required by the rule are only those that any creditor would demand before lending money.

Potential ownership and tax problems that may result from loans to the S Corporation by shareholders, or to shareholders from the S Corporation, are discussed in greater detail in Chapter 9.

SMALL BUSINESS CORPORATION

The term "Small Business Corporation" has never been clearly defined. In fact, we define a Small Business Corporation by defining the type of businesses that do not qualify.

Contrary to common belief, the phrase "Small Business Corporation" does not place any ceiling on the sales volume or asset value of the business. And for the most part, a Small Business Corporation (S Corporation) is not restricted to the type business in which it may engage.

The only forms of business that may not take advantage of S incorporation are:

1. Financial institutions such as banks, insurance companies, building and loan associations, or mutual savings and loan associations.
2. Foreign corporations (S Corporation must be incorporated under the laws of any state, possession, or territory of the United States).
3. Corporations that operate in possessions of the United States and use the possession's tax credit against their United States income tax.
4. Domestic International Sales Corporations (DISCs) or former DISCs and Foreign Service Corporations (FSCs).

A fifth category of ineligible corporations includes affiliated corporations. An S Corporation may not be a subsidiary of a parent corporation. This follows from the fact that shareholders of an S Corporation must be natural persons, estates, or certain trusts.

Moreover, a corporation that owns 80 percent or more of all of the stock of another corporation is an ineligible affiliated corporation. If, however, the second corporation has two classes of stock (e.g., voting and nonvoting common stock), the S Corporation must own 80 percent or more of each class of stock in order to be disqualified as an affiliated corporation.

ADDITIONAL REQUIREMENTS FOR EXISTING CORPORATIONS

If an existing C Corporation elects to become an S Corporation it must—in addition to the above requirements—satisfy two additional requirements as well.

The Five Year Rule

If the regular C Corporation has previously been an S Corporation and revoked or lost its S Status within the past five years, it will not be qualified to become an S Corporation. This provision exists to deter shareholders from electing S status in only those years during which their business loses money.

Therefore, the IRS will not approve of an election to be taxed as an S Corporation if the shareholders of the corporation revoked or lost their S Corporation election during the past five years. A possible exception to this rule exists if the corporation shares (or at least a controlling interest) are held by different shareholders than those who revoked or lost the election to be treated as an S Corporation

Planning Tip:
There is no penalty if shareholders choose to be treated as an S Corporation during the enterprise's first year (when it is likely to lose money because of start-up costs) and then switch to regular C status the following year. At most, the shareholders will be barred from making an S Corporation election for another five years.

Passive Investment Income

If a C Corporation elects to become an S Corporation and has no accumulated earnings and profits (prior profits not distributed as dividends to shareholders), it can qualify for S status regardless of the type or sources of income the corporation has had.

However, if the regular C Corporation does have accumulated earnings and profits when it makes its election for S status, its election may not be recognized. Under this rule, if an S Corporation has (1) accumulated earnings and profits from its C Corporation operations at the end of the S Corporation tax year, and (2) more than 25 percent of its gross income comes from passive investment income sources (dividends, interest, annuities, rents, royalties, and gain from the sale of securities), the election will be lost.

For the passive income rule to apply, the corporation must fall within both sides of the test for three years. In other words, during each of the first three years starting with the election year, the corporation must have accumulated C Corporation earnings and profits and must have passive investment income that is more than 25 percent of its gross income. Should that occur, the S Corporation election is lost in the fourth year but is in effect for the prior three years. For the fourth year the corporation will be taxed as a C Corporation and will remain unable to elect S Corporation status for another five years.

5 | FILING FOR S CORPORATION STATUS

OVERVIEW

It is relatively simple to qualify and elect to have your corporation become an S Corporation.

The IRS requires you to do very little work other than to timely file an easily completed Form 2553 (Election by a Small Business Corporation), and satisfy the other eligibility requirements.

These requirements, however, should be taken seriously because if the corporation fails to file on time, or improperly completes its forms, the corporation's election will be delayed and this may be costly in terms of taxes.

This chapter will explain the proper procedures for filing and will provide all the needed forms to help you create your own S Corporation.

This chapter, however, only discusses federal requirements. Each state may have its own requirements for recognition as an S Corporation at the state level, and several states do not recognize S Corporation status at all. In these states an S Corporation will be subject to state taxes in the same manner as a C Corporation, although the S Corporation will still enjoy the benefits of S Corporation status as to federal taxes. Appendix 3 lists those states that do and do not recognize S Corporation status.

DOCUMENTS THAT MUST BE FILED

To satisfy federal requirements, only one document is essential to convert an existing C Corporation to an S Corporation—Form 2553.

A Form 2553 (Election by a Small Business Corporation) is available at any IRS office. However, a current Form 2553 is included at the end of this chapter and may be used for filing purposes.

Instructions for completing Form 2553 require you to provide the following information:

- The corporation's name and address. If the address is the same as someone else's, enter the name of that individual.

- Employer identification number. If you have a new business and applied for an Employer Identification Number (EIN) but have not received it, enter "applied for." If the corporation does not have an EIN, apply for one using Form SS-4 found at the end of this chapter. (Mail duplicate copies.)

- The principal business activity and principal product or service is entered by code and the code is contained in instructions for Form 1120S (see Appendix 2). Your principal business activity is the one that accounts for the largest percentage of total receipts.

- If the filing is made for the corporation's first year of existence, the earliest of the dates the corporation (1) had shareholders, (2) had assets, or (3) began doing business.

- The total number of shares held by shareholders and have not been reacquired by the corporation.

- The date of incorporation and state of incorporation.

- The corporation's tax year. A new corporation may automatically elect a tax year ending December 31. If you prefer a tax year other than a calendar year, then parts 2–4 of Form 2553 must be completed. Noncalendar tax years are generally not permitted for S Corporations, and will be allowed only in limited circumstances.

- Each shareholder must consent to the election and complete the corresponding information relative to the stock owned, social security number, and individual tax year.

Finally, Form 2553 must be signed by an authorized corporate officer and mailed to the IRS office where the corporation files its tax returns.

It is recommended that Form 2553 be sent by certified mail, return receipt requested, so you have proof of filing should a question arise.

OBTAINING SHAREHOLDER CONSENT

All shareholders must consent to an S Corporation election (although only a majority of the outstanding shares are needed to revoke the election. Furthermore, all necessary consents must be filed within the time limit for filing Form 2553.

The following rules apply in determining who must sign and file consents:

- Every person who owned shares during the taxable year must file a consent—even if the person sold his or her shares before the election was filed.

- If shares are held for the benefit of another person, the beneficiary should file a consent. A beneficial owner of stock is ordinarily held by the courts to be the person who is entitled to the financial benefits (dividends or other distributions) of the shares. However, you may want consents from both the beneficiary and the person who holds the stock for the beneficiary.

- Owners of nonvoting common stock must also file consents with owners of voting stock.

- If stock is held jointly by husbands and wives, or others, each joint owner or tenant in common should file a consent. In community property states, even if shares of stock are listed in the name of only one spouse, both husband and wife should file consents.

- If shares have passed to an estate, it is generally safe to cover all possibilities by obtaining consents from both the executor of the estate as well as the beneficiaries or legatees of the stock.

If certain shareholders are not available for the filing of the Form 2553 itself, then file extensions for the filing of shareholder consents. In no event should you defer filing the 2553 beyond the required date. An acceptable form for obtaining an extension to filing a shareholder consent is found at the end of this chapter.

It is also possible to obtain shareholders consent using a consent form other than Form 2553. If, for example, a shareholder resides in a distant location, it may be more convenient to obtain his or her consent using the "shareholders consent" contained at the end of this chapter.

WHEN TO FILE

There are strict rules that govern the filing of Form 2553 for the election of S Corporation status.

- If the election is to be effective for the corporation's present tax year, then Form 2553 must be filed no later than the fifteenth day of the third month of the corporation's taxable year.

- An existing corporation that wants to elect S Corporation status for 1992 could have filed anytime during 1991, but not later than March 15, 1993.

Caution:
Be certain you allow enough time to meet the two month and fifteen day filing date from the beginning of the tax year. The IRS will not grant an extension for filing the election under any circumstances. Remember, time is of the essence.

FORMS IN THIS SECTION

1. *Form 2553* (with instructions) is the basic application to elect S Corporation status. Be particularly careful to complete all information *and* to file it on time. Note that the 2553 form is to be signed by all the stockholders of the corporation (see Column D of instructions).

2. Shareholder consent may also be submitted on the form—*Shareholder's Consent to S Corporation Election*—when the shareholder cannot conveniently sign Form 2553.

3. Use the *Request for Extension to File Shareholder's Consent* if for any reason you cannot obtain the signature of a shareholder within the time required to file 2553. Complete and file the Request For Extension together with the Form 2553, and as soon as possible obtain the shareholder's signature on the Shareholder's Consent and file with the IRS.

4. This section also contains Form SS-4, an *Application for Employer Identification Number*. If the corporation does not have an EIN when it files its 2553 application, it should mark "applied for" in the appropriate box.

Instructions for Form 2553

(Revised December 1990)

Election by a Small Business Corporation

(Section references are to the Internal Revenue Code unless otherwise noted.)

Paperwork Reduction Act Notice.—We ask for the information on this form to carry out the Internal Revenue laws of the United States. You are required to give us the information. We need it to ensure that you are complying with these laws and to allow us to figure and collect the right amount of tax.

The time needed to complete and file this form will vary depending on individual circumstances. The estimated average time is:

Recordkeeping	.6 hrs., 28 min.
Learning about the law or the form	.3 hrs., 16 min.
Preparing, copying, assembling, and sending the form to IRS	.3 hrs., 31 min.

If you have comments concerning the accuracy of these time estimates or suggestions for making this form more simple, we would be happy to hear from you. You can write to both the **Internal Revenue Service,** Washington, DC 20224, Attention: IRS Reports Clearance Officer, T:FP, and the **Office of Management and Budget,** Paperwork Reduction Project (1545-0146), Washington, DC 20503. **DO NOT** send the tax form to either of these offices. Instead, see the instructions below for information on where to file.

General Instructions

A. Purpose.—To elect to be treated as an "S Corporation," a corporation must file Form 2553. The election permits the income of the S corporation to be taxed to the shareholders of the corporation rather than to the corporation itself, except as provided in Subchapter S of the Code. For more information, see **Publication 589,** Tax Information on S Corporations.

B. Who May Elect.—Your corporation may make the election to be treated as an S corporation only if it meets **all** of the following tests:

1. It is a domestic corporation.

2. It has no more than 35 shareholders. A husband and wife (and their estates) are treated as one shareholder for this requirement. All other persons are treated as separate shareholders.

3. It has only individuals, estates, or certain trusts as shareholders. See the instructions for Part III regarding qualified subchapter S trusts.

4. It has no nonresident alien shareholders.

5. It has only one class of stock. See sections 1361(c)(4) and (5) for additional details.

6. It is not one of the following ineligible corporations:

(a) a corporation that owns 80% or more of the stock of another corporation, unless the other corporation has not begun business and has no gross income;

(b) a bank or thrift institution;

(c) an insurance company subject to tax under the special rules of Subchapter L of the Code;

(d) a corporation that has elected to be treated as a possessions corporation under section 936; or

(e) a domestic international sales corporation (DISC) or former DISC.

See section 1361(b)(2) for details.

7. It has a permitted tax year as required by section 1378 or makes a section 444 election to have a tax year other than a permitted tax year. Section 1378 defines a permitted tax year as a tax year ending December 31, or any other tax year for which the corporation establishes a business purpose to the satisfaction of the IRS. See Part II for details on requesting a fiscal tax year based on a business purpose or on making a section 444 election.

8. Each shareholder consents as explained in the instructions for Column K.

See sections 1361, 1362, and 1378 for additional information on the above tests.

C. Where To File.—File this election with the Internal Revenue Service Center listed below.

If the corporation's principal business, office, or agency is located in ▼	Use the following Internal Revenue Service Center address ▼
New Jersey, New York (New York City and counties of Nassau, Rockland, Suffolk, and Westchester)	Holtsville, NY 00501
New York (all other counties), Connecticut, Maine, Massachusetts, New Hampshire, Rhode Island, Vermont	Andover, MA 05501
Florida, Georgia, South Carolina	Atlanta, GA 39901
Indiana, Kentucky, Michigan, Ohio, West Virginia	Cincinnati, OH 45999
Kansas, New Mexico, Oklahoma, Texas	Austin, TX 73301
Alaska, Arizona, California (counties of Alpine, Amador, Butte, Calaveras, Colusa, Contra Costa, Del Norte, El Dorado, Glenn, Humboldt, Lake, Lassen, Marin, Mendocino, Modoc, Napa, Nevada, Placer, Plumas, Sacramento, San Joaquin, Shasta, Sierra, Siskiyou, Solano, Sonoma, Sutter, Tehama, Trinity, Yolo, and Yuba), Colorado, Idaho, Montana, Nebraska, Nevada, North Dakota, Oregon, South Dakota, Utah, Washington, Wyoming	Ogden, UT 84201
California (all other counties), Hawaii	Fresno, CA 93888
Illinois, Iowa, Minnesota, Missouri, Wisconsin	Kansas City, MO 64999
Alabama, Arkansas, Louisiana, Mississippi, North Carolina, Tennessee	Memphis, TN 37501
Delaware, District of Columbia, Maryland, Pennsylvania, Virginia	Philadelphia, PA 19255

D. When To Make the Election.—Complete Form 2553 and file it either: **(1)** at any time during that portion of the first tax year the election is to take effect which occurs before the 16th day of the third month of that tax year (if the tax year has 2½ months or less, and the election is made not later than 2 months and 15 days after the first day of the tax year, it shall be treated as timely made during such year), or **(2)** in the tax year before the first tax year it is to take effect. An election made by a small business corporation after the 15th day of the third month but before the end of the tax year is treated as made for the next year. For example, if a calendar year corporation makes the election in April 1991, it is effective for the corporation's 1992 calendar tax year. See section 1362(b) for more information.

E. Acceptance or Non-Acceptance of Election.—The Service Center will notify you if your election is accepted and when it will take effect. You will also be notified if your election is not accepted. You should generally receive a determination on your election within 60 days after you have filed Form 2553. If the Q1 box in Part II is checked on page 2, the corporation will receive a ruling letter from IRS in Washington, DC, which approves or denies the selected tax year. When Item Q1 is checked, it will generally take an additional 90 days for the Form 2553 to be accepted.

Do not file Form 1120S until you are notified that your election is accepted. If you are now required to file **Form 1120,** U.S. Corporation Income Tax Return, or any other applicable tax return, continue filing it until your election takes effect.

Care should be exercised to ensure that the election is received by the Internal Revenue Service. If you are not notified of acceptance or nonacceptance of your election within 3 months of date of filing (date mailed), or within 6 months if Part II, Item Q1, is checked, you should take follow-up action by corresponding with the Service Center where the election was filed. If filing of Form 2553 is questioned by IRS, an acceptable proof of filing is: **(1)** certified receipt (timely filed); **(2)** Form 2553 with accepted stamp; **(3)** Form 2553 with stamped IRS received date; or **(4)** IRS letter stating that Form 2553 had been accepted.

F. End of Election.—Once the election is made, it stays in effect for all years until it is terminated. During the 5 years after the election is terminated under section 1362(d), the corporation can make another election on Form 2553 only with IRS consent.

Specific Instructions
Part I

Part I must be completed by all corporations.

Name and Address of Corporation.—Enter the true corporate name as set forth in the corporate charter or other legal document creating it. If the corporation's mailing address is the same as someone else's, such as a shareholder's, please enter this person's name below the name of the corporation. Include the suite, room, or other unit number after the street address. If the Post Office does not deliver to the street address and the corporation has a P.O. box, show the P.O. box number instead of the street address. If the corporation has changed its name or address since applying for its EIN (filing Form SS-4), be sure to check the box in item F of Part I.

A. Employer Identification Number.—If you have applied for an employer identification number (EIN) but have not received it, enter "applied for." If the corporation does not have an EIN, you should apply for one on **Form SS-4**, Application for Employer Identification Number, available from most IRS and Social Security Administration offices.

C. Effective Date of Election.—Enter the beginning effective date (month, day, year) of the tax year that you have requested for the S corporation. Generally, this will be the beginning date of the tax year for which the ending effective date is required to be shown in item I, Part I. For a new corporation (first year the corporation exists) it will generally be the date required to be shown in item H, Part I. The tax year of a new corporation starts on the date that it has shareholders, acquires assets, or begins doing business, whichever happens first. If the effective date for item C for a newly formed corporation is later than the date in item H, the corporation should file Form 1120 or Form 1120-A, for the tax period between these dates.

Column K. Shareholders' Consent Statement.—Each shareholder who owns (or is deemed to own) stock at the time the election is made must consent to the election. If the election is made during the corporation's first tax year for which it is effective, any person who held stock at any time during the portion of that year which occurs before the time the election is made, must consent to the election although the person may have sold or transferred his or her stock before the election is made. Each shareholder consents by signing and dating in column K or signing and dating a separate consent statement described below. If stock is owned by a trust that is a qualified shareholder, the deemed owner of the trust must consent. See section 1361(c)(2) for details regarding qualified trusts that may be shareholders and rules on determining who is the deemed owner of the trust.

An election made during the first 2½ months of the tax year is considered made for the following tax year if one or more of the persons who held stock in the corporation during such tax year and before the election was made did not consent to the election. See section 1362(b)(2).

If a husband and wife have a community interest in the stock or in the income from it, both must consent. Each tenant in common, joint tenant, and tenant by the entirety also must consent.

A minor's consent is made by the minor or the legal representative of the minor, or by a natural or adoptive parent of the minor if no legal representative has been appointed. The consent of an estate is made by an executor or administrator.

Continuation sheet or separate consent statement.—If you need a continuation sheet or use a separate consent statement, attach it to Form 2553. The separate consent statement must contain the name, address, and employer identification number of the corporation and the shareholder information requested in columns J through N of Part I.

If you want, you may combine all the shareholders' consents in one statement.

Column L.—Enter the number of shares of stock each shareholder owns and the dates the stock was acquired. If the election is made during the corporation's first tax year for which it is effective, do not list the shares of stock for those shareholders who sold or transferred all of their stock before the election was made. However, these shareholders must still consent to the election for it to be effective for the tax year.

Column M.—Enter the social security number of each shareholder who is an individual. Enter the employer identification number of each shareholder that is an estate or a qualified trust.

Column N.—Enter the month and day that each shareholder's tax year ends. If a shareholder is changing his or her tax year, enter the tax year the shareholder is changing to, and attach an explanation indicating the present tax year and the basis for the change (e.g., automatic revenue procedure or letter ruling request).

If the election is made during the corporation's first tax year for which it is effective, you do not have to enter the tax year of any shareholder who sold or transferred all of his or her stock before the election was made.

Signature.—Form 2553 must be signed by the president, treasurer, assistant treasurer, chief accounting officer, or other corporate officer (such as tax officer) authorized to sign.

Part II

Complete Part II if you selected a tax year ending on any date other than December 31 (other than a 52-53-week tax year ending with reference to the month of December).

Box P1.—Attach a statement showing separately for each month the amount of gross receipts for the most recent 47 months as required by section 4.03(3) of

Revenue Procedure 87-32, 1987-2 C.B. 396. A corporation that does not have a 47-month period of gross receipts cannot establish a natural business year under section 4.01(1).

Box Q1.—For examples of an acceptable business purpose for requesting a fiscal tax year, see Revenue Ruling 87-57, 1987-2 C.B. 117.

In addition to a statement showing the business purpose for the requested fiscal year, you must attach the other information necessary to meet the ruling request requirements of Revenue Procedure 90-1, 1990-1 C.B. 356 (updated annually). Also attach a statement that shows separately the amount of gross receipts from sales or services (and inventory costs, if applicable) for each of the 36 months preceding the effective date of the election to be an S corporation. If the corporation has been in existence for fewer than 36 months, submit figures for the period of existence.

If you check box Q1, you must also pay a user fee of $200 (subject to change). Do not pay the fee when filing Form 2553. The Service Center will send Form 2553 to the IRS in Washington, DC, who, in turn, will notify the corporation that the fee is due. See Revenue Procedure 90-17, 1990-1 C.B. 479.

Box Q2.—If the corporation makes a back-up section 444 election for which it is qualified, then the election must be exercised in the event the business purpose request is not approved. Under certain circumstances, the tax year requested under the back-up section 444 election may be different than the tax year requested under business purpose. See **Form 8716**, Election To Have a Tax Year Other Than a Required Tax Year, for details on making a back-up section 444 election.

Boxes Q2 and R2.—If the corporation is not qualified to make the section 444 election after making the item Q2 back-up section 444 election or indicating its intention to make the election in item R1, and therefore it later files a calendar year return, it should write "Section 444 Election Not Made" in the top left corner of the 1st calendar year Form 1120S it files.

Part III

Certain Qualified Subchapter S Trusts (QSSTs) may make the QSST election required by section 1361(d)(2) in Part III. Part III may be used to make the QSST election only if corporate stock has been transferred to the trust on or before the date on which the corporation makes its election to be an S corporation. However, a statement can be used in lieu of Part III to make the election.

Note: *Part III may be used only in conjunction with making the Part I election (i.e., Form 2553 cannot be filed with only Part III completed).*

The deemed owner of the QSST must also consent to the S corporation election in column K, page 1, of Form 2553. See section 1361(c)(2).

✦U.S. GPO:1991-518-941/20363

Election by a Small Business Corporation
(Under section 1362 of the Internal Revenue Code)
▶ **For Paperwork Reduction Act Notice, see page 1 of instructions.**
▶ **See separate instructions.**

OMB No. 1545-0146

Expires 11-30-93

Notes: 1. *This election, to be treated as an "S corporation," can be accepted only if all the tests in General Instruction B are met; all signatures in Parts I and III are originals (no photocopies); and the exact name and address of the corporation and other required form information are provided.*

2. *Do not file Form 1120S until you are notified that your election is accepted. See General Instruction E.*

Part I Election Information

Please Type or Print

Name of corporation (see instructions)

XYZ Corporation

Number, street, and room or suite no. (If a P.O. box, see instructions.)

100 Main Street

City or town, state, and ZIP code

Anytown, USA 00000

A Employer identification number (see instructions)

81-4039261

B Name and telephone number (including area code) of corporate officer or legal representative who may be called for information

C Election is to be effective for tax year beginning (month, day, year)

1/1/92

D Is the corporation the outgrowth or continuation of any form of predecessor? . . ☐ Yes ☒ No

If "Yes," state name of predecessor, type of organization, and period of its existence ▶ ....

E Date of incorporation

7/15/91

F Check here ▶ ☐ if the corporation has changed its name or address since applying for the employer identification number shown in item A above.

G State of incorporation

New York

H If this election takes effect for the first tax year the corporation exists, enter month, day, and year of the **earliest** of the following: (1) date the corporation first had shareholders, (2) date the corporation first had assets, or (3) date the corporation began doing business. ▶ 7/15/91

I Selected tax year: Annual return will be filed for tax year ending (month and day) ▶ ......December 31......

If the tax year ends on any date other than December 31, except for an automatic 52-53-week tax year ending with reference to the month of December, you **must** complete Part II on the back. If the date you enter is the ending date of an automatic 52-53-week tax year, write "52-53-week year" to the right of the date. See Temporary Regulations section 1.441-2T(e)(3).

J Name of each shareholder, person having a community property interest in the corporation's stock, and each tenant in common, joint tenant, and tenant by the entirety. (A husband and wife (and their estates) are counted as one shareholder in determining the number of shareholders without regard to the manner in which the stock is owned.)	**K** Shareholders' Consent Statement. We, the undersigned shareholders, consent to the corporation's election to be treated as an "S corporation" under section 1362(a). (Shareholders sign and date below.)*		**L** Stock owned		**M** Social security number or employer identification number (see instructions)	**N** Shareholder's tax year ends (month and day)
	Signature	Date	Number of shares	Dates acquired		
Robert Brown	*Robert Brown*	7/15/91	50	7/15/91	111-11-1111	Dec. 31
Mary Brown	*Mary Brown*	7/15/91	50	7/15/91	111-12-1222	Dec. 31
	SAMPLE					

*For this election to be valid, the consent of each shareholder, person having a community property interest in the corporation's stock, and each tenant in common, joint tenant, and tenant by the entirety must either appear above or be attached to this form. (See instructions for Column K if continuation sheet or a separate consent statement is needed.)

Under penalties of perjury, I declare that I have examined this election, including accompanying schedules and statements, and to the best of my knowledge and belief, it is true, correct, and complete.

Signature of officer ▶ *Robert Brown* ▶   Date ▶ *July 15, 1991*

See Parts II and III on back.

Form **2553** (Rev. 12-90)

Form **2553**

(Rev. December 1990)

Department of the Treasury
Internal Revenue Service

Election by a Small Business Corporation

(Under section 1362 of the Internal Revenue Code)

▶ For Paperwork Reduction Act Notice, see page 1 of instructions.

▶ See separate instructions.

OMB No. 1545-0146

Expires 11-30-93

Notes: 1. *This election, to be treated as an "S corporation," can be accepted only if all the tests in General Instruction B are met; all signatures in Parts I and III are originals (no photocopies); and the exact name and address of the corporation and other required form information are provided.*

2. *Do not file Form 1120S until you are notified that your election is accepted. See General Instruction E.*

Part I — Election Information

Name of corporation (see instructions)		**A** **Employer identification number** (see instructions)	
Number, street, and room or suite no. (If a P.O. box, see instructions.)		**B** Name and telephone number (including area code) of corporate officer or legal representative who may be called for information	
City or town, state, and ZIP code		**C** Election is to be effective for tax year beginning (month, day, year)	

D Is the corporation the outgrowth or continuation of any form of predecessor? . . ☐ **Yes** ☐ **No**   **E** Date of incorporation

If "Yes," state name of predecessor, type of organization, and period of its existence ▶ ....

F Check here ▶ ☐ if the corporation has changed its name or address since applying for the employer identification number shown in item A above.   **G** State of incorporation

H If this election takes effect for the first tax year the corporation exists, enter month, day, and year of the **earliest** of the following: (1) date the corporation first had shareholders, (2) date the corporation first had assets, or (3) date the corporation began doing business. ▶

I Selected tax year: Annual return will be filed for tax year ending (month and day) ▶ ....

If the tax year ends on any date other than December 31, except for an automatic 52-53-week tax year ending with reference to the month of December, you **must** complete Part II on the back. If the date you enter is the ending date of an automatic 52-53-week tax year, write "52-53-week year" to the right of the date. See Temporary Regulations section 1.441-2T(e)(3).

J Name of each shareholder, person having a community property interest in the corporation's stock, and each tenant in common, joint tenant, and tenant by the entirety. (A husband and wife (and their estates) are counted as one shareholder in determining the number of shareholders without regard to the manner in which the stock is owned.)	K Shareholders' Consent Statement. We, the undersigned shareholders, consent to the corporation's election to be treated as an "S corporation" under section 1362(a). (Shareholders sign and date below.)*		L Stock owned		M Social security number or employer identification number (see instructions)	N Share- holder's tax year ends (month and day)
	Signature	Date	Number of shares	Dates acquired		

*For this election to be valid, the consent of each shareholder, person having a community property interest in the corporation's stock, and each tenant in common, joint tenant, and tenant by the entirety must either appear above or be attached to this form. (See instructions for Column K if continuation sheet or a separate consent statement is needed.)

Under penalties of perjury, I declare that I have examined this election, including accompanying schedules and statements, and to the best of my knowledge and belief, it is true, correct, and complete.

Signature of officer ▶ _____ **Title** ▶ _____ **Date** ▶ _____

See Parts II and III on back.

Form **2553** (Rev. 12-90)

Part II Selection of Fiscal Tax Year (All corporations using this Part must complete item O and one of items P, Q, or R.)

O Check the applicable box below to indicate whether the corporation is:

1. ☐ A new corporation adopting the tax year entered in item I, Part I.

2. ☐ An existing corporation retaining the tax year entered in item I, Part I.

3. ☐ An existing corporation changing to the tax year entered in item I, Part I.

P Complete item P if the corporation is using the expeditious approval provisions of Revenue Procedure 87-32, 1987-2 C.B. 396, to request: **(1)** a natural business year (as defined in section 4.01(1) of Rev. Proc. 87-32), or **(2)** a year that satisfies the ownership tax year test in section 4.01(2) of Rev. Proc. 87-32. Check the applicable box below to indicate the representation statement the corporation is making as required under section 4 of Rev. Proc. 87-32.

1. Natural Business Year ► ☐ I represent that the corporation is retaining or changing to a tax year that coincides with its natural business year as defined in section 4.01(1) of Rev. Proc. 87-32 and as verified by its satisfaction of the requirements of section 4.02(1) of Rev. Proc. 87-32. In addition, if the corporation is changing to a natural business year as defined in section 4.01(1), I further represent that such tax year results in less deferral of income to the owners than the corporation's present tax year. I also represent that the corporation is not described in section 3.01(2) of Rev. Proc. 87-32. (See instructions for additional information that must be attached.)

2. Ownership Tax Year ► ☐ I represent that shareholders holding more than half of the shares of the stock (as of the first day of the tax year to which the request relates) of the corporation have the same tax year or are concurrently changing to the tax year that the corporation adopts, retains, or changes to per item I, Part I. I also represent that the corporation is not described in section 3.01(2) of Rev. Proc. 87-32.

Note: *If you do not use item P and the corporation wants a fiscal tax year, complete either item Q or R below. Item Q is used to request a fiscal tax year based on a business purpose and to make a back-up section 444 election. Item R is used to make a regular section 444 election.*

Q **Business Purpose**—To request a fiscal tax year based on a business purpose, you must check box Q1 and pay a user fee. See instructions for details. You may also check box Q2 and/or box Q3.

1. Check here ► ☐ if the fiscal year entered in item I, Part I, is requested under the provisions of section 6.03 of Rev. Proc. 87-32. Attach to Form 2553 a statement showing the business purpose for the requested fiscal year. See instructions for additional information that must be attached.

2. Check here ► ☐ to show that the corporation intends to make a back-up section 444 election in the event the corporation's business purpose request is not approved by the IRS. (See instructions for more information.)

3. Check here ► ☐ to show that the corporation agrees to adopt or change to a tax year ending December 31 if necessary for the IRS to accept this election for S corporation status in the event: (1) the corporation's business purpose request is not approved and the corporation makes a back-up section 444 election, but is ultimately not qualified to make a section 444 election, or (2) the corporation's business purpose request is not approved and the corporation did not make a back-up section 444 election.

R **Section 444 Election**—To make a section 444 election, you must check box R1 and you may also check box R2.

1. Check here ► ☐ to show the corporation will make, if qualified, a section 444 election to have the fiscal tax year shown in item I, Part I. To make the election, you must complete **Form 8716**, Election To Have a Tax Year Other Than a Required Tax Year, and either attach it to Form 2553 or file it separately.

2. Check here ► ☐ to show that the corporation agrees to adopt or change to a tax year ending December 31 if necessary for the IRS to accept this election for S corporation status in the event the corporation is ultimately not qualified to make a section 444 election.

Part III Qualified Subchapter S Trust (QSST) Election Under Section 1361(d)(2)**

Income beneficiary's name and address	Social security number
Trust's name and address	Employer identification number

Date on which stock of the corporation was transferred to the trust (month, day, year) ►

In order for the trust named above to be a QSST and thus a qualifying shareholder of the S corporation for which this Form 2553 is filed, I hereby make the election under section 1361(d)(2). Under penalties of perjury, I certify that the trust meets the definition requirements of section 1361(d)(3) and that all other information provided in Part III is true, correct, and complete.

_____   _____
Signature of income beneficiary or signature and title of legal representative or other qualified person making the election   Date

**Use of Part III to make the QSST election may be made only if stock of the corporation has been transferred to the trust on or before the date on which the corporation makes its election to be an S corporation. The QSST election must be made and filed separately if stock of the corporation is transferred to the trust after the date on which the corporation makes the S election.

*U.S. GPO:1991-518-943/20365

SHAREHOLDER'S CONSENT TO S CORPORATION
ELECTION—SAMPLE

Date: August 1, 1991

Director
Internal Revenue Service Center
10 Oak Street
Anytown, USA   00000

Dear Sir:

By means of this letter, I state my consent to have
the   XYZ Corporation   (name), a
      New York   corporation with offices at
   100 Main Street, Anywhere, New York   treated as
S Corporation under Section 1362 of the Internal Revenue
Code. Pursuant to Form 2553, I offer the following data:

SAMPLE

1.   My name is Mary Brown   .

2.   I own   50   shares of stock of the XYZ
     Corporation   .

3.   I acquired that stock on   July 15, 1991   .

4.   My Social Security number is   111-12-1222   .

5.   My tax year ends on   December 31   .

6.   The Corporation EIN number is   81-4039261   .

Mary Brown
_____
Signature

Mary Brown
_____
Name (Print)

50 Maple Street
_____
Address

Anywhere, USA   00000
_____

555-5555
_____
Tel. No.

SHAREHOLDER'S CONSENT TO
S CORPORATION ELECTION—FORM

Date:

Director
Internal Revenue Service Center

Dear Sir:

By means of this letter, I state my consent to have the _____ (name), a corporation with offices at _____ treated as S Corporation under Section 1362 of the Internal Revenue Code. Pursuant to Form 2553, I offer the following data:

1. My name is _____ .

2. I own _____ shares of stock of the _____ .

3. I acquired that stock on _____ .

4. My Social Security number is _____ .

5. My tax year ends on _____ .

6. The Corporation EIN number is _____ .

_____
Signature

_____
Name (Print)

_____
Address

_____

_____
Tel. No.

REQUEST FOR EXTENSION TO FILE
SHAREHOLDER'S CONSENT TO
S CORPORATION ELECTION—SAMPLE

July 15, 1991

Director
Internal Revenue Service
10 Oak Street
Anywhere, USA 00000

Dear Sir:

Be advised XYZ Corporation
("Corporation") requests an extension of the time for
the filing of shareholder consents with respect to the
Corporation's election to be subject to the S incorporation provisions of the Internal Revenue Code. In
support of this request, the following information is
furnished:

1. The Corporation was incorporated under the laws
of the State of New York   , on July 15   , 19 90   .

2. The Corporation first* had assets   on
July 15   , 19 90   .

3. All of the shareholders' consents to the
Corporation election to be subject under the S incorporation provisions of the Internal Revenue Code have not
and could not be filed on Form 2553, submitted with this
letter, for the following reason:

Mary Brown, holder of 50 shares out of 100 shares issued,
consented to election, however, she is presently out of the
country for one month.

4. Other than Mary Brown   , all other
shareholders have consented to the election, and each of
those shareholders has consented in writing on Form
2553.

5. The government's interest will not be prejudiced by treating the election of the Corporation to
be chaptered under the S incorporation provisions of the
Internal Revenue Code as valid.

By:_____
                          Robert Brown
                          Title: President

* had assets, or
  had shareholders, or
  did business

REQUEST FOR EXTENSION TO FILE SHAREHOLDER'S CONSENT TO S CORPORATION ELECTION—FORM

Director
Internal Revenue Service

Dear Sir:

Be advised
("Corporation") requests an extension of the time for the filing of shareholder consents with respect to the Corporation's election to be subject to the S incorporation provisions of the Internal Revenue Code. In support of this request, the following information is furnished:

1. The Corporation was incorporated under the laws of the State of _____ , on _____ , 19__ .

2. The Corporation first* _____ on _____ , 19__ .

3. All of the shareholders' consents to the Corporation election to be taxed under the S incorporation provisions of the Internal Revenue Code have not and could not be filed on Form 2553, submitted with this letter, for the following reason:

4. Other than _____ , all other shareholders have consented to the election, and each of those shareholders has consented in writing on Form 2553.

5. The government's interest will not be prejudiced by treating the election of the Corporation to be chaptered under the S incorporation provisions of the Internal Revenue Code as valid.

By:_____

Title:_____

* had assets, or
  had shareholders, or
  did business

SS-4

Application for Employer Identification Number

(For use by employers and others. Please read the attached instructions before completing this form.)

EIN

OMB No. 1545-0003
Expires 4-30-94

Please type or print clearly.

1 Name of applicant (True legal name) (See instructions.)	

2 Trade name of business, if different from name in line 1	**3** Executor, trustee, "care of" name

4a Mailing address (street address) (room, apt., or suite no.)	**5a** Address of business (See instructions.)
4b City, state, and ZIP code	**5b** City, state, and ZIP code

6 County and state where principal business is located

7 Name of principal officer, grantor, or general partner (See instructions.) ▶

8a Type of entity (Check only one box.) (See instructions.)

- ☐ Individual SSN _____
- ☐ REMIC   ☐ Personal service corp.
- ☐ State/local government   ☐ National guard
- ☐ Other nonprofit organization (specify) _____
- ☐ Other (specify) ▶ _____
- ☐ Estate
- ☐ Plan administrator SSN _____
- ☐ Other corporation (specify) _____
- ☐ Federal government/military   ☐ Church or church controlled organization
- If nonprofit organization enter GEN (if applicable) _____
- ☐ Trust
- ☐ Partnership
- ☐ Farmers' cooperative

8b If a corporation, give name of foreign country (if applicable) or state in the U.S. where incorporated ▶

Foreign country	State

9 Reason for applying (Check only one box.)

- ☐ Started new business
- ☐ Hired employees
- ☐ Created a pension plan (specify type) ▶ _____
- ☐ Banking purpose (specify) ▶
- ☐ Changed type of organization (specify) ▶ _____
- ☐ Purchased going business
- ☐ Created a trust (specify) ▶ _____
- ☐ Other (specify) ▶

10 Date business started or acquired (Mo., day, year) (See instructions.)

11 Enter closing month of accounting year. (See instructions.)

12 First date wages or annuities were paid or will be paid (Mo., day, year). **Note:** *If applicant is a withholding agent, enter date income will first be paid to nonresident alien. (Mo., day, year)* . . . . ▶

13 Enter highest number of employees expected in the next 12 months. **Note:** *If the applicant does not expect to have any employees during the period, enter "0."* . . . . ▶

Nonagricultural	Agricultural	Household

14 Principal activity (See instructions.) ▶

15 Is the principal business activity manufacturing? . . . . ☐ **Yes** ☐ **No**
If "Yes," principal product and raw material used ▶

16 To whom are most of the products or services sold? Please check the appropriate box.   ☐ Business (wholesale)
☐ Public (retail)   ☐ Other (specify) ▶   ☐ N/A

17a Has the applicant ever applied for an identification number for this or any other business? . . . . ☐ **Yes** ☐ **No**
Note: *If "Yes," please complete lines 17b and 17c.*

17b If you checked the "Yes" box in line 17a, give applicant's true name and trade name, if different than name shown on prior application.

True name ▶   Trade name ▶

17c Enter approximate date, city, and state where the application was filed and the previous employer identification number if known.

Approximate date when filed (Mo., day, year)	City and state where filed	Previous EIN

Under penalties of perjury, I declare that I have examined this application, and to the best of my knowledge and belief, it is true, correct, and complete. | Telephone number (include area code)

Name and title (Please type or print clearly.) ▶

Signature ▶   Date ▶

Note: *Do not write below this line.   For official use only.*

Please leave blank ▶	Geo.	Ind.	Class	Size	Reason for applying

For Paperwork Reduction Act Notice, see attached instructions.   Cat. No. 16055N   Form **SS-4** (Rev. 4-91)

General Instructions

(Section references are to the Internal Revenue Code unless otherwise noted.)

Paperwork Reduction Act Notice.—We ask for the information on this form to carry out the Internal Revenue laws of the United States. You are required to give us this information. We need it to ensure that you are complying with these laws and to allow us to figure and collect the right amount of tax.

The time needed to complete and file this form will vary depending on individual circumstances. The estimated average time is:

Recordkeeping	7 min.
Learning about the law or the form	21 min.
Preparing the form	42 min.
Copying, assembling, and sending the form to IRS	20 min.

If you have comments concerning the accuracy of these time estimates or suggestions for making this form more simple, we would be happy to hear from you. You can write to both the **Internal Revenue Service,** Washington, DC 20224, Attention: IRS Reports Clearance Officer, T:FP; and the **Office of Management and Budget,** Paperwork Reduction Project (1545-0003), Washington, DC 20503. **DO NOT** send the tax form to either of these offices. Instead, see **Where To Apply.**

Purpose.—Use Form SS-4 to apply for an employer identification number (EIN). The information you provide on this form will establish your filing requirements.

Who Must File.—You must file this form if you have not obtained an EIN before and

● You pay wages to one or more employees.

● You are required to have an EIN to use on any return, statement, or other document, even if you are not an employer.

● You are required to withhold taxes on income, other than wages, paid to a nonresident alien (individual, corporation, partnership, etc.). For example, individuals who file **Form 1042,** Annual Withholding Tax Return for U.S. Source Income of Foreign Persons, to report alimony paid to nonresident aliens must have EINs.

Individuals who file **Schedule C,** Profit or Loss From Business, or **Schedule F,** Profit or Loss From Farming, of **Form 1040,** U.S. Individual Income Tax Return, must use EINs if they have a Keogh plan or are required to file excise, employment, or alcohol, tobacco, or firearms returns.

The following must use EINs even if they do not have any employees:

● Trusts, except an IRA trust, unless the IRA trust is required to file **Form 990-T,** Exempt Organization Business Income Tax Return, to report unrelated business taxable income or is filing Form 990-T to obtain a refund of the credit from a regulated investment company.

● Estates

● Partnerships

● REMICS (real estate mortgage investment conduits)

● Corporations

● Nonprofit organizations (churches, clubs, etc.)

● Farmers' cooperatives

● Plan administrators

New Business.—If you become the new owner of an existing business, **DO NOT** use the EIN of the former owner. If you already have an EIN, use that number. If you do not have an EIN, apply for one on this form. If you become the "owner" of a corporation by acquiring its stock, use the corporation's EIN.

If you already have an EIN, you may need to get a new one if either the organization or ownership of your business changes. If you incorporate a sole proprietorship or form a partnership, you must get a new EIN. However, **DO NOT** apply for a new EIN if you change only the name of your business.

File Only One Form SS-4.—File only one Form SS-4, regardless of the number of businesses operated or trade names under which a business operates. However, each corporation in an affiliated group must file a separate application.

If you do not have an EIN by the time a return is due, write "Applied for" and the date you applied in the space shown for the number. **DO NOT** show your social security number as an EIN on returns.

If you do not have an EIN by the time a tax deposit is due, send your payment to the Internal Revenue service center for your filing area. (See **Where To Apply** below.) Make your check or money order payable to Internal Revenue Service and show your name (as shown on Form SS-4), address, kind of tax, period covered, and date you applied for an EIN.

For more information about EINs, see **Pub. 583,** Taxpayers Starting a Business.

How To Apply.—You can apply for an EIN either by mail or by telephone. You can get an EIN immediately by calling the Tele-TIN phone number for the service center for your state, or you can send the completed Form SS-4 directly to the service center to receive your EIN in the mail.

Application by Tele-TIN.—The Tele-TIN program is designed to assign EINs by telephone. Under this program, you can receive your EIN over the telephone and use it immediately to file a return or make a payment.

To receive an EIN by phone, complete Form SS-4, then call the Tele-TIN phone number listed for your state under **Where To Apply.** The person making the call must be authorized to sign the form (see **Signature block** on page 3).

An IRS representative will use the information from the Form SS-4 to establish your account and assign you an EIN. Write the number you are given on the upper right-hand corner of the form, sign and date it, and promptly mail it to the Tele-TIN Unit at the service center address for your state.

Application by mail.—Complete Form SS-4 at least 4 to 5 weeks before you will need an EIN. Sign and date the application and mail it to the service center address for your state. You will receive your EIN in the mail in approximately 4 weeks.

Note: *The Tele-TIN phone numbers listed below will involve a long-distance charge to callers outside of the local calling area, and should only be used to apply for an EIN. Use 1-800-829-1040 to ask about an application by mail.*

Where To Apply.—

If your principal business, office or agency, or legal residence in the case of an individual, is located in: ▼	Call the Tele-TIN phone number shown or file with the Internal Revenue service center at: ▼
Florida, Georgia, South Carolina	Atlanta, GA 39901 (404) 455-2360
New Jersey, New York City and counties of Nassau, Rockland, Suffolk, and Westchester	Holtsville, NY 00501 (516) 447-4955
New York (all other counties), Connecticut, Maine, Massachusetts, New Hampshire, Rhode Island, Vermont	Andover, MA 05501 (508) 474-9717
Illinois, Iowa, Minnesota, Missouri, Wisconsin	Kansas City, MO 64999 (816) 926-5999
Delaware, District of Columbia, Maryland, Pennsylvania, Virginia	Philadelphia, PA 19255 (215) 961-3980
Indiana, Kentucky, Michigan, Ohio, West Virginia	Cincinnati, OH 45999 (606) 292-5467
Kansas, New Mexico, Oklahoma, Texas	Austin, TX 73301 (512) 462-7845
Alaska, Arizona, California (counties of Alpine, Amador, Butte, Calaveras, Colusa, Contra Costa, Del Norte, El Dorado, Glenn, Humboldt, Lake, Lassen, Marin, Mendocino, Modoc, Napa, Nevada, Placer, Plumas, Sacramento, San Joaquin, Shasta, Sierra, Siskiyou, Solano, Sonoma, Sutter, Tehama, Trinity, Yolo, and Yuba), Colorado, Idaho, Montana, Nebraska, Nevada, North Dakota, Oregon, South Dakota, Utah, Washington, Wyoming	Ogden, UT 84201 (801) 625-7645
California (all other counties), Hawaii	Fresno, CA 93888 (209) 456-5900
Alabama, Arkansas, Louisiana, Mississippi, North Carolina, Tennessee	Memphis, TN 37501 (901) 365-5970

If you have no legal residence, principal place of business, or principal office or agency in any Internal Revenue District, file your form with the Internal Revenue Service Center, Philadelphia, PA 19255 or call (215) 961-3980.

Specific Instructions

The instructions that follow are for those items that are not self-explanatory. Enter N/A (nonapplicable) on the lines that do not apply.

Line 1.—Enter the legal name of the entity applying for the EIN.

Individuals.—Enter the first name, middle initial, and last name.

Trusts.—Enter the name of the trust.

Estate of a decedent.—Enter the name of the estate.

Partnerships.—Enter the legal name of the partnership as it appears in the partnership agreement.

Corporations.—Enter the corporate name as set forth in the corporation charter or other legal document creating it.

Plan administrators.—Enter the name of the plan administrator. A plan administrator who already has an EIN should use that number.

Line 2.—Enter the trade name of the business if different from the legal name.

Note: *Use the full legal name entered on line 1 on all tax returns to be filed for the entity. However, if a trade name is entered on line 2, use only the name on line 1 **or** the name on line 2 consistently when filing tax returns.*

Line 3.—Trusts enter the name of the trustee. Estates enter the name of the executor, administrator, or other fiduciary. If the entity applying has a designated person to receive tax information, enter that person's name as the "care of" person. Print or type the first name, middle initial, and last name.

Lines 5a and 5b.—If the physical location of the business is different from the mailing address (lines 4a and 4b), enter the address of the physical location on lines 5a and 5b.

Line 7.—Enter the first name, middle initial, and last name of a principal officer if the business is a corporation; of a general partner if a partnership; and of a grantor if a trust.

Line 8a.—Check the box that best describes the type of entity that is applying for the EIN. If not specifically mentioned, check the "other" box and enter the type of entity. Do not enter N/A.

Individual.—Check this box if the individual files Schedule C or F (Form 1040) and has a Keogh plan or is required to file excise, employment, or alcohol, tobacco, or firearms returns. If this box is checked, enter the individual's SSN (social security number) in the space provided.

Plan administrator.—The term plan administrator means the person or group of persons specified as the administrator by the instrument under which the plan is operated. If the plan administrator is an individual, enter the plan administrator's SSN in the space provided.

New withholding agent.—If you are a new withholding agent required to file Form 1042, check the "other" box and enter in the space provided "new withholding agent."

REMICs.—Check this box if the entity is a real estate mortgage investment conduit (REMIC). A REMIC is any entity

1. To which an election to be treated as a REMIC applies for the tax year and all prior tax years,

2. In which all of the interests are regular interests or residual interests,

3. Which has one class of residual interests (and all distributions, if any, with respect to such interests are pro rata),

4. In which as of the close of the 3rd month beginning after the startup date and at all times thereafter, substantially all of its assets consist of qualified mortgages and permitted investments,

5. Which has a tax year that is a calendar year, and

6. With respect to which there are reasonable arrangements designed to ensure that: (a) residual interests are not held by disqualified organizations (as defined in section 860E(e)(5)), and (b) information necessary for the application of section 860E(e) will be made available.

For more information about REMICs see the Instructions for **Form 1066,** U. S. Real Estate Mortgage Investment Conduit Tax Return.

Personal service corporations.—Check this box if the entity is a personal service corporation. An entity is a personal service corporation for a tax year only if

1. The entity is a C corporation for the tax year.

2. The principal activity of the entity during the testing period (as defined in Temporary Regulations section 1.441-4T(f)) for the tax year is the performance of personal service.

3. During the testing period for the tax year, such services are substantially performed by employee-owners.

4. The employee-owners own 10 percent of the fair market value of the outstanding stock in the entity on the last day of the testing period for the tax year.

For more information about personal service corporations, see the instructions to **Form 1120,** U.S. Corporation Income Tax Return, and Temporary Regulations section 1.441-4T.

Other corporations.—This box is for any corporation other than a personal service corporation. If you check this box, enter the type of corporation (such as insurance company) in the space provided.

Other nonprofit organizations.—Check this box if the nonprofit organization is other than a church or church-controlled organization and specify the type of nonprofit organization (for example, an educational organization.)

Group exemption number (GEN).—If the applicant is a nonprofit organization that is a subordinate organization to be included in a group exemption letter under Revenue Procedure 80-27, 1980-1 C.B. 677, enter the GEN in the space provided. If you do not know the GEN, contact the parent organization for it. GEN is a four-digit number. Do not confuse it with the nine-digit EIN.

Line 9.—Check only one box. Do not enter N/A.

Started new business.—Check this box if you are starting a new business that requires an EIN. If you check this box, enter the type of business being started. **DO NOT** apply if you already have an EIN and are only adding another place of business.

Changed type of organization.—Check this box if the business is changing its type of organization, for example, if the business was a sole proprietorship and has been incorporated or has become a partnership. If you check this box, specify in the space provided the type of change made, for example, "from sole proprietorship to partnership."

Purchased going business.—Check this box if you acquired a business through purchase. Do not use the former owner's EIN. If you already have an EIN, use that number.

Hired employees.—Check this box if the existing business is requesting an EIN because it has hired or is hiring employees and is therefore required to file employment tax return for which an EIN is required. **DO NOT** apply if you already have an EIN and are only hiring employees.

Created a trust.—Check this box if you created a trust, and enter the type of trust created.

Created a pension plan.—Check this box if you have created a pension plan and need this number for reporting purposes. Also, enter the type of plan created.

Banking purpose.—Check this box if you are requesting an EIN for banking purpose only and enter the banking purpose (for example, checking, loan, etc.).

Other (specify).—Check this box if you are requesting an EIN for any reason other than those for which there are checkboxes and enter the reason.

Line 10.—If you are starting a new business, enter the starting date of the business. If the business you acquired is already operating, enter the date you acquired the business. Trusts should enter the date the trust was legally created. Estates should enter the date of death of the decedent whose name appears on line 1.

Line 11.—Enter the last month of your accounting year or tax year. An accounting year or tax year is usually 12 consecutive months. It may be a calendar year or a fiscal year (including a period of 52 or 53 weeks). A calendar year is 12 consecutive months ending on December 31. A fiscal year is either 12 consecutive months ending on the last day of any month other than December or a 52-53 week year. For more information

on accounting periods, see Pub. 538, Accounting Periods and Methods.

Individuals.—Your tax year generally will be a calendar year.

Partnerships.—Partnerships generally should conform to the tax year of either (1) its majority partners; (2) its principal partners; (3) the tax year that results in the least aggregate deferral of income (see Temporary Regulations section 1.706-1T); or (4) some other tax year, if (a) a business purpose is established for the fiscal year, or (b) the fiscal year is a "grandfather" year, or (c) an election is made under section 444 to have a fiscal year. (See the Instructions for **Form 1065,** U.S. Partnership Return of Income, for more information.)

REMICs.—Remics must have a calendar year as their tax year.

Personal service corporations.—A personal service corporation generally must adopt a calendar year unless:

1. It can establish to the satisfaction of the Commissioner that there is a business purpose for having a different tax year, or

2. It elects under section 444 to have a tax year other than a calendar year.

Line 12.—If the business has or will have employees, enter on this line the date on which the business began or will begin to pay wages to the employees. If the business does not have any plans to have employees, enter N/A on this line.

New withholding agent.—Enter the date you began or will begin to pay income to a nonresident alien. This also applies to individuals who are required to file Form 1042 to report alimony paid to a nonresident alien.

Line 14.—Generally, enter the exact type of business being operated (for example, advertising agency, farm, labor union, real estate agency, steam laundry, rental of coin-operated vending machine, investment club, etc.).

Governmental.—Enter the type of organization (state, county, school district, or municipality, etc.)

Nonprofit organization (other than governmental).—Enter whether organized for religious, educational, or humane purposes, and the principal activity (for example, religious organization—hospital, charitable).

Mining and quarrying.—Specify the process and the principal product (for example, mining bituminous coal, contract drilling for oil, quarrying dimension stone, etc.).

Contract construction.—Specify whether general contracting or special trade contracting. Also, show the type of work normally performed (for example, general contractor for residential buildings, electrical subcontractor, etc.).

Trade.—Specify the type of sales and the principal line of goods sold (for example, wholesale dairy products, manufacturer's representative for mining machinery, retail hardware, etc.).

Manufacturing.—Specify the type of establishment operated (for example, sawmill, vegetable cannery, etc.).

Signature block.—The application must be signed by: (1) the individual, if the person is an individual, (2) the president, vice president, or other principal officer, if the person is a corporation, (3) a responsible and duly authorized member or officer having knowledge of its affairs, if the person is a partnership or other unincorporated organization, or (4) the fiduciary, if the person is a trust or estate.

*U.S. Government Printing Office: 1991 — 523-733/40128

6 | OPERATING YOUR S CORPORATION

OVERVIEW

Operating an S Corporation is no more difficult than operating a C Corporation. There are, however, certain rules that must be followed if the business is to properly fulfill its responsibilities as an S Corporation and maintain its status.

Questions that often arise are: Do I need an attorney? Do I need a tax advisor? Do I need an accountant? The answer to each of these questions is *yes*, but not on staff. You will need to be able to consult with an attorney for contracts, from as simple a form as leasing space or a truck, to as complicated a form as a major construction project. There are traps for those who are not fully versed in the nuances and customs of contract language. You will need to consult a tax advisor who is either a tax attorney or a certified public accountant (CPA). The tax advisor will set up your tax recording and reporting system, provide tax-saving advice (such as deferral or acceleration of income and deductions), and other tax-saving strategies available to you. (The strategies are discussed in greater detail in Chapters 9, 10, and 11.)

Find experts with whom you are comfortable. Be sure that they specialize in the areas of importance to you, and that they are conscious of the very special needs of both a new business operation and an S Corporation. Check with other businesses in your area, or call your state bar association (contacts are listed in Appendix 3) for assistance in making your selection. Ask about costs and how you will be charged. Don't wait until you are surprised by an unexpected fee.

IMMEDIATE STEPS

1. *Transfer Personal Assets to the Corporation*

If you have been operating a business or service prior to S incorporation (as many people do), you can transfer the assets, financial instruments, accounts and debts of the old business to the new corporation, at an agreed sum or consideration and receive shares of stock in exchange. You cannot, however, burden the corporation with more debts than assets. Further, you cannot sell your personal property to the corporation at inflated prices, or exchange its stock for personal property that is overvalued. Be certain to obtain an appraisal so you can establish a "basis" for your shares and to determine the appreciation of the assets after it becomes part of the S Corporation.

You will run into the term "basis" frequently in other sections of this book, particularly as related to shareholder rights and taxation. Basis in its most simple term refers to what you have invested in the company. It can be cash, property, or securities. It can come from what you own, or what you borrow for the purposes of the corporation, if you are liable for its repayment.

Your basis can vary, particularly if there is more than one shareholder. Basis will increase from income passed through to you by the S Corporation. Basis will decrease by nonincome distributions to you as a shareholder, as well as by corporation losses, expenses, and depletion (oil and gas) deductions. A loan made to the corporation at an unreasonably low interest rate may become "interest income" to the corporation, and become either taxable compensation or a dividend to the person making the loan that, in turn, may change the shareholder's basis. These aspects will be discussed in greater detail later.

You should also check to determine whether the state will impose a sales tax or transfer tax on the sale of assets.

It will also be necessary to obtain approval from the shareholders and directors of the S Corporation, authorizing the acquisition of assets, assumption of debts, and issuance of shares in consideration of the transfer.

2. *Notify All Existing Business Affiliates and Customers or Clients of the New Change to a Corporate Status*

This can be done by personal communication (telephone or letter), or by a small newspaper notice. Generally, all subsequent company records and transactions should be changed to reflect the new "corporate" status of the organization, including the printing of new letterheads, business cards, stationery, and sign.

As a seller of assets to the corporation, you should also comply with the Bulk Sales Act in your state that generally provides that creditors of the seller be notified of the intended transfer at least 10 days in advance. As a practical matter, however, this need not be complied with if the existing liabilities are to be fully paid in the ordinary course of business. Similarly, if any assets to be transferred are encumbered or subject to lien or security interest, then authorization to transfer the encumbered asset must be obtained from the lienholder.

3. Determine State and Local Requirements

Not only should the parties starting a new business look into the formalities for incorporation, but other possible regulation and clearances must also be considered. Permits and licenses are required for such businesses as real estate brokers, barbers, hairdressers, private investigators, cosmetologists, billiard rooms, pharmacies, nursing homes, notaries, peddlers, newsstands, employment agencies, businesses serving or selling alcoholic beverages, health concerns and hospitals, and educational institutions. Many businesses are regulated by federal agencies, such as brokerage and securities businesses, air transportation, banking, and drug manufacturing companies. Before commencing any new business, you should consider what regulations are applicable so that your business will not be conducted in violation of these rules and regulations. Bear in mind that an S Corporation cannot engage in certain business activities (i.e., banking). The state offices to contact are listed in Appendix 3.

4. Determine Withholding Taxes

Any business that hires employees must consider whether it is subject to rules relating to withholding of taxes for local, state, and the federal government, whether it must pay social security tax, unemployment insurance, or worker's compensation, and whether any unions have jurisdiction and what pension or other payments must be made to them. Minimum wage requirements and their applicability should be considered together with the permissibility of hiring minors, and any occupational safety and health regulations. There are, however, no special withholding tax requirements for an S Corporation as compared to a C Corporation. You will be expected to file a W-2 withholding form for each of your paid employees, as noted in Chapter 9, and shown in Appendix 2.

5. Keep Separate Financial Records

Remember that your corporation is viewed in the eyes of the law as a different "legal entity" separate and apart from the owner(s). Hence, to avoid potential IRS problems, you must maintain separate sets of records—one for your personal affairs, and one for the affairs of the corporation. As a rule, however, it is not necessary to maintain an elaborate bookkeeping system. A separate banking account, and a bookkeeping system that clearly shows what you and the corporation separately earn and pay out, is usually sufficient. A local bookkeeper or accountant can easily set up a convenient accounting and tax system for your business. An S Corporation requires no special bookkeeping procedure. (Chapter 9 describes the basic tax records you will need for your S Corporation bookkeeping.)

6. Set Up Your Corporate Bank Accounts

To open a corporate bank account, you will need an Employer Identification Number (EIN) for your corporation. To obtain this, file an application,

Form SS-4, with the IRS. (See Chapter 5 for SS-4 form.) Another item you'll most probably be required to have by the bank, is a "corporate resolution" duly signed and impressed with the "corporate seal" as an official corporate indication of authorization to open such an account(s). Most banks will provide you with the appropriate corporate resolutions, and a corporate seal can be ordered as part of the corporate kit. (See Chapter 3, "Forming the Corporation" for names of firms that can provide corporate kits with corporate seals.)

7. *Qualify in Other States*

If your new S Corporation is a local business only, it is unlikely that you will have any questions as to whether you need to be authorized or qualified to do business in another state. You clearly are doing business in only one place. But what happens if you start advertising in magazines and you get orders from other states? Are you now doing business in more than one state? Or, what if you are in sales and have a store or sales office only in one place, but have sales representatives who drive to other states and call on potential customers? Does this mean you are now doing business elsewhere? If you start expanding and open up new stores, then you would clearly be doing business in these other locations.

Before we go further into how you decide whether you are "doing business" in another state, let's look at why it matters. If you are doing business in another state, but have not qualified by filing the proper papers and paying the fees, the consequences can be serious. In all states, an unqualified foreign corporation is denied access to the courts of the state, which would mean you could not sue someone in that state in order to enforce a contract or obligation. In addition, fines are imposed by many states when they discover a corporation doing business there without having qualified, and in some cases directors, officers, or agents may be subject to these fines. These consequences could be very serious to your business.

The statutes of many states define what constitutes "doing business" within that state, and these statutes should be consulted.

The model corporation act gives a list of activities, which, in and of themselves alone, do not constitute doing business. Since this act is the basis for the state laws in many states, it is a good guide as to what you can do without having to qualify:

(a) Maintaining or defending any action or suit or any administrative or arbitration proceeding, or effecting settlement thereof, or the settlement of claims or disputes.

(b) Holding meetings of its directors or shareholders, or carrying on other activities concerning its internal affairs.

(c) Maintaining bank accounts.

(d) Maintaining offices or agencies for the transfer, exchange, and registration of its securities, or appointing and maintaining trustees or depositaries with relation to its securities.

(e) Effecting sales through independent contractor

(f) Soliciting or procuring orders, whether by mail or through employees or agents or otherwise, where such orders must be approved for acceptance by an office located in another state before becoming binding contracts.

(g) Creating as borrower or lender, or acquiring, indebtedness or mortgages or other security interests in real or personal property.

(h) Securing or collecting debts or enforcing any rights in property securing the same.

(i) Transacting any business in interstate commerce.

(j) Conducting an isolated transaction completed within a period of thirty days and not in the course of a number of repeated transactions of like nature.

If you do have to become authorized to do business as a foreign corporation, the procedure is relatively simple. You obtain from the Secretary of State the application form, complete it, and file it with the proper fees.

MAINTAINING CORPORATE RECORDS

Once organized, the S Corporation must maintain a continuous and accurate record of all authorized actions—whether approved by its stockholders or directors.

A complete and detailed record of stockholders and directors meeting—"minutes" as they are called—is important for many reasons:

1. Parties dealing with the corporation may want evidence that the corporate action was approved.

2. Officers and employees within the corporation are entitled to the protection their acts were approved.

3. Accurate minutes is frequently necessary to preserve certain tax benefits or to avoid tax liabilities and penalties.

4. Minutes are oftentimes necessary to prove the corporation is operated as an entity, independent of its principals.

5. Actions that change a shareholder's basis (ownership) of the S Corporation, even for a single day of the year, can have tax consequences, as discussed in Chapters 9 and 11.

Stockholders' Actions

Stockholders can usually vote on the broadest issues relating to the S Corporation. These typically include change of corporate name, address, purpose, the amount of authorized or type shares, and other matters involving the corporate structure. Stockholders' action may also be needed on major legal or financial issues such as to mortgage, encumber, pledge, or lease all or substantially all of the corporate assets, or to file bankruptcy, merge, or consolidate. There are, of course, many other actions that can be taken by stockholders and many of these resolutions can be found within this section. The primary function of the stockholders, however, is to elect the board of directors, through whose governance the S Corporation is actually managed. Stockholders can act officially only as a group. This means that a formal meeting is needed before they can legally bind the corporation. There are some exceptions where the stockholders can consent in writing to a particular action without having to hold a meeting, such as in the election to become an S Corporation.

Certain rules and procedures have to be followed for stockholders to properly conduct an official stockholder meeting.

1. Every stockholder has to be properly notified about the time and place of the meeting, who is calling the meeting, and any matters that will be considered at the meeting. It is common in small corporations for the stockholders to do without a formal notice, especially where the bylaws set out the time and place of the regular annual meeting of stockholders. This can be done by having all the stockholders sign a waiver of notice at the meeting. Unscheduled or special meetings of stockholders may require notice, although a signed waiver of notice can also be used at these meetings. For an unscheduled meeting to be legally convened, it is essential that the records show that proper notice was given, or that the stockholders signed a waiver of notice requirement.

   Your articles of incorporation or bylaws will specify where and when a stockholders' meeting can legally be held, and the book of minutes should show the time and place of each meeting. In this way, you can prove that the meeting complied with the legal requirements.

2. No business can be transacted at a stockholders' meeting unless a quorum is present. Therefore, it is essential that the book of minutes reflect a quorum of stockholders attended the meeting. The articles of incorporation or the bylaws will usually state the size of the quorum, either in terms of the number of stockholders, or the number of shares that must be represented at the meeting. For example, a bylaw that "two-thirds of all stockholders shall constitute a quorum" applies to the number of stockholders, and not to the amount of stock they own. On the other hand, a bylaw that "a majority of the outstanding stock shall constitute a quorum" means that a certain number of shares of stock must be represented, regardless of whether the stock is owned by one person or by thousands of people. If there is no rule on a quorum, then whatever number of stockholders shows up for the meeting will constitute a quo-

rum; however, some states require a stated percentage of the outstanding shares be represented at a shareholders' meeting to be valid.

3. Stockholder meetings must have a chairperson to preside over the meeting. It must also have a secretary to record what happened at the meeting. The bylaws will ordinarily designate these officials, such as by specifying that the president serve as chairperson, and the secretary act as secretary; however, substitutes are usually allowable.

4. The first items of business at every stockholders' meeting should be to read and approve the minutes of the previous meeting. Once the minutes are approved, they legally document what occurred at the meeting. They are the most nearly conclusive proof of what the corporation is authorized to do. That is why it is important to show that the minutes have been read and approved as accurate, or that necessary changes have been made.

Directors' Actions

Most of the rules and procedures that apply to stockholders' meetings apply equally to meetings of the board of directors with several exceptions:

1. Directors will meet far more often than stockholders, and in larger S Corporations may even meet monthly. The directors can also hold special meetings for interim board action, and in more active S Corporations they will routinely meet more often.

2. The board—as with stockholders—can only function through a duly-called meeting where a quorum of directors (as defined in the bylaws) are present. Directors who may be in conflict with the interests of the S Corporation may, however, not be counted towards the quorum or entitled to vote. An example of this is when the corporation plans to enter into a contract with a company with which the director is affiliated.

3. The board must be particularly careful to document not only its actions but why the action was taken. Because the board has responsibility to stockholders—and potential liability to other constituencies—it may be called upon to show why its action was prudent—particularly in areas of dividends, loans to officers, major contracts, compensation, and policy-making. It is especially critical for the minutes to include or refer to reports, arguments, opinions, and other documents to support the reasonableness of the board's actions.

4. Frequently the board will be called upon to issue "certified resolutions" or "certificates of vote," which conclusively show to third parties dealing with the corporation that the person acting on behalf of the corporation has the required authority. These forms are contained in Appendix 1, and can be easily completed with notary seal and/or corporate seal.

All records, resolutions, and minutes should be kept within the corporate minute book and kept for no less than six years—although retaining the records longer is recommended considering the numerous types of claims that are possible and the varying statute of limitations in the various states.

7 COMPENSATION STRATEGIES

OVERVIEW

Another major advantage of an S Corporation is that it allows for greater flexibility in how compensation to officers and key employees can be structured, often reducing personal tax liability or allowing more net income to remain within the family.

COMPENSATION TYPES

You might think that the least of your worries will be how your S Corporation will compensate you. The challenge is how to obtain maximum tax benefits for yourself while at the same time assuring maximum profits and minimum tax liability for the S Corporation. If you are an officer or employee of the S Corporation as well as a shareholder, you can be compensated by salary, by distribution of profits based on the amount of stock you own (your stock basis), by a distribution of stock itself, or by some combination of all these methods.

Your basic choices are: cash (present or deferred, salary or profits distribution); stock (actual or options); corporation note (as evidence or as payment); tax-free fringe benefits (those allowed by the IRS as corporate deductions); or property (at fair market value).

The combinations can be complicated. There is no simple formula for the creation of maximum income with minimum tax. Each choice affects the shareholder's tax bill, or the profitability or unprofitability of the S Corporation, or both. For best results, you will need the advice and guidance of a tax consultant (CPA or attorney) who has specific experience and knowhow in the field of S Corporation tax law.

Cash or Distribution?

The S Corporation's profitability for the year will have a significant effect on the shareholder-employee's income. Should compensation be a cash salary or a profits distribution? Other factors include the shareholder-employee's ownership basis, and the presence or absence of an Accumulated Adjustments Account (AAA).

Note that the AAA is created as a potential source for return of capital distributions to the shareholders. The AAA is the sum of net income (not including tax-exempt income) taxed to shareholders, minus net deductions (but not disallowed deductions relating to tax-exempt income), and minus prior distributions out of the AAA.

Distributions out of the AAA equal return of capital to the shareholders, whereas distributions not out of the AAA are dividends.

Profitable Year. The choice is between salary and distribution:

1. A cash compensation salary becomes an expense deduction for the S Corporation, reducing the corporation's pass-through profit.

2. A distribution of profits may have the same effect as the payment of a deductible salary if the salary does not exceed the shareholder-employee's stock basis. If the basis is exceeded, the payment becomes a stock distribution, changing the recipient's stock basis.

Nonprofitable Year. The choices become less clear:

1. Does the shareholder-employee have enough stock basis for the compensation to pass through as a salary deduction for the corporation?

2. Does the S Corporation have accumulated earnings and profits equal to or greater than the shareholder-employee's cash distribution respective to his or her stock basis?

3. If the answer to Question 2 is yes, does the S Corporation have an AAA at least equal to the possible cash distribution?

Here are the decision possibilities and their tax and/or deduction consequences:

1. *When there are no S Corporation earnings and the shareholder basis is sufficient to allow pass-through of losses.* The tax effect is the same from either salary payment or a distribution with respect to stock basis. Salary payment increases the corporation's loss by the amount of the salary. Distribution, on the other hand, reduces the shareholder's stock basis.

2. *When there are no S Corporation earnings and zero shareholder basis, both for stock and for loans to the corporation.* As before, a cash salary compensation increases the corporate loss, but the loss is "suspended" as a deduction because of the shareholder's lack of stock basis. This means that the shareholder has ordinary income along with an equal but suspended (postponed) ordinary deduction for the corporation. In contrast, a distribution normally equals a capital gain for the shareholder, instead of a salary payment.

3. *When there are S Corporation earnings, shareholder basis exists, and there is an AAA.* The results are the same as for a above.

4. *When there are S Corporation earnings and a shareholder basis exists, but there is no AAA.* Payment by salary gives better tax results than is possible with a distribution. A salary is taxable as ordinary income to the shareholder, with an equal loss (deductible expense) to the corporation.

5. *When there are S Corporation earnings and no shareholder basis, but there is an AAA.* The results are the same as for b above.

6. *When there are S Corporation earnings, but no shareholder basis and no AAA.* A salary payment equals ordinary income to the shareholder. Corporate loss is increased, but suspended. Distribution, on the other hand, equals a dividend from accumulated earnings and profits. It appears that ordinary income with suspended deduction for the corporation is better than distribution income with no deduction. But a dividend distribution has the benefit of reducing corporate earnings and profits.

A Matter of Timing

The simplest situation is where both the S Corporation and the shareholder have the same tax year, as discussed in Chapter 9. If the tax years differ, however, several consequences may result. Tax deductions that pass through to the shareholder may be delayed for as long as 11 months, and the time to report income may be accelerated.

The S Corporation may not deduct as an expense the salary owed to a *related* person until the day the salary is includable in that person's income. By definition, in this situation a related person is someone who owns, directly or indirectly, any stock in the S Corporation; ergo, any shareholder is considered to be a related person.

Compensation and Withholding Taxes

The form elected for shareholder income will affect federal tax consequences, and, depending on the state in which you are situated, local taxes.

Salaries and wages are subject to S Corporation withholding of taxes for income (W-2), Social Security (FICA), and unemployment (FUTA). Also, earning a salary may reduce future Social Security benefits.

Distributions ordinarily do not trigger S Corporation withholding or unemployment taxes. Recipients are responsible for their own Social Security payments. Note that if the shareholder recipient is also a salaried employee, and if the IRS determines that the salary is inadequate, part of the distribution may be redefined as salary, triggering S Corporation withholding for income, Social Security, and unemployment taxes on the salary amount. The problems of inadequate salaries are discussed later in this chapter.

Income pass-through is not salary. It does not trigger any of the three withholding taxes by the corporation.

Noncash Compensation

Noncash compensation in lieu of cash salary payments includes stock, stock options, property, notes, and tax-free fringe benefits.

Stock Compensation. If the S Corporation uses its own stock as compensation, the employee-recipient generally must include the current value of that stock as personal gross income. The tax basis for the stock is equal to its reported value.

Ordinary, the S Corporation can deduct the value of the stock as an operating expense, with benefits of the deduction passing through to all shareholders. The problem is that as S Corporation stock is not publicly traded, its value is subjective and subject to IRS valuation procedures.

While stock distributions to shareholders generally are tax-free, stock compensation usually is currently taxable.

Stock Option Compensation. The S Corporation may issue stock options as compensation. Fortunately for S Corporation status, such distributions ordinarily do not constitute a second class of stock. As was true for payment by stock compensation, there is the problem of valuation of the stock.

Property Compensation. When property is used as compensation, the S Corporation generally can deduct the value of the property in the year in which the employee reports it as income. The corporation then recognizes a loss (expense) on the property transfer.

Corporate Notes as Compensation. If the S corporation issues its own note as *evidence* of its debt for unpaid salary, the employee normally does not have taxable income until the amount of the note is actually paid. If the employee is also a shareholder, there is no corporate level deduction until the employee can report the property as income.

If, on the other hand, the S Corporation issues its own note as *payment* (not merely evidence of debt) of the employee's salary, the employee must take the fair market value of that note as income. If the note is issued to a shareholder with respect to stock, receipt of the note may be tax free, ordinary income, or capital gain.

Tax-Free Fringe Benefits as Compensation. As will be discussed in Chapter 8, there are strict rules concerning the S Corporation's ability to deduct the costs of fringe benefits as expenses. Shareholders who own more than 2 percent of the S Corporation's stock may not deduct prohibited fringe benefits from income. A shareholder is deemed to be a 2 percent holder for the entire year if on *any single day of the year* that person owns in excess of 2 percent.

The federal tax code definition of fringe benefits is vague, but they are generally deemed to include group-term life insurance premiums, certain health and accident benefits, death benefits, meals, and lodging. There is still some question about the deductibility of qualified transportation, cafeteria plans, and education assistance programs.

Qualified Deferred Compensation Plans

Deferred compensation rules are generally the same for S Corporations, C Corporations, and Partnerships. Principal tax advantages of deferred compensation plans include:

1. The amount of the deferred compensation contributions by the S Corporation ordinarily may be currently deducted.
2. Employee beneficiaries of a deferred compensation plan generally are not taxed until they actually receive the distribution.
3. Income for the money held in the plan generally accumulates without any tax during the period of accumulation.
4. A lump-sum distribution to a beneficiary under the plan may be taxed under favorable rules.

But there are drawbacks. The employee must wait to receive the money.

Also, the corporation cannot discriminate. The plan must cover non-shareholder-employees as well as shareholder-employees. And, for the S Corporation in particular, the corporation may not make a loan to a shareholder-employee, specifically referring to an employee or officer who owns directly or indirectly more than 5 percent of the S Corporation's stock on *any single day of the entire tax year.*

Impact on Basis

We noted that S Corporation losses flow through to the corporation shareholders and may be used as deductions against their other income. We also noted a limitation on that rule: losses can only be used as a deduction if the shareholder has sufficient basis in his or her stock and debt to cover the amount of the loss at risk. If a shareholder-employee draws all of his or her income from the S Corporation in the form of wages, the basis in his or her stock remains unchanged. If, on the other hand, the shareholder draws only a portion of his or her income as wages, the part that is not drawn will become corporate profit at the end of the year. If the money is removed as a distribution of profits, the amount taken in this form will be added to the shareholder's basis in his or her stock, and can, therefore, be later used against corporate losses.

> *Example:*
> *Assume that the S Corporation has two equal shareholders, John and Jane, and that they are unrelated familywise. Together, they own 100 percent of the shares of S Corporation. Although they agree that both will share profits equally, John, who had put up most of the money to get the business off the ground, does not work for the corporation nor does he draw a salary. Jane works for the corporation full time and is compensated for her services:*
>
> *Let's now assume that the IRS determines that Jane's salary was unreasonable and that they conclude it was unreasonable to the extent of $20,000. The result would be that the payment to Jane would be considered a distribution. She would not have to include the $20,000 when reporting her taxable income. However, since the $20,000 payment to Jane is a distribution, the corporation cannot claim it as a deduction for salary. That means the corporation will have an additional $20,000 of income that will flow through to its shareholders. John and Jane will each have to report an extra $10,000 of income—in John's case, he will be paying tax on money he never received; Jane, on the other hand, will receive $20,000 and pay tax on $10,000*
>
> *Nor do the consequences end there. John's basis in his stock will be increased by $10,000—his share of the distribution that was treated as a corporate profit. Jane, however, will see her basis reduced by $10,000 (the $20,000 decrease because the distribution is partially offset by a $10,000 increase attributable to her share of the $20,000 distribution treated as a corporate profit).*

DETERMINING REASONABLE COMPENSATION

Because an S Corporation avoids the double taxation of a C Corporation, there is little incentive for a shareholder-employee to increase salary simply for purposes of escaping the corporate tax on corporate profits. In an S Corporation, the overall tax liability is precisely the same whether the shareholder-employee takes his or her payment as salary or profits.

For that reason, the IRS is not as concerned with the "reasonableness" of compensation with an S Corporation as it is with a C Corporation. On the other hand, the IRS frequently challenges C Corporation shareholder-employees who pay themselves high salaries to avoid the double tax on corporate profits. If the IRS is successful in arguing the compensation level is "unreasonable," the excess salary is recalculated as corporate profits on which it must pay the corporate tax.

Should the S Corporation seek to avoid withholding taxes by not paying its owner-employees a salary, it would do so by making a distribution to those employees. Distributions, since they are not wages, would not be subject to withholding taxes, but each distribution affects the shareholder's stock basis, as discussed below.

Both the IRS and the Social Security Administration are alert to this possibility. Both will be quick to take the position that distributions are disguised wages subject to withholding. And both have been successful in making this argument. Shareholders, otherwise entitled to Social Security benefits, have another concern: if they do, in fact, work for their S Corporation without salary, the Social Security Administration will take the position that distributions they receive are, in fact, wages, and that those wages should be applied to reduce the amount of Social Security benefits the shareholder-employee will be entitled to receive. (This problem, it should be noted, exists for both C and S Corporations.)

One way to minimize the impact of the withholding problem is to minimize the amount of wages received by the shareholder-employee. Wages can be reduced to the lowest reasonable amount that can be justified for the services in question. It should be noted, however, that monies taken as salary will reduce passive profits and, therefore, there will be less earnings to be shielded by passive losses.

Although there is no one fixed guideline that establishes precisely what constitutes reasonable compensation, there are accepted standards. The most objective test looks to salaries paid to individuals performing comparable services for comparable businesses. Even this test is subject to other considerations. For example, the executive in question may have offered services far greater in effort or scope than would ordinarily be expected. In such cases, a bonus may very well be in order. Straight salary (or bonuses) can be tied to performance standards, (e.g., gross sales, an approach that may lead to justifiably high, or low salaries). Other factors that may be considered when determining whether compensation is reasonable include:

1. Business Performance: If the business enjoys a significant increase in sales volume or net profits, higher compensation can be justified.

2. Extensive Experience: An employee with years of experience or special knowledge in a given field generally justifies higher compensation than a less experienced person.

If you anticipate a problem with the salary level, it may be wise to prepare a formal employment contract between yourself and the corporation. This employment contract can then spell out the responsibilities that may help justify the salary level.

While the IRS may look at the level of compensation, as a practical matter, it seldom contests salary levels within a small corporation unless there is a clear case of abuse.

INCOME SPLITTING

Starting in 1988, the Tax Reform Act of 1986 provides two basic tax rates for individuals: 15 percent and 28 percent. Given the difference of 13 percent, many taxpayers who form small businesses will be tempted to underpay themselves and maximize the salary they pay to family members, usually children, who are in a lower tax bracket.

To prevent this, the Internal Revenue Code allows the IRS to reallocate income in situations where a family member draws an unreasonably low salary for his or her efforts. The family member in question does not have to be a shareholder in the S Corporation but may be a spouse, parent, grandparent, child, or grandchild of a shareholder. A parent, for example, may be willing to work full time to assist a child and may prefer not to draw a salary to perhaps avoid reducing Social Security benefits.

But there are commonly encountered situations where you can, with some degree of safety, spread income within the family so it is taxed at the lower 15 percent rate.

For example, you have two children and want each to receive $100 monthly. If you pay it to them as an allowance, you must pay tax on the earnings before you give them the remainder. Assuming you are in the 28 percent bracket, you must earn $280 monthly to give them $200. A better strategy may be to hire your children as employees of the S Corporation. Pay them by the hour to maintain, paint, clean, or otherwise perform services for your S Corporation. Their earnings now become a deduction to the business thereby increasing the deductions you add to your personal return.

And don't forget, your children could earn up to $3250 in 1990 ($3,000 in 1988) without owning any tax. In fact, each could earn $5,250 tax-free if he or she contributed $2,000 to an IRA.

This means that when you pay each child $100 monthly as wages, absolutely no taxes are paid on it. Whatever bracket you are in, you need earn only $200 monthly to give them $200.

Be careful to maintain employment records, showing dates and hours worked. Be sure wages paid are reasonable when compared to work done. If your S Corporation is ever audited, you will need solid backup information prove your deductions.

In another example, you can also use your S Corporation to split *investment income* with family members, cutting your tax bill and keeping more cash in the family. Assume you earn $10,000 annually from investments and that you are in the 28 percent tax bracket, so the IRS takes $2,800.

If you form an S Corporation instead, and give half the stock to your three children, they can now record their proportionate share of the income on their returns. Each child will report $1,667 of income (one-third of $5,000). Under the 1986 Tax Reform Act each child will be entitled to a $500 standard deduction (assuming the child had no other earnings). Each child will pay tax on $1,167 at a rate of 15 percent. The total tax paid by your children will be $525. Your tax on the $5,000 of income would have been $1,400, a savings to your family of $875.

Tax Warning:
The examples described above will only work if the children with whom you split your investments are over 14 years of age. Under the Tax Reform Act of 1986, the unearned income of children under the age of 14 will be treated as follows: the first $500 is excluded, the next $500 is taxes at the child's tax rate (assume 15 percent), the remainder is taxed at the parent's rate.

Tax Warning:
If the shareholder-employee's salary appears unreasonably low, the IRS can reallocate income between family members. The criteria for determining whether compensation is too low is the same as determining whether it is too high.

Another income splitting approach is to give your spouse $2,000 to help keep corporate records. If your spouse opens an IRA account and invests the $2,000 in the account each year it will grow to $144,000 in 20 years. And, of course, it will all be tax deferred until mandatory withdrawal begins at age 70 ½.

Tax Warning:
This plan will work only if neither you nor your spouse currently participates in a qualified retirement program. The Tax Reform Act of 1986 denies IRAs for individuals who are covered by a retirement plan or who are married to someone who participates in a qualified plan. Note also the income limits imposed for purposes of IRAs.

8 FRINGE BENEFITS AND THE S CORPORATION

OVERVIEW

The legislative history of S Corporations show several changes in the rules regarding fringe benefits.

Prior to 1982 an S Corporation could provide the same fringe benefits—medical, accident, disability, life insurance plans—that a C Corporation could, and do so on the same terms. Premiums paid by the corporation were deductible as a business expense; benefits received by the employee were excluded from taxable income. Therefore, in terms of fringe benefits the S Corporation featured no disadvantage.

However, in 1982 Congress sought to provide the S Corporation with as many partnership tax features as possible. Most of the changes worked to help entrepreneurs who sought the benefits of limited liability associated with incorporation and the single tax on earnings available in the sole proprietorship or partnership.

When S Corporations were taxed on a par with partnerships, Congress applied the rule on partnerships and fringe benefits to S Corporations. This means that the S Corporation cannot deduct as a business expense the cost of fringe benefits provided to most shareholder-employees. As is the case with partnerships, the shareholder-employee who receives a benefit must include the benefit when reporting taxable income.

Such benefits include:

1. Premiums paid by the S Corporation for medical and disability plans.

2. Premiums paid for $50,000 group life insurance policies.

3. Meals and lodging furnished by the S Corporation to the employee but for the convenience of the company.

4. The $5,000 death benefit exclusion available to the estate of an employee whose employer provides this benefit.

If the S Corporation pays for health or medical insurance policies for a 2 percent shareholder-employee, the cost of the policy becomes income to the beneficiary, and cannot be claimed as an expense deduction for the S Corporation. The policy beneficiary is, however, treated as self-employed, and may deduct 25 percent of the dollar value of the policy at the bottom of Form 1040 (line 26 for 1991), with the remainder of the policy as a medical expense. One warning, the amount of the 25 percent deduction cannot exceed wages as an S Corporation employee.

WHO IS QUALIFIED TO RECEIVE BENEFITS?

The important point to remember is that fringe benefits may be provided to nonshareholder-employees. As with a regular C Corporation the cost of those benefits are deductible by the S Corporation and nontaxable to the employee. Therefore, an S Corporation features absolutely no disadvantage in recruiting and retaining valuable employees who, of course, will expect a competitive fringe benefit package.

Therefore, only employees who are stockholders of the S Corporation are ineligible to receive tax-free fringe benefits. If the corporation provides fringe benefits to stockholder-employees, the cost of the fringe benefits would not be deductible by the S Corporation and would be taxable to the stockholder-employee.

The rule described above applies to all shareholder-employees who own more than 2 percent of the S Corporation stock or, if the corporation has both voting and nonvoting stock, more than 2 percent of the corporation's total combined voting stock. If either of these ownership requirements is satisfied for just one day of the corporation tax year, the rule applies.

Example:
On January 1, 1988, Mary Smith owned 3 percent of S Corporation stock. On January 2, 1988, she sold her stock interest but continued to remain employed by the corporation for the rest of the year.

Under these circumstances, Mary would be ineligible to receive tax-free fringe benefits for all of 1988 (as she owned over 2 percent during a part of 1988); however, she may receive tax-free benefits starting January 1, 1989.

The disqualification of stockholder-employees who own over 2 percent of the shares also extends to an employed relative who owns no shares. The term "relative" includes spouse, parents, grandparents, children, and grandchildren. Furthermore, this disqualification extends to an employed relative who owns no shares but is related to a disqualified shareholder who is not an employee of the corporation.

The obvious legislative intent in disqualifying "relatives" is to prevent a disqualified stockholder from indirectly benefitting from tax-free fringe benefits provided the relative, and, of course, it also avoids a stockholder from using a relative as a "straw" so as to frustrate the intent of the law.

The drawback to a stockholder-employee of not obtaining tax-free fringe benefits is, of course, relatively minor when measured against the many positive attributes of an S Corporation.

There are, however, two approaches that may even resolve this fringe benefit problem:

1. A common solution is to divide your business activities into two corporations—a C Corporation and an S Corporation. The C Corporation may provide a service, or perhaps sell a product to the S Corporation. The C Corporation—with nominal income—may provide the fringe benefits and operate at a break-even or near break-even basis. Essentially, the C Corporation becomes a conduit for furnishing tax-exempt, tax-deductible fringe benefits.

The fact that the same individual owns both corporations would not be a disqualification for this strategy, provided the corporations were operated as separate and distinct entities.

2. It is always possible to adjust a stockholder-employee's compensation levels so that the stockholder-employee can purchase a comparable package of benefits designed for his or her specific needs. While this compensation would be deductible by the corporation (as salary), it would, nevertheless, be taxable to the stockholder-employee.

YOUR BENEFIT PLANS

Should you provide fringe benefits for your employees—those who are eligible because they own less than 2 percent of the S Corporation? Yes, just as soon as you can. It is difficult to hire and keep a quality employee without a basic health/medical plan, even though they are expensive. Other fringe benefits to be considered are group life insurance policies, paid vacation and sick time, moving expenses, education support, and more.

You can start modestly with basic medical coverage, then, as you can afford it, you can add other benefits. How can you control costs? Look for "affinity" programs, such as may be offered by the trade association for your industry or profession. Let your employees pay part or all of the medical coverage costs out of salary or wages. The benefit from lower-cost group rates, and you are spared the expense.

What Kind of Benefits Plan?

In tax language, your plan can be "defined benefit" or "defined contribution." The defined benefit plan is paid by the company and guarantees specified benefits to the employee. The defined contribution plan is paid by the employee, either out of salary or with credits from the employer, and guarantees only those benefits selected by and paid for by the employee.

Your plan can be fixed or flexible. The flexible plan, usually called a "cafeteria" plan, presents a "menu" of choices to the employee, allowing that person to choose a combination of benefits most nearly meeting personal needs. Not only does the employee have a choice of benefits, but those that are chosen are available at attractive group rates.

The Cafeteria Benefits Plan. There are several types of cafeteria plans: core-plus, prepackaged, and flexible-spending account. The latter plan is the one most often used by small companies, as it costs less than other plans. The employee is allowed to pay for selected benefits on a before-tax basis through a salary reduction. One warning: If the employee does not dedicate all of the salary reduction to specific benefits, the undedicated amount is forfeited back to the employer.

The immediate advantage of the flexible-spending account plan, other than group rates, is the lower wage base on which the employee must pay income and Social Security taxes. The disadvantage is that by paying less in Social Security taxes, future Social Security benefits after retirement will be reduced.

The core-plus approach is another variation of the cafeteria plan. A basic list of benefits is offered to all eligible employees. With this is a list of optional benefits the employee may "purchase" with dollars or credits given the employee as part of the overall benefits package. With this amount, additional coverage may be acquired, or the employee may take this amount as an increase in income.

Prepackaged cafeteria plans are less flexible. They offer a choice from several predesigned benefit plan packages. One plan will be a bare-bones group of benefits provided without additional payment by the employee. Other packages may be more expensive, with payment by credits or actual cash out of wages.

There are limitations to the cafeteria-plan approach, however. Under current tax law, they cannot cover scholarships and fellowships, transportation benefits, educational assistance, employee discounts, and no-additional-cost services. Group term life insurance coverage greater than $50,000 can be included, but retirement benefits cannot, except for a 401(k) savings plan. But tax laws change, and the IRS and Tax Court interpretations of tax laws change. Your tax advisor can keep you abreast of new opportunities, or new restrictions.

RETIREMENT PLANS

Unlike other fringe benefits, stockholder-employees may participate along with other employees in qualified retirement plans set up by the S Corporation.

In 1982 when the Tax Equity and Fiscal Responsibility Act (TEFRA) was passed, Congress placed S Corporations, C Corporations, and partnerships on equal footing with respect to qualified retirement plans. In large measure, there are few significant differences in the treatment accorded the three types of business forms.

The benefits provided by a qualified retirement plan are:

1. The corporation is permitted to take a deduction for the full amount of its contribution to the plan.

2. The shareholder-employee does not include as income either the contribution made on his or her behalf by the corporation or the earnings on the contribution until the time he or she receives a distribution from the qualified plan.

However, there are limits on the amount an employer may contribute on behalf of shareholder-employees. Those limits are very similar to the requirements concerning compensation—only a reasonable salary will be treated as compensation when paid to a shareholder-employee. Similarly, the contribution made on behalf of a shareholder-employee must be reasonable when considered along with other compensation paid to the shareholder-employee.

If the S Corporation has an HR 10 (Keogh) Plan, it may deduct that portion of contributions it uses to purchase life insurance for shareholder-employees. To that extent, the use of a qualified plan may, at least partially solve the problem of fringe benefits for stockholder-employees.

There are, however, two serious considerations in adopting a qualified retirement plan by an S Corporation.

1. Should the stockholder-employees choose to form an Employee Stock Ownership Plan (ESOP), formation of a trust will be necessary. However, trusts are not eligible to own shares in an S Corporation and such ownership would cause the S Corporation to lose its status. Many companies are establishing ESOPs with the idea of encouraging the ESOP to take over ownership of the company at a future date. When this becomes the primary objective of an ESOP the corporation should consider switching from S status to C status.

2. Shareholders of an S Corporation may not receive loans from a qualified plan if they hold 5 percent or more of the corporate shares. C Corporations do not have this restriction. In determining the percentages of stock ownership listed above, the employee is considered the owner of shares owned by a spouse, children, parents, grandparents, and grandchildren.

Tax Warning:
There are other rules that govern retirement plans.

One caution is to avoid a "top heavy" plan that imposes complex requirements. A "top heavy" plan exists if 60 percent or more of the plan's benefits are for the benefit of key employees. A key employee who (1) is an officer of the corporation, or (2) owns 5 percent or more of the S Corporation stock, or (3) is one of ten employees who owns the greatest interest in the corporation, or (4) *receives more than $150,000 a year in compensation from the corporation.*

Another problem may arise with retirement plans when a C Corporation converts to S Corporation status. Loans made by the pension plan while the entity was a C Corporation become disqualified for an S Corporation exposing the plan to potential penalties.

Because retirement plans are so technical, consider seeking professional advice—often provided free of charge from most banks and financial institutions.

AVAILABILITY OF FRINGE BENEFIT

FRINGE BENEFIT	C CORP. EMPLOYEE	2% S CORP. SHAREHOLDER	EARNED INCOME PARTNER	PASSIVE PARTNER	SELF-EMPLOYED
Health & Accident	Yes	No	No	No Yes under new law to 25%	No
Group-Term Life	Yes	No	No	No	No
Qualified Group Legal	Yes	Yes	Yes	No	Yes
Education Assistance	Yes	Yes	Yes	No	Yes
Dependent Care Assistance	Yes	Yes	Yes	No	Yes
No-Additional-Cost Services	Yes	Yes	Yes	No	No
Qualified Employee Discounts	Yes	Yes	Yes	No	No
Working Condition Fringes	Yes	Yes	Yes	No	No
Diminimus Fringe Benefits	Yes	Yes	Yes	No	No

9 SETTING UP AND BENEFITTING FROM YOUR TAX RECORDS SYSTEM

OVERVIEW

When we say that your S Corporation is taxed the same as for a partnership or for your personal tax records, there are exceptions. While you are not subject to double taxation (as you would be for a C Corporation), the S Corporation pass-through of profits or losses to the shareholders is subject to a number of rules and restrictions, which we will discuss below.

A few words of advice: The tax recordkeeping for an S Corporation is not simple. You will be wading into dangerous waters if you are not an experienced accountant or do not have assistance from an experienced accountant when you first set up your bookkeeping procedures, and also later when you must determine timing and handling of corporation and personal incomes and deductions. Careless bookkeeping could jeopardize the continuing status of your S Corporation.

So why do we bother? The more you understand, the better you will be able to work with and communicate with your accountant—both in establishing the system that will best serve your needs, and in obtaining maximum tax advantage from your system.

YOUR TAX YEAR

The IRS standard tax year for an S Corporation is the calendar year. If you feel the need for a different tax year, you must have IRS approval, using IRS Form 2553. Before you will be allowed to have a noncalendar tax year, you must show the IRS that you have a substantial business purpose. For example, the IRS will look at your annual business cycle. Is it seasonal, such as a summertime business for installation of swimming pools? Also, would a noncalendar tax year distort your overall tax liability picture? IRS Publication 538 discusses the S Corporation tax year in greater detail. (See Appendix 3 on how to order IRS publications.)

To change your tax year, apply for the change using IRS Form 1128 (see Appendix 2), along with a $200 fee.

KEEPING RECORDS

The types of records and ledgers you will need for your S Corporation depends on the nature of your business, whether or not you have employees for whom you will withhold income taxes and Social Security payments, and more. Both federal and state laws require a careful system of recordkeeping regarding taxes, income, deductions, and other business expenses.

There are two primary bookkeeping systems: *single-entry* and *double-entry*. Single-entry is the easiest to use, particularly if you intend to keep your own books. The double-entry system is more complex, but has the advantage of checking its own accuracy through what is called self-balancing. In single-entry bookkeeping, you keep track of income and expenses with daily and monthly summaries of receipts, then a monthly summary of disbursements. In double-entry bookkeeping, credit and debit transactions are entered into a journal. Summary totals are then entered monthly into ledger accounts, such as income, expense, liability, net worth, and inventory. The sums of the debits must equal the sums of the credits, making the system self-balancing.

One mistake often made by those new to the business world is to try to keep business and personal records in the same set of ledgers. In banking, keep your business life and your personal life separate by establishing separate checking accounts. Set up a company petty cash fund for small disbursements.

Here are some general rules that, if followed, will simplify your life, and will provide the type of records you will need to track the status of your business and to prove yourself should the IRS or state tax regulators challenge you with an audit:

- When you withdraw income from your business, make a business check payable to yourself.

- Do not write a check to *cash*, but if you do, attach a note or receipt to explain its purpose.

- Support all recordkeeping entries with cancelled checks, receipts, duplicate deposit slips, and so forth. Don't expect tax auditors to accept vague memoranda or sketchy reports of approximate income, deductions, or other items that affect your tax liability.

- Classify your accounts by ledgers—for example, income, expenses, assets, liabilities, equity (net worth), and so forth.

- Classify assets as current or fixed, and record the date of acquisition, the cost (or other original basis), and depreciation or depletion as well as anything else that affects their basis.
- Always keep books and records available for inspection.
- Never discard or destroy records that support your reporting of income and expenses for your tax records until the statute of limitation expires—usually (except in charges of fraud) three years after the date the tax was paid, or when your return was due or filed, whichever is later.
- Keep all records that verify your basis in property as long as you own that property, plus the statute of limitation period. You will need these records to verify your basis for the property when that property is sold, lost, or destroyed.
- Employee tax records (income tax withholding, Social Security, unemployment) must be held for at least four years after the due date or the date the tax is paid, whichever is later.
- Keep copies of past tax returns.

YOUR ACCOUNTING METHOD

The IRS also controls the accounting method you may use for your business. In general, you may use either the *cash method* or the *accrual method*. In special cases you may be allowed to use a hybrid cash-accrual method.

The *cash method* is the simplest. It is the one used most often by small businesses with no inventory. This method is concerned only with actual income and actual expenses during the tax year. Note, however, the IRS considers that you have income when it is available for you to use, even if you delay taking advantage of it. For example, a check in payment for services received late in the tax year is income for that year, even if you delay cashing it until the following tax year.

The *accrual method* is more complex. If your business carries a constantly changing inventory, you will need to use the accrual method. The objective is to match income and expenses in the correct year. For example, income is recorded for the tax year in which it is earned, even though actual payment may not be received until the following tax year. Business expenses are deducted or capitalized in the tax year during which you become liable for them, even though you may pay them in another tax year.

BASIS AND AT-RISK LIMITATIONS

Your benefits from S Corporation profits and losses are limited by your *basis*, your *adjusted basis*, and your *at-risk basis* in the S Corporation.

Basis, as discussed earlier, represents what you have invested in the corporation, both cash contributions and loans to the corporation. In brief, basis is your invested ownership in the corporation.

Adjusted basis represents changes in basis. Your basis in the S Corporation is increased when corporate income (including tax-exempt income) is passed through to you. If your business has properties eligible for depletion allowances, such as oil wells, you may have an increase in basis if you claim a depletion amount that is greater than the basis of the depleted property; that is, you are profiting from it.

Your basis is decreased by corporate distributions to nonshareholders, by losses and deductions passed through to you, and for your depletion claims where they are equal to or smaller than the basis of the depleted property.

At-risk in simple terms means that the IRS will limit pass-through from the S Corporation to the amount you have risked (could lose) in the corporation. Your at-risk limit is your cash contribution plus the adjusted basis of other property you have contributed to the corporation, plus amounts you borrow for use by the corporation, and for which you are liable for repayment. Summarized, the IRS says you cannot deduct losses that are greater than your investment in the corporation.

BASIS AND LOANS

One of the advantages of your own S Corporation is to use it as a source or repository for loans. While it sounds simple, loans to or from the S Corporation can change your basis in the corporation.

As noted earlier, loans you make to the corporation are part of your investment in the corporation and are counted as part of your basis. If it is a loan you have taken out from a lender, you must be liable for its repayment.

Suppose you make a loan to the S Corporation but at an interest rate that is below the free-market loan rate. The IRS will "recharacterize" a part of this loan to create a fair-market interest rate and call it your contribution to the corporation. This will, of course, increase your basis in the corporation.

Suppose, on the other hand, that the S Corporation makes a loan to you at an interest rate that is below the free-market loan rate. The IRS may well consider that the corporation has made a payment to you for the amount that the interest rate is short, decreasing your basis. The shortfall in interest payments by you to the corporation now becomes compensation, and you will be taxed on this amount.

THE BASIS OF TAXATION

If you are the sole shareholder in the S Corporation, income and loss calculations will be greatly simplified. Everything comes either from or to you. If, however, there are several shareholders, income and deductions will be shared according to shareholder basis (ownership). In either case, deductions will be in two basic forms: (1) those deductions that are subtracted from corporation gross revenues with the remaining profit (or loss) distributed pro rata to the shareholders according to their relative basis, and (2) those deductions that are passed through separately for inclusion in the individual personal tax returns of the shareholders.

This combination of corporate-level deductions and pass-through for personal deductions can create confusion and may require expert interpretation for the preparation of both the corporation and personal tax returns. A pass-through deduction (called a *separately stated item*) of $1,000 for a shareholder with 25 percent basis would be $250. But it's not that simple. The calculation is made on a per-day/per-share basis to allow for changes in individual shareholder basis during the tax year, as discussed elsewhere. Here is how the tax calculation for a specific ITEM is made:

1. $ITEM/(days/yr) = $DAI (daily dollar amount of ITEM)
2. $DAI x PSB (percent of shareholder basis on a specific day) = $SHDD (shareholder deduction for that day)
3. $TSHDY (total shareholder deduction for the year) = summation of each $SHDD

If you want to simplify your tax-record bookkeeping, you will either prevent any change in individual shareholder basis, or, if such change is to be made, make it on the first day of the tax year. Remember, if the basis for one shareholder changes, the bases for each of the other shareholders will be changed accordingly as total ownership of the corporation cannot be either more than or less than 100 percent.

Examples of pass-through *separately stated* items include:

- Net income or loss from real estate activity.
- Net income or loss from rental activity.
- Income, loss, or expense related to portfolio interest income, dividend income, royalty income, and short-term and long-term capital gains or losses.
- Section 1231 gain or loss.
- Charitable contributions.
- Health insurance premiums.
- Section 179 expense deductions.
- Investment interest expense.
- Tax preference adjustment items needed to figure shareholders' alternative minimum tax.

Each of the preceding items is subject to tax regulations and must follow personal deduction requirements for personal income tax returns.

Examples of corporation-level deductions include payments for:

- Supplies and materials.
- Facility and equipment rentals.
- Salaries, wages, and contractor or consultant fees.
- Telephone, computer time, telecommunications, and postage.
- Certain travel and entertainment.
- Certain business gifts up to $25 each.
- Maintenance, repairs, and cleaning.
- Magazine subscriptions and reference materials.
- Professional and association dues.
- Bank fees for checking and safety deposit vaults.
- Office furnishings (up to $10,000).
- Car mileage for business purposes.
- Certain retirement fund contributions.

There are, of course, more deductible items than listed above. Also, there are special rules regarding deductions for farming syndicates, groves and orchards, film-making and publishing, and vacation homes for dual personal-corporation use.

TAX BENEFITS FOR YOU

There are legal tax strategies through which you can benefit with your corporation, in addition to the straightforward pass-through profits or losses. Some of these apply to all types of corporations, others are specific to the S Corporation.

Strategy 1: Split your income. Hire your children to work for the corporation. Your child's income, if not excessive, will be taxed at a rate lower than yours. Don't try to cheat; be sure that the child actually performs a useful chore for the corporation in return for his or her pay. See Chapter 7 for more details.

Strategy 2: Another form of income splitting is to transfer partial ownership of the corporation to your spouse or children. See Chapter 7 for more details.

Strategy 3: A Keogh Plan through the S Corporation allows you to save up to 20 percent of your income, up to $30,000 a year, in a tax-deferred retirement account. You pay no taxes on your contributions or the interest earned until you start withdrawing funds (starting no sooner than age 59.5 and no later than age 70.5). Early withdrawal means a 10 percent penalty.

Strategy 4: Section 179 of the tax code allows you to deduct ("capitalize") the cost of new equipment up to a maximum of $10,000 for the year, instead of depreciating it over several years. You can make the purchase on the last day of the tax year, charge it to your credit card, and pick up the item during the next tax year.

Strategy 5: Normally, an S Corporation cannot make charitable contributions. Such contributions become separately stated items, credited back to the individual shareholders. But the corporation can contribute old equipment to a charity and be credited for a charitable deduction. Note: You cannot do this with equipment you have already capitalized or depreciated; that would be taking a deduction twice on the same item.

Strategy 6: Reduce your income for the year by deferring income until the following tax year. You can do this by delaying the mailing of invoices until late in the tax year. Remember, once you have control over the money, such as a check in hand, the IRS considers it to be that year's income even though you have not cashed the check.

Strategy 7: Speed up the payment of debts and for materials recently received or to be received during the next tax year. This will give you added deductions for the current tax year.

Strategy 8: You'll save taxes if you use the LIFO (last-in, first-out) method of inventory accounting. LIFO lets you deduct the higher (inflated) cost of newer goods in your inventory before you deduct the cost of older less-costly goods. Note: If you are not now using LIFO, you'll need IRS approval to switch inventory accounting methods.

Strategy 9: Increase your basis for deductions for loss pass-through by either an additional cash contribution to the corporation or by a qualified direct loan to the corporation.

There are more sophisticated ways to receive tax benefits from an S Corporation, but you will need the help of a tax advisor or accountant (not a bookkeeper) with specific S Corporation tax law experience. For example, consider how to benefit from a precontribution loss through formation of an S Corporation:

Suppose that you own land with a basis of $300,000 but a current fair market value of only $100,000. Suppose also that your current income is not large enough to allow you to write off the entire $200,000 loss. A developer, let's call him Jones, is in a high income bracket and is looking for losses to offset against income.

You and Jones form an S Corporation. You contribute your property at a fair market value of $100,000 in return for 25 percent of the S Corporation stock. Jones contributes $300,000 for the remaining 75 percent of the stock. The corporation takes over your basis of $300,000 for the contributed property. The $300,000 contributed to the corporation by Jones is now used to build roads, sewers, and pay other subdivision costs. Now the property has the $300,000 acquisition basis plus the improvement investment of $300,000, or a total basis of $600,000. The corporation then sells the lots for a total price of $400,000, resulting in an ordinary loss of $200,000. Of this, 75 percent ($150,000) is *allocated to Jones, and 25 percent ($50,000) to you. Both of you can now apply these allocated losses against your income from other sources.*

How does this affect the basis for you and for Jones? The $50,000 loss you took reduces your basis in the corporation from $300,000 to $250,000. Jones, having taken a $150,000 loss, now has a basis of only $150,000 in the corporation. If the corporation is liquidated at this time for $400,000, you would have a loss of $150,000 (the 25 percent or $100,000 of the liquidation minus your $250,000 basis in corporation stock) and Jones would have a gain of $150,000 (the 75 percent or $300,000 of the liquidation amount minus his $150,000 basis in corporation stock).

Tax credits offer another way to receive tax benefits. Your tax advisor can tell you which credits might apply to your operation. There are federal tax credits that apply in all 50 states, plus local tax credits unique to each of the 50 states. A sampling on the federal level includes credits for small businesses that make themselves more accessible to persons with disabilities, that renovate industrial and commercial buildings and income-producing historic structures, that use alcohol fuels, that conserve energy, that use nonconventional fuels (such as biomass), that perform research, or that create specific types of jobs.

What you cannot do is juggle things within a family group to create fallacious tax deductions, such as a father working for the corporation without sufficient compensation in order to shift income to other members of the family in lower income tax brackets. If you do try this, don't be surprised if the IRS reallocates items among your family members to reflect the full reasonable value of the services you render to the corporation. The subject of adequate compensation is discussed in Chapter 7.

CALCULATING S CORPORATION TAXES

For reasons unexplained, although S Corporation income is to pass though to shareholders with tax liability computed on individual shareholder tax returns, you are still required to compute and file Form 1120S with Schedules K and K-1 (shown in Appendix 2). In general, the S Corporation taxable income is calculated in the same way as that of individuals. Exceptions to this rule are:

1. A separate statement is required for items of income, loss, deductions, or credit that could affect the tax liability of any shareholder.

2. Deductions that generally pass through to individual shareholders are disallowed in the S Corporation tax return. These include certain personal exemptions, taxes paid or accrued to foreign countries and U.S. possessions, charitable contributions, proratable net operating losses, and itemized deductions, including income-production expenses, alimony payments, moving expenses, and adoption expenses.

3. An S Corporation can amortize its organizational expenses as a deduction over a 60-month period. Note: This is not allowed to partnerships and individuals.

4. The S Corporation is liable for C Corporate tax preference items accrued prior to S Corporation election. (See Chapter 11.)

When using a *cash-basis tax reporting* system, income and expenses must actually occur during the tax year. For *accrual-basis tax reporting*, certain deductions may be accrued. For example, an S Corporation may not deduct an amount payable to a shareholder until the day such item is includable in the gross income of the shareholder. That is, the corporation may not deduct a 1991 salary payable to a shareholder-employee in 1991 if the salary is not paid until 1992. Similarly, the shareholder will not receive the deduction benefit of salary payment until the amount is actually transferred to the shareholder.

Pass-through items have been discussed earlier. The reason for pass-through items, in contrast to pro rata items, is that each shareholder will have different personal limits and deductibles that, as such, cannot be shared equally by deducting at the corporate level. In addition to the pass-through items already listed, see Schedule K-1 (Appendix 2) for a list of other pass-through items, including dividends, net gain or loss from theft, and expenses for meals, travel, and entertainment.

NET OPERATING LOSSES

There are obstacles to overcome before you can benefit personally from an S Corporation net operating loss (NOL). Here are some general rules:

1. Items must be characterized (identified) on a corporate level as belonging to corporate tax accounting (for pro rata allocation to shareholders) or to individual shareholder tax accounting (for separately stated pass through to shareholders).

2. The corporate income/expense/deduction items must be calculated and allocated to shareholders based on stock ownership. As discussed elsewhere, ownership is determined on a daily basis.

3. If there is an operating loss, it is necessary to determine if the loss is of value to one or more of the shareholders as related to these shareholder bases (ownerships).

4. Are the shareholders at-risk regarding their investments in the corporation? Could any of the shareholders lose everything, or do they have some promised collateral that will protect them from corporation losses?

5. For the shareholders that meet the at-risk test, Do they merit the loss under the passive-activity loss rule?

6. After passing each of the above tests, a shareholder may use whatever remains of his or her authorized and pro rata share of the NOL against personal income from other sources, if any. If the NOL share exceeds a shareholder's income for the current tax year, that shareholder can take advantage of carryback and carryforward rules.

7. Good luck!

10 TAX BENEFITS FROM CORPORATE LOSSES

OVERVIEW

One of the great benefits of the S Corporation is that its stockholders have several ways to personally take advantage of the corporate losses. Of course, stockholders will—at least in most cases—prefer that their corporation earn a profit, but the fact they can "write off" at least a portion of the losses can be somewhat consoling.

SECTION 1244 STOCK

One tax benefit stockholders of either a C or S Corporation can take advantage of is to use Section 1244 Stock.

Summarily, Section 1244 Stock allows shareholders of a failed corporation to write off up to $50,000 in any one year, against either capital gains or ordinary income ($100,000 if the taxpayers file a joint return).

Under present tax rules, losses suffered by a shareholder when his stock becomes worthless are capital losses and can be used only in a limited manner. If the losses are long-term losses (held for more than six months), they can be applied to offset capital gains, and then if there are excess capital losses, they can be used to offset ordinary income but only up to a maximum of $3,000. This means that if a taxpayer has $2,000 of capital gains and $20,000 of long-term capital losses, $15,000 of capital losses cannot be used in the current tax year but must be carried forward. The $2,000 gain will be offset by $2,000 of the losses, and another $3,000 can be used to offset ordinary income; that leaves a balance of $15,000 of the total $20,000 loss that is unused in the current tax year, and must be held over to be applied to future years earnings.

However, if the shareholder had the same $20,000 loss on 1244 shares, he or she could have applied the $20,000 against an equivalent amount of income in that year. Assuming this shareholder has $20,000 in earnings he or she could have eliminated his or her total tax liability for the year through the accelerated write off.

The advantages of 1244 Stock are obvious and there are absolutely no disadvantages; therefore it is important that every corporation that qualifies issue stock pursuant to Section 1244 of the Internal Revenue Code.

The procedure is simple. Reference to the 1244 Stock issue may be contained in the bylaws or minutes of Incorporators of Directors (see Appendix 1), and any attorney can have the paperwork properly documented.

In order to use Section 1244 Stock, the corporation must satisfy five criteria, none of which conflict with S Corporation requirements. The five criteria are:

1. The corporation must be a U.S. corporation.
2. The corporation may not be a holding company.
3. The total amount paid by shareholders for their stock must not be more than $1 million.
4. The stock must have been issued for cash or property, and may not have been issued for services or in exchange for other shares of stock.
5. During the five tax years that preceded the year in which the stock became worthless, the corporation derived more than half of its income from nonpassive sources. (Passive sources include income from royalties, rents, dividends, interest, annuities, and sales or exchanges of stock or other securities.)

It should be noted that although the benefits of capital have been eliminated under the Tax Reform Act, the concept of capital gains as well as limits on capital losses remain. Also, under the new law the differential between short-term losses and long-term losses is no longer in effect.

OPERATING LOSSES

Although S Corporation losses flow through to its shareholders, those losses can be deducted by shareholders on their returns only if they do not exceed the total of shareholders' basis in their stock and any debt owed to them by the corporation. "Basis" is a tax term that generally means the cost of the asset.

However, if an S Corporation's losses exceed a shareholder's basis, the shareholder cannot deduct his or her full loss but must limit it to his or her basis, and any excess must be carried over until such time as he or she has a sufficient basis to cover the loss.

Therefore, to fully take advantage of the S Corporation tax loss provisions it is important to understand how basis is determined, how basis increases or decreases and how the tax loss carryover provisions work.

DETERMINING BASIS

Basis is determined by combining the cost of the stock together with any debts made to the corporation. We can, however, consider each separately.

The general rule is that a shareholder's basis in S Corporation stock is the price paid for the stock. If, for example, a shareholder paid $500 for 50 shares of stock, the basis per share is $50 and the total or aggregate basis is $500.

However, if the shareholder transfers property to the S Corporation in exchange for shares, the shareholder's basis is determined by whether the transfer is a taxable event. Typically when a new business is formed, the transfer of property for shares is not a taxable event. In those cases, basis equals: (1) the basis of the property in the shareholder's hands when he or she transferred it to the corporation, (2) less the amount of any cash paid to the shareholder for the property, and (3) plus any gain the shareholder recognizes on the transfer.

If the stock was simply exchanged for property and the transfer was a taxable event, the basis of the stock would be the fair market value of the property at the time of transfer. It should be noted, however, that a transfer property to the corporation generally results in a nontaxable event.

Tax Tip:
When transferring property to your own corporation always obtain a professional appraisal to establish value.

Of course, if the stock is inherited by a stockholder, the basis to the stockholder is the fair market value of the shares at the time of the decedent's death. Similarly, if the shares were gifted, the transferee accepts the shares at the transferors basis at the time of the gift.

Loans made to a corporation constitute part of the basis.

If a shareholder lends money to an S Corporation, his or her basis is the amount of the loan. If a shareholder renders services or property in exchange for a note, the shareholder's basis is the amount of the note.

Of course, a shareholder has a basis only in money actually loaned to the corporation, not money loaned to the corporation by a third-party.

The mere fact that a shareholder guarantees a corporate note is not sufficient for that debt to become part of the shareholder's basis. The shareholder must be more than "at risk." The shareholder actually has to expend the funds in payment of the debt before it becomes part of his or her basis.

Therefore, if a corporation defaults on a note and the shareholder as guarantor is required to pay the note, he or she will have obtained a basis in corporate debt by the amount actually paid on the guarantee.

"At-risk" has a specific meaning to the IRS. It refers to the amount you are risking in the S Corporation activity, including: (1) cash and property you contribute to the activity; (2) amounts borrowed, and for which you are liable, for use in the activity; and (3) your share of the S Corporation net operating income that you haven't yet withdrawn, but is yours for the asking.

CHANGES IN BASIS

An S Corporation's shareholder will experience a change in his or her stock basis annually to reflect the corporation's profit or loss for the year. For example, if a shareholder has a stock basis of $20,000 and the corporation earns a profit of $5,000 for the year, the new basis will be $25,000. Conversely, if the corporation lost $5,000 the basis would have been reduced to $15,000 at the end of the year.

Therefore, to determine annual adjustments in basis, each S Corporation shareholder should increase or decrease his or her basis by the proportionate share of any profit or loss. However, if the S Corporation makes a nontaxable distribution (dividend payment) to shareholders, their basis is reduced by the amount of the distribution.

If a shareholder has basis in both stock and debt, there is a formula for determining which of the two bases change when the corporation operates at a profit or loss. The general rule is that both accounts are determined separately unless operating losses exceed the shareholder's basis in his or her stock. In that case, the shareholder may deduct the loss only if he or she has sufficient basis in debt owed to him or her by the corporation to cover the loss. If the corporation operates at a profit the next year, the increase in basis would be applied to the debt basis first and the excess, if any, to stock.

A simple formula is as follows:

1. Decreases in basis caused by operating losses are applied first to the basis in stock and then to the basis in debt.

2. If operating losses have been used to decrease the basis in debt and there is a profit in a succeeding year, the debt basis must be increased until it is completely replaced; then remaining profits can increase the basis of stock.

3. A shareholder can deduct losses only if the losses do not exceed the total amount of the shareholder's basis in stock and debt. If losses do exceed the combined basis, the shareholder may carry them forward indefinitely and until such times as (i) the shareholder has increased his or her basis through additional investments in stock or loans to the corporation, or (ii) operating profits supply sufficient basis to cover the losses.

Tax Tip:
If you are an S Corporation's sole stockholder, and anticipate losses for the year, you may want to loan or invest further funds into the corporation so as to increase your basis to match the losses and thereby take the entire loss in the current year.

As a shareholder of an S Corporation, you cannot, however, repay loans to yourself without it being a taxable event. Because loans made to an S Corporation will be treated unlike loans made to a C Corporation, you should review the tax consequences with an advisor before loaning money to the S Corporation. In many cases the taxable consequences associated with debt repayment are sufficiently significant to determine whether an S Corporation or some other form of organization will be used.

11 TAX PROBLEMS TO AVOID

OVERVIEW

The one distinguishing feature of the S Corporation is that its profits are not subject to taxation at the corporate level. However, there are exceptions to this general rule; an S Corporation may be taxed under several circumstances discussed in this chapter.

However, it should be first pointed out that the tax possibilities discussed in the first section of the chapter apply only to corporations that previously operated as C Corporations and later switched to S Corporation status. Corporations that start out as S Corporations can most likely bypass this chapter.

The three tax-creating situations we will cover in this chapter include:

1. Excess passive investment income.
2. Capital gains.
3. Taxes arising from a sale or disposition of property in a liquidation.

EXCESS PASSIVE INVESTMENT INCOME

An S Corporation is obligated to pay a tax on excess passive investment income earned during a tax year when it also operated as a regular C Corporation and had earnings or profits from other sources or business activities.

Obviously, this tax can only apply to corporations that began as a C Corporation and later switched to S Corporation status.

Passive investment income, for purposes of an S Corporation tax include:

- Rents
- Dividends
- Interest
- Annuities
- Royalties
- Proceeds from the sale or exchange of stock or other securities

Although this problem most commonly occurs when shareholders of a C Corporation elect to switch to S Corporation in a year during which the C Corporation had earnings, it may also occur when there is a merger between a C and S Corporation.

Tax Tip:
The way to avoid the tax on passive investment is to have the corporation distribute its accumulated earnings and profits to its shareholders before the end of the tax year. Although the shareholders will be required to declare the distribution as taxable dividend income, the corporation will escape tax liability if the distribution is made before the end of the tax year.

CAPITAL GAINS

A capital gain occurs when a "capital asset" is sold for more than its basis. (Cost plus improvements less depreciation.) Typically, a capital asset usually is a fixed asset (real estate, equipment, etc.) used to produce income.

The Tax Reform Act of 1986 provides that capital gains are to be taxed as if they constitute ordinary income. However, the Tax Reform Act left undisturbed the procedures for determining capital gains as part of a taxpayers income. This was probably done so the concept of capital gains can be reintroduced in future tax changes, if warranted.

Because capital gains enjoyed favorable treatment, Congress was concerned that S Corporations would be organized solely to take advantage of a one-time capital gain benefit. To avoid this the new tax law pre–scribes an S Corporation will have to pay a tax on capital gains if four criteria exist:

1. The net capital gain must be in excess of $25,000.
2. The corporation has taxable income in excess of $25,000.
3. The net capital gain must constitute more than 50 percent of the corporation's taxable income for the year.
4. The corporation (a) was not an S Corporation for each of the three years prior to the tax year in question, or (b) has been in business for less than four years and has not been an S Corporation throughout the period.

All four criteria must be present before the S Corporation has a liability for capital gain tax. The tax applies only to the capital gain in excess of $25,000. Further, the tax rate is the lower of (a) 28 percent, or (b) the tax if the corporation had not been an S Corporation.

Tax Tip:
To avoid the capital gains tax consider one of these options:
1. Wait at least three years before selling capital assets at a gain.
2. Sell capital assets with values of less than $25,000 in any one taxable year.

LIQUIDATION OF ASSETS

Prior to the Tax Reform Act of 1986, if a corporation sold appreciated property for a gain as part of a complete liquidation, the corporation would not be taxed on the gain. Alternatively, the gain would pass through to the shareholders and be taxable to them if the gain received was greater than their investment in their shares. This is no longer the situation.

Since passage of the new Tax Act, if a regular C Corporation disposes of an appreciated asset, it must pay a tax on the gain, and the shareholders will pay a tax at their level if the distribution received represents a gain to them.

Unfortunately, switching to an S Corporation does not totally solve the problem. The 1986 tax law requires the S Corporation to pay a tax on any appreciation of its property that occurred before the switch to S status, but only if the sale or distribution that is part of the liquidation occurs within ten years of the day the S Corporation becomes effective. Therefore, the tax that can be assessed against the S Corporation is limited to the appreciation that took place before the conversion. Appreciation that occurs after the conversion to S status is gain that flows through to the shareholders of the S Corporation. It should be noted, however, that C Corporations that converted to S Corporation status by December 31, 1986, avoided this problem.

Tax Tip:
If a C Corporation is to convert to S status, it should obtain an appraisal on its capital assets so the appreciation occurring after conversion can be distinguished from the appreciation prior to conversion.

Note:
The 1986 Tax Reform Act has provided limited relief from this provision for C Corporations whose assets do not exceed $10 million if more than 50 percent of their stock is owned by fewer than 11 individuals. If the corporation's assets total $5 million or less, the new provisions do not affect it at all. The exemption for these $5- and $10-million-dollar corporations, however, applies only to liquidating sales that were completed before January 1, 1989.

RECAPTURE OF INVESTMENT TAX CREDITS

Another problem area is that of Investment Tax Credits (ITCs). The new tax laws effectively eliminated ITCs; however, it still applies in a more limited way.

If an S Corporation has an ITC, the unused credit is automatically passed through to the shareholders. However, if the S Corporation sells property on which it took an ITC as a C Corporation, the S Corporation becomes liable for the recapture of the ITC. Of course, this only applies to corporations that switch from C status to S status.

12 SELLING S CORPORATION SHARES

OVERVIEW

A shareholder may sell or transfer his or her shares to a third-party, or as is often the case with an S Corporation, the shareholder may elect to transfer part or all of his or her shares back to the corporation.

Frequently, there are important tax ramifications based on how a sale is structured, and this is certainly true in the case of an S Corporation where the rules are particularly complex.

REDEMPTIONS

A "redemption" occurs when a shareholder transfers all or part of his or her shares back to the corporation. The corporation then owns the shares; however, as is typically the case, the corporation retires the shares as nonvoting treasury stock.

A shareholder may redeem or transfer his or her shares to the corporation for a variety of reasons:

1. The shareholder's basis in his or her stock has been reduced, and he or she wants to take a long-term capital loss by selling a portion of his or her shares in a year when long-term gains on other holdings will be realized.

2. An existing shareholder, because of the desire to retire from active business, wishes to sell all of his or her shareholdings back to the corporation, so the corporation can issue new shares to the buyer of the business.

3. Planning reduced participation in the business, a majority shareholder is willing to sell a portion of his or her shares back to the corporation in order to equalize his or her holdings with those of the minority shareholder.

4. The selling shareholder, wishing to obtain a tax-free distribution from the S Corporation, sells a portion of his or her shareholdings back to the business for the distribution.

The transfer of shares back to the corporation may be treated either as a distribution or a sale (or exchange).

How the transaction is characterized is critical to the selling shareholder because of the difference in tax treatments of a distribution versus a sale or exchange.

If the transfer of stock is treated as a distribution, the shareholder may receive a tax-free payment of money from the corporation. If a transfer is found to be a sale or exchange, the shareholder will end up with either a capital gain or loss, depending upon the basis he or she had in the stock before the transfer. A shareholder receiving a distribution may have to recognize the distribution as ordinary income if the distribution exceeds his or her basis.

In large measure we can define a distribution as all transactions that do not meet the criteria of a sale or exchange.

The key criteria for a sale or exchange (and hence taxable) is if, upon completion of the transfer, there will be a meaningful or significant change at the corporate or shareholder level. That determination, in turn, rests on five points:

1. The shareholder transfers all of his or her stock;
2. There is a substantially disproportionate redemption of stock;
3. The redemption takes place as part of a partial liquidation of the S Corporation;
4. The transfer is viewed as a redemption that is not equivalent to a dividend;
5. The shareholder's stock in the S Corporation exceeds 35 percent of his or her estate and the shares are sold back to the corporation in order to provide the estate with money to pay death taxes.

(i) Sale of All Shares: If a shareholder sells all of his or her shares back to the corporation, there has been a meaningful change at both the shareholder and corporate levels. Such a transfer will constitute a sale or exchange only if the selling shareholder completely severs his or her relationship with the S Corporation. In order to satisfy this requirement, the selling shareholder may not continue as an officer, employee, or director of the S Corporation. The selling shareholder may, however, serve the corporation as an independent contractor. It is cautioned, however, that the Internal Revenue Service carefully scrutinizes independent contractor arrangement, and it is wise to have counsel prepare appropriate independent contractor agreements to document the nature of the relationship.

The selling shareholder will not be considered as having completely terminated his or her interest if the shareholder's spouse, children, grandchildren, or parents will continue to own stock in the corporation. In that case, the sale to the corporation will be viewed as a distribution. The same result is obtained if the selling shareholder retains an option to purchase shares in the S Corporation.

(ii) Transfer Is Not a Dividend: This test is satisfied if the shareholder can show that as a result of the transfer there has been a meaningful reduction in the shareholder's pro rata interest in the S Corporation. This test, therefore, only applies to situations where the corporation has more than one shareholder and the comparative ownership of the shareholders can be evaluated.

In determining whether there has been a meaningful reduction in the shareholder's proportionate interest, the IRS looks at voting power. For example, if a shareholder who owns 95 percent of the corporation stock sells 44 percent back to the corporation, the IRS will probably view the transfer as a distribution rather than a sale because the transferring shareholder will end up with 51 percent of the stock and will retain voting control.

If, instead, that shareholder had sold sufficient outstanding stock so that he or she retained exactly half the voting stock, the transfer would be considered as a sale or exchange since the selling shareholder would no longer have voting control.

The IRS claims most other partial share redemptions, even those involving a minority shareholder, may qualify as sales or exchanges. Of course, if there is a pro rata transfer by all shareholders, there will not be a meaningful change, and the transfers will be treated as distributions.

(iii) Disproportionate Reductions: A transfer of shares back to the S Corporation will be treated as a sale or exchange if the selling shareholder can show:

1. The selling shareholder will then own less than 50 percent of the total voting power of the corporation after the transfer.

2. After the transfer the selling shareholder will not own more than 79 percent of the percentage of voting stock the shareholder had before the transfer.

3. If the S Corporation has nonvoting common stock, the selling shareholder may not be left with more than 79 percent of the total amount of stock he or she held before the transfer. In this test, the percentages are based on the fair market value of the shares.

TAX TREATMENT

Based on the factors described above, the primary difference between a distribution and a sale or exchange occurs when a shareholder transfers fewer than all of his or her shares to the corporation. In such a case the shareholder will receive an immediate benefit (tax-free money) if the transfer is viewed as a distribution; the cost, however, will be a reduced basis in stock. This means the shareholder's use of operating losses of the S Corporation in subsequent years will be limited. Should the shareholder be viewed as having sold or exchanged his or her shares, he or she may have a capital gain or loss on the shares he or she transfers; the shareholder's basis in his or her remaining shares will be unchanged and he or she will be in a position to use subsequent losses, if they occur, to the extent of that basis.

If a transfer is considered a sale or exchange the following tax implications will occur:

1. If the selling shareholder transfers all of his or her shares back to the corporation, he or she will lose the benefit of all unused carryover losses (i.e., losses the shareholder was unable to use in previous years because he had an insufficient basis in his stock). Should there be unused losses, the selling shareholder might instead sell fewer than all his or her shares and hold the remainder until such time that his or her basis can permit him or her to make use of the losses.

2. If the shareholder receives more for his or her stock than his or her basis in the shares, he or she will have capital gain. If he or she receives less than his or her basis, he or she will have a capital loss. If the shareholder sells fewer than all of his or her shares and remains with an ownership interest of more than 50 percent of the corporation value, the capital loss will not be allowed by the IRS.

3. If the S Corporation holds property on which it took an investment tax credit, the selling shareholder may be liable for the recapture of the credit.

If the shareholder is viewed as receiving a distribution when he or she redeems his or her shares to the corporation: (1) The amount received from the corporation is tax-free to the extent of the shareholder's basis in his or her shares, and, (2) If the distribution exceeds the shareholder's basis in his or her shares, the excess is treated as a capital gain—the shareholder may not apply the excess against any basis he or she may have in corporate debt.

SALE TO THIRD PARTIES

Instead of redeeming shares back to the corporation, the selling shareholder may sell to a third party—either another shareholder or a person within the corporation.

Of course, the new stockholder must be one qualified to be an S Corporation stockholder, otherwise the S status election will be subject to revocation.

If there is a sale to a third-party, the tax consequences to the selling shareholder are precisely the same as a sale or exchange to the corporation.

The shareholder who purchases the shares will be obligated to pro rate with the selling stockholder his or her pro rata share of income and loss that flows through to him or her.

CLOSING THE BOOKS

Whenever there is a sale and exchange (whether to the corporation or a third-party) the selling stockholder and buyer have the option to:

1. Keep the corporate books (financial) open, thereby adjusting the pro rata share of profits and losses.

2. Close the books as of the transfer date. This will essentially create two short tax years and the selling shareholder will report only his or her share of flow-through profits or losses for that portion of the year during which shares were owned.

Since there is no way to predict what will happen after a shareholder leaves the corporation, it is impossible to determine which approach will work best in a given situation. If, however, the S Corporation is running in the red when the shareholder sells his or her stock back to the business, a prudent approach might be to close the books as of the date of the sale. That way the shareholder gets the benefit of those losses. This approach makes even more sense if the corporation business is seasonal and its high season will follow the sale.

When the selling shareholder and buyer agree to close the books the parties should complete the forms that follow.

INSTRUCTIONS TO CLOSE CORPORATE BOOKS WHEN A SHAREHOLDER SELLS ALL HIS OR HER SHARES

The form that appears on the next page must be used if a shareholder sells all of his or her shares in the S Corporation, and the selling and buyer shareholders agree to create two short tax years.

When completed, the form must be attached to the corporate income tax form (Form 1120S). Every shareholder who owned the S Corporation stock at any time during the course of the tax year, even if only for one day, must consent to the closing of the corporation books upon the transfer of all of the shareholder's shares.

This form may be used when the shareholder sells his or her shares to either the S Corporation or to an individual.

ELECTION TO CLOSE CORPORATE BOOKS—SAMPLE

Date: July 18, 1991

XYZ Corporation
_____
Corporate Name

100 Main Street
_____
Address

Anytown, USA 00000
_____

Employer Identification Number: 81-4039261

    This Election is hereby made as an Attachment to Form 1120S for the above captioned Corporation's Tax Year which ends   December 31   , 1991   .

    The above Corporation hereby elects to have the provisions of Internal Revenue Code Section 1377(a)(1) enforced as if the Corporation's taxable year consisted of two taxable years, the first of which shall end   July 1   , 1991   .

    The reason for this election is that   Robert Brown , a shareholder of the Corporation sold all of his shares in the Corporation, and terminated his interest in the Corporation, on July 1   , 1991   .

    Pursuant to this election, the Corporation's tax year, which runs a calendar year from January 1 through December 31, will consist of the following two parts:
(1) January 1 , 1991   , through June 30   , 1991   , and
(2) July 1   , 1991   , through December 30 , 1991   .

                      XYZ Corporation

By: *Adam Smith*
                Adam Smith, President

SHAREHOLDERS' CONSENT

    The undersigned who include every person or party who was a shareholder of the above Corporation at any time during calendar year 1991   all consent to the above election.

Shareholder Name	Shareholder Signature
Robert Brown	*Robert Brown*
Mary Brown	*Mary Brown*
Adam Smith	*Adam Smith*

ELECTION TO CLOSE CORPORATE BOOKS—FORM

Date:

_____
Corporate Name

_____
Address

_____

Employer Identification Number:

    This Election is hereby made as an Attachment to
Form 1120S for the above captioned Corporation's Tax
Year which ends _____, 19___.

    The above Corporation hereby elects to have the
provisions of Internal Revenue Code Section 1377(a)(1)
enforced as if the Corporation's taxable year consisted
of two taxable years, the first of which shall end
_____, 19___.

    The reason for this election is that
_____, a shareholder of the Corporation sold all of
his shares in the Corporation, and terminated his
interest in the Corporation, on _____, 19___.

    Pursuant to this election, the Corporation's tax
year, which runs a calendar year from January 1 through
December 31, will consist of the following two parts:
(1) _____, 19___, through _____, 19___, and
(2) _____, 19___, through _____, 19___.

By:_____

SHAREHOLDERS' CONSENT

    The undersigned who include every person or party
who was a shareholder of the above Corporation at any
time during calendar year 19___ all consent to the
above election.

Shareholder Name   Shareholder Signature

_____   _____

_____   _____

_____   _____

13 | TERMINATING THE S CORPORATION ELECTION

OVERVIEW

Once having made the decision to elect S Corporation status, the shareholders retain the right to switch back to C Corporation status, just as a C Corporation may elect to become an S Corporation. However, when the decision is made to switch from S Corporation status to C Corporation status, it is termed a revocation of S status.

It is also possible to lose the benefits of S Corporation status if the corporation fails to comply with Internal Revenue Code requirements necessary to maintain S Corporation status. When the IRS ends the S Corporation status for noncompliance the involuntary ending is referred to as a termination of election.

REVOCATION OF S STATUS

Revocation of S Status automatically occurs when shareholders who own more than 50 percent of all outstanding shares of corporate stock notify the IRS of the election to discontinue as an S Corporation. For purposes of determining a majority, both voting and nonvoting shares are included as one class.

Example:
Ralph owns 100 shares of stock in S Corporation. Henry and Mary each own 40 shares. Ralph controls the decision to revoke the S status election since he owns more than one-half the outstanding shares (100 out of 180 shares). Of course, a shareholder's agreement may provide that the vote of a higher percentage of shares is necessary to revoke S Corporation status.

91

A sample and blank "Revocation Notice" is included at the end of this chapter. It should be addressed to the nearest regional office of the IRS and, of course, must be signed by the shareholders electing to reovke S Corporation status. The notice must also be signed on behalf of the Corporation by an authorized corporate officer (President or Treasurer), notwithstanding that such officer may also be a shareholder who personally does not elect revocation.

EFFECTIVE DATE OF REVOCATION

When shareholders decide to revoke the S status election, there are three possible dates upon which the revocation will become effective, and the corporation will thereinafter be taxed as a regular C Corporation.

The three possibilities include:

1. *On the date the consent form is filed, or some later date.*

Example:
You file the revocation notice form on April 10, 1991, and ask that S Corporation status end on June 30, 1991. One tax return is filed for the enterprise as an S Corporation (January1–June 30). Another tax return is filed for it as a regular corporation (July 1–December 31).

2. *The first day of the corporation's taxable year.* The filing deadline is the 15th of the 4th month of the corporation's taxable year; (April 15 for calendar year corporations).

Example:
Your corporation operates on a December 31 calendar year for tax purposes. In early 1991, you decide to give up S corporation tax status. If you want your business to be taxed as a regular corporation for all of 1991, file the revocation notice on or before April 15, 1991. The corporation will then be taxed as a regular C Corporation beginning January 1, 1992.

3. *On the first day of the next year.*

Example:
You file the revocation notice form on April 10, 1991, and ask that S Corporation status end on December 31, 1991. The 1992 tax return is filed for a regular C Corporation.

INVOLUNTARY TERMINATIONS

In order to remain an S Corporation, the corporation must continue in all respects to qualify as a small business corporation, with the same requirements as when it first obtained S Corporation status.

Should the S Corporation fail to satisfy one or more requirements needed to qualify it as a small business corporation, its S Status ends as of the day the disqualifying event occurs.

Therefore, it's worthwhile to review the qualifications for S election if you are to avoid an involuntary termination by the IRS.

1. *Do not permit more than 35 shareholders in your S Corporation.* Once a corporation has the maximum number of shareholders (35), you should keep track of what your other shareholders do with their stock. For example, should a married couple divorce and each take half the shares they jointly held, they will count as two shareholders, not one. Similarly, if a parent gives shares to his or her children, each child adds to the total of shareholders. Therefore, each shareholder must understand these restrictions to avoid the corporation inadvertently ending up with more than 35 shareholders.

2. *Do not issue shares to ineligible shareholders.* S Corporation status is terminated when organizations have ineligible shareholders. Therefore, do not issue shares to:

- A corporation.
- Any person who is a nonresident alien of the United States.
- A trust (certain trusts are eligible to be shareholders in an S Corporation, but you should check with your tax advisor before issuing shares to a trust).
- A partnership.

Similarly, a shareholder cannot transfer his or her shares to any of the above ineligible parties.

The best way to avoid these problems is to enter into a buy-sell agreement that requires a shareholder to offer his or her shares to the corporation before transferring them to any other buyer. If such an agreement is used, you should take care to place a legend on each share certificate indicating the shares are subject to a restriction on their transferability; a similar statement should be placed in the corporation articles of incorporation and in its by-laws. An appropriate legend is found on the sample stock certificate found in Appendix 1.

A buy-sell agreement of the type described above will insure that no shareholder transfers shares to an ineligible purchaser such as a corporation or a partnership. A sample buy-sell agreement ("Shareholders' Agreement") is included at the end of this chapter. Shareholders should also be reminded to review their S Corporation ownership with their estate planner to avoid transfer to nonqualifying trusts.

3. *Avoid disqualifying loans.* If a corporation's shareholders lend too much money to the corporation (rather than putting their investment in at risk in exchange for common stock), the IRS may treat the loan as an investment in stock—and hold that stock to be of a different class than the one originally

issued. The result is that the corporation will be viewed as having more than one class of stock and will be ineligible for S Corporation treatment. The rules for permissible lending limits are the same for S Corporations as they are for regular C Corporations. Further, loans must carry legitimate loan terms—a fair interest rate, an unconditional promise to repay, a definite repayment date, and not be subordinated to other debts. If your loan carries normal lending terms, the likelihood is that it will not be treated as a second class of stock. If you intend lending money to your corporation in amounts greater than your investment in its stock, you should consider clearing the amount and terms of the loan with your tax advisor before completing the arrangement.

Of course, issuance of a second class of stock is a disqualifying event. An S Corporation is permitted to have only one class of stock. The exception to this rule allows an S Corporation to create a second class of common stock that differs from the first class only with respect to voting rights.

4. *Comply with tax year requirements.* Although not a violation of the requirements concerning a small business corporation, an S Corporation may lose its status if it does not use a proper tax year. In most instances, S Corporations are required to use a calendar year since they are obliged to use the year that is the same as their owner's tax year.

5. *Avoid intracorporate relationships.* Another way to lose S Corporation status is to permit the S Corporation to enter into a parent-subsidiary with another corporation. And you should not allow it to enter into an affiliation with another corporation (i.e., owning 80 percent of the stock in another corporation). And remember: S Corporation status is available only to domestic (U.S.) corporations.

6. *Watch passive income limits.* If you are switching from a regular corporation to an S corporation and the regular corporation was profitable, not more than 25 percent of its gross receipts can be "passive income." In general, the term "passive income" includes all nonoperating income (e.g., interest, dividends, or rent). If your passive income begins to approach 25 percent of total corporate revenues, then confer with your accountant for ways to redistribute passive earnings so the corporation can continue to qualify. The test for excessive passive income applies to an S Corporation that has (i) accumulated earnings and profits from its C Corporation operations, and those earnings and profits remain in the S Corporation for three consecutive S Corporation tax years, and (ii) passive income for three consecutive tax years, and the passive income exceeds 25 percent of the S Corporation gross receipts for each of those years.

7. *Avoid disqualifying business activities.* For example, an S Corporation cannot become a banking or financial institution or become an insurance company. If there is a question whether a new business activity would disqualify the S status, the corporation should obtain a ruling from the IRS.

WHEN YOU LOSE YOUR S STATUS

When a terminating or disqualifying event occurs, the corporation has the responsibility to report it to the IRS. The statement must include the date the disqualifying event occurred and the nature of the event (i.e., sold shares to an ineligible purchaser, exceeded passive income limits, and so forth).

However, if you can show the IRS that you inadvertently violated one of the above rules, the Service may allow you to correct the problem, and keep your business an S Corporation.

Example:
One of your 35 stockholders (a married couple) divorces and divides their stock, so there are now 36 stockholders. But other stockholders quickly move to purchase the stock held by the ex-husband or ex-wife.

Result:
The number of stockholders returns to 35. Since no tax is avoided, the IRS will most likely allow S Corporation status to continue.

It is important to show your willingness to spot and correct any violation of S Corporation rules.

EFFECT OF TERMINATION

If a corporation's election to be taxed as an S Corporation is revoked or terminated, it then becomes a C Corporation. As a general rule, it cannot elect to return to S status until the fifth year after the year in which the revocation or termination occurred. For example, if an S Corporation revoked its S election on April 15, 1992, and it was a calendar year corporation, it cannot become an S Corporation again until January 1, 1997.

Although the IRS can waive the five-year rule, it seldom does so where there was a revocation or an intentional termination unless there has been a change of ownership amongst a majority of the corporation's shareholders.

THE FORMS IN THIS SECTION

1. The *Revocation Notice* is used to terminate the S Corporation election. It must be signed by the shareholders who own fifty percent or more of the outstanding shares, and mailed to the IRS.

2. The *Shareholders' Agreement* should be signed by all shareholders when they first elect to adopt S Corporation status. This agreement essentially prevents a shareholder from transferring his or her shares to a stockholder who would disqualify the S Corporation status. The shares of stock should carry a legend making reference to the restriction on transfer.

REVOCATION NOTICE—SAMPLE

Date: December 31, 1992

Director
Internal Revenue Service Center
10 Oak Street
Anytown, USA 00000

Re: <u>XYZ Corporation</u>
        Corporation
<u>100 Main St., Anywhere,</u> USA 00000
        Address
<u>81-4039261</u>
        EIN Number

SAMPLE

Dear Sir:

Please be advised that the above   XYZ
Corporation   , (Corporation) hereby revokes
its election to be taxed as an S Corporation under the
provisions of Section 1362 of the Internal Revenue Code.
The Corporation has a total of   100   shares of stock
issued and outstanding as of this date. This revocation
shall be effective as of   December 31 , 1992 . The
consent by a requisite number of stockholders is contained below.

Sincerely,
XYZ Corporation

By: _Adam Smith_____
Authorized Officer

SHAREHOLDERS' CONSENT

The undersigned, record owners of more than fifty
percent of the outstanding stock of XYZ Corporation
(Corporation) as of the date of this notice, have
consented to the revocation of the Corporation's
election to be treated as an S Corporation under Section
1362 of the Internal Revenue Code.

Name	Signature	Number of Shares Owned
Robert Brown	*Robert Brown*	50
Adam Smith	*Adam Smith*	50

REVOCATION NOTICE—FORM

Date:

Director
Internal Revenue Service Center

Re:_____
                    Corporation

    _____
                    Address

    _____
                    EIN Number

Dear Sir:

Please be advised that the above
_____, (Corporation) hereby revokes
its election to be taxed as an S Corporation under the
provisions of Section 1362 of the Internal Revenue Code.
The Corporation has a total of _____ shares of stock
issued and outstanding as of this date. This revocation
shall be effective as of _____, 19___. The
consent by a requisite number of stockholders is contained below.

                        Sincerely,

                        By:_____
                            Authorized Officer

SHAREHOLDERS' CONSENT

The undersigned, record owners of more than fifty
percent of the outstanding stock of _____
(Corporation) as of the date of this notice, have
consented to the revocation of the Corporation's
election to be treated as an S Corporation under Section
1362 of the Internal Revenue Code.

Name	Signature	Number of Shares Owned
_____	_____	_____
_____	_____	_____
_____	_____	_____

SHAREHOLDERS' AGREEMENT—SAMPLE

This agreement is made on the 15th day of
July   , 1991 , by and between
XYZ Corporation   , a   New York   corporation,
and   Robert Brown and Mary Brown   , who are all
shareholders (Shareholders) of   XYZ Corporation.   .

Whereas, the Corporation has elected to be taxed as
an S Corporation as permitted by the Internal Revenue
Code of the United States, and that each Shareholder has
consented to that election; and

Whereas, the Shareholders believe it is in their
mutual interests for the Corporation to continue as an S
Corporation as long as the holders of   55   percent of
the outstanding shares of stock agree the Corporation
shall be an S Corporation, it is hereby mutually agreed
that:

1.   Unless the approval of all of the Shareholders
is first obtained, no Shareholder shall gift, hypo-
thecate, encumber, sell, donate, or in any way transfer
shares of stock in the Corporation without first obtaining (a) the written opinion of the legal counsel to the
corporation that the transfer will not cause the corporation to lose its status as an S Corporation and (b) the
transferee's written consent that he or she will be
bound by all the terms of this Agreement. Any actual or
attempted transfer of shares of stock in violation of
paragraph 1 above will be null, void and without legal
effect.

2.   No Shareholder shall refuse to provide any
consent or execute other document that may now or hereinafter be required by the Internal Revenue Code, any
regulations promulgated under the Internal Revenue Code
or the Internal Revenue Service that may be as a condi-
tion for maintaining the Corporation election to be
taxed as an S Corporation.

3.   In the event any Shareholder violates or
refuses to perform in accordance with the provisions of
paragraphs 1 and/or 2 above, the other Shareholders
shall, in addition to monetary damages, enforce this
Agreement by requesting any form of legal or equitable
relief or remedy that requires specific performance from
the Shareholder in accordance with this Agreement.

4. In the event that the Corporation loses its S Corporation status and such loss is attributable in whole or in any part to the failure of one or more Shareholders to act in accordance with the provisions of paragraphs 1 and/or 2 above, then each Shareholder who failed to comply with the provisions of paragraphs 1 and/or 2 above shall be jointly and severally liable for all losses incurred by the Corporation and the other Shareholders as a result or consequence of said violation.

5. Each Shareholder, upon the signing of this Agreement, shall return to the Secretary of the Corporation, all stock certificates he or she may now own and shall receive in substitution therefor a share certificate for the same number of shares. The new certificate shall contain a printed legend stating that the shares represented by the certificate are subject to the restrictions on transfer set out in this Agreement.

6. In the event that the Internal Revenue Code provisions governing S Corporation status are amended or changed in any way, this Agreement will be modified by such modification or modifications are necessary in order for the Shareholders to continue to receive the benefit of S incorporation status.

7. This Agreement shall terminate upon the occurrence of any one of the following events:

    a. The written agreement of the holders of 51 percent of the outstanding shares of the Corporation or

    b. The repeal of the Internal Revenue Code provisions allowing for the election of S Corporation status and the failure of the Internal Revenue Code, or any future law replacing the Internal Revenue Code, to provide a substitute for the single taxation approach to corporate profits and dividends currently provided by the existing S Corporation provisions of the Internal Revenue Code.

8. This Agreement will be binding upon and exists for the benefit of the parties to this Agreement, and, subject to the restrictions set out in this Agreement, upon their heirs, assigns, personal representatives and successors.

9. This Agreement is governed by the laws of New York

IN WITNESS WHEREOF, the parties have executed this Agreement on the date first above written.

XYZ Corporation

By: *Robert Brown, Pres.*

ATTEST:

SAMPLE

By: *Henry Jones*

WITNESS: SHAREHOLDERS:

Henry Jones   *Robert Brown*
Henry Jones   Robert Brown
                                        Mary Brown
                                        Mary Brown

SHAREHOLDERS' AGREEMENT—FORM

This agreement is made on the   day of
        , 19   , by and between
                          , a   corporation,
and   , who are all
shareholders (Shareholders) of   .

Whereas, the Corporation has elected to be taxed as
an S Corporation as permitted by the Internal Revenue
Code of the United States, and that each Shareholder has
consented to that election; and

Whereas, the Shareholders believe it is in their
mutual interests for the Corporation to continue as an S
Corporation as long as the holders of   percent of
the outstanding shares of stock agree the Corporation
shall be an S Corporation, it is hereby mutually agreed
that:

1.   Unless the approval of all of the Shareholders
is first obtained, no Shareholder shall gift, hypo-
thecate, encumber, sell, donate, or in any way transfer
shares of stock in the Corporation without first obtaining (a) the written opinion of the legal counsel to the
corporation that the transfer will not cause the corporation to lose its status as an S Corporation and (b) the
transferee's written consent that he or she will be
bound by all the terms of this Agreement. Any actual or
attempted transfer of shares of stock in violation of
paragraph 1 above will be null, void and without legal
effect.

2.   No Shareholder shall refuse to provide any
consent or execute other document that may now or hereinafter be required by the Internal Revenue Code, any
regulations promulgated under the Internal Revenue Code
or the Internal Revenue Service that may be as a condi-
tion for maintaining the Corporation election to be
taxed as an S Corporation.

3.   In the event any Shareholder violates or
refuses to perform in accordance with the provisions of
paragraphs 1 and/or 2 above, the other Shareholders
shall, in addition to monetary damages, enforce this
Agreement by requesting any form of legal or equitable
relief or remedy that requires specific performance from
the Shareholder in accordance with this Agreement.

4.   In the event that the Corporation loses its S Corporation status and such loss is attributable in whole or in any part to the failure of one or more Shareholders to act in accordance with the provisions of paragraphs 1 and/or 2 above, then each Shareholder who failed to comply with the provisions of paragraphs 1 and/or 2 above shall be jointly and severally liable for all losses incurred by the Corporation and the other Shareholders as a result or consequence of said violation.

5.   Each Shareholder, upon the signing of this Agreement, shall return to the Secretary of the Corporation, all stock certificates he or she may now own and shall receive in substitution therefor a share certificate for the same number of shares. The new certificate shall contain a printed legend stating that the shares represented by the certificate are subject to the restrictions on transfer set out in this Agreement.

6.   In the event that the Internal Revenue Code provisions governing S Corporation status are amended or changed in any way, this Agreement will be modified by such modification or modifications are necessary in order for the Shareholders to continue to receive the benefit of S incorporation status.

7.   This Agreement shall terminate upon the occurrence of any one of the following events:

   a.   The written agreement of the holders of   percent of the outstanding shares of the Corporation or

   b.   The repeal of the Internal Revenue Code provisions allowing for the election of S Corporation status and the failure of the Internal Revenue Code, or any future law replacing the Internal Revenue Code, to provide a substitute for the single taxation approach to corporate profits and dividends currently provided by the existing S Corporation provisions of the Internal Revenue Code.

8.   This Agreement will be binding upon and exists for the benefit of the parties to this Agreement, and, subject to the restrictions set out in this Agreement, upon their heirs, assigns, personal representatives and successors.

9.   This Agreement is governed by the laws of

IN WITNESS WHEREOF, the parties have executed this Agreement on the date first above written.

By:_____

ATTEST:

By:_____

WITNESS: SHAREHOLDERS:

_____   _____

_____   _____

_____   _____

_____   _____

_____   _____

_____

APPENDIX 1
CORPORATE DOCUMENTS

THE FORMS IN THIS SECTION

This section contains numerous forms designed to simplify the procedures for maintaining proper corporate records:

1. Notice of Organization Meeting
2. Waiver of Notice of Organization Meeting
3. Minutes of Organization Meeting of Directors
4. Waiver of Notice—Shareholders' Meeting
5. Minutes, First Shareholders' Meeting
6. Minutes, Special Stockholders' Meeting
7. Stockholders' Resolution for S Corporation
8. Bylaws
9. Stock Certificate
10. Stock Transfer Ledger

NOTICE OF ORGANIZATION MEETING
OF INCORPORATORS AND DIRECTORS

TO: _____

_____

_____

PLEASE BE ADVISED THAT:

We, the undersigned, do hereby constitute a
majority of the directors named in the Articles of
Incorporation of _____,
a   corporation;

Pursuant to state law, we are hereby calling an
organization meeting of the Board of Directors and
incorporators named in the Articles of Incorporation of
the above named corporation; for the purpose of adopting
by-laws, electing officers, and transacting such other
business as may come before the meeting; and

Said organization meeting shall be held at _____

_____

on _____, 19____, at _____ o'clock ____.m.

_____   _____

_____   _____

RECEIPT OF NOTICE

_____   _____
Addressee-Director   Date Received

WAIVER OF NOTICE OF ORGANIZATION
MEETING OF INCORPORATORS AND DIRECTORS

OF_____

        We do hereby constitute the incorporators and
directors of the above named corporation and do hereby
waive notice of the organization meeting of directors
and incorporators of the aforesaid corporation.

        Furthermore, we hereby agree that said meeting
shall be held at   o'clock   .m. on
                   , 19   at the following place:

_____.

        We do hereby affix our names to show our waiver of
notice of said meeting.

_____   _____

_____   _____

Dated:

MINUTES OF ORGANIZATION MEETING
OF BOARD OF DIRECTORS OF

_____

The organizational meeting of the Board of

Directors of   , was held

at   on

                , 19   , at   :00   .m.

Present was   ,

              ,   , being

the persons designated as the Directors in the Articles

of Incorporation.

                    acted as temporary Chairman of

the meeting and   acted as

temporary Secretary.

The Chairman announced that the meeting had been

duly called by the Incorporators of the Corporation.

The Chairman reported that the Articles of Incor-

poration of the Corporation had been duly filed with the

State of   on   , 19   .

The Certificate of Incorporation and a copy of said

Articles of Incorporation were ordered to be inserted in

the Minutes as a part of the records of the meeting.

A proposed form of Bylaws for the regulation and

the management of the affairs of the Corporation was

then presented at the meeting. The Bylaws were read

and considered and, upon motion duly made and seconded,

it was:

RESOLVED, that the form of Bylaws of the Corporation, as presented to this meeting, a copy of which is directed to be inserted in the Minute Book of the Corporation be, and the same are hereby approved and adopted as the Bylaws of the Corporation.

The following persons were nominated officers of the Corporation to serve until their respective successors are chosen and qualify:

PRESIDENT:

VICE PRESIDENT:

SECRETARY:

TREASURER:

The Chairman announced that the aforenamed persons had been elected to the office set opposite their respective names.

The President thereupon took the chair and the Secretary immediately assumed the discharge of the duties of that office.

The President then stated that there were a number of organizational matters to be considered at the meeting and a number of resolutions to be adopted by the Board of Directors.

The form of stock certificates was then exhibited at the meeting. Thereupon, a motion duly made and seconded, it was:

RESOLVED, that the form of stock certificates presented at this meeting be, and the same is hereby adopted and approved as the stock certificate of the Corporation, a specimen copy of the stock certificate to be inserted with these Minutes

FURTHER RESOLVED, that the officers are hereby authorized to pay or reimburse the payment of all fees and expenses incident to and necessary for the organization of this Corporation.

The Board of Directors then considered the opening of a corporate bank account to serve as a depository for the funds of the Corporation. Following discussion, on motion duly made and seconded, it was:

RESOLVED, that the Treasurer be authorized, empowered and directed to open an account with

and to deposit all funds of the Corporation, all drafts, checks and notes of the Corporation, payable on said account to be made in the corporate name signed by

FURTHER RESOLVED, that officers are hereby authorized to execute such resolutions (including formal Bank Resolutions), documents and other instruments as may be necessary or advisable in opening or continuing said bank account. A copy of the applicable printed form of Bank Resolution hereby adopted to supplement these Minutes is ordered appended to the Minutes of this meeting.

It is announced that the following persons have offered to transfer the property listed below in exchange for the following shares of the stock of the Corporation:

Name	Payment Consideration, or Property	Number of Shares

Upon motion duly made and seconded, it was:

RESOLVED, that acceptance of the offer of the above-named person is in the best interest of the Corporation and necessary for carrying out the corporate business, and in the judgement of the Board of Directors, the assets proposed to be transferred to the Corporation are reasonably worth the amount of consideration deemed therefor, and the same hereby is accepted, and that upon receipt of the consideration indicated above, the President

and the Secretary are authorized to issue certifi-

cates of fully-paid, nonassessable capital stock of

this Corporation in the amounts indicated to the

above-named persons.

In order to provide for the payment of expenses of

incorporation and organization fo the Corporation, on

motion duly made, seconded and unanimously carried, the

following resolution was adopted:

RESOLVED, that the President and the Secretary

and/or Treasurer of this Corporation be and they

are hereby authorized and directed to pay the

expenses of this Corporation, including attorney's

fees for incorporation, and to reimburse the per-

sons who have made disbursements thereof.

After consideration of the pertinent issues with

regard to the tax year and accounting basis, on motion

duly made, and seconded and unanimously carried, the

following resolution was adopted:

RESOLVED, that the first fiscal year of the

Corporation shall commence on

and end on   .

FURTHER RESOLVED, that the President be and is hereby authorized and directed to enter into employment contracts with certain employees, such contract shall be for the term and the rate stated in the attached Employment Agreements.

FURTHER RESOLVED, that it shall be the policy of the Corporation to reimburse each employee or to pay directly on his behalf all expenses incidental to his attendance at conventions and seminars as may be approved by the President. Reimbursement shall include full reimbursement for commercial and private transportation expenses, plus other necessary and ordinary out-of-pocket expenses incidental to the said travel, including meals and lodging.

A general discussion was then held concerning the immediate commencement of business operations as a Corporation and it was determined that business operations of the Corporation would commence as of

It was agreed that no fixed date would be set for holding meetings of the Board of Directors except the regular meetings to be held immediately after the annual meetings of shareholders as provided in the By-laws of the Corporation but that meetings of the Directors would be periodically called by the President and Secretary or others as provided by the Bylaws.

Upon motion duly made, seconded and unanimously carried, it was:

RESOLVED, that the officers of the Corporation are hereby authorized to do any and all things necessary to conduct the business of the Corporation as set forth in the Articles of Incorporation and Bylaws of the Corporation.

Upon motion duly made, seconded, and unanimously carried the following resolution was adopted:

RESOLVED, that, if required, that be, and hereby is, appointed Resident Agent in the State of . The office of the Resident Agent will be located at .

The Chairman then presented to the meeting the question of electing the provisions of Section 1244 of the Internal Revenue Code. He noted that this Section permits ordinary loss treatment when either the holder of Section 1244 stock sells or exchanges such stock at a loss or when such stock becomes worthless. After a discussion, the following preamble was stated and the following resolution was unanimously:

RESOLVED, THAT:

WHEREAS, this Corporation qualifies as a small business corporation as defined in Section 1244, but

WHEREAS, the Board of Directors are concerned over future tax law changes modifying Section 1244 as presently enacted (subsequent to the Revenue Act of 1978) and thus desire to safeguard this Corporation's 1244 election by complying with prior law as well as present law, and

WHEREAS, pursuant to the requirements of Section 1244 and the Regulations issued thereunder, the following plan has been submitted to the Corporation by the Board of Directors of the Corporation:

(a) The plan as hereafter set forth shall, upon its adoption by the Board of Directors of the Corporation immediately become effective.

(b) No more than _____ shares of common stock are authorized to be issued under this plan, such stock to have a par value of $ _____ per share.

(c) Stock authorized under this plan shall be issued only in exchange for money, or property susceptible to monetary valuation other than capital stock, securities or services rendered

114

or to be rendered. The aggregate dollar amount to be received for such stock shall not exceed $1,000,000, and the sum of each aggregate dollar amount and the equity capital of the Corporation (determined on the date of adoption of the plan) shall not exceed $1,000,000.

(d) Any stock options granted during the life of this plan which apply to the stock issuable hereunder shall apply solely to such stock and to no other and must be exercised within the period in which the plan is effective.

(e) Such other action as may be necessary shall be taken by the Corporation to qualify the stock to be offered and issued under this plan as "Section 1244 Stock", as such term is defined in the Internal Revenue Code and the regulations issued thereunder.

NOW, THEREFORE, the foregoing plan to issue Section 1244 Stock is adopted by the Corporation and the appropriate officers of the Corporation are authorized and directed to take all actions deemed by them necessary to carry out the intent and purpose of the recited plan.

There being no further business requiring Board action or consideration;

On motion duly made, seconded and carried, the
meeting was adjourned.

Dated:

_____
Secretary of the Meeting

WAIVER OF NOTICE,
FIRST MEETING OF SHAREHOLDERS

We the undersigned, being the shareholders of the_____, agree that the first meeting of shareholders be held on the date and at the time and place stated below in order to elect officers and transact such other business as may lawfully come before the meeting. We hereby waive all notice of such meeting and of any adjournment thereof.

Place of Meeting_____

Date of Meeting_____

Time of Meeting_____

_____

_____

_____

_____

_____

Dated:_____ _____
                                              Shareholders

MINUTES, FIRST MEETING
OF SHAREHOLDERS

The first meeting of the shareholders of _____
_____ was held at _____
_____ on the _____
day of _____, 19_____, at _____
o'clock _____.m.

The meeting was duly called to order by the President. He stated the purpose of the meeting.

Next, the Secretary read the list of shareholders as they appear in the record book of the Corporation. He reported the presence of a quorum of shareholders.

Next, the Secretary read a waiver of notice of the meeting, signed by all shareholders. On a motion duly made, seconded and carried, the waiver was ordered appended to the minutes of this meeting.

Next, the President asked the Secretary to read:

(1) the minutes of the organization meeting of the Corporation; and (2) the minutes of the first meeting of the Board of Directors.

A motion was duly made, seconded and carried unanimously that the following resolution be adopted:

WHEREAS, the minutes of the organization meeting of the Corporation and the minutes of the first meeting of the Board of Directors have been read to this meeting, and

WHEREAS, Bylaws were adopted and directors and officers were elected at the organization meeting, it is hereby

RESOLVED that this meeting approves and ratifies the election of the said directors and officers of this Corporation for the term of _____ years, and approves, ratifies and adopts said Bylaws as the Bylaws of the corporation. It is further

RESOLVED that all acts taken and decisions made at the organization meeting and the first meeting of the Board are approved and ratified. It is further

RESOLVED that signing of these minutes constitutes full ratification by the signatories and waiver of notice of the meeting.

There being no further business, the meeting was adjourned, Dated the _____day of_____, 19_____.

_____
Secretary

_____

_____

_____

_____

Directors

Appended hereto:

Waiver of notice of meeting.

MINUTES OF SPECIAL MEETING OF STOCKHOLDERS

A special meeting of the stockholders of the Corporation was held at
in the City of   , in the State of
                        , on   , 19   ,
at   .m.

The meeting was called to order by   ,
the President of the Corporation, and   ,
the Secretary of the Corporation, kept the records of the meeting.

The Secretary reported that a quorum of stockholders were present in person or were represented by proxy, the aggregate amount representing more than
of the outstanding stock entitled to vote on the resolutions proposed at the meeting.

The Secretary reported that the following stockholders were present in person:

Names	Number of Shares
_____	_____
_____	_____
_____	_____
_____	_____

and that the following stockholders were represented by proxy:

Names	Names of Proxies	Number of Shares
_____	_____	_____
_____	_____	_____
_____	_____	_____
_____	_____	_____

The Secretary presented and read a waiver of notice of the meeting signed by each stockholder entitled to notice of the meeting, which waiver of notice was ordered to be filed with the minutes of the meeting.

On motion duly made and seconded, and after due deliberation, the following resolution(s) was/were unanimously voted upon:

That the Corporation elect to be subject to and taxed pursuant to Section 1362 of the Internal Revenue Code.

The Secretary reported that all shares of common stock had been voted in favor of the foregoing resolution(s) and no shares of common stock had been voted against the resolutions, said vote therefore representing 100 percent of the outstanding shares entitled to vote thereon.

The President thereupon declared that the resolution(s) had been duly adopted.

There being no further business, upon motion, the meeting adjourned.

A True Record

Attest

_____
Secretary

RESOLUTION OF STOCKHOLDERS OF

_____

BE IT KNOWN, that at a special meeting of the Stockholders of the Corporation wherein all the Stockholders were present, in person or by proxy, and voting throughout, it was upon motion duly made and seconded that it be <u>unanimously</u>

<u>Voted</u>:   That the Corporation elect to be subject to the provisions of Section 1362 of the Internal Revenue Code and be deemed and taxed as an S Corporation.

<u>Voted</u>:   That the President of the Corporation execute and file all documents and undertake such further acts which in his discretion is deemed necessary or advisable to carry out the tenor and performance of the foregoing vote.

IN WITNESS WHEREOF, I have affixed my name as Secretary and have caused the corporate seal of said Corporation to be hereunto affixed, this   day of , 19   .

A True Record

Attest

_____
Secretary

BYLAWS
OF

_____

ARTICLE I
OFFICES

Thr principal office of the Corporation in the
State of   shall be located in
                    , County of   .
The Corporation may have such other offices, either
within or without the State of   , as
the Board of Directors may designate or as the business
of the Corporation may require from time to time.

ARTICLE II
SHAREHOLDERS

SECTION 1. <u>Annual Meeting</u>. The annual meeting of
the shareholders shall be held on the   day in the
month of   in each year, beginning with
the year 19   , at the hour of   o'clock   .m.,
for the purpose of electing Directors and for the
transaction of such other business as may come before
the meeting. If the day fixed for the annual meeting
shall be a legal holiday in the State of   ,
such meeting shall be held on the next succeeding
business day. If the election of Directors shall not be
held on the day designated herein for any annual meeting
of the shareholders, or at any adjournment thereof, the
Board of Directors shall cause the election to be held
at a special meeting of the shareholders as soon
thereafter as conveniently may be.

SECTION 2. <u>Special Meetings</u>. Special meetings of
the shareholders, for any purpose or purposes, unless
otherwise prescribed by statute, may be called by the
President or by the Board of Directors, and shall be
called by the President at the request of the holders of
not less than   percent (%) of all the
outstanding shares of the Corporation entitled to vote
at the meeting.

SECTION 3. <u>Place of Meeting</u>. The Board of Directors
may designate any place, either within or without the
State of   , unless otherwise prescribed
by statute, as the place of meeting for any annual
meeting or for any special meeting. A waiver of notice
signed by all shareholders entitled to vote at a meeting
may designate any place, either within or without the
State of   , unless otherwise prescribed

by statute, as the place for the holding of such meeting. If no designation is made, the place of meeting shall be the principal office of the Corporation.

SECTION 4. Notice of Meeting. Written notice stating the place, day and hour of the meeting and, in case of a special meeting, the purpose or purposes for which the meeting is called, shall unless otherwise prescribed by statute, be delivered not less than (   ) nor more than (   ) days before the date of the meeting, to each shareholder of record entitled to vote at such meeting. If mailed, such notice shall be deemed to be delivered when deposited in the United States Mail, addressed to the shareholder at his address as it appears on the stock transfer books of the Corporation, with postage thereon prepaid.

SECTION 5. Closing of Transfer Books or Fixing of Record. For the purpose of determining shareholders entitled to notice of or to vote at any meeting of shareholders or any adjournment thereof, or shareholders entitled to receive payment of any dividend, or in order to make a determination of shareholders for any other proper purpose, the Board of Directors of the Corporation may provide that the stock transfer books shall be closed for a stated period, but not to exceed in any case fifty (50) days. If the stock transfer books shall be closed for the purpose of determining shareholders entitled to notice of or to vote at a meeting of shareholders, such books shall be closed for at least (   ) days immediately preceding such meeting. In lieu of closing the stock transfer books, the Board of Directors may fix in advance a date as the record date for any such determination of shareholders, such date in any case to be not more than (   ) days and, in case of a meeting of shareholders, not less than (   ) days, prior to the date on which the particular action requiring such determination of shareholders is to be taken. If the stock transfer books are not closed and no record date is fixed for the determination of shareholders entitled to notice of or to vote at a meeting of shareholders, or shareholders entitled to receive payment of a dividend, the date on which notice of the meeting is mailed or the date on which the resolution of the Board of Directors declaring such dividend is adopted, as the case may be, shall be the record date for such determination of shareholders. When a determination of shareholders entitled to vote at any meeting of shareholders has been made as provided in this section, such determination shall apply to any adjournment thereof.

SECTION 6. Voting Lists. The officer or agent
having charge of the stock transfer books for shares of
the corporation shall make a complete list of the
shareholders entitled to vote at each meeting of
shareholders or any adjournment thereof, arranged in
alphabetical order, with the address of and the number
of shares held by each. Such list shall be produced and
kept open at the time and place of the meeting and shall
be subject to the inspection of any shareholder during
the whole time of the meeting for the purposes thereof.

SECTION 7. Quorum. A majority of the outstanding
shares of the Corporation entitled to vote, represented
in person or by proxy, shall constitute a quorum at a
meeting of shareholders. If less than a majority of the
outstanding shares are represented at a meeting, a
majority of the shares so represented may adjourn the
meeting from time to time without further notice. At
such adjourned meeting at which a quorum shall be
present or represented, any business may be transacted
which might have been transacted at the meeting as
originally noticed. The shareholders present at a duly
organized meeting may continue to transact business
until adjournment, notwithstanding the withdrawal of
enough shareholders to leave less than a quorum.

SECTION 8. Proxies. At all meetings of
shareholders, a shareholder may vote in person or by
proxy executed in writing by the shareholder or by his
duly authorized attorney-in-fact. Such proxy shall be
filed with the secretary of the Corporation before or at
the time of the meeting. A meeting of the Board of
Directors may be had by means of a telephone conference
or similar communications equipment by which all persons
participating in the meeting can hear each other, and
participation in a meeting under such circumstances
shall constitute presence at the meeting.

SECTION 9. Voting of Shares. Each outstanding share
entitled to vote shall be entitled to one vote upon each
matter submitted to a vote at a meeting of shareholders.

SECTION 10. Voting of Shares by Certain Holders.
Shares standing in the name of another corporation may
be voted by such officer, agent or proxy as the Bylaws
of such corporation may prescribe or, in the absence of
such provision, as the Board of Directors of such
corporation may determine.

Shares held by an administrator, executor, guardian
or conservator may be voted by him, either in person or
by proxy, without a transfer of such shares into his
name. Shares standing in the name of a trustee may be
voted by him, either in person or by proxy, but no

trustee shall be entitled to vote shares held by him without a transfer of such shares into his name.

Shares standing in the name of a receiver may be voted by such receiver, and shares held by or under the control of a receiver may be voted by such receiver without the transfer thereof into his name, if authority so to do be contained in an appropriate order of the court by which such receiver was appointed.

A shareholder whose shares are pledged shall be entitled to vote such shares until the shares have been transferred into the name of the pledgee, and thereafter the pledgee shall be entitled to vote the shares so transferred.

Shares of its own stock belonging to the Corporation shall not be voted, directly or indirectly, at any meeting, and shall not be counted in determining the total number of outstanding shares at any given time.

SECTION 11. _Informal Action by Shareholders_. Unless otherwise provided by law, any action required to be taken at a meeting of the shareholders, or any other action which may be taken at a meeting of the shareholders, may be taken without a meeting if a consent in writing, setting forth the action so taken, shall be signed by all of the shareholders entitled to vote with respect to the subject matter thereof.

ARTICLE III
BOARD OF DIRECTORS

SECTION 1. _General Powers_. The business and affairs of the Corporation shall be managed by its Board of Directors.

SECTION 2. _Number, Tenure and Qualifications_. The number of directors of the Corporation shall be fixed by the Board of Directors, but in no event shall be less than (   ). Each director shall hold office until the next annual meeting of shareholders and until his successor shall have been elected and qualified.

SECTION 3. _Regular Meetings_. A regular meeting of the Board of Directors shall be held without other notice than this By-Law immediately after, and at the same place as, the annual meeting of shareholders. The Board of Directors may provide, by resolution, the time and place for the holding of additional regular meetings without notice other than such resolution.

SECTION 4. Special Meetings. Special meetings of the Board of Directors may be called by or at the request of the President or any two directors. The person or persons authorized to call special meetings of the Board of Directors may fix the place for holding any special meeting of the Board of Directors called by them.

SECTION 5. Notice. Notice of any special meeting shall be given at least one (1) day previous thereto by written notice delivered personally or mailed to each director at his business address, or by telegram. If mailed, such notice shall be deemed to be delivered when deposited in the United States Mail so addressed, with postage thereon prepaid. If notice be given by telegram, such notice shall be deemed to be delivered when the telegram is delivered to the telegraph company. Any directors may waive notice of any meeting. The attendance of a director at a meeting shall constitute a waiver of notice of such meeting, except where a director attends a meeting for the express purpose of objecting to the transaction of any business because the meeting is not lawfully called or convened.

SECTION 6. Quorum. A majority of the number of directors fixed by Section 2 of this Article III shall constitute a quorum for the transaction of business at any meeting of the Board of Directors, but if less than such majority is present at a meeting, a majority of the directors present may adjourn the meeting from time to time without further notice.

SECTION 7. Manner of Acting. The act of the majority of the directors present at a meeting at which a quorum is present shall be the act of the Board of Directors.

SECTION 8. Action Without a Meeting. Any action that may be taken by the Board of Directors at a meeting may be taken without a meeting if a consent in writing, setting forth the action so to be taken, shall be signed before such action by all of the directors.

SECTION 9. Vacancies. Any vacancy occurring in the Board of Directors may be filled by the affirmative vote of a majority of the remaining directors though less than a quorum of the Board of Directors, unless otherwise provided by law. A director elected to fill a vacancy shall be elected for the unexpired term of his predecessor in office. Any directorship to be filled by reason of an increase in the number of directors may be filled by election by the Board of Directors for a term of office continuing only until the next election of directors by the shareholders.

SECTION 10. <u>Compensation</u>. By resolution of the Board of Directors, each director may be paid his expenses, if any, of attendance at each meeting of the Board of Directors, and may be paid a stated salary as director or a fixed sum for attendance at each meeting of the Board of Directors or both. No such payment shall preclude any director from serving the Corporation in any other capacity and receiving compensation therefor.

SECTION 11. <u>Presumption of Assent</u>. A director of the Corporation who is present at a meeting of the Board of Directors at which action on any corporate matter is taken shall be presumed to have assented to the action taken unless his dissent shall be entered in the minutes of the meeting or unless he shall file his written dissent to such action with the person acting as the Secretary of the meeting before the adjournment thereof, or shall forward such dissent by registered mail to the Secretary of the Corporation immediately after the adjournment of the meeting. Such right to dissent shall not apply to a director who voted in favor of such action.

ARTICLE IV
OFFICERS

SECTION 1. <u>Number</u>. The officers of the Corporation shall be a President, one or more Vice Presidents, a Secretary and a Treasurer, each of whom shall be elected by the Board of Directors. Such other officers and assistant officers as may be deemed necessary may be elected or appointed by the Board of Directors, including a Chairman of the Board. In its discretion, the Board of Directors may leave unfilled for any such period as it may determine any office except those of President and Secretary. Any two or more offices may be held by the same person, except for the offices of President and Secretary which may not be held by the same person. Officers may be directors or shareholders of the Corporation.

SECTION 2. <u>Election and Term of Office</u>. The officers of the Corporation to be elected by the Board of Directors shall be elected annually by the Board of Directors at the first meeting of the Board of Directors held after each annual meeting of the shareholders. If the election of officers shall not be held at such meeting, such election shall be held as soon thereafter as conveniently may be. Each officer shall hold office until his successor shall have been duly elected and shall have qualified, or until his death, or until he shall resign or shall have been removed in the manner hereinafter provided.

SECTION 3. Removal. Any officer or agent may be removed by the Board of Directors whenever, in its judgement, the best interests of the Corporation will be served thereby, but such removal shall be without prejudice to the contract rights, if any, of the person so removed. Election or appointment of an officer or agent shall not of itself create contract rights, and such appointment shall be terminable at will.

SECTION 4. Vacancies. A vacancy in any office because of death, resignation, removal, disqualification or otherwise, may be filled by the Board of Directors for the unexpired portion of the term.

SECTION 5. President. The President shall be the principal executive officer of the Corporation and, subject to the control of the Board of Directors, shall in general supervise and control all of the business and affairs of the Corporation. He shall, when present, preside at all meetings of the shareholders and of the Board of Directors, unless there is a Chairman of the Board, in which case the Chairman shall preside. He may sign, with the Secretary or any other proper officer of the Corporation thereunto authorized by the Board of Directors, certificates for shares of the Corporation, any deeds, mortgages, bonds, contracts, or other instruments which the Board of Directors has authorized to be executed, except in cases where the signing and execution thereof shall be expressly delegated by the Board of Directors or by these Bylaws to some other officer or agent of the Corporation, or shall be required by law to be otherwise signed or executed; and in general shall perform all duties incident to the office of President and such other duties as may be prescribed by the Board of Directors from time to time.

SECTION 6. Vice President. In the absence of the President or in event of his death, inability or refusal to act, the Vice President shall perform the duties of the President, and when so acting, shall have all the powers of and be subject to all the restrictions upon the President. The Vice President shall perform such other duties as from time to time may be assigned to him by the President or by the Board of Directors. If there is more than one Vice President, each Vice President shall succeed to the duties of the President in order of rank as determined by the Board of Directors. If no such rank has been determined, then each Vice President shall succeed to the duties of the President in order of date of election, the earliest date having the first rank.

SECTION 7. Secretary. The Secretary shall: (a) keep the minutes of the proceedings of the shareholders and of the Board of Directors in one or more minute books provided for that purpose; (b) see that all notices are duly given in accordance with the provisions of these By-Laws or as required by law; (c) be custodian of the corporate records and of the seal of the Corporation and see that the seal of the Corporation is affixed to all documents, the execution of which on behalf of the Corporation under its seal is duly authorized; (d) keep a register of the post office address of each shareholder which shall be furnished to the Secretary by such shareholder; (e) sign with the President certificates for shares of the Corporation, the issuance of which shall have been authorized by resolution of the Board of Directors; (f) have general charge of the stock transfer books of the Corporation; and (g) in general perform all duties incident to the office of the Secretary and such other duties as from time to time may be assigned to him by the President or by the Board of Directors.

SECTION 8. Treasurer. The Treasurer shall: (a) have charge and custody of and be responsible for all funds and securities of the Corporation; (b) receive and give receipts for moneys due and payable to the Corporation from any source whatsoever, and deposit all such moneys in the name of the Corporation in such banks, trust companies or other depositaries as shall be selected in accordance with the provisions of Article VI of these Bylaws; and (c) in general perform all of the duties incident to the office of Treasurer and such other duties as from time to time may be assigned to him by the President or by the Board of Directors. If required by the Board of Directors, the Treasurer shall give a bond for the faithful discharge of his duties in such sum and with such sureties as the Board of Directors shall determine.

SECTION 9. Salaries. The salaries of the officers shall be fixed from time to time by the Board of Directors, and no officer shall be prevented from receiving such salary by reason of the fact that he is also a director of the Corporation.

ARTICLE V
INDEMNITY

The Corporation shall indemnify its directors, officers and employees as follows:

(a) Every director, officer, or employee of the Corporation shall be indemnified by the Corporation

131

against all expenses and liabilities, including counsel fees, reasonably incurred by or imposed upon him in connection with any proceeding to which he may be made a party, or in which he may become involved, by reason of his being or having been a director, officer, employee or agent of the Corporation or is or was serving at the request of the Corporation as a director, officer, employee or agent of the corporation, partnership, joint venture, trust or enterprise, or any settlement thereof, whether or not he is a director, officer, employee or agent at the time such expenses are incurred, except in such cases wherein the director, officer, or employee is adjudged guilty of willful misfeasance or malfeasance in the performance of his duties; provided that in the event of a settlement the indemnification herein shall apply only when the Board of Directors approves such settlement and reimbursement as being for the best interests of the Corporation.

(b) The Corporation shall provide to any person who is or was a director, officer, employee, or agent of the Corporation or is or was serving at the request of the Corporation as a director, officer, employee or agent of the corporation, partnership, joint venture, trust or enterprise, the indemnity against expenses of suit, litigation or other proceedings which is specifically permissible under applicable law.

(c) The Board of Directors may, in its discretion, direct the purchase of liability insurance by way of implementing the provisions of this Article V.

ARTICLE VI
CONTRACTS, LOANS, CHECKS AND DEPOSITS

SECTION 1. Contracts. The Board of Directors may authorize any officer or officers, agent or agents, to enter into any contract or execute and deliver any instrument in the name of and on behalf of the Corporation, and such authority may be general or confined to specific instances.

SECTION 2. Loans. No loans shall be contracted on behalf of the Corporation and no evidences of indebtedness shall be issued in its name unless authorized by a resolution of the Board of Directors. Such authority may be general or confined to specific instances.

SECTION 3. Checks, Drafts, etc. All checks, drafts or other orders for the payment of money, notes or other evidences of indebtedness issued in the name of the Corporation, shall be signed by such officer or officers, agent or agents of the Corporation and in such manner as shall from time to time be determined by resolution of the Board of Directors.

SECTION 4. _Deposits_. All funds of the Corporation not otherwise employed shall be deposited from time to time to the credit of the Corporation in such banks, trust companies or other depositaries as the Board of Directors may select.

ARTICLE VII
CERTIFICATES FOR SHARES AND THEIR TRANSFER

SECTION 1. _Certificates for Shares_. Certificates representing shares of the Corporation shall be in such form as shall be determined by the Board of Directors. Such certificates shall be signed by the President and by the Secretary or by such other officers authorized by law and by the Board of Directors so to do, and sealed with the corporate seal. All certificates for shares shall be consecutively numbered or otherwise identified. The name and address of the person to whom the shares represented thereby are issued, with the number of shares and date of issue, shall be entered on the stock transfer books of the Corporation. All certificates surrendered to the Corporation for transfer shall be cancelled and no new certificate shall be issued until the former certificate for a like number of shares shall have been surrendered and cancelled, except that in case of a lost, destroyed or mutilated certificate, a new one may be issued therefor upon such terms and indemnity to the Corporation as the Board of Directors may prescribe.

SECTION 2. _Transfer of Shares_. Transfer of shares of the Corporation shall be made only on the stock transfer books of the Corporation by the holder of record thereof or by his legal representative, who shall furnish proper evidence of authority to transfer, or by his attorney thereunto authorized by power of attorney duly executed and filed with the Secretary of the Corporation, and on surrender for cancellation of the certificate for such shares. The person in whose name shares stand on the books of the Corporation shall be deemed by the Corporation to be the owner thereof for all purposes. Provided, however, that upon any action undertaken by the shareholders to elect S Corporation status pursuant to Section 1362 of the Internal Revenue Code and upon any shareholders agreement thereto restricting the transfer of said shares so as to dis-qualify said S Corporation status, said restriction on transfer shall be made a part of the Bylaws so long as said agreement is in force and effect.

ARTICLE VIII
FISCAL YEAR

The fiscal year of the Corporation shall begin on the   day of   and end on the day of   of each year.

ARTICLE IX
DIVIDENDS

The Board of Directors may from time to time declare, and the Corporation may pay, dividends on its outstanding shares in the manner and upon the terms and conditions provided by law and its Articles of Incorporation.

ARTICLE X
CORPORATE SEAL

The Board of Directors shall provide a corporate seal which shall be circular in form and shall have inscribed thereon the name of the Corporation and the state of incorporation and the words, "Corporate Seal".

ARTICLE XI
WAIVER OF NOTICE

Unless otherwise provided by law, whenever any notice is required to be given to any shareholder or director of the Corporation under the provisions of these Bylaws or under the provisions of the Articles of Incorporation or under the provisions of the applicable Business Corporation Act, a waiver thereof in writing, signed by the person or persons entitled to such notice, whether before or after the time stated therein, shall be deemed equivalent to the giving of such notice.

ARTICLE XII
AMENDMENTS

These Bylaws may be altered, amended or repealed and new Bylaws may be adopted by the Board of Directors at any regular or special meeting of the Board of Directors.

The above Bylaws are certified to have been adopted by the Board of Directors of the Corporation on the   day of   , 19   .

_____
Secretary

These shares are subject to restrictions on transfer pursuant to a shareholder agreement

SHARES

NUMBER

This Certifies that

is the owner of

non-assessable Shares of the above Corporation transferable only on the books of the Corporation by the holder hereof in person or by duly authorized Attorney upon surrender of this Certificate properly endorsed.

In Witness Whereof, the said Corporation has caused this Certificate to be signed by its duly authorized officers and to be sealed with the Seal of the Corporation.

Dated

STOCK TRANSFER LEDGER

NAME OF STOCKHOLDER	PLACE OF RESIDENCE		CERTIFICATES ISSUED		FROM WHOM SHARES WERE TRANSFERRED	
			CERTIF. NOS.	NO. SHARES	(IF ORIGINAL ISSUE ENTER AS SUCH)	

AMOUNT PAID THEREON	DATE OF TRANSFER OF SHARES	TO WHOM SHARES ARE TRANSFERRED	CERTIFICATES SURRENDERED		NUMBER OF SHARES HELD (BALANCE)	VALUE OF STOCK TRANSFER TAX STAMP AFFIXED
			CERTIF. NOS.	NO. SHARES		

APPENDIX 2
IRS TAX FORMS

THE FORMS IN THIS SECTION

1. *Form 1120S: U.S. Income Tax Return for an S Corporation*
   This form contains complete instructions for preparing and filing the corporation's income tax returns at the end of its fiscal year, together with a sample tax return.

2. *Form 4562: Depreciation and Amortization*
   This form contains both instructions and depreciation and amortization attachment to the year end Form 1120S tax return.

3. *Schedule K-1: Shareholder's Share of Income*
   This form is used by shareholders of the S Corporation to report their shares of income, credits, deductions, and other "pass-through" items.

4. *Schedule D: Capital Gains and Losses and Built-In Gains*
   This form is used by shareholders of the S Corporation to report both short- and long-term capital gains and losses, and to calculate the capital gains taxes.

5. *Form 8716: Election to Have a Tax Year Other Than a Required Tax Year*
   This form is filed by partnerships, S corporations, and personal service corporations that elect to have a tax year other than a required tax year; namely, the calendar year for the S Corporation.

6. *Form 1128: Application to Adopt, Change, or Retain a Tax Year*
   This form is used to make a change in the already established tax year of the S Corporation. Note that a $200 user fee must accompany this application.

7. *Form 940: Employer's Annual Federal Unemployment (FUTA) Tax Return*
   If your S Corporation has paid employees, federal law requires that you pay FUTA taxes, using this form for reporting.

8. *Form 940-EZ: Employer's Annual Federal Unemployment (FUTA) Tax Return*
   You may be entitled to use this less complicated form during the early years of your S Corporation. An example of how to use this form is included.

9. *Form W-2: Wage and Tax Statement 1991*
   Each wage- or salary-earning employee must have federal taxes withheld and reported on this form.

10. *Form 1099-MISC: Miscellaneous Income*
    This form must be used for payments to nonemployees of at least $600 in rents, services (including parts and materials), prizes and awards, medical and health care payments, and other income payments.

1991

**Department of the Treasury
Internal Revenue Service**

Instructions for Form 1120S

U.S. Income Tax Return for an S Corporation

(Section references are to the Internal Revenue Code unless otherwise noted.)

Paperwork Reduction Act Notice

We ask for the information on these forms to carry out the Internal Revenue laws of the United States. You are required to give us the information. We need it to ensure that you are complying with these laws and to allow us to figure and collect the right amount of tax.

The time needed to complete and file the following forms will vary depending on individual circumstances. The estimated average times are:

Form	Recordkeeping	Learning about the law or the form	Preparing the form	Copying, assembling, and sending the form to the IRS
1120S	62 hr., 40 min.	18 hr., 38 min.	34 hr., 26 min.	4 hr., 1 min.
Sch. D (1120S)	7 hr., 53 min.	4 hr., 31 min.	9 hr., 31 min.	1 hr., 20 min.
Sch. K-1 (1120S)	13 hr., 39 min.	9 hr., 43 min.	14 hr., 5 min.	1 hr., 4 min.

If you have comments concerning the accuracy of these time estimates or suggestions for making these forms more simple, we would be happy to hear from you. You can write to both the **Internal Revenue Service,** Washington, DC 20224, Attention: IRS Reports Clearance Officer, T:FP; and the **Office of Management and Budget,** Paperwork Reduction Project (1545-0130), Washington, DC 20503. **DO NOT** send the tax forms to either of these offices. Instead, see the instructions on page 2 for information on where to file.

Contents

Voluntary Contributions To Reduce the Public Debt

Quite often, inquiries are received about how to make voluntary contributions to reduce the public debt. A corporation may contribute by enclosing with the tax return a check made payable to "Bureau of the Public Debt."

A Change You Should Note

Corporations may claim a credit on **Form 8830,** Enhanced Oil Recovery Credit, for 15% of qualified enhanced oil recovery costs paid or incurred in tax years beginning after 1990. These costs generally include amounts paid or incurred in connection with a qualified enhanced oil recovery project for:

1. Certain tangible property for which the corporation can claim a deduction for depreciation or amortization,

2. Intangible drilling and development costs eligible for the election under section 263(c) or required to be capitalized under section 291(b)(1), and

3. Qualified tertiary injectant expenses for which a deduction is allowed under section 193.

If a corporation claims this credit, the amounts otherwise deductible (or required to be capitalized and recovered through depreciation, depletion, or amortization), for costs that were used in figuring the credit must be reduced by the amount of the credit attributable to such costs.

For more information, see section 43 and Form 8830.

General Instructions

Note: *In addition to the publications listed throughout these instructions, you may wish to get:* **Pub. 334,** *Tax Guide for Small Business;* **Pub. 535,** *Business Expenses;* **Pub. 550,** *Investment Income and Expenses;* **Pub. 556,** *Examination of Returns, Appeal Rights, and Claims for Refund; and* **Pub. 589,** *Tax Information on S Corporations.*

The above publications and other publications referenced throughout these instructions may be obtained at most IRS offices. To order publications and forms, call our toll-free number 1-800-TAX-FORM (829-3676).

Purpose of Form

Form 1120S is used to report the income, deductions, gains, losses, etc., of a domestic corporation that has filed **Form 2553,** Election by a Small Business Corporation, to be treated as an S corporation, and whose election is in effect for the tax year.

Who Must File

A corporation must file Form 1120S if **(a)** it elected by filing Form 2553 to be treated as an S corporation, **(b)** IRS accepted the election, and **(c)** the election remains in effect. Do not file Form 1120S until the

Cat. No. 11515K

corporation has been notified by the IRS that the election has been accepted.

Termination of Election

Once the election is made, it stays in effect until it is terminated. During the 5 years after the tax year the election has been terminated, the corporation may make another election on Form 2553 only with IRS consent. See section 1362(g).

The election terminates **automatically** in any of the following cases:

1. The corporation is no longer a small business corporation as defined in section 1361(b). The termination of an election in this manner is effective as of the day on which the corporation ceases to be a small business corporation. See sections 1362(d)(2) and 1362(e) for more information.

2. If, for each of three consecutive tax years, the corporation has both subchapter C earnings and profits and gross receipts more than 25% of which are derived from passive investment income as defined in section 1362(d)(3)(D), the election terminates on the first day of the first tax year beginning after the third consecutive tax year. The corporation must pay a tax for each year it has excess net passive income. See specific instructions for line 22a for details on how to figure the tax.

3. The election may be revoked if shareholders who collectively own a majority of the stock in the corporation on the day on which the revocation is made consent to the revocation. If the revocation specifies a date for revocation that is on or after the date that the revocation is made, the revocation is effective as of the specified date. If no date is specified, the revocation is effective as of the beginning of a tax year if it is made during the tax year and on or before the 15th day of the 3rd month of such tax year. If no date is specified and the revocation is made during the tax year but after the 15th day of the 3rd month, it is not effective until the beginning of the following tax year. See section 1362(d)(1) for more information.

When To File

In general, file Form 1120S by the 15th day of the 3rd month after the end of the tax year.

Extension

Use **Form 7004,** Application for Automatic Extension of Time To File Corporation Income Tax Return, to request an automatic 6-month extension of time to file Form 1120S.

Period Covered

File the 1991 return for calendar year 1991 and fiscal years beginning in 1991 and ending in 1992. If the return is for a fiscal year, fill in the tax year space at the top of the form.

Note: *The 1991 Form 1120S may also be used if (a) the corporation has a tax year of less than 12 months that begins and ends*

Page 2

in 1992 and (b) the 1992 Form 1120S is not available by the time the corporation is required to file its return. However, the corporation must show its 1992 tax year on the 1991 Form 1120S and incorporate any tax law changes that are effective for tax years beginning after December 31, 1991.

Where To File

Use the preaddressed envelope. If you do not use the envelope, file your return at the applicable IRS address listed below.

If the corporation's principal business, office, or agency is located in ▼	Use the following Internal Revenue Service Center address ▼
New Jersey, New York (New York City and counties of Nassau, Rockland, Suffolk, and Westchester)	Holtsville, NY 00501
Connecticut, Maine, Massachusetts, New Hampshire, New York (all other counties), Rhode Island, Vermont	Andover, MA 05501
Florida, Georgia, South Carolina	Atlanta, GA 39901
Indiana, Kentucky, Michigan, Ohio, West Virginia	Cincinnati, OH 45999
Kansas, New Mexico, Oklahoma, Texas	Austin, TX 73301
Alaska, Arizona, California (counties of Alpine, Amador, Butte, Calaveras, Colusa, Contra Costa, Del Norte, El Dorado, Glenn, Humboldt, Lake, Lassen, Marin, Mendocino, Modoc, Napa, Nevada, Placer, Plumas, Sacramento, San Joaquin, Shasta, Sierra, Siskiyou, Solano, Sonoma, Sutter, Tehama, Trinity, Yolo, and Yuba), Colorado, Idaho, Montana, Nebraska, Nevada, North Dakota, Oregon, South Dakota, Utah, Washington, Wyoming	Ogden, UT 84201
California (all other counties), Hawaii	Fresno, CA 93888
Illinois, Iowa, Minnesota, Missouri, Wisconsin	Kansas City, MO 64999
Alabama, Arkansas, Louisiana, Mississippi, North Carolina, Tennessee	Memphis, TN 37501
Delaware, District of Columbia, Maryland, Pennsylvania, Virginia	Philadelphia, PA 19255

Who Must Sign

The return must be signed and dated by the president, vice president, treasurer, assistant treasurer, chief accounting officer, or any other corporate officer (such as tax officer) authorized to sign. A receiver, trustee, or assignee must sign and date any return he or she is required to file on behalf of a corporation.

If a corporate officer filled in Form 1120S, the Paid Preparer's space under

"Signature of Officer" should remain blank. If someone prepares Form 1120S and does not charge the corporation, that person should not sign the return. Certain others who prepare Form 1120S should not sign. For example, a regular, full-time employee of the corporation such as a clerk, secretary, etc., should not sign.

Generally, anyone paid to prepare Form 1120S must sign the return and fill in the other blanks in the Paid Preparer's Use Only area of the return.

The preparer required to sign the return MUST complete the required preparer information and:

● Sign it, by hand, in the space provided for the preparer's signature. (Signature stamps or labels are not acceptable.)

● Give a copy of Form 1120S to the taxpayer in addition to the copy filed with the IRS.

Accounting Information

Accounting Methods

Figure ordinary income using the method of accounting regularly used in keeping the corporation's books and records. Generally, permissible methods include the cash receipts and disbursements method, the accrual method, or any other method permitted by the Internal Revenue Code. In all cases, the method adopted must clearly reflect income. (See section 446.)

Generally, an S corporation may not use the cash method of accounting if the corporation is a tax shelter (as defined in section 448(d)(3)). See section 448 for details.

Generally, an accrual basis taxpayer can deduct accrued expenses in the tax year that all events have occurred that determine the liability, the amount of the liability can be determined with reasonable accuracy, and economic performance takes place with respect to the expense. There are exceptions for recurring items.

For long-term contracts (except certain real property construction contracts), taxpayers must generally use the percentage of completion method described in section 460. However, for purposes of the percentage of completion method, the corporation may elect to postpone recognition of income and expense under a long-term contract entered into after July 10, 1989, until the first tax year as of the end of which at least 10% of the estimated total contract costs have been incurred.

Unless otherwise allowed by law, a corporation may change the method of accounting used to report income in earlier years (for income as a whole or for any material item) only by first getting consent on **Form 3115,** Application for Change in Accounting Method. See **Pub. 538,** Accounting Periods and Methods, for more information.

Change in Accounting Period

Generally, an S corporation may not change its accounting period to a tax year that is not a permitted year. A "permitted year" is a calendar year or any other accounting period for which the corporation can establish to the satisfaction of the IRS that there is a business purpose for the tax year.

To change an accounting period, see Regulations section 1.442-1 and **Form 1128,** Application to Adopt, Change, or Retain a Tax Year. Also see Pub. 538.

Election of a tax year other than a required year.—Under the provisions of section 444, an S corporation may elect to have a tax year other than a permitted year, but only if the deferral period of the tax year is not longer than 3 months. This election is made by filing **Form 8716,** Election To Have a Tax Year Other Than a Required Tax Year.

An S corporation may not make or continue an election under section 444 if it is a member of a tiered structure, other than a tiered structure that consists entirely of partnerships and S corporations all of which have the same tax year. For the S corporation to have a section 444 election in effect, it must make the payments required by section 7519 and file **Form 8752,** Required Payment or Refund Under Section 7519.

Rounding Off to Whole-Dollar Amounts

You may show the money items on the return and accompanying schedules as whole-dollar amounts. To do so, drop any amount less than 50 cents, and increase any amount from 50 cents through 99 cents to the next higher dollar.

Depositary Method of Tax Payment

The corporation must pay the tax due (line 25, page 1) in full, no later than the 15th day of the 3rd month after the end of the tax year.

Deposit corporation income tax payments (and estimated tax payments) with **Form 8109,** Federal Tax Deposit Coupon. Be sure to darken the "1120" box on the coupon. Make these tax deposits with either a financial institution qualified as a depositary for Federal taxes or the Federal Reserve bank or branch servicing the geographic area where the corporation is located. Do not submit deposits directly to an IRS office; otherwise, the corporation may be subject to a penalty. Records of deposits will be sent to the IRS for crediting to the corporation's account. See the instructions contained in the coupon book (Form 8109) for more information.

To help ensure proper crediting to your account, write the corporation's employer identification number, "Form 1120S," and the tax year to which the deposit applies on the corporation's check or money order.

To get more deposit forms, use the reorder form **(Form 8109A)** provided in the coupon book.

For additional information concerning deposits, see **Pub. 583,** Taxpayers Starting a Business.

Estimated Tax

Generally, the corporation must make estimated tax payments for the following taxes, if the total of these taxes is $500 or more: **(a)** the tax on certain capital gains, **(b)** the tax on built-in gains, **(c)** the excess net passive income tax, and **(d)** the investment credit recapture tax.

The amount of estimated tax required to be paid annually is the lesser of **(a)** 90% of the above taxes shown on the return for the tax year (or if no return is filed, 90% of these taxes for the year); or **(b)** the sum of **(i)** 90% of the sum of the investment credit recapture tax and the built-in gains tax (or the tax on certain capital gains) shown on the return for the tax year (or if no return is filed, 90% of these taxes for the year), and **(ii)** 100% of any excess net passive income tax shown on the corporation's return for the preceding tax year. If the preceding tax year was less than 12 months, the estimated tax must be determined under (a).

The estimated tax is generally payable in four equal installments. However, the corporation may be able to lower the amount of one or more installments by using the annualized income installment method or adjusted seasonal installment method under section 6655(e).

For a calendar year corporation, the installments are due by April 15, June 15, September 15, and December 15. For a fiscal year corporation, they are due by the 15th day of the 4th, 6th, 9th, and 12th months of the fiscal year.

The installments are made using the depositary method of tax payment.

Interest and Penalties

Interest

Interest is charged on taxes not paid by the due date, even if an extension of time to file is granted. Interest is also charged from the due date (including extensions) to the date of payment on the failure to file penalty, the accuracy-related penalty, and the fraud penalty. The interest charge is figured at a rate determined under section 6621.

Late Filing of Return

Form 1120S is required to be filed under sections 6037(a) and 6012. A corporation that does not file its tax return by the due date, including extensions, generally may have to pay a penalty of 5% a month, or fraction of a month, up to a maximum of 25%, for each month the return is not filed. The penalty is imposed on the net amount due. See section 6651(a)(1). The minimum penalty for not filing a tax return within 60 days of the due date for filing (including extensions) is the lesser of the underpayment of tax or $100.

The penalty will not be imposed if the corporation can show that failure to file a timely return was due to reasonable cause

and not due to willful neglect. If the failure was due to reasonable cause, attach an explanation to the return.

Late Payment of Tax

A corporation that does not pay the tax when due generally may have to pay a penalty of ½ of 1% a month or fraction of a month, up to a maximum of 25%, for each month the tax is not paid. The penalty is imposed on the net amount due. See section 6651(a)(2).

The penalty will not be imposed if the corporation can show that failure to pay on time was due to reasonable cause and not due to willful neglect.

Underpayment of Estimated Tax

A corporation that fails to make estimated tax payments when due may be subject to an underpayment penalty for the period of underpayment. Use **Form 2220,** Underpayment of Estimated Tax by Corporations, to see if the corporation owes a penalty and to figure the amount of the penalty. If you attach Form 2220 to Form 1120S, be sure to check the box on line 24, page 1, and enter the amount of any penalty on this line.

Failure To Furnish Information Timely

Section 6037(b) requires an S corporation to furnish to each shareholder a copy of such information shown on Schedule K-1 (Form 1120S) that is attached to Form 1120S. The Schedule K-1 must be furnished to each shareholder on or before the day on which the Form 1120S was filed.

For each failure to furnish Schedule K-1 to a shareholder when due and each failure to include on Schedule K-1 all of the information required to be shown (or the inclusion of incorrect information), a penalty of $50 may be imposed with respect to each Schedule K-1 for which a failure occurs. If the requirement to report correct information is intentionally disregarded, each $50 penalty is increased to $100 or, if greater, 10% of the aggregate amount of items required to be reported. See sections 6722 and 6724 for more information.

The penalty will not be imposed if the corporation can show that not furnishing information timely was due to reasonable cause and not due to willful neglect.

Unresolved Tax Problems

The IRS has a Problem Resolution Program for taxpayers who have been unable to resolve their problems with the IRS. If the corporation has a tax problem it has been unable to resolve through normal channels, write to the corporation's local IRS district director or call the corporation's local IRS office and ask for Problem Resolution Assistance. Hearing-impaired persons who have access to TDD equipment may call 1-800-829-4059 to ask for help. The Problem Resolution office will take responsibility for your problem and ensure that it receives proper attention. Although the office cannot change the tax law or make technical decisions, it can frequently clear up misunderstandings that may have resulted from previous contacts.

Other Forms, Returns, Schedules, and Statements That May Be Required

Forms W-2 and **W-3,** Wage and Tax Statement; and Transmittal of Income and Tax Statements.

Form 720, Quarterly Federal Excise Tax Return. Use Form 720 to report the 10% excise tax on the first retail sale of the following items sold to the extent the sales price exceeds the amounts shown: **(a)** passenger vehicles, $30,000; **(b)** boats and yachts, $100,000; **(c)** aircraft, $250,000; and **(d)** jewelry and furs, $10,000. Form 720 is also used to report environmental excise taxes, communications and air transportation taxes, fuel taxes, manufacturers taxes, ship passenger tax, and certain other excise taxes.

Form 966, Corporate Dissolution or Liquidation.

Forms 1042 and **1042S,** Annual Withholding Tax Return for U.S. Source Income of Foreign Persons; and Foreign Person's U.S. Source Income Subject to Withholding. Use these forms to report and transmit withheld tax on payments made to nonresident alien individuals, foreign partnerships, or foreign corporations to the extent such payments constitute gross income from sources within the United States (see sections 861 through 865). For more information, see sections 1441 and 1442, and **Pub. 515,** Withholding of Tax on Nonresident Aliens and Foreign Corporations.

Form 1096, Annual Summary and Transmittal of U.S. Information Returns.

Form 1098, Mortgage Interest Statement. This form is used to report the receipt from any individual of $600 or more of mortgage interest and points in the course of the corporation's trade or business.

Forms 1099-A, B, DIV, INT, MISC, OID, PATR, S, and **R.** You may have to file these information returns to report abandonments, acquisitions through foreclosure, proceeds from broker and barter exchange transactions, certain dividends, interest payments, medical and dental health care payments, miscellaneous income payments, original issue discount, patronage dividends, distributions from pensions, annuities, retirement or profit-sharing plans, IRAs, insurance contracts, etc., and proceeds from real estate transactions. Also use certain of these returns to report amounts that were received as a nominee on behalf of another person.

Use Form 1099-DIV to report actual dividends paid by the corporation. Only distributions from accumulated earnings and profits are classified as dividends. Do not issue Form 1099-DIV for dividends received by the corporation that are allocated to shareholders on line 4b of Schedule K-1.

For more information, see the separate **Instructions for Forms 1099, 1098, 5498, and W-2G.**

Note: *Every corporation must file Forms 1099-MISC if it makes payments of rents, commissions, or other fixed or determinable income (see section 6041) totaling $600 or more to any one person in the course of its trade or business during the calendar year.*

Form 5713, International Boycott Report. Every corporation that had operations in, or related to, a "boycotting" country, company, or national of a country must file Form 5713. In addition, persons who participate in or cooperate with an international boycott may have to complete Schedule A or Schedule B and Schedule C of Form 5713 to compute their loss of the foreign tax credit, the deferral of earnings of a controlled foreign corporation, IC-DISC benefits, and FSC benefits.

Form 8264, Application for Registration of a Tax Shelter, is used by tax shelter organizers to register tax shelters with the IRS for the purpose of receiving a tax shelter registration number.

Form 8271, Investor Reporting of Tax Shelter Registration Number, is used by corporations that have acquired an interest in a tax shelter that is required to be registered to report the tax shelter's registration number. Form 8271 must be attached to any return on which a deduction, credit, loss, or other tax benefit attributable to a tax shelter is taken or any income attributable to a tax shelter is reported.

Form 8281, Information Return for Publicly Offered Original Issue Discount Instruments. This form is used by issuers of publicly offered debt instruments having OID to provide the information required by section 1275(c).

Forms 8288 and **8288-A,** U.S. Withholding Tax Return for Dispositions by Foreign Persons of U.S. Real Property Interests; and Statement of Withholding on Dispositions by Foreign Persons of U.S. Real Property Interests. Use these forms to report and transmit withheld tax on the sale of U.S. real property by a foreign person. See section 1445 and the related regulations for additional information.

Form 8300, Report of Cash Payments Over $10,000 Received in a Trade or Business. This form is used to report the receipt of more than $10,000 in cash or foreign currency in one transaction (or a series of related transactions).

Form 8594, Asset Acquisition Statement, is to be filed by both the purchaser and seller of a group of assets constituting a trade or business if goodwill or a going concern value attaches, or could attach, to such assets and if the purchaser's basis in the assets is determined only by the amount paid for the assets.

Form 8697, Interest Computation Under the Look-Back Method for Completed Long-Term Contracts. Certain S corporations that are not closely held may have to file Form 8697. Form 8697 is used to figure the interest due or to be refunded under the look-back method of section 460(b)(3) on certain long-term contracts entered into after February 28, 1986, that are accounted for under either the percentage of completion-capitalized cost method or the percentage of completion method. Closely held corporations should see the instructions for line 20, item 13, of Schedule K-1 for details on the Form 8697 information they must provide to their shareholders.

Stock ownership in foreign corporations.—If the corporation owned at least 5% in value of the outstanding stock of a foreign personal holding company, attach the statement required by section 551(c).

A corporation that (a) controls a foreign corporation; (b) is a 10%-or-more shareholder of a controlled foreign corporation; or (c) acquires, disposes of, or owns 5% or more in value of the outstanding stock of a foreign corporation, may have to file **Form 5471,** Information Return of U.S. Persons With Respect to Certain Foreign Corporations.

Transfers to corporation controlled by transferor.—If a person acquires stock of a corporation in exchange for property, and no gain or loss is recognized under section 351, the transferor and transferee must attach to their respective tax returns the information required by Regulations section 1.351-3.

Attachments

Attach **Form 4136,** Credit for Federal Tax on Fuels, after page 4, Form 1120S. Attach schedules in alphabetical order and other forms in numerical order after Form 4136.

To assist us in processing the return, **please complete every applicable entry space on Form 1120S and Schedule K-1.** Do not attach statements and write "See attached" in lieu of completing the entry spaces on Form 1120S and Schedule K-1.

If you need more space on the forms or schedules, attach separate sheets and show the same information in the same order as on the printed forms. **But show your totals on the printed forms.** Please use sheets that are the same size as the forms and schedules. Attach these separate sheets after all the schedules and forms. Be sure to put the corporation's name and employer identification number (EIN) on each sheet.

Amended Return

To correct an error in a Form 1120S already filed, file an amended Form 1120S and check box F(4). If the amended return results in a change to income, or a change in the distribution of any income or other information provided to shareholders, an amended Schedule K-1 (Form 1120S) must also be filed with the amended Form 1120S and given to each shareholder. Be sure to check box D(2) on each Schedule K-1 to indicate that it is an amended Schedule K-1.

Note: If an S corporation does not meet the small S corporation exception under Temporary Regulations section 301.6241-1T or if it is a small S corporation that has made the election described in Temporary Regulations section 301.6241-1T(c)(2)(v), and such corporation files an amended return, the amended return will be a request for administrative adjustment and **Form 8082,** Notice of Inconsistent Treatment or Amended Return (Administrative Adjustment Request (AAR)), must be filed by the tax matters person. See the Temporary Regulations under section 6241 for more information.

Passive Activity Limitations

In general, section 469 limits the amount of losses, deductions, and credits that shareholders may claim from "passive activities." The passive activity limitations do not apply to the corporation. Instead, they apply to each shareholder's share of any income or loss and credit attributable to a passive activity. Because the treatment of each shareholder's share of corporation income or loss and credit depends upon the nature of the activity that generated it, the corporation must report income or loss and credits separately for each activity.

The instructions below (pages 5 through 8) and the instructions for Schedules K and K-1 (pages 13 through 20) explain the applicable passive activity limitation rules and specify the type of information the corporation must provide to its shareholders for each activity. If the corporation had more than one activity, it must report information for each activity on an attachment to Schedules K and K-1.

Generally, passive activities include **(a)** activities that involve the conduct of a trade or business in which the shareholder does not materially participate, and **(b)** any rental activity (see definition on page 6) even if the shareholder materially participates. The level of each shareholder's participation in an activity must be determined by the shareholder.

The passive activity rules provide that losses and credits from passive activities can generally be applied only against income and tax from passive activities. Thus, passive losses and credits cannot be applied against income from salaries, wages, professional fees, or a business in which the shareholder materially participates; against "portfolio income" (see definition on page 7); or against the tax related to any of these types of income.

Special transitional rules apply to losses incurred by investors in qualified low-income housing projects. In addition, special rules require that net income from certain activities that would otherwise be treated as passive income must be recharacterized as nonpassive income for purposes of the passive activity limitations.

To allow each shareholder to apply the passive activity limitations at the individual level, the corporation must report income or loss and credits separately for each of the following: trade or business activities, rental real estate activities, rental activities other than rental real estate, and portfolio income. For definitions of each type of activity or income, see **Types of Activities and Income,** below. For details on the special reporting requirements for passive activities, see **Passive Activity Reporting Requirements** on page 7.

Identifying Activities

Generally, each undertaking the corporation owns is a separate activity.

An undertaking includes all the business or rental operations owned at the same location. Operations not actually conducted at the same location are treated as conducted at the location with which they are most closely associated under all the facts and circumstances. For example, if a business sends employees from a central office to perform services at the customer's home, the operations are treated as conducted at the central office. If the corporation conducts all its business or rental operations at the same location directly or through one entity, the corporation has only one undertaking and one activity.

Rental undertakings.—If the corporation owns an undertaking that conducts both rental and nonrental operations, it must treat the two types of operations as two separate undertakings unless **(a)** the rental operations, if treated as a separate activity, would not be a rental activity (see **Rental activities** on page 6) or **(b)** one type of operation produces more than 80% of the combined undertaking's gross income.

Combining corporate undertakings into activities.—Once corporate undertakings are identified, treat each undertaking as a separate activity unless one of the following rules requires or permits the corporation to combine undertakings into a larger activity:

Trade or business undertakings.— Generally, the corporation must combine trade or business undertakings into a larger activity if the undertakings are similar and commonly controlled. For details, see Temporary Regulations sections 1.469-4T(f) and (j). Trade or business undertakings include all nonrental undertakings except professional service undertakings (described in the next paragraph) and oil or gas wells treated as separate undertakings under Temporary Regulations section 1.469-4T(e). Trade or business activities that constitute an integrated business may have to be combined into an even larger activity under Temporary Regulations section 1.469-4T(g).

Professional service undertakings.— Professional service undertakings principally provide services in the fields of health, law, engineering, architecture, accounting, actuarial science, the performing arts, or consulting. Generally, the corporation must combine its interests in professional service undertakings into a single activity if the undertakings provide services in the same field or earn more than 20% of their gross income from serving the same customers, or if the undertakings are controlled by the same interests. For details, see Temporary Regulations section 1.469-4T(h).

The corporation can elect to treat combined nonrental undertakings acquired in 1991 as separate activities for purposes other than determining participation in activities. To make this election, the corporation must attach to Form 1120S a statement that **(a)** gives the corporation name, address, and employer identification number; **(b)** declares that the election is being made under Temporary Regulations section 1.469-4T(o); **(c)** identifies the undertaking that is treated as a separate activity; and **(d)** identifies the rest of the activity from which the undertaking was separated.

If the corporation wants to treat as separate activities any undertakings it acquired in 1991 that these rules would otherwise combine into a larger activity, it must attach this statement to its 1991 return or it will not be able to treat the undertakings as separate activities for 1991 or any later year. For details, see Temporary Regulations section 1.469-4T(o).

If undertakings the corporation acquired in a previous year were combined into a larger activity on a prior return, those undertakings cannot be divided into separate activities in 1991 or any later year.

Rental real estate undertakings.—A rental real estate undertaking is a rental undertaking in which at least 85% of the unadjusted basis of the property made available for use by customers is real property. The corporation may treat a single rental real estate undertaking as a single activity, or it may treat any combination of rental real estate undertakings as a single activity. Under certain circumstances, the corporation may also elect to divide a single rental real estate undertaking into separate undertakings. For details, see Temporary Regulations section 1.469-4T(k)(2)(iii).

Generally, the corporation must attach a statement to Form 1120S if it combines separate rental real estate undertakings or portions of undertakings into the same activity or divides a single rental real estate undertaking into separate undertakings. If the corporation wants to divide a single rental real estate undertaking it acquired in 1991 into separate undertakings, it must attach this statement to its 1991 Form 1120S or it will not be able to treat the undertaking as separate undertakings for 1991 or any later year.

If the corporation divided a single rental real estate undertaking it acquired in a previous year into separate undertakings on a prior year return, it must treat the undertakings as separate undertakings in 1991 and any later year.

Futhermore, if the corporation combined rental real estate undertakings it acquired in a previous year into a larger activity on a prior year return, the larger activity cannot be divided into separate activities in 1991 or any later year.

Page 5

Types of Activities and Income

Trade or business activities.—A trade or business activity involves the conduct of a trade or business within the meaning of section 162.

If the shareholder does not materially participate in the activity, a trade or business activity of the corporation is a passive activity for the shareholder.

Note: *The section 469(c)(3) exception for a working interest in oil and gas properties is not applicable to an S corporation because state law generally limits the liability of corporate shareholders, including shareholders of an S corporation.*

Accordingly, an activity of holding a working interest in oil or gas properties is a trade or business activity and the material participation rules apply to determine if the activity is a passive activity. See Temporary Regulations section 1.469-1T(e)(4).

The determination whether a shareholder materially participated in an activity must be made by each shareholder. As a result, while the corporation's overall trade or business income (loss) is reported on page 1 of Form 1120S, the specific income and deductions from each separate trade or business activity must be reported on attachments to Form 1120S. Similarly, while each shareholder's allocable share of the corporation's overall trade or business income (loss) is reported on line 1 of Schedule K-1, each shareholder's allocable share of the income and deductions from each trade or business activity must be reported on attachments to each Schedule K-1. See **Passive Activity Reporting Requirements** on page 7 for more information.

Rental activities.—Generally, except as noted below, if the gross income from an activity consists of amounts paid principally for the use of real or personal tangible property held by the corporation, the activity is a rental activity. There are several exceptions to this general rule. Under these exceptions, an activity involving the use of real or personal tangible property is not a rental activity if **(a)** the average period of customer use (see definition below) for such property is 7 days or less; **(b)** the average period of customer use for such property is 30 days or less and significant personal services (see definition below) are provided by or on behalf of the corporation; **(c)** extraordinary personal services (see definition below) are provided by or on behalf of the corporation; **(d)** the rental of such property is treated as incidental to a nonrental activity of the corporation under Temporary Regulations section 1.469-1T(e)(3)(vi); or **(e)** the corporation customarily makes the property available during defined business hours for nonexclusive use by various customers. In addition, if a corporation owns an interest in a partnership that conducts a nonrental activity, and the corporation provides property for use in that activity in the corporation's capacity as an owner of an interest in the partnership, the provision of the property is not a rental activity. Consequently, the corporation's distributive share of income

from the activity is not income from a rental activity. A guaranteed payment described in section 707(c) is not income from a rental activity under any circumstances.

Whether the corporation provides property used in an activity of a partnership in the corporation's capacity as an owner of an interest in the partnership is based on all the facts and circumstances.

Average period of customer use.—The average period of customer use of property is computed by dividing the total number of days in all rental periods by the number of rentals during the tax year. If the activity involves renting more than one class of property, multiply the average period of customer use of each class by the ratio of the gross rental income from that class to the activity's total gross rental income. The activity's average period of customer use equals the sum of these class-by-class average periods weighted by gross income. See Temporary Regulations section 1.469-1T(e)(3)(iii).

Significant personal services.— Personal services include only services performed by individuals. In determining whether personal services are significant personal services, all of the relevant facts and circumstances are considered. Relevant facts and circumstances include the frequency that the services are provided, the type and amount of labor required to perform the services, and the value of the services in relation to the amount charged for the use of the property. The following services are excluded from consideration in determining whether personal services are significant: **(a)** services necessary to permit the lawful use of the rental property; **(b)** services performed in connection with improvements or repairs to the rental property that extend the useful life of the property substantially beyond the average rental period; and **(c)** services provided in connection with the use of any improved real property that are similar to those commonly provided in connection with long-term rentals of high-grade commercial or residential property (e.g., cleaning and maintenance of common areas, routine repairs, trash collection, elevator service, and security at entrances).

Extraordinary personal services.— Services provided in connection with making rental property available for customer use are extraordinary personal services only if the services are performed by individuals and the customers' use of the rental property is incidental to their receipt of the services. For example, a patient's use of a hospital room generally is incidental to the care that the patient receives from the hospital's medical staff. Similarly, a student's use of a dormitory room in a boarding school is incidental to the personal services provided by the school's teaching staff.

Rental property incidental to a nonrental activity.—An activity is not a rental activity if the rental of the property is incidental to a nonrental activity, such as the activity of holding property for

investment, a trade or business activity, or the activity of dealing in property.

Rental property is incidental to an activity of holding property for investment if the main purpose for holding the property is to realize a gain from the appreciation of the property and the gross rental income from such property for the tax year is less than 2% of the smaller of the unadjusted basis of the property or the fair market value of the property.

Rental property is incidental to a trade or business activity if **(a)** the corporation owns an interest in the trade or business at all times during the year; **(b)** the rental property was mainly used in the trade or business activity during the tax year or during at least two of the five preceding tax years; and **(c)** the gross rental income from the property is less than 2% of the smaller of the unadjusted basis of the property or the fair market value of the property.

The sale or exchange of property that is also rented during the tax year (where the gain or loss is recognized) is treated as incidental to the activity of dealing in property if, at the time of the sale or exchange, the property was held primarily for sale to customers in the ordinary course of the corporation's trade or business.

See Temporary Regulations section 1.469-1T(e)(3) for more information on the definition of rental activities for purposes of the passive activity limitations.

Reporting of rental activities.—In reporting the corporation's income or losses and credits from rental activities, the corporation must separately report **(a)** rental real estate activities and **(b)** rental activities other than rental real estate activities.

Shareholders who actively participate in a rental real estate activity may be able to deduct part or all of their rental real estate losses (and the deduction equivalent of rental real estate credits) against income (or tax) from nonpassive activities. Generally, the combined amount of rental real estate losses and the deduction equivalent of rental real estate credits from all sources (including rental real estate activities not held through the corporation) that may be claimed is limited to $25,000.

Special transitional rules apply to investors in qualified low-income housing projects. See section 502 of the Tax Reform Act of 1986 and **Pub. 925,** Passive Activity and At-Risk Rules, for more information.

Rental real estate activity income (loss) is reported on **Form 8825,** Rental Real Estate Income and Expenses of a Partnership or an S Corporation, and on line 2 of Schedules K and K-1 rather than on page 1 of Form 1120S.

Credits related to rental real estate activities are reported on lines 12c and 12d of Schedules K and K-1. Low-income housing credits are reported on line 12b of Schedules K and K-1.

Income (loss) from rental activities other than rental real estate is reported on line 3 of Schedules K and K-1. Credits related to rental activities other than rental real estate are reported on line 12e of Schedules K and K-1.

Portfolio income.—Generally, portfolio income includes all gross income, other than income derived in the ordinary course of a trade or business, that is attributable to interest; dividends; royalties; income from a real estate investment trust, a regulated investment company, a real estate mortgage investment conduit, a common trust fund, a controlled foreign corporation, a qualified electing fund, or a cooperative; income from the disposition of property that produces income of a type defined as portfolio income; and income from the disposition of property held for investment.

Solely for purposes of the preceding paragraph, gross income derived in the ordinary course of a trade or business includes **(and portfolio income, therefore, does not include)** only the following types of income: (a) interest income on loans and investments made in the ordinary course of a trade or business of lending money; (b) interest on accounts receivable arising from the performance of services or the sale of property in the ordinary course of a trade or business of performing such services or selling such property, but only if credit is customarily offered to customers of the business; (c) income from investments made in the ordinary course of a trade or business of furnishing insurance or annuity contracts or reinsuring risks underwritten by insurance companies; (d) income or gain derived in the ordinary course of an activity of trading or dealing in any property if such activity constitutes a trade or business (unless the dealer held the property for investment at any time before such income or gain is recognized); (e) royalties derived by the taxpayer in the ordinary course of a trade or business of licensing intangible property; (f) amounts included in the gross income of a patron of a cooperative by reason of any payment or allocation to the patron based on patronage occurring with respect to a trade or business of the patron; and (g) other income identified by the IRS as income derived by the taxpayer in the ordinary course of a trade or business.

See Temporary Regulations section 1.469-2T(c)(3) for more information on portfolio income.

Portfolio income is reported on line 4 of Schedules K and K-1, rather than on page 1 of Form 1120S.

Expenses related to portfolio income are reported on line 9 of Schedules K and K-1.

Recharacterization of Passive Income

Under the provisions of Temporary Regulations section 1.469-2T(f), net passive income from certain passive activities must be treated as nonpassive income. Income from the six sources listed below is subject to recharacterization. In addition, any net passive income from an activity of renting substantially nondepreciable property from an equity-financed lending activity, or from an activity related to an interest in a pass-through entity that licenses intangible property that is recharacterized as nonpassive income, is treated as investment income for purposes of computing investment interest expense limitations. "Net passive income" means the excess of passive activity gross income from the activity over passive activity deductions (current year deductions and prior year unallowed losses) from the activity.

1. Significant participation passive activities.—A significant participation passive activity is any trade or business activity in which the shareholder both participates for more than 100 hours during the tax year and does not materially participate. Because each shareholder must determine his or her level of participation, the corporation will not be able to identify significant participation passive activities.

2. Certain nondepreciable rental property activities.—Net passive income from a rental activity is nonpassive income if less than 30% of the unadjusted basis of the property used or held for use by customers in the activity is subject to depreciation under section 167.

3. Passive equity-financed lending activities.—If the corporation has net income from a passive equity-financed lending activity, the lesser of the net passive income or equity-financed interest income from the activity is nonpassive income.

Note: *The amount of income from the activities in items 1 through 3, above, that any shareholder will be required to recharacterize as nonpassive income may be limited under Temporary Regulations section 1.469-2T(f)(8). Because the corporation will not have information regarding all of a shareholder's activities, it must identify all corporate activities meeting the definitions in items 1 through 3 as activities that may be subject to recharacterization.*

4. Rental activities incidental to a development activity.—Net rental activity income is nonpassive income for a shareholder if all of the following apply: (a) the corporation recognizes gain from the sale, exchange, or other disposition of the rental property during the tax year; (b) the use of the item of property in the rental activity started less than 12 months before the date of disposition (the use of an item of rental property begins on the first day on which (i) the corporation owns an interest in the property; (ii) substantially all of the property is either rented or held out for rent and ready to be rented; and (iii) no significant value-enhancing services remain to be performed), and (c) the shareholder materially participated or significantly participated for any tax year in an activity that involved the performance of services for the purpose of enhancing the value of the property (or any other item of property, if the basis of the property disposed of is determined in whole or in part by reference to the basis of that item of property). "Net rental activity income" means the excess of passive activity gross income from renting or disposing of property over passive activity deductions (current year deductions and prior year unallowed losses) that are reasonably allocable to the rented property.

Because the corporation cannot determine a shareholder's level of participation, the corporation must identify net income from property described in items (a) and (b) above as income that may be subject to recharacterization.

5. Activities involving property rented to a nonpassive activity.—If a taxpayer rents property to a trade or business activity in which the taxpayer materially participates, the taxpayer's net rental activity income from the property is nonpassive income. "Net rental activity income" means the excess of passive activity gross income from renting or disposing of property over passive activity deductions (current year deductions and prior year unallowed losses) that are reasonably allocable to the rented property.

6. Acquisition of an interest in a pass-through entity that licenses intangible property.—Generally, net royalty income from intangible property is nonpassive income if the taxpayer acquired an interest in the pass-through entity after the pass-through entity created the intangible property or performed substantial services or incurred substantial costs in developing or marketing the intangible property. "Net royalty income" means the excess of passive activity gross income from licensing or transferring any right in intangible property over passive activity deductions (current year deductions and prior year unallowed losses) that are reasonably allocable to the intangible property.

See Temporary Regulations section 1.469-2T(f)(7)(iii) for exceptions to this rule.

Passive Activity Reporting Requirements

To allow shareholders to correctly apply the passive activity loss and credit limitation rules, any corporation that carries on more than one activity must:

1. Provide an attachment for each activity conducted through the corporation that identifies the type of activity conducted (trade or business, rental real estate, rental activity other than rental real estate, or investment).

2. On the attachment for each activity, provide a schedule, using the same line numbers as shown on Schedule K-1, detailing the net income (loss), credits, and all items required to be separately stated under section 1366(a)(1) from each trade or business activity, from each rental real estate activity, from each rental activity other than a rental real estate activity, and from investments.

3. Identify the net income (loss) and the shareholder's share of corporation interest expense from each activity of renting a dwelling unit that the shareholder also uses for personal purposes during the year for

Page 7

more than the greater of 14 days or 10% of the number of days that the residence is rented at fair rental value.

4. Identify the net income (loss) and the shareholder's share of interest expense from each activity of trading personal property conducted through the corporation.

5. With respect to any gain (loss) from the disposition of an interest in an activity or of an interest in property used in an activity (including dispositions before 1987 from which gain is being recognized after 1986):

a. Identify the activity in which the property was used at the time of disposition;

b. If the property was used in more than one activity during the 12 months preceding the disposition, identify the activities in which the property was used and the adjusted basis allocated to each activity; and

c. For gains only, if the property was substantially appreciated at the time of the disposition and the applicable holding period specified in Temporary Regulations section 1.469-2T(c)(2)(iii)(A) was not satisfied, identify the amount of the nonpassive gain and indicate whether or not the gain is investment income under the provisions of Temporary Regulations section 1.469-2T(c)(2)(iii)(E).

6. Specify the amount of gross portfolio income, the interest expense properly allocable to portfolio income, and expenses other than interest expense that are clearly and directly allocable to portfolio income.

7. Identify the ratable portion of any section 481 adjustment (whether a net positive or a net negative adjustment) allocable to each corporate activity.

8. Identify any gross income from sources that are specifically excluded from passive activity gross income, including income from intangible property if the shareholder is an individual and the shareholder's personal efforts significantly contributed to the creation of the property; income from a qualified low-income housing project (as defined in section 502 of the Tax Reform Act of 1986) conducted through the corporation; income from state, local, or foreign income tax refunds; and income from a covenant not to compete (in the case of a shareholder who is an individual and who contributed the covenant to the corporation).

9. Identify any deductions that are not passive activity deductions.

10. If the corporation makes a full or partial disposition of its interest in another entity, identify the gain (loss) allocable to each activity conducted through the entity, and the gain allocable to a passive activity that would have been recharacterized as nonpassive gain had the corporation disposed of its interest in property used in the activity (because the property was substantially appreciated at the time of the disposition, and the gain represented more than 10% of the shareholder's total gain from the disposition).

11. Identify the following items with respect to activities which may be subject to the recharacterization rules under Temporary Regulations section 1.469-2T(f):

a. Net income from an activity of renting substantially nondepreciable property;

b. The lesser of equity-financed interest income or net passive income from an equity-financed lending activity;

c. Net rental activity income from property that was developed (by the shareholder or the corporation), rented, and sold within 12 months after the rental of the property commenced;

d. Net rental activity income from the rental of property by the corporation to a trade or business activity in which the shareholder had an interest (either directly or indirectly); and

e. Net royalty income from intangible property if the shareholder acquired the shareholder's interest in the corporation after the corporation created the intangible property or performed substantial services or incurred substantial costs in developing or marketing the intangible property.

12. With respect to credits, identify separately the credits from the corporation that are associated with each activity conducted by or through the corporation.

Specific Instructions

General Information

Name, Address, and Employer Identification Number

Use the label on the package that was mailed to the corporation. If the corporation's name, address, or employer identification number is wrong on the label, mark through it and write the correct information on the label.

If the corporation does not have a package with a label, print or type the corporation's true name (as set forth in the corporate charter or other legal document creating it), address, and employer identification number on the appropriate lines.

Include the suite, room, or other unit number after the street address. If a preaddressed label is used, please include the information on the label. If the Post Office does not deliver to the street address and the corporation has a P.O. box, show the P.O. box number instead of the street address.

Item B—Business Code No.

See **Codes for Principal Business Activity** on page 22 of these instructions.

Item E—Total Assets

Enter the total assets, as determined by the accounting method regularly used in maintaining the corporation's books and records, at the end of the corporation's tax year. If there are no assets at the end of the tax year, enter the total assets as of the beginning of the tax year.

Item F—Initial Return, Final Return, Change in Address, and Amended Return

If this is the corporation's first return, check box F(1). If the corporation has ceased to exist, check box F(2). Also check box D(1) on each Schedule K-1 to indicate that it is a final Schedule K-1. Indicate a change in address by checking box F(3). If the corporation has a change of mailing address after filing its return, it can notify the IRS by filing **Form 8822,** Change of Address. If this amends a previously filed return, check box F(4).

Item G—Consolidated Audit Procedures

With certain exceptions, the tax treatment of S corporation items is determined at the S corporation level in a consolidated audit proceeding, rather than in separate proceedings with individual shareholders. Check the box for item G if any of the following apply.

● The S corporation had more than five shareholders at any time during the tax year (for this purpose a husband and wife, and their estates, are treated as one shareholder).

● Any shareholder was other than a natural person or estate.

● The small S corporation (five or fewer shareholders) has elected as provided in Temporary Regulations section 301.6241-1T(c)(2)(v) to be subject to the rules for consolidated proceedings.

Note: *The S corporation does not make the section 301.6241-1T(c)(2)(v) election when it checks the box for item G. This election must be made separately.*

For more information on the consolidated audit procedures for S corporations, see sections 6241 through 6245, Temporary Regulations section 301.6241-1T, and **Pub. 556,** Examination of Returns, Appeal Rights, and Claims for Refund.

Income

Caution: *Report only trade or business activity income or loss on lines 1a through 6.* ***Do not report rental activity income or portfolio income or loss on these lines.*** *(See the instructions on **Passive Activity Limitations** beginning on page 5 for definitions of rental income and portfolio income.) Rental activity income and portfolio income are reported on Schedules K and K-1 (rental real estate activities are also reported on Form 8825).*

Note: *Do not include any tax exempt income on lines 1 through 5, or any nondeductible expenses on lines 7 through 19. However, these income and expense items are used in figuring the accumulated adjustments account and the other adjustments account in Schedule M-2. Also, see instructions for line 18 of Schedule K and line 20 of Schedule K-1.*

A corporation that receives any exempt income other than interest, or holds any property or engages in an activity that produces exempt income, must attach to its return an itemized statement showing the amount of each type of exempt income and the expenses allocated to each type.

Line 1—Gross Receipts or Sales

Enter gross receipts or sales from all trade or business operations except those you report on lines 4 and 5. For reporting advance payments, see Regulations section 1.451-5. To report income from long-term contracts, see section 460.

Generally, the installment method cannot be used for dealer dispositions of property. A "dealer disposition" means any disposition of personal property by a person who regularly sells or otherwise disposes of personal property of the same type on the installment plan or any disposition of real property held for sale to customers in the ordinary course of the taxpayer's trade or business. The disposition of property used or produced in a farming business is not included as a dealer disposition. See section 453(l) for details and exceptions. For dealer dispositions of property before March 1, 1986, dispositions of property used or produced in the trade or business of farming, and certain dispositions of timeshares and residential lots reported under the installment method, enter on line 1a the gross profit on collections from installment sales and carry the same amount to line 3. Attach a schedule showing the following for the current year and the 3 preceding years: (a) gross sales, (b) cost of goods sold, (c) gross profits, (d) percentage of gross profits to gross sales, (e) amount collected, and (f) gross profit on amount collected.

Line 2—Cost of Goods Sold

See the instructions for Schedule A.

Line 4—Net Gain (Loss) From Form 4797

Caution: *Include only ordinary gains or losses from the sale, exchange, or involuntary conversion of assets used in a trade or business activity. Ordinary gains or losses from the sale, exchange, or involuntary conversions of assets of rental activities must be reported separately on Schedule K as part of the net income (loss) from the rental activity in which the property was used.*

In addition to the ordinary gains or losses reported on line 4 from the corporation's attached **Form 4797,** Sales of Business Property, a corporation that is a partner in a partnership must include its partnership share of ordinary gains (losses) from sales, exchanges, or involuntary or compulsory conversions (other than casualties or thefts) of the partnership's trade or business assets.

Do not include any recapture of the section 179 expense deduction. See the Instructions for Schedule K-1, line 20, item 5, and for Form 4797 for more information.

Line 5—Other Income

Enter on line 5 trade or business income (loss) that is not included on lines 1a through 4. Examples of such income include: **(a)** interest income derived in the ordinary course of the corporation's trade or business, such as interest charged on receivable balances; **(b)** recoveries of bad debts deducted in earlier years under the specific charge-off method; **(c)** taxable income from insurance proceeds; and **(d)** the amount of credit figured on **Form 6478,** Credit for Alcohol Used as Fuel.

Also include on line 5 all section 481 income adjustments resulting from changes in accounting methods. Show the computation of the section 481 adjustment on an attached schedule. Do not include items requiring separate computations by shareholders that must be reported on Schedule K. (See the instructions for Schedules K and K-1.) Do not offset current year's taxes with tax refunds.

The corporation must include as other income the recapture amount for section 280F if the business use of listed property drops to 50% or less. See section 280F(b)(2). To figure the recapture amount, the corporation must complete Part V of Form 4797.

If "other income" consists of only one item, identify it by showing the account caption in parentheses on line 5. A separate schedule need not be attached to the return in this case.

Do not net any expense item (such as interest) with a similar income item. Report all trade or business expenses on lines 7 through 19.

Deductions

Caution: *Report only trade or business activity expenses on lines 7 through 19. Do not report rental activity expenses or deductions allocable to portfolio income on these lines. Rental activity expenses are separately reported on Form 8825 or line 3 of Schedules K and K-1. Deductions allocable to portfolio income are separately reported on line 9 of Schedules K and K-1. See the instructions on Passive Activity Limitations beginning on page 5 for more information on rental activities and portfolio income.*

Limitations on Deductions

Section 263A uniform capitalization rules.—The uniform capitalization rules of section 263A require corporations to capitalize or include in inventory certain costs incurred in connection with the production of real and personal tangible property held in inventory or held for sale in the ordinary course of business. Tangible personal property produced by a corporation includes a film, sound recording, video tape, book, or similar property. The rules also apply to personal property (tangible and intangible) acquired for resale. Corporations subject to the rules are required to capitalize not only direct costs but an allocable portion of most indirect costs (including taxes) that benefit the assets produced or acquired for resale.

Interest expense paid or incurred during the production period of certain property must be capitalized and is governed by special rules. For more information, see Notice 88-99, 1988-2 C.B. 422. The uniform capitalization rules also apply to the production of property constructed or improved by a corporation for use in its trade or business or in an activity engaged in for profit.

Section 263A does not apply to personal property acquired for resale if the taxpayer's annual average gross receipts are $10 million or less. It does not apply to timber or to most property produced under a long-term contract. Special rules apply to certain corporations engaged in farming (see below). The rules do not apply to property that is produced for use by the taxpayer if substantial construction occurred before March 1, 1986.

In the case of inventory, some of the indirect costs that must be capitalized are: administration expenses; taxes; depreciation; insurance; compensation paid to officers attributable to services; rework labor; and contributions to pension, stock bonus, and certain profit-sharing, annuity, or deferred compensation plans.

The costs required to be capitalized under section 263A are not deductible until the property to which the costs relate is sold, used, or otherwise disposed of by the corporation.

Research and experimental costs under section 174, intangible drilling costs for oil and gas and geothermal property, and mining exploration and development costs are separately reported to shareholders for purposes of determinations under section 59(e). Temporary Regulations section 1.263A-1T specifies other indirect costs that may be currently deducted and those that must be capitalized with respect to production or resale activities. For more information, see Temporary Regulations section 1.263A-1T; Notice 88-86, 1988-2 C.B. 401; and Notice 89-67, 1989-1 C.B. 723.

Special rules for certain corporations engaged in farming.—For S corporations not required to use the accrual method of accounting, the rules of section 263A do **not** apply to expenses of raising **(a)** any animal or **(b)** any plant that has a preproductive period of 2 years or less. Shareholders of S corporations not required to use the accrual method of accounting may elect to currently deduct the preproductive period expenses of certain plants that have a preproductive period of more than 2 years. Because the election to deduct these expenses is made by the shareholder, the farming corporation should not capitalize such preproductive expenses but should separately report these expenses on line 18 of Schedule K, and each shareholder's share on line 20 of Schedule K-1. See sections 263A(d) and (e) and Temporary Regulations section 1.263A-1T(c) for definitions and other details. Also see Notice 88-24, 1988-1 C.B. 491 and Notice 89-67.

Transactions between related taxpayers.—Generally, an accrual basis S

Page 9

148

corporation may deduct business expenses and interest owed to a related party (including any shareholder) **only** in the tax year of the corporation that includes the day on which the payment is includible in the income of the related party. See section 267 for details.

Section 291 limitations.—If the S corporation was a C corporation for any of the 3 immediately preceding years, the corporation may be required to adjust deductions allowed to the corporation for depletion of iron ore and coal, and the amortizable basis of pollution control facilities. See section 291 to determine the amount of the adjustment.

Business start-up expenses.—Business start-up expenses must be capitalized. An election may be made to amortize them over a period of not less than 60 months. See section 195.

Line 7—Compensation of Officers

Enter on line 7 the total compensation of all officers paid or incurred in the trade or business activities of the corporation, including fringe benefit expenditures made on behalf of officers owning more than 2% of the corporation's stock. Also report these fringe benefits as wages in Box 10 of Form W-2. Do not include on line 7 amounts paid or incurred for fringe benefits of officers owning 2% or less of the corporation's stock. These amounts are reported on line 18, page 1, of Form 1120S. See the instructions for that line for information on the types of expenditures that are treated as fringe benefits and for the stock ownership rules.

If you report amounts on line 7 that were paid for insurance that constitutes medical care for a more than 2% shareholder, that shareholder's spouse, and that shareholder's dependents, the shareholder may be allowed a deduction of up to 25% of such amounts on Form 1040, line 26. Report the amount paid for medical insurance for that shareholder as an information item in Box 18 of his or her Form W-2.

Do not include on line 7 compensation reported elsewhere on the return, such as amounts included in cost of goods sold, elective contributions to a section 401(k) cash or deferred arrangement, or amounts contributed under a salary reduction SEP agreement.

Line 8—Salaries and Wages

Enter on line 8a the amount of salaries and wages paid or incurred for the tax year, including fringe benefit expenditures made on behalf of employees (other than officers) owning more than 2% of the corporation's stock. Also report these fringe benefits as wages in Box 10 of Form W-2. Do not include on line 8a amounts paid or incurred for fringe benefits of employees owning 2% or less of the corporation's stock. These amounts are reported on line 18, page 1, of Form 1120S. See the instructions for that line for information on the types of expenditures that are treated as fringe benefits and for the stock ownership rules.

If you report amounts on line 8a that were paid for insurance that constitutes medical care for a more than 2% shareholder, that shareholder's spouse, and that shareholder's dependents, the shareholder may be allowed a deduction of up to 25% of such amounts on Form 1040, line 26. Report the amount paid for medical insurance for that shareholder as an information item in Box 18 of his or her Form W-2.

Do not include on line 8a salaries and wages reported elsewhere on the return, such as amounts included in cost of goods sold, elective contributions to a section 401(k) cash or deferred arrangement, or amounts contributed under a salary reduction SEP agreement.

Enter on line 8b the applicable jobs credit from **Form 5884,** Jobs Credit. See the instructions for Form 5884 for more information.

If a shareholder or a member of the family of one or more shareholders of the corporation renders services or furnishes capital to the corporation for which reasonable compensation is not paid, the IRS may make adjustments in the items taken into account by such individuals and the value of such services or capital. See section 1366(e).

Line 9—Repairs

Enter the cost of incidental repairs, such as labor and supplies, that do not add to the value of the property or appreciably prolong its life, but only to the extent that such repairs relate to a trade or business activity and are not claimed elsewhere on the return. New buildings, machinery, or permanent improvements that increase the value of the property are not deductible. They are chargeable to capital accounts and may be depreciated or amortized.

Do not include any section 179 expense deduction on this line. See the instructions for line 8 of Schedules K and K-1 for details on reporting these items to shareholders.

Line 10—Bad Debts

Enter the total debts that became worthless in whole or in part during the year, but only to the extent such debts relate to a trade or business activity.

Caution: *Cash method taxpayers cannot take a bad debt deduction unless the amount was previously included in income.*

Line 11—Rents

If the corporation rented or leased a vehicle, enter the total annual rent or lease expense paid or incurred in the trade or business activities of the corporation. Also complete Part V of **Form 4562,** Depreciation and Amortization. If the corporation leased a vehicle for a term of 30 days or more, the deduction for vehicle lease expense may have to be reduced by an amount called the **inclusion amount.** You may have an inclusion amount if—

The lease term began:	And the vehicle's fair market value on the first day of the lease exceeded:
After 12/31/86	$12,800
After 4/2/85 but before 1/1/87 .	$28,000
After 6/18/84 but before 4/3/85 .	$40,500

See **Pub. 917,** Business Use of a Car, for instructions on how to figure the inclusion amount.

Line 12—Taxes

Enter taxes paid or incurred in the trade or business activities of the corporation, if not reflected in cost of goods sold. Federal import duties and Federal excise and stamp taxes are deductible only if paid or incurred in carrying on the trade or business of the corporation. Taxes incurred in the production or collection of income, or for the management, conservation, or maintenance of property held for the production of income are not deductible on line 12. Report these taxes separately on Schedules K and K-1, line 10.

Do not deduct taxes, including state and local sales taxes, paid or accrued in connection with the acquisition or disposition of business property. These taxes must be added to the cost of the property, or in the case of a disposition, subtracted from the amount realized. See section 164.

Do not deduct taxes assessed against local benefits that increase the value of the property assessed (such as for paving, etc.); Federal income taxes; estate, inheritance, legacy, succession, and gift taxes; or taxes reported elsewhere on the return.

Do not deduct section 901 foreign taxes. These taxes are reported separately on line 15e, Schedule K.

See section 263A(a) for information on capitalization of allocable costs (including taxes) for any property.

Line 13—Interest

Include on line 13 only interest incurred in the trade or business activities of the corporation that is not claimed elsewhere on the return.

Do not include interest expense on debt used to purchase rental property or debt used in a rental activity. Interest allocable to a rental real estate activity is reported on Form 8825 and is used in arriving at net income (loss) from rental real estate activities on line 2 of Schedules K and K-1. Interest allocable to a rental activity other than a rental real estate activity is included on line 3b of Schedule K and is used in arriving at net income (loss) from a rental activity (other than a rental real estate activity). This net amount is reported on line 3c of Schedule K and line 3 of Schedule K-1.

Do not include interest expense that is clearly and directly allocable to portfolio or investment income. This interest expense is reported separately on line 11a of Schedule K.

Page 10

Do not include interest on debt proceeds allocated to distributions made to shareholders during the tax year. Instead, report such interest on line 10 of Schedules K and K-1. To determine the amount to allocate to distributions to shareholders, see Notice 89-35, 1989-1 C.B. 675.

Do not include interest expense on debt required to be allocated to the production of qualified property. Interest that is allocable to certain property produced by an S corporation for its own use or for sale must be capitalized. The corporation must also capitalize any interest on debt that is allocable to an asset used to produce the above property. A shareholder may have to capitalize interest that the shareholder incurs during the tax year for the production expenditures of the S corporation. Similarly, interest incurred by an S corporation may have to be capitalized by a shareholder for the shareholder's own production expenditures. The information required by the shareholder to properly capitalize interest for this purpose must be provided by the corporation in an attachment for line 20 of Schedule K-1 (see the instructions for Schedule K-1, line 20, item 12). See section 263A(f) and Notice 88-99 for additional information.

Temporary Regulations section 1.163-8T gives rules for allocating interest expense among activities so that the limitations on passive activity losses, investment interest, and personal interest can be properly figured. Generally, interest expense is allocated in the same manner as debt is allocated. Debt is allocated by tracing disbursements of the debt proceeds to specific expenditures. These regulations give rules for tracing debt proceeds to expenditures.

Generally, prepaid interest can only be deducted over the period to which the prepayment applies. See section 461(g) for details.

Line 14—Depreciation

Enter on line 14a only the depreciation claimed on assets used in a trade or business activity. See the Instructions for Form 4562 or **Pub. 534,** Depreciation, to figure the amount of depreciation to enter on this line. For depreciation, you must complete and attach Form 4562 only if the corporation placed property in service during 1991 or claims depreciation on any car or other listed property.

Do not include any section 179 expense deduction on this line. This amount is not deductible by the corporation. Instead, it is passed through to the shareholders on line 8 of Schedule K-1.

Line 15—Depletion

If the corporation claims a deduction for timber depletion, complete and attach **Form T,** Forest Industries Schedules.

Caution: *Do not report depletion deductions for oil and gas properties on this line. Each shareholder figures depletion on these properties under section 613A(c)(11). See the instructions for line 20*

of Schedule K-1 for information on oil and gas depletion that must be supplied to the shareholders by the corporation.

Line 17—Pension, Profit-Sharing, etc., Plans

Enter the deductible contributions not claimed elsewhere on the return made by the corporation for its employees under a qualified pension, profit-sharing, annuity, or simplified employee pension (SEP) plan, and under any other deferred compensation plan.

If the corporation contributes to an individual retirement arrangement (IRA) for employees, include the contribution in salaries and wages on page 1, line 8a, or Schedule A, line 3, and not on line 17.

Employers who maintain a pension, profit-sharing, or other funded deferred compensation plan, whether or not qualified under the Internal Revenue Code and whether or not a deduction is claimed for the current tax year, generally are required to file one of the forms listed below:

Form 5500, Annual Return/Report of Employee Benefit Plan (with 100 or more participants).

Form 5500-C/R, Return/Report of Employee Benefit Plan (with fewer than 100 participants).

Form 5500EZ, Annual Return of One-Participant (Owners and Their Spouses) Pension Benefit Plan. Complete this form for a one-participant plan.

There are penalties for failure to file these forms on time and for overstating the pension plan deduction.

Line 18—Employee Benefit Programs

Enter amounts for fringe benefits paid or incurred on behalf of employees owning 2% or less of the corporation's stock. These fringe benefits include **(a)** up to $5,000 paid by reason of an employee's death to his estate or beneficiary, **(b)** employer contributions to certain accident and health plans, **(c)** the cost of up to $50,000 of group-term life insurance on an employee's life, and **(d)** meals and lodging furnished for the employer's convenience.

Do not deduct amounts that are an incidental part of a pension, profit-sharing, etc., plan included on line 17 or amounts reported elsewhere on the return.

Report amounts paid on behalf of more than 2% shareholders on line 7 or 8 of Form 1120S, whichever applies. A shareholder is considered to own more than 2% of the corporation's stock if that person owns on any day during the tax year more than 2% of the outstanding stock of the corporation or stock possessing more than 2% of the combined voting power of all stock of the corporation. See section 318 for attribution rules.

Line 19—Other Deductions

Attach a separate sheet listing all allowable deductions related to any trade or business activity for which there is no line on page 1 of the return. Enter the total on this line. Do not include those items that must be reported separately on Schedules K and K-1.

An S corporation may not take the deduction for net operating losses provided by section 172 or the special deductions in sections 241 through 249 (except the election to amortize organizational expenditures under section 248). Subject to limitations, the corporation's net operating loss is allowed as a deduction from the shareholders' gross income. See section 1366.

Do not include qualified expenditures to which an election under section 59(e) may apply. See instructions for lines 16a and 16b of Schedule K-1 for details on treatment of these items.

Include on line 19 the deduction taken for amortization. See instructions for Form 4562 for more information. You must complete and attach Form 4562 if the corporation is claiming amortization of costs that begin during its 1991 tax year.

In most cases, you may not take a deduction for any part of any item allocable to a class of exempt income. (See section 265 for exceptions.) Items directly attributable to wholly exempt income must be allocated to that income. Items directly attributable to any class of taxable income must be allocated to that taxable income.

If an item is indirectly attributable both to taxable income and to exempt income, allocate a reasonable proportion of the item to each, based on all the facts in each case.

Attach a statement showing **(a)** the amount of each class of exempt income and **(b)** the amount of expense items allocated to each such class. Show the amount allocated by apportionment separately.

Section 464(f) limits the deduction for certain expenditures of S corporations engaged in farming that use the cash method of accounting, and whose prepaid expenses for feed, seed, fertilizer, and other farm supplies, and the cost of poultry are more than 50% of other deductible farming expenses. Generally, any excess (amount over 50%) may be deducted only in the tax year the items are actually used or consumed. See section 464(f) for more information.

Generally, the corporation can deduct only 80% of the amount otherwise allowable for meals and entertainment expenses paid or incurred in its trade or business. In addition, meals must not be lavish or extravagant; a bona fide business discussion must occur during, immediately before, or immediately after the meal; and an employee of the corporation must be present at the meal. See section 274(k)(2) for exceptions.

Additional limitations apply to deductions for gifts, skybox rentals, luxury water

Page 11

travel, convention expenses, and entertainment tickets. See section 274 and **Pub. 463,** Travel, Entertainment, and Gift Expenses, for details.

Generally, a corporation can deduct all other ordinary and necessary travel and entertainment expenses paid or incurred in its trade or business. However, it cannot deduct an expense paid or incurred for a facility (such as a yacht or hunting lodge) that is used for an activity that is usually considered entertainment, amusement, or recreation.

Note: *The corporation may be able to deduct the expense if the amount is treated as compensation and reported on Form W-2 for an employee or on Form 1099-MISC for an independent contractor.*

Do not deduct penalties imposed on the corporation such as those included in the General Instruction on **Interest and Penalties.**

Line 21—Ordinary Income (Loss)

This is nonseparately computed income or loss as defined in section 1366(a)(2) attributable to trade or business activities of the corporation. This income or loss is entered on line 1 of Schedule K.

Line 21 income is not used in figuring the tax on line 22a or 22b. See the instructions for line 22a for figuring taxable income for purposes of line 22a or 22b tax.

Line 22a—Excess Net Passive Income Tax

If the corporation has always been an S corporation, the excess net passive income tax does not apply to the corporation. If the corporation has subchapter C earnings and profits (defined in section 1362(d)(3)(B)) at the close of its tax year, has passive investment income for the tax year that is in excess of 25% of gross receipts, and has taxable income at year end, the corporation must pay a tax on the excess net passive income. Complete lines 1 through 3 and line 9 of the worksheet below to make this determination. If line 2 is greater than line 3 and the corporation has taxable income (see instructions for line 9 of worksheet), it must pay the tax. Complete a separate schedule using the format of lines 1 through 11 of the worksheet below to figure the tax. Enter the tax on line 22a, page 1, Form 1120S, and attach the computation schedule to Form 1120S.

Reduce each item of passive income passed through to shareholders by its portion of tax on line 22a. See section 1366(f)(3).

Worksheet for Line 22a

1. Enter gross receipts for the tax year (see section 1362(d)(3)(C) for gross receipts from the sale of capital assets)* . . . . _____
2. Enter passive investment income as defined in section 1362(d)(3)(D)* . _____
3. Enter 25% of line 1 (If line 2 is less than line 3, stop here. You are not liable for this tax.) . . . . _____
4. Excess passive investment income—Subtract line 3 from line 2 . . _____
5. Enter deductions directly connected with the production of income on line 2 (see section 1375(b)(2)* . . . _____
6. Net passive income—Subtract line 5 from line 2 . . . . _____
7. Divide amount on line 4 by amount on line 2 . . . . _____ %
8. Excess net passive income—Multiply line 6 by line 7 . . . . . . _____
9. Enter taxable income (see instructions for taxable income below) . . . _____
10. Enter smaller of line 8 or line 9 . . _____
11. Excess net passive income tax—Enter 34% of line 10. Enter here and on line 22a, page 1, Form 1120S . . . _____

*Income and deductions on lines 1, 2, and 5 are from total operations for the tax year. This includes applicable income and expenses from page 1, Form 1120S, as well as those reported separately on Schedule K. See sections 1362(d)(3)(D) and 1375(b)(4) for exceptions regarding lines 2 and 5.

Line 9 of Worksheet.—Taxable income.—

Line 9 taxable income is defined in Regulations section 1.1374-1A(d). Figure this income by completing lines 1 through 28 of **Form 1120,** U.S. Corporation Income Tax Return. Include the Form 1120 computation with the worksheet computation you attach to Form 1120S. You do not have to attach the schedules, etc., called for on Form 1120. However, you may want to complete certain Form 1120 schedules, such as Schedule D (Form 1120), if you have capital gains or losses.

Line 22b—Tax From Schedule D (Form 1120S)

If the corporation elected to be an S corporation before 1987 (or elected to be an S corporation during 1987 or 1988 and qualifies for transitional relief from the built-in gains tax), see instructions for Part III of Schedule D (Form 1120S) to determine if the corporation is liable for the capital gains tax.

If the corporation made its election to be an S corporation after 1986, see the instructions for Part IV of Schedule D to determine if the corporation is liable for the built-in gains tax.

Note: *For purposes of line 13 of Part III and line 17 of Part IV of Schedule D, taxable income is defined in section 1375(b)(1)(B) and is generally figured in the same manner as taxable income for line 9 of the worksheet above for line 22a of Form 1120S.*

Line 22c

Include in the total for line 22c the following:

Investment credit recapture tax.— Section 1371(d) provides that an S corporation is liable for investment credit recapture attributable to credits allowed for tax years for which the corporation was not an S corporation.

Figure the corporation's investment credit recapture tax by completing **Form 4255,** Recapture of Investment Credit. Include the tax in the total amount to be entered on line 22c. Write to the left of the line 22c total the amount of recapture tax and the words "Tax From Form 4255," and attach Form 4255 to Form 1120S.

LIFO recapture tax.—If the corporation used the LIFO inventory pricing method for its last tax year as a C corporation, the corporation may be liable for the additional tax due to LIFO recapture under section 1363(d).

The LIFO recapture tax is figured for the last tax year the corporation was a C corporation. See the Instructions for Forms 1120 and 1120-A for details. The LIFO tax is paid in four equal installments. The first installment is due with the corporation's Form 1120 (or 1120-A) for the corporation's last tax year as a C corporation, and each of the remaining installments is paid with the corporation's Form 1120S for the 3 succeeding tax years. Include this year's installment in the total amount to be entered on line 22c, page 1, Form 1120S. Write to the left of the total on line 22c the installment amount and the words "LIFO tax."

Interest due under the look-back method for completed long-term contracts.—If the corporation completed

Form 8697, Interest Computation Under the Look-Back Method for Completed Long-Term Contracts, and owes interest, write to the left of the line 22c total the amount of interest and "From Form 8697." Attach the completed form to Form 1120S.

Line 23d

If the S corporation is a beneficiary of a trust and the trust makes a section 643(g) election to credit its estimated tax overpayments to its beneficiaries, include the corporation's share of the overpayment (reported to the corporation on Schedule K-1 (Form 1041)) in the total amount entered on line 23d. Also, to the left of line 23d, write "T" and the amount of the overpayment.

Schedule A—Cost of Goods Sold

Section 263A Uniform Capitalization Rules

The uniform capitalization rules of section 263A are discussed under **Limitations on Deductions** on page 9. See those instructions before completing Schedule A.

Line 4—Additional Section 263A Costs

An entry is required on this line only for corporations that have elected a simplified method of accounting. For corporations that have elected the simplified production method, additional section 263A costs are generally those costs, other than interest, that were not capitalized or included in inventory costs under the corporation's method of accounting immediately prior to the effective date in Temporary Regulations section 1.263A-1T that are now required to be capitalized under section 263A. For corporations that have elected a simplified resale method, additional section 263A costs are generally those costs incurred with respect to the following categories: off-site storage or warehousing; purchasing; handling, processing, assembly, and repackaging; and general and administrative costs (mixed service costs). Enter on line 4 the balance of section 263A costs paid or incurred during the tax year not included on lines 2 and 3. See Temporary Regulations section 1.263A-1T for more information.

Line 5—Other Costs

Enter on line 5 any other inventoriable costs paid or incurred during the tax year not entered on lines 2 through 4.

Line 7—Inventory At End of Year

See Temporary Regulations section 1.263A-1T for details on figuring the amount of additional section 263A costs to be capitalized and added to ending inventory.

Lines 9a through 9e—Inventory Valuation Methods

Inventories can be valued at (a) cost, (b) cost or market value (whichever is lower), or (c) any other method approved by the IRS that conforms to the provisions of the applicable regulations cited below.

Taxpayers using erroneous valuation methods must change to a method permitted for Federal income tax purposes. To make this change, file Form 3115. For more information, see Regulations section 1.446-1(e)(3) and Rev. Proc. 84-74, 1984-2 C.B. 736; Notice 88-78, 1988-2 C.B. 394; and Notice 89-67.

On line 9a, check the method(s) used for valuing inventories. Under "lower of cost or market," *market* generally applies to normal market conditions when there is a current bid price prevailing at the date the inventory is valued. When no regular open market exists or when quotations are nominal because of inactive market conditions, use fair market prices from the most reliable sales or purchase transactions that occurred near the date the inventory is valued. For additional requirements, see Regulations section 1.471-4 and Notice 88-86, 1988-2 C.B. 401 (section IV(N)).

Inventory may be valued below cost when the merchandise is unsalable at normal prices or unusable in the normal way because the goods are "subnormal" (i.e., because of damage, imperfections, shop wear, etc.) within the meaning of Regulations section 1.471-2(c). Such goods may be valued at a current bona fide selling price less direct cost of disposition (but not less than scrap value) when the taxpayer can establish such a price. See Regulations section 1.471-2(c) for additional requirements.

If this is the first year the "last-in-first-out" (LIFO) inventory method was either adopted or extended to inventory goods not previously valued under the LIFO method, as provided in section 472, attach **Form 970**, Application To Use LIFO Inventory Method, or a statement showing the information required by Form 970, with Form 1120S and check the LIFO box in line 9b. On line 9c, enter the amount or percent (estimates may be used) of total closing inventories covered under section 472.

If you have changed or extended your inventory method to LIFO and have had to "write up" your opening inventory to cost in the year of election, report the effect of this writeup as income (line 5, page 1) proportionately over a 3-year period that begins in the tax year you made this election. (See section 472(d).)

Schedule B—Other Information

Be sure to answer the questions and provide other information in items 1 through 10.

Line 5—Foreign Financial Accounts

Check the "Yes" box if either 1 or 2 below applies to the corporation. Otherwise, check the "No" box.

1. At any time during the year, the corporation had an interest in or signature or other authority over a financial account in a foreign country (such as a bank account, securities account, or other financial account); AND

● The combined value of the accounts was more than $10,000 during the year; AND

● The account was NOT with a U.S. military banking facility operated by a U.S. financial institution.

2. The corporation owns more than 50% of the stock in any corporation that would answer "Yes" to item **1** above.

Get form **TD F 90-22.1**, Report of Foreign Bank and Financial Accounts, to see if the corporation is considered to have an interest in or signature or other authority over a financial account in a foreign country (such as a bank account, securities account, or other financial account).

If "Yes" is checked for this question, file form TD F 90-22.1 by June 30, 1992, with the Department of the Treasury at the address shown on the form. Form TD F 90-22.1 is not a tax return, so do not file it with Form 1120S. Form TD F 90-22.1 may be ordered by calling our toll-free number, 1-800-829-3676.

Also, if "Yes" is checked for this question, enter the name of the foreign country or countries. Attach a separate sheet if you need more space.

Line 9

Complete line 9 if the corporation: **(a)** filed its election to be an S corporation after 1986; **(b)** was a C corporation before it elected to be an S corporation **or** the corporation acquired an asset with a basis determined by reference to its basis (or the basis of any other property) in the hands of a C corporation; and **(c)** has net unrealized built-in gain (defined below) in excess of the net recognized built-in gain from prior years.

The corporation is liable for section 1374 tax if (a), (b), and (c) above apply and it has a net recognized built-in gain (section 1374(d)(2)) for its tax year.

Section 633(d)(8) of the Tax Reform Act of 1986 provides transitional relief from the built-in gains for certain corporations that elected to be S corporations in 1987 or 1988. However, the relief rule does **not** apply to ordinary gains or losses (determined without regard to section 1239), gains or losses from the disposition of capital assets held 6 months or less, and gains from the disposition of any asset acquired by the corporation with a substituted basis if a principal purpose for acquiring the asset was to secure transitional relief from the built-in gains tax. See the instructions for Part IV of Schedule D (Form 1120S) for more information.

The corporation's "net unrealized built-in gain" is the amount, if any, by which the fair market value of the assets of the corporation at the beginning of its first S corporation year (or as of the date the assets were acquired, for any asset with a basis determined by reference to its basis (or the basis of any other property) in the hands of a C corporation) exceeds the aggregate adjusted basis of such assets at that time.

Enter on line 9 the corporation's net unrealized built-in gain reduced by the net recognized built-in gain for prior years. See sections 1374(c)(2) and (d)(1).

Line 10

Check the box on line 10 if the corporation was a C corporation in a prior year and has subchapter C earnings and profits (E&P) at the close of its 1991 tax year. For this purpose, "subchapter C E&P" means E&P of any corporation for any tax year when it was not an S corporation. See sections 1362(d)(3)(B) and 312 for other details. If the corporation has subchapter C E&P, it may be liable for tax imposed on excess net passive income. See the instructions for line 22a, page 1, of Form 1120S for details on this tax.

Designation of Tax Matters Person (TMP)

If the S corporation is subject to sections 6241 through 6245 (consolidated audit procedures), it may designate a shareholder as the TMP for the tax year for which the return is filed by completing the **Designation of Tax Matters Person** section at the bottom of page 2 of Form 1120S. Temporary Regulations section 301.6241-1T provides an exception to the consolidated provisions for small S corporations with 5 or fewer shareholders each of whom is a natural person or an estate. See the instructions for **Item G, Consolidated Audit Procedures,** on page 8, sections 6241 through 6245, and Temporary Regulations section 301.6241-1T for other details.

General Instructions For Schedules K and K-1— Shareholders' Shares of Income, Credits, Deductions, Etc.

Purpose of Schedules

The corporation is liable for taxes on lines 22a, b, and c, page 1, Form 1120S. Shareholders are liable for income tax on their shares of the corporation's income (reduced by any taxes paid by the corporation on income) and must include their share of the income on their tax return whether or not it is distributed to them. Unlike most partnership income, S corporation income is **not** self-employment income and is not subject to self-employment tax.

Schedule K is a summary schedule of all the shareholders' shares of the corporation's income, deductions, credits, etc. Schedule K-1 shows each shareholder's separate share. A copy of each shareholder's Schedule K-1 must be attached to the Form 1120S filed with the IRS. A copy is kept as a part of the corporation's records, and the corporation must give each shareholder a separate copy.

The total pro rata share items (column (b)) of all Schedules K-1 should equal the amount reported on the same line of Schedule K. Lines 1 through 17 of Schedule K correspond to lines 1 through 17 of Schedule K-1. Other lines do not correspond, but instructions will explain the differences.

Be sure to give each shareholder a copy of the Shareholder's Instructions for Schedule K-1 (Form 1120S). These instructions are available, separately from Schedule K-1, at most IRS offices.

Note: *Instructions that apply only to line items reported on Schedule K-1 may be prepared and given to each shareholder in lieu of the instructions printed by the IRS.*

Substitute Forms

You do not need IRS approval to use a substitute Schedule K-1 if it is an exact facsimile of the IRS schedule, or if it contains only those lines the taxpayer is required to use, and the lines have the same numbers and titles and are in the

same order as on the comparable IRS Schedule K-1. In either case, your substitute schedule must include the OMB number, and either **(a)** the Shareholder's Instructions for Schedule K-1 (Form 1120S), or **(b)** instructions that apply to the items reported on Schedule K-1 (Form 1120S).

Other substitute Schedules K-1 require approval. You may apply for approval of a substitute form by writing to: Internal Revenue Service, Attention: Substitute Forms Program Coordinator, R:R:R, 1111 Constitution Avenue, NW, Washington, DC 20224.

You may be subject to a penalty if you file a substitute Schedule K-1 that does not conform to the specifications of Rev. Proc. 91-16, 1991-1 C.B. 487.

Shareholder's Pro Rata Share Items

Items of income, loss, deductions, etc., are allocated to a shareholder on a daily basis, according to the number of shares of stock held by the shareholder on each day during the tax year of the corporation. See **Item A** below.

A transferee shareholder (rather than the transferor) is considered to be the owner of stock on the day it is transferred.

Special rule.—If a shareholder terminates his or her interest in a corporation during the tax year, the corporation, with the consent of all shareholders (including the one whose interest is terminated), may elect to allocate income and expenses, etc., as if the corporation's tax year consisted of 2 tax years, the first of which ends on the date of the shareholder's termination. To make the election, the corporation must file a statement of election with the return for the tax year of election and attach a statement of consent signed by all shareholders. If the election is made, write "Section 1377(a)(2) Election Made" at the top of each Schedule K-1. See section 1377(a)(2) and Temporary Regulations section 18.1377-1 for details.

Specific Instructions (Schedule K Only)

Enter the total pro rata share amount for each applicable line item on Schedule K.

Specific Instructions (Schedule K-1 Only)

General Information

On each Schedule K-1, complete the date spaces at the top; enter the names, addresses, and identifying numbers of the shareholder and corporation; complete items A through D; and enter the shareholder's pro rata share of each item. **Schedule K-1 must be prepared and given to each shareholder on or before the day on which Form 1120S is filed.**

Note: *Space has been provided on line 20 (Supplemental Information) of Schedule*

K-1 for the corporation to provide additional information to shareholders. This space, if sufficient, should be used in place of any attached schedules required for any lines on Schedule K-1, or other amounts not shown on lines 1 through 19 of Schedule K-1. Please be sure to identify the applicable line number next to the information entered below line 20.

Specific Items

Item A

If there was no change in shareholders or in the relative interest in stock the shareholders owned during the tax year, enter the percentage of total stock owned by each shareholder during the tax year. For example, if shareholders X and Y each owned 50% for the entire tax year, enter 50% in item A for each shareholder. Each shareholder's pro rata share items (lines 1 through 17 of Schedule K-1) are figured by multiplying the Schedule K amount on the corresponding line of Schedule K by the percentage in item A.

If there was a change in shareholders or in the relative interest in stock the shareholders owned during the tax year, each shareholder's percentage of ownership is weighted for the number of days in the tax year that stock was owned. For example, A and B each held 50% for half the tax year and A, B, and C held 40%, 40%, and 20%, respectively, for the remaining half of the tax year. The percentage of ownership for the year for A, B, and C is figured as follows and is then entered in item A.

	a	b	c (a × b)
	% of total stock owned	% of tax year held	% of ownership for the year
A	50 40	50 50	25 +20	45
B	50 40	50 50	25 +20	45
C	20	50	10	10
Total 100%

If there was a change in shareholders or in the relative interest in stock the shareholders owned during the tax year, each shareholder's pro rata share items can also be figured on a daily basis, based on the percentage of stock held by the shareholder on each day. See sections 1377(a)(1) and (2) for details.

Item B

Enter the Internal Revenue service center address where the Form 1120S, to which a copy of this K-1 was attached, was or will be filed.

Item C

If the corporation is a registration-required tax shelter, it must enter its tax shelter registration number in item C(1) and identify the type of shelter in C(2). If the corporation invested in a registration-required shelter, the corporation must also attach a copy of its Form 8271 to Schedule K-1. See Form

8271 for a list of the types of tax shelters and for more information.

Special Reporting Requirements for Corporations With Multiple Activities

If items of income, loss, deduction, or credit from more than one activity (determined for purposes of the passive activity loss and credit limitations) are reported on lines 1, 2, or 3 of Schedule K-1, the corporation must provide information for each activity to its shareholders. See **Passive Activity Reporting Requirements** on page 7 for details on the reporting requirements.

Special Reporting Requirements for At-Risk Activities

If the corporation is involved in one or more at-risk activities for which a loss is reported on Schedule K-1, the corporation must report information separately for each at-risk activity. See section 465(c) for a definition of at-risk activities.

For each at-risk activity, the following information must be provided on an attachment to Schedule K-1:

1. A statement that the information is a breakdown of at-risk activity loss amounts.

2. The identity of the at-risk activity; the loss amount for the activity; other income, deductions; and other information that relates to the activity.

Specific Instructions (Schedules K and K-1, Except as Noted)

Income (Loss)

Reminder: Before entering income items on Schedule K or K-1, be sure to reduce the items of income for the following:

1. Built-in gains tax (Schedule D, Part IV, line 23).—Each recognized built-in gain item (within the meaning of section 1374(d)(3)) is reduced by its proportionate share of the built-in gains tax.

2. Capital gains tax (Schedule D, Part III, line 15).—The net long-term capital gain on line 6 of Schedule D or the section 1231 gain included on line 5 or 6 of Schedule K is reduced by this tax.

3. Excess net passive income tax (line 22a, page 1, Form 1120S).—Each item of passive investment income (within the meaning of section 1362(d)(3)(D)) is reduced by its proportionate share of the net passive income tax.

Line 1—Ordinary Income (Loss) From Trade or Business Activities

Enter the amount from line 21, page 1. Enter the income or loss without reference to **(a)** shareholders' basis in the stock of the corporation and in any indebtedness of the corporation to the shareholders (section 1366(d)), **(b)** shareholders' at-risk limitations, and **(c)** shareholders' passive activity limitations. These limitations, if

applicable, are determined at the shareholder level.

If the corporation is involved in more than one trade or business activity, see **Passive Activity Reporting Requirements** on page 7 for details on the information to be reported for each activity. If an at-risk activity loss is reported on line 1, see **Special Reporting Requirements for At-Risk Activities** on this page.

Line 2—Net Income (Loss) From Rental Real Estate Activities ·

Enter the net income or loss from rental real estate activities of the corporation from **Form 8825**, Rental Real Estate Income and Expenses of a Partnership or an S Corporation. Each Form 8825 has space for reporting the income and expenses of up to 8 properties.

If the corporation has income or loss from more than one rental real estate activity reported on line 2, see **Passive Activity Reporting Requirements** on page 7 for details on the information to be reported for each activity. If an at-risk activity loss is reported on line 2, see **Special Reporting Requirements for At-Risk Activities** on this page.

If a loss from a qualified low-income housing project is reported on line 2, identify this loss on a statement attached to the Schedule K-1 of each shareholder who is a qualified investor in the project. Any loss sustained by a qualified investor in a qualified low-income housing project for any tax year in the relief period is not subject to the passive activity loss limitations under section 502 of the Tax Reform Act of 1986. See Act section 502 for definitions and other information on qualified low-income housing projects.

Line 3—Income and Expenses of Other Rental Activities

Enter on lines 3a and 3b of Schedule K (line 3 of Schedule K-1) the income and expenses of rental activities other than the income and expenses reported on Form 8825. If the corporation has more than one rental activity reported on line 3, see **Passive Activity Reporting Requirements** on page 7 for details on the information to be reported for each activity. If an at-risk activity loss is reported on line 3, see **Special Reporting Requirements for At-Risk Activities** on this page. Also see **Rental activities** on page 6 for a definition and other details on other rental activities.

Lines 4a Through 4f—Portfolio Income (Loss)

Enter portfolio income (loss) on lines 4a through 4f. See **Portfolio Income** on page 6 for a definition of portfolio income. Do not reduce portfolio income by expenses allocated to it. Such expenses (other than interest expense) are reported on line 9 of Schedules K and K-1. Interest expense allocable to portfolio income is generally investment interest expense and is reported on line 11a of Schedules K and K-1.

Lines 4a and 4b.—Enter only taxable interest and dividends that are portfolio income. Interest income derived in the ordinary course of the corporation's trade or business, such as interest charged on receivable balances, is reported on line 5, page 1, Form 1120S. See Temporary Regulations section 1.469-2T(c)(3).

Lines 4d and 4e.—Enter on line 4d the net short-term capital gain or loss (reduced by any applicable taxes) from line 3 of Schedule D (Form 1120S) that is portfolio income. Enter on line 4e the net long-term capital gain or loss (reduced by any applicable taxes) from line 6 of Schedule D (Form 1120S) that is portfolio income. If any gain or loss from lines 3 and 6 of Schedule D is not portfolio income (e.g., gain or loss from the disposition of nondepreciable personal property used in a trade or business), do not report this income or loss on lines 4d and 4e. Instead, report it on line 6 of Schedules K and K-1. If the income or loss is attributable to more than one activity, report the income or loss amount separately for each activity on an attachment to Schedule K-1 and identify the activity to which the income or loss relates.

Line 4f.—Enter any other portfolio income not reported on lines 4a through 4e.

If the corporation holds a residual interest in a REMIC, report on an attachment for line 4f each shareholder's share of taxable income (net loss) from the REMIC (line 1b of Schedule Q (Form 1066)); excess inclusion (line 2c of Schedule Q (Form 1066)); and section 212 expenses (line 3b of Schedule Q (Form 1066)). Because Schedule Q (Form 1066) is a quarterly statement, the corporation must follow the Schedule Q (Form 1066) Instructions for Residual Holder to figure the amounts to report to shareholders for the corporation's tax year.

Line 5—Net Gain (Loss) Under Section 1231 (Other Than Due to Casualty or Theft)

Enter the gain (loss) under section 1231 shown on line 7 of Form 4797. Do not include net gains or losses from involuntary conversions due to casualties or thefts on this line. Instead, report them on line 6.

Line 6—Other Income (Loss)

Enter any other item of income or loss not included on lines 1 through 5, such as:

1. Recoveries of tax benefit items (section 111).

2. Gambling gains and losses (section 165(d)).

3. Net gain (loss) from involuntary conversions due to casualty or theft. The amount for this item is shown on **Form 4684**, Casualties and Thefts, Section B, line 20a or 20b.

4. Any net gain or loss from section 1256 contracts from **Form 6781**, Gains and Losses From Section 1256 Contracts and Straddles.

Page 15

154

Deductions

Line 7—Charitable Contributions

Enter the amount of charitable contributions paid by the corporation during its tax year. Attach an itemized list that separately shows the corporation's charitable contributions subject to the 50%, 30%, and 20% limitations.

If the corporation contributes property other than cash and the deduction claimed for such property exceeds $500, **Form 8283**, Noncash Charitable Contributions, must be completed and attached to Form 1120S. The corporation must give a copy of its Form 8283 to every shareholder if the deduction for any item or group of similar items of contributed property exceeds $5,000, even if the amount allocated to any shareholder is $5,000 or less. If this requirement is not met, the corporation does not have to furnish the shareholders with a copy of its Form 8283. However, the corporation must report each shareholder's pro rata share of the amount of noncash contributions to enable individual shareholders to complete their own Forms 8283. See the Instructions for Form 8283 for more information.

If the corporation made a qualified conservation contribution under section 170(h), also include the fair market value of the underlying property before and after the donation, as well as the type of legal interest contributed, and describe the conservation purpose furthered by the donation. Give a copy of this information to each shareholder.

Line 8—Section 179 Expense Deduction

An S corporation may elect to expense part of the cost of certain tangible property that the corporation purchased during the tax year for use in its trade or business or certain rental activities. See the instructions for Form 4562 for more information.

Complete Part I of Form 4562 to figure the corporation's section 179 expense deduction. The corporation does not deduct the expense itself but passes the expense through to its shareholders. Attach Form 4562 to Form 1120S and show the total section 179 expense deduction on Schedule K, line 8. Report each individual shareholder's pro rata share on Schedule K-1, line 8. Do not complete line 8 of Schedule K-1 for any shareholder that is an estate or trust.

See the instructions for line 20 of Schedule K-1, item 6, for any recapture of a section 179 amount.

Line 9—Deductions Related to Portfolio Income (Loss)

Enter on line 9 the deductions clearly and directly allocable to portfolio income (other than interest expense). Interest expense related to portfolio income is investment interest expense and is reported on line 11a of Schedules K and K-1. Generally, the line 9 expenses are section 212

expenses and are subject to section 212 limitations at the shareholder level.

Note: *No deduction is allowed under section 212 for expenses allocable to a convention, seminar, or similar meeting. Because these expenses are not deductible by shareholders, the corporation does not report these expenses on line 9 or line 10. The expenses are nondeductible and are reported as such on line 18 of Schedule K and line 20 of Schedule K-1.*

Line 10—Other Deductions

Enter any other deductions not included on lines 7, 8, 9, and 15e, such as:

● Amounts (other than investment interest required to be reported on line 11a of Schedules K and K-1) paid by the corporation that would be allowed as itemized deductions on a shareholder's income tax return if they were paid directly by a shareholder for the same purpose. These amounts include, but are not limited to, expenses under section 212 for the production of income other than from the corporation's trade or business.

● Any penalty on early withdrawal of savings not reported on line 9 because the corporation withdrew funds from its time savings deposit before its maturity.

● Soil and water conservation expenditures (section 175).

● Expenditures paid or incurred for the removal of architectural and transportation barriers to the elderly and disabled that the corporation has elected to treat as a current expense. See section 190.

● Interest expense allocated to debt-financed distributions. See Notice 89-35 for more information.

● If there was a gain (loss) from a casualty or theft to property not used in a trade or business or for income producing purposes, provide each shareholder with the needed information to complete Form 4684.

Investment Interest

Lines 11a and 11b must be completed for all shareholders.

Line 11a—Investment Interest Expense

Include on this line the interest properly allocable to debt on property held for investment purposes. Property held for investment includes property that produces investment income (interest, dividends, annuities, royalties, etc.).

Investment interest expense **does not** include interest expense allocable to a passive activity.

Report investment interest expense only on line 11a of Schedules K and K-1.

The amount on line 11a will be deducted by individual shareholders on Form 1040 after applying the investment interest expense limitations of section 163(d). The section 163(d) limitations are figured on **Form 4952**, Investment Interest Expense Deduction.

Lines 11b(1) and 11b(2)—Investment Income and Expenses

Enter on line 11b(1) only the investment income included on line 4 of Schedule K-1. Enter on line 11b(2) only the investment expense included on line 9 of Schedule K-1.

If there are items of investment income or expense included in the amounts that are required to be passed through separately to the shareholders on Schedule K-1 (items other than the amounts included on lines 4 and 9 of Schedule K-1), give each shareholder a schedule identifying these amounts.

Investment income includes gross income from property held for investment, gain attributable to the disposition of property held for investment, and other amounts that are gross portfolio income. Generally, investment income and investment expenses do not include any income or expenses from a passive activity. See Temporary Regulations section 1.469-2T(f)(10) for exceptions.

Property subject to a net lease is not treated as investment property because it is subject to the passive loss rules. Do not reduce investment income by losses from passive activities.

Investment expenses are deductible expenses (other than interest) directly connected with the production of investment income. See the Instructions for Form 4952 for more information on investment income and expenses.

Credits

Note: *If the corporation has credits from more than one trade or business activity on line 12a or 13, or from more than one rental activity on line 12b, 12c, 12d, or 12e, it must report separately on an attachment to Schedule K-1, the amount of each credit and provide any other applicable activity information listed in* **Passive Activity Reporting Requirements** *on page 7.*

Line 12a—Credit for Alcohol Used as Fuel

Enter on line 12a of Schedule K the credit for alcohol used as fuel computed by the corporation that is attributable to a trade or business activity. Enter on line 12d or 12e, the credit for alcohol used as fuel attributable to rental activities. The credit for alcohol used as fuel is figured on **Form 6478**, Credit for Alcohol Used as Fuel, and the form is attached to Form 1120S. The credit must be included as income on page 1, line 5, of Form 1120S. See section 40(f) for an election the corporation can make to have the credit not apply.

Enter each shareholder's share of the credit for alcohol used as fuel on line 12a, 12d, or 12e of Schedule K-1.

Line 12b—Low-Income Housing Credit

Section 42 provides for a low-income housing credit that may be claimed by owners of low-income residential rental buildings. If shareholders are eligible to claim the low-income housing credit, complete the applicable parts of **Form 8586,** Low-Income Housing Credit, and attach it to Form 1120S. Enter the credit figured by the corporation on Form 8586, and any low-income housing credit received from other entities in which the corporation is allowed to invest on the applicable line as explained below. The corporation must also complete and attach **Form 8609,** Low-Income Housing Credit Allocation Certification, and **Schedule A (Form 8609),** Annual Statement, to Form 1120S. See the Instructions for Form 8586 and Form 8609 for information on completing these forms.

Note: *No credit may be claimed for any building in a qualified low-income housing project for which any person was allowed to claim a loss from the project by reason of not being subject to the passive activity limitations (see section 502 of the Tax Reform Act of 1986 for details).*

Line 12b(1).—If the corporation invested in a partnership to which the provisions of section 42(j)(5) apply, report on line 12b(1) the credit the partnership reported to the corporation on line 13b(1) of Schedule K-1 (Form 1065). If the corporation invested **before 1990** in a section 42(j)(5) partnership, also include on this line any credit the partnership reported to the corporation on line 13b(3) of Schedule K-1 (Form 1065).

Line 12b(2).—Report on line 12b(2) any low-income housing credit for property placed in service before 1990 and not reported on line 12b(1). This includes any credit from a building placed in service before 1990 in a project owned by the corporation and any credit from a partnership reported to the corporation on line 13b(2) of Schedule K-1 (Form 1065). Also include on this line any credit from a partnership reported to the corporation on line 13b(4) of Schedule K-1 (Form 1065), if the corporation invested in that partnership **before 1990.**

Line 12b(3).—If the corporation invested **after 1989** in a partnership to which the provisions of section 42(j)(5) apply, report on line 12b(3) the credit the partnership reported to the corporation on line 13b(3) of Schedule K-1 (Form 1065).

Line 12b(4).—Report on line 12b(4) any low-income housing credit for property placed in service after 1989 and not reported on any other line. This includes any credit from a building placed in service after 1989 in a project owned by the corporation and any credit from a partnership reported to the corporation on line 13b(4) of Schedule K-1 (Form 1065), if the corporation invested in that partnership **after 1989.**

Line 12c—Qualified Rehabilitation Expenditures Related to Rental Real Estate Activities

Enter total qualified rehabilitation expenditures related to rental real estate activities of the corporation, and for line 12c of Schedule K, complete the applicable lines of **Form 3468,** Investment

Credit, that apply to qualified rehabilitation expenditures for property related to rental real estate activities of the corporation for which income or loss is reported on line 2 of Schedule K. See Form 3468 for details on qualified rehabilitation expenditures. Attach Form 3468 to Form 1120S.

For line 12c of Schedule K-1, enter each shareholder's pro rata share of the expenditures. On the dotted line to the left of the entry space for line 12c, enter the line number of Form 3468 on which the shareholder should report the expenditures. If there is more than one type of expenditure, or the expenditures are from more than one line 2 activity, report this information separately for each expenditure or activity on an attachment to Schedules K and K-1.

Note: *Qualified rehabilitation expenditures not related to rental real estate activities must be listed separately on line 20 of Schedule K-1.*

Line 12d—Credits (Other Than Credits Shown on Lines 12b and 12c) Related to Rental Real Estate Activities

Enter on line 12d any other credit (other than credits on lines 12b and 12c) related to rental real estate activities. On the dotted line to the left of the entry space for line 12d, identify the type of credit. If there is more than one type of credit or the credit is from more than one line 2 activity, report this information separately for each credit or activity on an attachment to Schedules K and K-1. These credits may include any type of credit listed in the instructions for line 13.

Line 12e—Credits Related to Other Rental Activities

Enter on line 12e any credit related to other rental activities for which income or loss is reported on line 3 of Schedules K and K-1. On the dotted line to the left of the entry space for line 12e, identify the type of credit. If there is more than one type of credit or the credit is from more than one line 3 activity, report this information separately for each credit or activity on an attachment to Schedules K and K-1. These credits may include any type of credit listed in the instructions for line 13.

Line 13—Other Credits

Enter on line 13 any other credit (other than credits or expenditures shown or listed for lines 12a through 12e of Schedules K and K-1). On the dotted line to the left of the entry space for line 13, identify the type of credit. If there is more than one type of credit or the credit is from more than one activity, report this information separately for each credit or activity on an attachment to Schedules K and K-1.

The credits to be reported on line 13 and other required attachments follow:

• Nonconventional source fuel credit. This credit is figured by the corporation on a separate schedule prepared by the

corporation. This computation schedule must also be attached to Form 1120S. See section 29 for computation provisions and other special rules for figuring this credit.

• Unused investment credit from cooperatives. If the corporation is a member of a cooperative that passes an unused investment credit through to its members, the credit is in turn passed through to the corporation's shareholders.

• Credit for backup withholding on dividends, interest, or patronage dividends.

• Credit for increasing research activities and orphan drug credit. Complete and attach **Form 6765,** Credit for Increasing Research Activities (or for claiming the orphan drug credit), to Form 1120S.

• Jobs credit. Complete and attach **Form 5884,** Jobs Credit, to Form 1120S.

• Disabled access credit. Complete and attach **Form 8826,** Disabled Access Credit, to Form 1120S.

• Enhanced oil recovery credit. Complete and attach **Form 8830,** Enhanced Oil Recovery Credit, to Form 1120S. This credit applies to costs paid or incurred in connection with qualified enhanced oil recovery projects located in the United States for which the first injection of liquids, gases, or other matter began after 1990.

See the instructions for line 18 (Schedule K) and line 20 (Schedule K-1) to report expenditures qualifying for the **(a)** rehabilitation credit not related to rental real estate activities, **(b)** energy credit, or **(c)** reforestation credit.

Adjustments and Tax Preference Items

Lines 14a through 14f must be completed for all shareholders.

Enter items of income and deductions that are adjustments or tax preference items. See **Form 6251,** Alternative Minimum Tax—Individuals, and **Pub. 909,** Alternative Minimum Tax for Individuals, to determine the amounts to enter and for other information.

Do not include as a tax preference item any qualified expenditures to which an election under section 59(e) may apply. Because these expenditures are subject to an election by each shareholder, the corporation cannot compute the amount of any tax preference related to them. Instead, the corporation must pass through to each shareholder on lines 16a and 16b of Schedule K-1 the information needed to compute the deduction. Each shareholder computes both the deduction he or she will claim and the resulting tax preference item, if any.

Line 14c—Depreciation Adjustment on Property Placed in Service After 1986

Figure the adjustment for line 14c based only on tangible property placed in service after 1986 (and tangible property placed in service after July 31, 1986 and before

1987 for which the corporation elected to use the General Depreciation System).

Refigure depreciation as follows: For property other than real property and property on which the straight line method was used, use the 150% declining balance method, switching to straight line method for the first tax year when that method gives a better result. (For property on which the straight line method was used, use the straight line method.) Use the class life (instead of the recovery period) and the same conventions as the corporation used on Form 4562. For personal property having no class life, use 12 years. For residential rental and nonresidential real property, use the straight line method over 40 years. Determine the depreciation adjustment by subtracting the recomputed depreciation from the depreciation claimed on Form 4562. If the recomputed depreciation exceeds the depreciation claimed on Form 4562, enter the difference as a negative amount. See the instructions for Form 6251 and Form 4562 for more information.

Line 14d—Depletion (Other Than Oil and Gas)

Do not include any depletion on oil and gas wells. The shareholders must compute their depletion deductions separately under section 613A.

In the case of mines, wells, and other natural deposits, other than oil and gas wells, enter the amount by which the deduction for depletion under section 611 (including percentage depletion for geothermal deposits) is more than the adjusted basis of such property at the end of the tax year. Figure the adjusted basis without regard to the depletion deduction and figure the excess separately for each property.

Lines 14e(1) and 14e(2)

Generally, the amounts to be entered on these lines are only the income and deductions for oil, gas, and geothermal properties that are used to figure the amount on line 21, page 1, Form 1120S.

If there are any items of income or deductions for oil, gas, and geothermal properties included in the amounts that are required to be passed through separately to the shareholders on Schedule K-1, give each shareholder a schedule for the line on which the income or deduction is included and which shows the amount of income or deductions included in the total amount for that line. Do not include any of these direct passthrough amounts on line 14e(1) or 14e(2). The shareholder is told in the Shareholder's Instructions for Schedule K-1 (Form 1120S) to adjust the amounts on lines 14e(1) and 14e(2) for any other income or deductions from oil, gas, or geothermal properties included on lines 2 through 10 and 20 of Schedule K-1 in order to determine the total income and deductions from oil, gas, and geothermal properties for the corporation.

Figure the amounts for lines 14e(1) and 14e(2) separately for oil and gas properties which are not geothermal deposits and for

all properties which are geothermal deposits.

Give the shareholders a schedule that shows the separate amounts that are included in the computation of the amounts on lines 14e(1) and 14e(2).

Line 14e(1). Gross income from oil, gas, and geothermal properties.— Enter the aggregate amount of gross income (within the meaning of section 613(a)) from all oil, gas, and geothermal properties received or accrued during the tax year and included on page 1, Form 1120S.

Line 14e(2). Deductions allocable to oil, gas, and geothermal properties.— Enter the amount of any deductions allocable to oil, gas, and geothermal properties reduced by the excess intangible drilling costs that were included on page 1, Form 1120S, on properties for which the corporation made an election to expense intangible drilling costs in tax years beginning before 1983. Do not include nonproductive well costs included on page 1.

Figure excess intangible drilling costs as follows: From the allowable intangible drilling and development costs (except for costs in drilling a nonproductive well), subtract the amount that would have been allowable if the corporation had capitalized these costs and either amortized them over the 120 months that started when production began, or treated them according to any election the corporation made under section 57(b)(2).

See section 57(a)(2) for more information.

Line 14f—Other Adjustments and Tax Preference Items

Attach a schedule that shows each shareholder's share of other items not shown on lines 14a through 14e(2) that are adjustments or tax preference items or that the shareholder needs to complete Form 6251 or Form 8656. See these forms and their instructions to determine the amount to enter. Other adjustments or tax preference items include the following:

● Amortization of certified pollution control facilities.—The deduction allowable under section 169 for any facility placed in service after 1986 must be refigured using the alternative depreciation system under section 168(g).

● Long-term contracts entered into after February 28, 1986.—Except for certain home construction contracts, the taxable income from these contracts must be figured using the percentage of completion method of accounting for alternative minimum tax purposes.

● Installment sales of inventory or stock in trade after March 1, 1986.—Generally, the installment method may not be used for these sales in computing alternative minimum taxable income.

● Charitable contributions of appreciated property.—Generally, the deduction for charitable contributions claimed on line 7 of Schedules K and K-1 is reduced by the difference between the fair market value and the adjusted basis of the capital gain

and section 1231 property donated to a charitable organization. For tax years beginning in 1991, no reduction is made for any contribution of tangible personal property.

● Losses from tax shelter farm activities.— No loss from any tax shelter farm activity is allowed for alternative minimum tax purposes.

Foreign Taxes

Lines 15a through 15g must be completed whether or not a shareholder is eligible for the foreign tax credit, if the corporation has foreign income, deductions, or losses, or has paid or accrued foreign taxes.

In addition to the instructions below, see **Form 1116,** Foreign Tax Credit (Individual, Fiduciary, or Nonresident Alien Individual), and the related instructions.

Line 15a—Type of Income

Enter the type of income from outside the United States as follows:

● Passive income.

● High withholding tax interest.

● Financial services income.

● Shipping income.

● Dividends from a DISC or former DISC.

● Certain distributions from a foreign sales corporation (FSC) or former FSC.

● Dividends from each noncontrolled section 902 corporation.

● Taxable income attributable to foreign trade income (within the meaning of section 923(b)).

● General limitation income (all other income from sources outside the United States, including income from sources within U.S. possessions).

If, for the country or U.S. possession shown on line 15b, the corporation had more than one type of income, enter "See attached" and attach a schedule for each type of income for lines 15b through 15g.

Line 15b—Foreign Country or U.S. Possession

Enter the name of the foreign country or U.S. possession. If, for the type of income shown on line 15a, the corporation had income from, or paid taxes to, more than one foreign country or U.S. possession, enter "See attached" and attach a schedule for each country for lines 15a and 15c through 15g.

Line 15c—Total Gross Income From Sources Outside the U.S.

Enter in U.S. dollars the total gross income from sources outside the United States. Attach a schedule that shows each type of income listed in the instructions for line 15a.

Line 15d—Total Applicable Deductions and Losses

Enter in U.S. dollars the total applicable deductions and losses attributable to income on line 15c. Attach a schedule that shows each type of deduction or loss as follows:

- Expenses directly allocable to each type of income listed above.
- Pro rata share of all other deductions not directly allocable to specific items of income.
- Pro rata share of losses from other separate limitation categories.

Line 15e—Total Foreign Taxes

Enter in U.S. dollars the total foreign taxes (described in section 901) that were paid or accrued by the corporation to foreign countries or U.S. possessions. Attach a schedule that shows the dates the taxes were paid or accrued, and the amount in both foreign currency and in U.S. dollars, as follows:

- Taxes withheld at source on dividends.
- Taxes withheld at source on rents and royalties.
- Other foreign taxes paid or accrued.

Line 15f—Reduction in Taxes Available for Credit

Enter in U.S. dollars the total reduction in taxes available for credit. Attach a schedule that shows separately the:

- Reduction for foreign mineral income.
- Reduction for failure to furnish returns required under section 6038.
- Reduction for taxes attributable to boycott operations (section 908).
- Reduction for foreign oil and gas extraction income (section 907(a)).
- Reduction for any other items (specify).

Line 15g—Other Foreign Tax Information

Enter in U.S. dollars any items not covered on lines 15c through 15f.

Other

Lines 16a and 16b

Generally, section 59(e) allows each shareholder to make an election to deduct the shareholder's pro rata share of the corporation's otherwise deductible qualified expenditures ratably over 10 years (3 years for circulation expenditures), beginning with the tax year in which the expenditures were made (or for intangible drilling and development costs, over the 60-month period beginning with the month in which such costs were paid or incurred). The term "qualified expenditures" includes only the following types of expenditures paid or incurred during the tax year: circulation expenditures, research and experimental expenditures, intangible drilling and development costs, and mining exploration and development costs. If a shareholder makes this election, these items are not treated as tax preference items.

Because the shareholders are generally allowed to make this election, the corporation cannot deduct these amounts or include them as adjustments or tax preference items on Schedule K-1. Instead, on lines 16a and 16b of Schedule K-1, the corporation passes through the information the shareholders need to compute their separate deductions.

Enter on line 16a the qualified expenditures paid or incurred during the tax year to which an election under section 59(e) may apply. Enter this amount for all shareholders whether or not any shareholder makes an election under section 59(e). On line 16b, enter the type of expenditure claimed on line 16a. If the expenditure is for intangible drilling and development costs, enter the month in which the expenditure was paid or incurred (after the type of expenditure on line 16b). If there is more than one type of expenditure included in the total shown on line 16a (or intangible drilling and development costs were paid or incurred for more than one month), report this information separately for each type of expenditure (or month) on an attachment to Schedules K and K-1.

Line 17

Enter total distributions made to each shareholder other than dividends reported on line 19 of Schedule K. Noncash distributions of appreciated property are valued at fair market value. See Schedule M-2 instructions for ordering rules on distributions.

Line 18 (Schedule K Only)

Attach a statement to Schedule K to report the corporation's total income, expenditures, or other information for items 1 through 16 of the line 20 (Schedule K-1 Only) instruction below.

Line 19 (Schedule K Only)

Enter total dividends paid to shareholders from accumulated earnings and profits. Report these dividends to shareholders on Form 1099-DIV. Do not report them on Schedule K-1.

Lines 19a and 19b (Schedule K-1 Only)—Recapture of Low-Income Housing Credit

If recapture of part or all of the low-income housing credit is required because: (1) prior year qualified basis of a building decreased, or (2) the corporation disposed of a building or part of its interest in a building, see Form 8611, Recapture of Low-Income Housing Credit. The instructions for Form 8611 indicate when Form 8611 is completed by the corporation and what information is provided to shareholders when recapture is required.

Note: If a shareholder's ownership interest in a building decreased because of a transaction at the shareholder level, the corporation must provide the necessary information to the shareholder to enable the shareholder to compute the recapture.

If the corporation posted a bond as provided in section 42(j)(6) to avoid recapture of the low-income housing credit, no entry should be made on line 19 of Schedule K-1.

See Form 8586, Form 8611, and section 42 for more information.

Supplemental Information

Line 20 (Schedule K-1 Only)

Enter in the line 20 Supplemental Information space of Schedule K-1, or on an attached schedule if more space is needed, each shareholder's share of any information asked for on lines 1 through 19 that is required to be reported in detail, and items 1 through 16 below. Please identify the applicable line number next to the information entered in the Supplemental Information space. Show income or gains as a positive number. Show losses in parentheses.

1. Tax-exempt interest income. Include exempt-interest dividends the corporation received as a shareholder in a mutual fund or other regulated investment company.

2. Nondeductible expenses incurred by the corporation.

3. Taxes paid on undistributed capital gains by a regulated investment company. As a shareholder of a regulated investment company, the corporation will receive notice on Form 2439, Notice to Shareholder of Undistributed Long-Term Capital Gains, that the company paid tax on undistributed capital gains.

4. Gross income and other information relating to oil and gas well properties that are reported to shareholders to allow them to figure the depletion deduction for oil and gas well properties. See section 613A(c)(11) for details.

The corporation cannot deduct depletion on oil and gas wells. Each shareholder must determine the allowable amount to report on his or her return. See Pub. 535 for more information.

5. Qualified exploratory costs. In order for each shareholder to compute the alternative minimum tax adjustment based on energy preferences, the corporation must identify the portion, if any, of intangible drilling and development costs shown on line 16a that is attributable to qualified exploratory costs. Identify this amount on line 20 as "Qualified exploratory costs included on line 16a." Qualified exploratory costs are intangible drilling and development costs paid or incurred in connection with the drilling of an exploratory well located in the United States. See section 56(h)(6) for more details.

6. Recapture of section 179 expense deduction. For property placed in service after 1986, the section 179 deduction is recaptured at any time the business use of property drops to 50% or less. Enter the amount that was originally passed through and the corporation's tax year in which it was passed through. Inform the shareholder if the recapture amount was caused by the disposition of the section 179 property. See section 179(d)(10) for more information. Do not include this amount on line 4 or 5, page 1, Form 1120S.

Page 19

7. Recapture of certain mining exploration expenditures (section 617).

8. Any information or statements the corporation is required to furnish to shareholders to allow them to comply with requirements under section 6111 (registration of tax shelters) or section 6662(d)(2)(B)(ii) (regarding adequate disclosure of items that may cause an understatement of income tax).

9. If the corporation is involved in farming or fishing activities, report the gross income from these activities to shareholders.

10. Any information needed by a shareholder to compute the interest due under section 453A(c). If an obligation arising from the disposition of property to which section 453A applies is outstanding at the close of the year, each shareholder's tax liability must be increased by the tax due under section 453(c) on the shareholder's pro rata share of the tax deferred under the installment method.

11. Any information needed by a shareholder to compute the interest due under section 453(l)(3). If the corporation elected to report the dispositions of certain timeshares and residential lots on the installment method, each shareholder's tax liability must be increased by the shareholder's pro rata share of the interest on tax attributable to the installment payments received during the tax year.

12. Any information needed by a shareholder to properly capitalize interest as required by section 263A(f). See **Section 263A uniform capitalization rules** on page 9 for additional information. See Notice 88-99 for more information.

13. If the corporation is a closely held S corporation (defined in section 460(b)) and it entered into any long-term contracts after February 28, 1986, that are accounted for under either the percentage of completion-capitalized cost method or the percentage of completion method, it must attach a schedule to Form 1120S showing the information required in items (a) and (b) of the instructions for lines 1 and 3 of Part II for **Form 8697,** Interest Computation Under the Look-Back Method for Completed Long-Term Contracts. It must also report the amounts for Part II, lines 1 and 3, to its shareholders. See the instructions for Form 8697 for more information.

14. Expenditures qualifying for the **(a)** rehabilitation credit not related to rental real estate activities, **(b)** energy credit, or **(c)** reforestation credit. Complete and attach Form 3468 to Form 1120S. See Form 3468 and related instructions for information on eligible property and the lines on Form 3468 to complete. Do not include that part of the cost of the property the corporation has elected to expense under section 179. Attach to each Schedule K-1 a separate schedule in a format similar to that shown on Form 3468 detailing each shareholder's pro rata share of qualified expenditures. Also indicate the lines of Form 3468 on which the shareholders should report these amounts.

15. Recapture of investment credit. Complete and attach **Form 4255,** Recapture of Investment Credit, when investment credit property is disposed of or it no longer qualifies for the credit. State the kind of property at the top of Form 4255, and complete lines 2, 3, 4, and 8, whether or not any shareholder is subject to recapture of the credit. Attach to each Schedule K-1 a separate schedule providing the information the corporation is required to show on Form 4255, but list only the shareholder's pro rata share of the cost of the property subject to recapture. Also indicate the lines of Form 4255 on which the shareholders should report these amounts.

The corporation itself is liable for investment credit recapture in certain cases. See the instructions for line 22c, page 1, Form 1120S, for details.

16. Any other information the shareholders need to prepare their tax returns.

Specific Instructions

Schedule L—Balance Sheets

The balance sheets should agree with the corporation's books and records. Include certificates of deposit as cash on line 1 of Schedule L.

Line 5—Tax-Exempt Securities

Include on this line:

1. State and local government obligations, the interest on which is excludible from gross income under section 103(a), and

2. Stock in a mutual fund or other regulated investment company that distributed exempt-interest dividends during the tax year of the corporation.

Line 24—Retained Earnings

If the corporation maintains separate accounts for appropriated and unappropriated retained earnings, it may want to continue such accounting for purposes of preparing its financial balance sheet. Also, if the corporation converts to C corporation status in a subsequent year, it will be required to report its appropriated and unappropriated retained earnings on separate lines of Schedule L of Form 1120.

Schedule M-1— Reconciliation of Income per Books With Income per Return

Line 3b—Travel and Entertainment

Include on this line: 20% of meals and entertainment not allowed under section 274(n); expenses for the use of an entertainment facility; the part of business gifts in excess of $25; expenses of an individual allocable to conventions on cruise ships in excess of $2,000; employee achievement awards in excess of $400; the cost of entertainment tickets in excess of face value (also subject to 20%

disallowance); the cost of skyboxes in excess of the face value of nonluxury box seat tickets; the part of the cost of luxury water travel not allowed under section 274(m); expenses for travel as a form of education; and other travel and entertainment expenses not allowed as a deduction.

Schedule M-2—Analysis of Accumulated Adjustments Account, Other Adjustments Account, and Shareholders' Undistributed Taxable Income Previously Taxed

Column (a)—Accumulated Adjustments Account

The accumulated adjustments account (AAA) is to be maintained by all S corporations.

At the end of the tax year, if the corporation **does not have accumulated earnings and profits (E&P),** the AAA is determined by taking into account all items of income, loss, and deductions for the tax year (including nontaxable income and nondeductible losses and expenses). See section 1368 for other details. After the year-end income and expense adjustments are made, the account is reduced by distributions made during the tax year. See **Distributions** below for distribution rules.

At the end of the tax year, if the corporation **has accumulated E&P,** the AAA is determined by taking into account the taxable income, deductible losses and expenses, and nondeductible losses and expenses for the tax year. Adjustments for nontaxable income are made to the other adjustments account as explained in the column (b) instruction below. See section 1368. After the year-end income and expense adjustments are made, the AAA is reduced by distributions made during the tax year. See **Distributions** below for distribution rules.

Note: *The AAA may have a negative balance at year end. See section 1368(e).*

Column (b)—Other Adjustments Account

The other adjustments account is maintained only by corporations that **have** accumulated E&P at year end. The account is adjusted for tax-exempt income (and related expenses) of the corporation. See section 1368. After adjusting for tax-exempt income, the account is reduced for any distributions made during the year. See **Distributions** below.

Column (c)—Shareholders' Undistributed Taxable Income Previously Taxed

The shareholders' undistributed taxable income previously taxed account, also called previously taxed income (PTI), is maintained only if the corporation had a balance in this account at the start of its 1991 tax year. If there is a beginning

Page 20

balance for the 1991 tax year, no adjustments are made to the account except to reduce the account for distributions made under section 1375(d) (as in effect before the enactment of the Subchapter S Revision Act of 1982). See **Distributions** below for the order of distributions from the account.

Each shareholder's right to nontaxable distributions from PTI is personal and cannot be transferred to another person. The corporation is required to keep records of each shareholder's net share of PTI.

Distributions

Generally, property distributions (including cash) are applied in the following order to reduce accounts of the S corporation that are used to compute the tax effect of distributions made by the corporation to its shareholders:

1. Reduce AAA (but not below zero). If distributions during the tax year exceed the AAA at the close of the tax year, the AAA is allocated pro rata to each distribution made during the tax year. See section 1368(c).

2. Reduce shareholders' PTI account for any section 1375(d) (as in effect before 1983) distributions. A distribution from the PTI account is tax free to the extent of a shareholder's basis in his or her stock in the corporation.

3. Reduce accumulated E&P. Generally, the S corporation has accumulated E&P only if it has not distributed E&P accumulated in prior years when the S corporation was a C corporation (section 1361(a)(2)) or a small business corporation prior to 1983 (section 1371 of prior law).

See section 312 for information on E&P. The only adjustments that can be made to the accumulated E&P of an S corporation are: **(a)** reductions for dividend distributions; **(b)** adjustments for redemptions, liquidations, reorganizations, etc.; and **(c)** reductions for investment credit recapture tax for which the corporation is liable. See sections 1371(c) and (d)(3).

4. Reduce the other adjustments account.

5. Reduce any remaining shareholders' equity accounts.

If the corporation has accumulated E&P and wants to distribute this E&P before making distributions from the AAA, it may elect to do so with the consent of all its affected shareholders (section 1368(e)(3)). If the corporation has PTI and wants to make distributions from retained earnings before making distributions from PTI, it may elect to do so with the consent of all its shareholders. The statement of election must be attached to a timely filed Form 1120S for the tax year during which the distributions are made. The election must be made separately for each tax year.

In the case of either election, after all accumulated E&P in the retained earnings are distributed, the above general order of distributions applies except that item **3** is eliminated.

Example

The following example for a corporation that has accumulated E&P shows how the Schedule M-2 accounts are adjusted for items of income (loss), deductions, and distributions reported on Form 1120S.

Items per return are:

1. Page 1, line 21 income—$219,000

2. Schedule K, line 2 loss—($3,000)

3. Schedule K, line 4a income—$4,000

4. Schedule K, line 4b income—$16,000

5. Schedule K, line 7 deduction—$24,000

6. Schedule K, line 11a deduction—$3,000

7. Schedule K, line 13 jobs credit—$6,000

8. Schedule K, line 17 distributions—$65,000, and

9. Schedule K, line 18 scheduled items:

a. Tax-exempt income—$5,000, and

b. Nondeductible expense—$6,000 (reduction in salaries and wages for jobs credit).

Based on return items 1 through 9 and starting balances of zero, the columns for the AAA and the other adjustments account are completed as shown in the Schedule M-2 Worksheet below.

Note: *For the AAA account, the worksheet line 3—$20,000 amount is the total of the Schedule K, lines 4a and 4b incomes of $4,000 and $16,000. The worksheet line 5—$36,000 amount is the total of the Schedule K, line 2 loss of ($3,000), line 7 deduction of $24,000, line 11a deduction of $3,000, and the line 18 nondeductible expense item of $6,000. For the other adjustments account, the worksheet line 3 amount is the Schedule K, line 18, tax-exempt income of $5,000. Other worksheet amounts are self-explanatory.*

Schedule M-2 Worksheet

		(a) Accumulated adjustments account	(b) Other adjustments account	(c) Shareholders' undistributed taxable income previously taxed
1	Balance at beginning of tax year . . .	-0-	-0-	
2	Ordinary income from page 1, line 21 .	219,000		
3	Other additions	20,000	5,000	
4	Loss from page 1, line 21	( )		
5	Other reductions	(36,000)	( )	
6	Combine lines 1 through 5	203,000	5,000	
7	Distributions other than dividend distributions	65,000	-0-	
8	Balance at end of tax year. Subtract line 7 from line 6	138,000	5,000	

Codes for Principal Business Activity

These codes for the Principal Business Activity are designed to classify enterprises by the type of activity in which they are engaged to facilitate the administration of the Internal Revenue Code. Though similar in format and structure to the Standard Industrial Classification (SIC) codes, they should not be used as SIC codes.

Using the list below, enter on page 1, under B, the code number for the specific industry group from which the largest percentage of "total receipts" is derived. "Total receipts" means the total of: gross receipts on line 1a, page 1; all other income on lines 4 and 5, page 1; all income on lines 2, 19, and 20a of Form 8825; and income (receipts only) on lines 3a and 4a through 4f of Schedule K.

On page 2, Schedule B, line 2, state the principal business activity and principal product or service that account for the largest percentage of total receipts. For example, if the principal business activity is "Grain mill products," the principal product or service may be "Cereal preparations."

If, as its principal business activity, the corporation: (1) purchases raw materials, (2) subcontracts out for labor to make a finished product from the raw materials, and (3) retains title to the goods, the corporation is considered to be a manufacturer and must enter one of the codes (2010–3998) under "Manufacturing."

Agriculture, Forestry, and Fishing
Code
0400 Agricultural production.
0600 Agricultural services (except veterinarians), forestry, fishing, hunting, and trapping.

Mining
Metal mining:
1010 Iron ores.
1070 Copper, lead and zinc, gold and silver ores.
1098 Other metal mining.
1150 Coal mining.
Oil and gas extraction:
1330 Crude petroleum, natural gas, and natural gas liquids.
1380 Oil and gas field services.
Nonmetallic minerals, except fuels:
1430 Dimension, crushed and broken stone; sand and gravel.
1498 Other nonmetallic minerals, except fuels.

Construction
General building contractors and operative builders:
1510 General building contractors.
1531 Operative builders.
1600 Heavy construction contractors.
Special trade contractors:
1711 Plumbing, heating, and air conditioning.
1731 Electrical work.
1798 Other special trade contractors.

Manufacturing
Food and kindred products:
2010 Meat products.
2020 Dairy products.
2030 Preserved fruits and vegetables.
2040 Grain mill products.
2050 Bakery products.
2060 Sugar and confectionery products.
2081 Malt liquors and malt.
2088 Alcoholic beverages, except malt liquors and malt.
2089 Bottled soft drinks, and flavorings.
2096 Other food and kindred products.

2100 Tobacco manufacturers.

Textile mill products:
2228 Weaving mills and textile finishing.
2250 Knitting mills.
2298 Other textile mill products.

Apparel and other textile products:
2315 Men's and boys' clothing.
2345 Women's and children's clothing.
2388 Other apparel and accessories.
2390 Miscellaneous fabricated textile products.

Lumber and wood products:
2415 Logging, sawmills, and planing mills.
2430 Millwork, plywood, and related products.
2498 Other wood products, including wood buildings and mobile homes.

2500 Furniture and fixtures.

Paper and allied products:
2625 Pulp, paper, and board mills.
2699 Other paper products.

Printing and publishing:
2710 Newspapers.
2720 Periodicals.
2735 Books, greeting cards, and miscellaneous publishing.
2799 Commercial and other printing, and printing trade services.

Chemicals and allied products:
2815 Industrial chemicals, plastics materials and synthetics.
2830 Drugs.
2840 Soap, cleaners, and toilet goods.
2850 Paints and allied products.
2898 Agricultural and other chemical products.

Petroleum refining and related industries (including those integrated with extraction):
2910 Petroleum refining (including integrated).
2998 Other petroleum and coal products.

Rubber and misc. plastics products:
3050 Rubber products: plastics footwear, hose, and belting.
3070 Misc. plastics products.

Leather and leather products:
3140 Footwear, except rubber.
3198 Other leather and leather products.

Stone, clay, and glass products:
3225 Glass products.
3240 Cement, hydraulic.
3270 Concrete, gypsum, and plaster products.
3298 Other nonmetallic mineral products.

Primary metal industries:
3370 Ferrous metal industries; misc. primary metal products.
3380 Nonferrous metal industries.

Fabricated metal products:
3410 Metal cans and shipping containers.
3428 Cutlery, hand tools, and hardware; screw machine products, bolts, and similar products.
3430 Plumbing and heating, except electric and warm air.
3440 Fabricated structural metal products.
3460 Metal forgings and stampings.
3470 Coating, engraving, and allied services.
3480 Ordnance and accessories, except vehicles and guided missiles.
3490 Misc. fabricated metal products.

Machinery, except electrical:
3520 Farm machinery.
3530 Construction and related machinery.
3540 Metalworking machinery.
3550 Special industry machinery.
3560 General industrial machinery.
3570 Office, computing, and accounting machines.
3598 Other machinery except electrical.

Electrical and electronic equipment:
3630 Household appliances.
3665 Radio, television, and communications equipment.
3670 Electronic components and accessories.
3698 Other electrical equipment.

3710 Motor vehicles and equipment.

Transportation equipment, except motor vehicles:
3725 Aircraft, guided missiles and parts.
3730 Ship and boat building and repairing.
3798 Other transportation equipment, except motor vehicles.

Instruments and related products:
3815 Scientific instruments and measuring devices; watches and clocks.
3845 Optical, medical, and ophthalmic goods.
3860 Photographic equipment and supplies.

3998 Other manufacturing products.

Transportation and Public Utilities
Code
Transportation:
4000 Railroad transportation.
4100 Local and interurban passenger transit.
4200 Trucking and warehousing.
4400 Water transportation.
4500 Transportation by air.
4600 Pipe lines, except natural gas.
4700 Miscellaneous transportation services.
Communication:
4825 Telephone, telegraph, and other communication services.
4830 Radio and television broadcasting.
Electric, gas, and sanitary services:
4910 Electric services.
4920 Gas production and distribution.
4930 Combination utility services.
4990 Water supply and other sanitary services.

Wholesale Trade
Durable:
5008 Machinery, equipment, and supplies.
5010 Motor vehicles and automotive equipment.
5020 Furniture and home furnishings.
5030 Lumber and construction materials.
5040 Sporting, recreational, photographic, and hobby goods, toys and supplies.
5050 Metals and minerals, except petroleum and scrap.
5060 Electrical goods.
5070 Hardware, plumbing and heating equipment and supplies.
5098 Other durable goods.
Nondurable:
5110 Paper and paper products.
5129 Drugs, drug proprietaries, and druggists' sundries.
5130 Apparel, piece goods, and notions.
5140 Groceries and related products.
5150 Farm-product raw materials.
5160 Chemicals and allied products.
5170 Petroleum and petroleum products.
5180 Alcoholic beverages.
5190 Misc. nondurable goods.

Retail Trade
Building materials, garden supplies, and mobile home dealers:
5220 Building materials dealers.
5251 Hardware stores.
5265 Garden supplies and mobile home dealers.

5300 General merchandise stores.

Food stores:
5410 Grocery stores.
5490 Other food stores.

Automotive dealers and service stations:
5515 Motor vehicle dealers.
5541 Gasoline service stations.
5598 Other automotive dealers.

5600 Apparel and accessory stores.

5700 Furniture and home furnishings stores.

5800 Eating and drinking places.

Misc. retail stores:
5912 Drug stores and proprietary stores.
5921 Liquor stores.
5995 Other retail stores.

Finance, Insurance, and Real Estate
Code
Banking:
6030 Mutual savings banks.
6060 Bank holding companies.
6090 Banks, except mutual savings banks and bank holding companies.

Credit agencies other than banks:
6120 Savings and loan associations.
6140 Personal credit institutions.
6150 Business credit institutions.
6199 Other credit agencies.

Security, commodity brokers and services:
6210 Security brokers, dealers, and flotation companies.
6299 Commodity contracts brokers and dealers; security and commodity exchanges; and allied services.

Insurance:
6355 Life insurance.
6356 Mutual insurance, except life or marine and certain fire or flood insurance companies.
6359 Other insurance companies.
6411 Insurance agents, brokers, and service.

Real estate:
6511 Real estate operators and lessors of buildings.
6516 Lessors of mining, oil, and similar property.
6518 Lessors of railroad property and other real property.
6530 Condominium management and cooperative housing associations.
6550 Subdividers and developers.
6599 Other real estate.

Holding and other investment companies, except bank holding companies:
6744 Small business investment companies.
6749 Other holding and investment companies, except bank holding companies.

Services
7000 Hotels and other lodging places.
7200 Personal services.

Business services:
7310 Advertising.
7389 Business services, except advertising.

Auto repair; miscellaneous repair services:
7500 Auto repair and services.
7600 Misc. repair services.

Amusement and recreation services:
7812 Motion picture production, distribution, and services.
7830 Motion picture theaters.
7900 Amusement and recreation services, except motion pictures.

Other services:
8015 Offices of physicians, including osteopathic physicians.
8021 Offices of dentists.
8040 Offices of other health practitioners.
8050 Nursing and personal care facilities.
8060 Hospitals.
8071 Medical laboratories.
8099 Other medical services.
8111 Legal services.
8200 Educational services.
8300 Social services.
8600 Membership organizations.
8911 Architectural and engineering services.
8930 Accounting, auditing, and bookkeeping.
8980 Miscellaneous services (including veterinarians).

☆ U.S. Government Printing Office: 1991-285-274

Form 1120S — U.S. Income Tax Return for an S Corporation

Form 1120S
Department of the Treasury
Internal Revenue Service

For calendar year 1991, or tax year beginning ...., 1991, and ending ...., 19 .....
▶ See separate instructions.

OMB No. 1545-0130

1991

A Date of election as an S corporation
12-1-90

B Business code no. (see Specific Instructions)
5008

Use IRS label. Otherwise, please print or type.

10-4487965   DEC91 D74 3070
STRATOTECH, INC.
482 WINSTON STREET
METRO CITY   OH   43705

C Employer Identification number
10-4487965

D Date incorporated
3-1-73

E Total assets (see Specific Instructions)
$ **825,714**

F Check applicable boxes: (1) ☑ Initial return (2) ☐ Final return (3) ☐ Change in address (4) ☐ Amended return
G Check this box if this S corporation is subject to the consolidated audit procedures of sections 6241 through 6245 (see instructions before checking this box) . ▶ ☐
H Enter number of shareholders in the corporation at end of the tax year .... ▶ **6**

Caution: *Include only trade or business income and expenses on lines 1a through 21. See the instructions for more information.*

Income

1a	Gross receipts or sales **1,545,700**	b Less returns and allowances **21,000**	c Bal ▶ 1c **1,524,700**
2	Cost of goods sold (Schedule A, line 8)		2 **954,700**
3	Gross profit. Subtract line 2 from line 1c		3 **570,000**
4	Net gain (loss) from Form 4797, Part II, line 18 (attach Form 4797)		4 **-0-**
5	Other income (see instructions) (attach schedule)		5 **-0-**
6	Total income (loss). Combine lines 3 through 5 ▶		6 **570,000**

Deductions (See instructions for limitations.)

7	Compensation of officers		7 **170,000**
8a	Salaries and wages **144,000**	b Less jobs credit **6,000**	c Bal ▶ 8c **138,000**
9	Repairs		9 **800**
10	Bad debts		10 **1,600**
11	Rents		11 **9,200**
12	Taxes		12 **15,000**
13	Interest		13 **24,200**
14a	Depreciation (see instructions)	14a **5,200**	
b	Depreciation claimed on Schedule A and elsewhere on return	14b **-0-**	
c	Subtract line 14b from line 14a		14c **5,200**
15	Depletion (Do not deduct oil and gas depletion.)		15 **-0-**
16	Advertising		16 **8,700**
17	Pension, profit-sharing, etc., plans		17 **-0-**
18	Employee benefit programs		18 **-0-**
19	Other deductions (attach schedule)		19 **78,300**
20	Total deductions. Add lines 7 through 19 ▶		20 **451,000**
21	Ordinary income (loss) from trade or business activities. Subtract line 20 from line 6		21 **119,000**

Tax and Payments

22	**Tax:**		
a	Excess net passive income tax (attach schedule)	22a	
b	Tax from Schedule D (Form 1120S)	22b	
c	Add lines 22a and 22b (see instructions for additional taxes)		22c **-0-**
23	**Payments:**		
a	1991 estimated tax payments	23a	
b	Tax deposited with Form 7004	23b	
c	Credit for Federal tax on fuels (attach Form 4136)	23c	
d	Add lines 23a through 23c		23d **-0-**
24	Estimated tax penalty (see page 3 of instructions). Check if Form 2220 is attached . . ▶ ☐		24
25	Tax due. If the total of lines 22c and 24 is larger than line 23d, enter amount owed. See instructions for depositary method of payment ▶		25 **-0-**
26	Overpayment. If line 23d is larger than the total of lines 22c and 24, enter amount overpaid ▶		26 **-0-**
27	Enter amount of line 26 you want: Credited to 1992 estimated tax ▶ Refunded ▶		27 **-0-**

Please Sign Here

Under penalties of perjury, I declare that I have examined this return, including accompanying schedules and statements, and to the best of my knowledge and belief, it is true, correct, and complete. Declaration of preparer (other than taxpayer) is based on all information of which preparer has any knowledge.

Signature of officer: *John H. Green*   Date: **3-10-92**   Title: **President**

Paid Preparer's Use Only

Preparer's signature ▶		Date	Check if self-employed ▶ ☐	Preparer's social security number
Firm's name (or yours if self-employed) and address ▶			E.I. No ▶	
			ZIP code ▶	

For Paperwork Reduction Act Notice, see page 1 of separate instructions.   Cat. No. 11510H   Form **1120S** (1991)

15

Schedule A   Cost of Goods Sold (See instructions.)

1	Inventory at beginning of year	**1** 126,000
2	Purchases.	**2** 1,127,100
3	Cost of labor	**3** -0-
4	Additional section 263A costs (see instructions) *(attach schedule)*	**4** -0-
5	Other costs *(attach schedule)*.	**5** -0-
6	Total. Add lines 1 through 5	**6** 1,253,100
7	Inventory at end of year	**7** 298,400
8	Cost of goods sold. Subtract line 7 from line 6. Enter here and on line 2, page 1 . . .	**8** 954,700

9a   Check all methods used for valuing closing inventory:

  (i) ☐ Cost

  (ii) ☑ Lower of cost or market as described in Regulations section 1.471-4

  (iii) ☐ Writedown of "subnormal" goods as described in Regulations section 1.471-2(c)

  (iv) ☐ Other (specify method used and attach explanation) ▶ .... ☐

  b   Check if the LIFO inventory method was adopted this tax year for any goods *(if checked, attach Form 970)*. . . . . . ▶ ☐

  c   If the LIFO inventory method was used for this tax year, enter percentage (or amounts) of closing
      inventory computed under LIFO **9c**

  d   Do the rules of section 263A (for property produced or acquired for resale) apply to the corporation? . . . . ☐ Yes ☑ No

  e   Was there any change in determining quantities, cost, or valuations between opening and closing inventory? . . ☐ Yes ☑ No
      If "Yes," attach explanation.

Schedule B   Other Information

		Yes	No
1	Check method of accounting: (a) ☐ Cash (b) ☑ Accrual (c) ☐ Other (specify) ▶		
2	Refer to the list in the instructions and state your principal: (a) Business activity ▶ **5008 – Distributor** (b) Product or service ▶ **Heavy Equipment**		
3	Did you at the end of the tax year own, directly or indirectly, 50% or more of the voting stock of a domestic corporation? (For rules of attribution, see section 267(c).) If "Yes," attach a schedule showing: (a) name, address, and employer identification number and (b) percentage owned.		✓
4	Were you a member of a controlled group subject to the provisions of section 1561?		✓
5	At any time during the tax year, did you have an interest in or a signature or other authority over a financial account in a foreign country (such as a bank account, securities account, or other financial account)? (See instructions for exceptions and filing requirements for form TD F 90-22.1.) . . . . If "Yes," enter the name of the foreign country ▶		✓
6	Were you the grantor of, or transferor to, a foreign trust that existed during the current tax year, whether or not you have any beneficial interest in it? If "Yes," you may have to file Forms 3520, 3520-A, or 926		✓
7	Check this box if the corporation has filed or is required to file **Form 8264**, Application for Registration of a Tax Shelter . . . . ▶ ☐		
8	Check this box if the corporation issued publicly offered debt instruments with original issue discount . . . ▶ ☐ If so, the corporation may have to file **Form 8281**, Information Return for Publicly Offered Original Issue Discount Instruments.		
9	If the corporation: (a) filed its election to be an S corporation after 1986, (b) was a C corporation before it elected to be an S corporation or the corporation acquired an asset with a basis determined by reference to its basis (or the basis of any other property) in the hands of a C corporation, and (c) has net unrealized built-in gain (defined in section 1374(d)(1)) in excess of the net recognized built-in gain from prior years, enter the net unrealized built-in gain reduced by net recognized built-in gain from prior years (see instructions) . . . . . . ▶ $ 37,200		
10	Check this box if the corporation had subchapter C earnings and profits at the close of the tax year (see instructions) . . . . ▶ ☑		

Designation of Tax Matters Person (See instructions.)

Enter below the shareholder designated as the tax matters person (TMP) for the tax year of this return:

Name of
designated TMP ▶ **John H. Green**   Identifying
                                            number of TMP ▶ **458-00-0327**

Address of
designated TMP ▶ **4340 Holmes Parkway, Metro City, OH 43704**

Schedule K — Shareholders' Shares of Income, Credits, Deductions, etc.

	(a) Pro rata share items		(b) Total amount
Income (Loss)	**1** Ordinary income (loss) from trade or business activities (page 1, line 21)	**1**	119,000
	2 Net income (loss) from rental real estate activities (attach Form 8825)	**2**	
	3a Gross income from other rental activities **3a**		
	b Less expenses (attach schedule). **3b**		
	c Net income (loss) from other rental activities	**3c**	
	4 Portfolio income (loss):		
	a Interest income	**4a**	4,000
	b Dividend income.	**4b**	16,000
	c Royalty income	**4c**	
	d Net short-term capital gain (loss) (attach Schedule D (Form 1120S))	**4d**	
	e Net long-term capital gain (loss) (attach Schedule D (Form 1120S)).	**4e**	
	f Other portfolio income (loss) (attach schedule)	**4f**	
	5 Net gain (loss) under section 1231 (other than due to casualty or theft) (attach Form 4797)	**5**	
	6 Other income (loss) (attach schedule)	**6**	
Deductions	**7** Charitable contributions (see instructions) (attach list)	**7**	24,000
	8 Section 179 expense deduction (attach Form 4562).	**8**	
	9 Deductions related to portfolio income (loss) (see instructions) (itemize)	**9**	
	10 Other deductions (attach schedule).	**10**	
Investment Interest	**11a** Interest expense on investment debts	**11a**	3,000
	b (1) Investment income included on lines 4a through 4f above	**11b(1)**	20,000
	(2) Investment expenses included on line 9 above	**11b(2)**	
Credits	**12a** Credit for alcohol used as a fuel (attach Form 6478)	**12a**	
	b Low-income housing credit (see instructions):		
	(1) From partnerships to which section 42(j)(5) applies for property placed in service before 1990	**12b(1)**	
	(2) Other than on line 12b(1) for property placed in service before 1990.	**12b(2)**	
	(3) From partnerships to which section 42(j)(5) applies for property placed in service after 1989	**12b(3)**	
	(4) Other than on line 12b(3) for property placed in service after 1989	**12b(4)**	
	c Qualified rehabilitation expenditures related to rental real estate activities (attach Form 3468)	**12c**	
	d Credits (other than credits shown on lines 12b and 12c) related to rental real estate activities (see instructions).	**12d**	
	e Credits related to other rental activities (see instructions)	**12e**	
	13 Other credits (see instructions) . . . Jobs Credit.	**13**	6,000
Adjustments and Tax Preference Items	**14a** Accelerated depreciation of real property placed in service before 1987	**14a**	
	b Accelerated depreciation of leased personal property placed in service before 1987	**14b**	
	c Depreciation adjustment on property placed in service after 1986	**14c**	
	d Depletion (other than oil and gas)	**14d**	
	e (1) Gross income from oil, gas, or geothermal properties	**14e(1)**	
	(2) Deductions allocable to oil, gas, or geothermal properties	**14e(2)**	
	f Other adjustments and tax preference items (attach schedule)	**14f**	
Foreign Taxes	**15a** Type of income ▶		
	b Name of foreign country or U.S. possession ▶		
	c Total gross income from sources outside the United States (attach schedule)	**15c**	
	d Total applicable deductions and losses (attach schedule)	**15d**	
	e Total foreign taxes (check one): ▶ ☐ Paid ☐ Accrued	**15e**	
	f Reduction in taxes available for credit (attach schedule)	**15f**	
	g Other foreign tax information (attach schedule)	**15g**	
Other	**16a** Total expenditures to which a section 59(e) election may apply	**16a**	
	b Type of expenditures ▶		
	17 Total property distributions (including cash) other than dividends reported on line 19 below	**17**	65,000
	18 Other items and amounts required to be reported separately to shareholders (see instructions) (attach schedule)		
	19 Total dividend distributions paid from accumulated earnings and profits	**19**	
	20 Income (loss) (Required only if Schedule M-1 must be completed.). Combine lines 1 through 6 in column (b). From the result, subtract the sum of lines 7 through 11a, 15e, and 16a	**20**	112,000

17

Schedule L　Balance Sheets

	Beginning of tax year		End of tax year	
Assets	(a)	(b)	(c)	(d)
1 Cash		14,700		14,514
2a Trade notes and accounts receivable	98,400		33,700	
b Less allowance for bad debts		98,400		33,700
3 Inventories		126,000		298,400
4 U.S. Government obligations				
5 Tax-exempt securities		100,000		120,000
6 Other current assets (attach schedule)		26,300		26,300
7 Loans to shareholders				
8 Mortgage and real estate loans				
9 Other investments (attach schedule)		100,000		100,000
10a Buildings and other depreciable assets	204,700		198,700	
b Less accumulated depreciation	6,000	198,700	5,200	193,500
11a Depletable assets				
b Less accumulated depletion				
12 Land (net of any amortization)		20,000		20,000
13a Intangible assets (amortizable only)				
b Less accumulated amortization				
14 Other assets (attach schedule)		14,800		19,300
15 Total assets		698,900		825,714
Liabilities and Shareholders' Equity				
16 Accounts payable		28,500		34,834
17 Mortgages, notes, bonds payable in less than 1 year		4,300		4,300
18 Other current liabilities (attach schedule)		6,800		7,400
19 Loans from shareholders				
20 Mortgages, notes, bonds payable in 1 year or more		191,300		265,180
21 Other liabilities (attach schedule)		200,000		200,000
22 Capital stock				
23 Paid-in or capital surplus				
24 Retained earnings		268,000		314,000
25 Less cost of treasury stock		( )		( )
26 Total liabilities and shareholders' equity		698,900		825,714

Schedule M-1　Reconciliation of Income per Books With Income per Return (You are not required to complete this schedule if the total assets on line 15, column (d), of Schedule L are less than $25,000.)

1 Net income per books	102,270	5 Income recorded on books this year not included on Schedule K, lines 1 through 6 (itemize):		
2 Income included on Schedule K, lines 1 through 6, not recorded on books this year (itemize):		a Tax-exempt interest $ 5,000		5,000
	-0-			
3 Expenses recorded on books this year not included on Schedule K, lines 1 through 11a, 15e, and 16a (itemize):		6 Deductions included on Schedule K, lines 1 through 11a, 15e, and 16a, not charged against book income this year (itemize):		
a Depreciation $		a Depreciation $ 1,620		
b Travel and entertainment $ (Itemized statement attached)				1,620
	16,350	7 Add lines 5 and 6		6,620
4 Add lines 1 through 3	118,620	8 Income (loss) (Schedule K, line 20). Line 4 less line 7		112,000

Schedule M-2　Analysis of Accumulated Adjustments Account, Other Adjustments Account, and Shareholders' Undistributed Taxable Income Previously Taxed (See instructions.)

	(a) Accumulated adjustments account	(b) Other adjustments account	(c) Shareholders' undistributed taxable income previously taxed
1 Balance at beginning of tax year	-0-	-0-	
2 Ordinary income from page 1, line 21	119,000		
3 Other additions	20,000	5,000	
4 Loss from page 1, line 21	(-0-)		
5 Other reductions	(33,000)	(-0-)	
6 Combine lines 1 through 5	106,000	5,000	
7 Distributions other than dividend distributions	65,000	-0-	
8 Balance at end of tax year. Subtract line 7 from line 6	41,000	5,000	

20

Form **1120S**

Department of the Treasury
Internal Revenue Service

U.S. Income Tax Return for an S Corporation

For calendar year 1991, or tax year beginning .... , 1991, and ending .... , 19 .....
► **See separate instructions.**

OMB No. 1545-0130

19 91

A Date of election as an S corporation	**Use IRS label. Other-wise, please print or type.**	Name
		Number, street, and room or suite no. (If a P.O. box, see page 8 of the instructions.)
B Business code no. (see Specific Instructions)		City or town, state, and ZIP code

C Employer identification number

D Date incorporated

E Total assets (see Specific Instructions)
$

F Check applicable boxes: (1) ☐ Initial return (2) ☐ Final return (3) ☐ Change in address (4) ☐ Amended return

G Check this box if this S corporation is subject to the consolidated audit procedures of sections 6241 through 6245 (see instructions before checking this box) . ► ☐

H Enter number of shareholders in the corporation at end of the tax year . . . . ►

Caution: *Include **only** trade or business income and expenses on lines 1a through 21. See the instructions for more information.*

Income

1a Gross receipts or sales		**b** Less returns and allowances	**c** Bal ►	**1c**
2	Cost of goods sold (Schedule A, line 8)		**2**
3	Gross profit. Subtract line 2 from line 1c		**3**
4	Net gain (loss) from Form 4797, Part II, line 18 *(attach Form 4797)*		**4**
5	Other income (see instructions) *(attach schedule)*		**5**
6	**Total income (loss).** Combine lines 3 through 5 . . . . ►		**6**

Deductions (See instructions for limitations.)

7	Compensation of officers	**7**
8a Salaries and wages	**b** Less jobs credit	**c** Bal ►	**8c**
9	Repairs	**9**
10	Bad debts	**10**
11	Rents	**11**
12	Taxes	**12**
13	Interest	**13**
14a	Depreciation (see instructions) **14a**	
b	Depreciation claimed on Schedule A and elsewhere on return **14b**	
c	Subtract line 14b from line 14a	**14c**
15	Depletion **(Do not deduct oil and gas depletion.)**	**15**
16	Advertising	**16**
17	Pension, profit-sharing, etc., plans	**17**
18	Employee benefit programs	**18**
19	Other deductions *(attach schedule)*	**19**
20	**Total deductions.** Add lines 7 through 19 . . . . ►	**20**
21	Ordinary income (loss) from trade or business activities. Subtract line 20 from line 6	**21**

Tax and Payments

22	**Tax:**	
a	Excess net passive income tax *(attach schedule)* **22a**	
b	Tax from Schedule D (Form 1120S) **22b**	
c	Add lines 22a and 22b (see instructions for additional taxes)	**22c**
23	**Payments:**	
a	1991 estimated tax payments **23a**	
b	Tax deposited with Form 7004 . . . . **23b**	
c	Credit for Federal tax on fuels *(attach Form 4136)* . **23c**	
d	Add lines 23a through 23c	**23d**
24	Estimated tax penalty (see page 3 of instructions). Check if Form 2220 is attached . . ► ☐	**24**
25	**Tax due.** If the total of lines 22c and 24 is larger than line 23d, enter amount owed. See instructions for depositary method of payment . . . . ►	**25**
26	**Overpayment.** If line 23d is larger than the total of lines 22c and 24, enter amount overpaid ►	**26**
27	Enter amount of line 26 you want: **Credited to 1992 estimated tax ►**	**Refunded ►**	**27**

Please Sign Here

Under penalties of perjury, I declare that I have examined this return, including accompanying schedules and statements, and to the best of my knowledge and belief, it is true, correct, and complete. Declaration of preparer (other than taxpayer) is based on all information of which preparer has any knowledge.

► _____ Signature of officer | Date | ► _____ Title

Paid Preparer's Use Only

Preparer's signature ►		Date	Check if self-employed ► ☐	Preparer's social security number
Firm's name (or yours if self-employed) and address ►			E.I. No. ►
			ZIP code ►

For Paperwork Reduction Act Notice, see page 1 of separate instructions.   Cat. No. 11510H   Form **1120S** (1991)

Schedule A   **Cost of Goods Sold** (See instructions.)

1	Inventory at beginning of year	**1**
2	Purchases.	**2**
3	Cost of labor	**3**
4	Additional section 263A costs (see instructions) *(attach schedule)*	**4**
5	Other costs *(attach schedule)*.	**5**
6	**Total.** Add lines 1 through 5	**6**
7	Inventory at end of year	**7**
8	**Cost of goods sold.** Subtract line 7 from line 6. Enter here and on line 2, page 1	**8**

9a Check all methods used for valuing closing inventory:

    (i) ☐ Cost

    (ii) ☐ Lower of cost or market as described in Regulations section 1.471-4

    (iii) ☐ Writedown of "subnormal" goods as described in Regulations section 1.471-2(c)

    (iv) ☐ Other (specify method used and attach explanation) ▶ ....

  b Check if the LIFO inventory method was adopted this tax year for any goods *(if checked, attach Form 970).* . . . . . ▶ ☐

  c If the LIFO inventory method was used for this tax year, enter percentage (or amounts) of closing inventory computed under LIFO **9c**

  d Do the rules of section 263A (for property produced or acquired for resale) apply to the corporation? . . . . ☐ Yes ☐ No

  e Was there any change in determining quantities, cost, or valuations between opening and closing inventory? . . ☐ Yes ☐ No

    If "Yes," attach explanation.

Schedule B   **Other Information**

		Yes	No
1	Check method of accounting: **(a)** ☐ Cash **(b)** ☐ Accrual **(c)** ☐ Other (specify) ▶		
2	Refer to the list in the instructions and state your principal:		
	(a) Business activity ▶ .... **(b)** Product or service ▶		
3	Did you at the end of the tax year own, directly or indirectly, 50% or more of the voting stock of a domestic corporation? (For rules of attribution, see section 267(c).) If "Yes," attach a schedule showing: **(a)** name, address, and employer identification number and **(b)** percentage owned.		
4	Were you a member of a controlled group subject to the provisions of section 1561?		
5	At any time during the tax year, did you have an interest in or a signature or other authority over a financial account in a foreign country (such as a bank account, securities account, or other financial account)? (See instructions for exceptions and filing requirements for form TD F 90-22.1.)		
	If "Yes," enter the name of the foreign country ▶		
6	Were you the grantor of, or transferor to, a foreign trust that existed during the current tax year, whether or not you have any beneficial interest in it? If "Yes," you may have to file Forms 3520, 3520-A, or 926		
7	Check this box if the corporation has filed or is required to file **Form 8264,** Application for Registration of a Tax Shelter . . . . ▶ ☐		
8	Check this box if the corporation issued publicly offered debt instruments with original issue discount . . . ▶ ☐		
	If so, the corporation may have to file **Form 8281,** Information Return for Publicly Offered Original Issue Discount Instruments.		
9	If the corporation: **(a)** filed its election to be an S corporation after 1986, **(b)** was a C corporation before it elected to be an S corporation **or** the corporation acquired an asset with a basis determined by reference to its basis (or the basis of any other property) in the hands of a C corporation, and **(c)** has net unrealized built-in gain (defined in section 1374(d)(1)) in excess of the net recognized built-in gain from prior years, enter the net unrealized built-in gain reduced by net recognized built-in gain from prior years (see instructions) . . . . ▶ $..................		
10	Check this box if the corporation had subchapter C earnings and profits at the close of the tax year (see instructions) . . . . ▶ ☐		

Designation of Tax Matters Person (See instructions.)

Enter below the shareholder designated as the tax matters person (TMP) for the tax year of this return:

Name of designated TMP ▶	Identifying number of TMP ▶

Address of designated TMP ▶ _____

Schedule K　Shareholders' Shares of Income, Credits, Deductions, etc.

	(a) Pro rata share items		(b) Total amount
Income (Loss)	1　Ordinary income (loss) from trade or business activities (page 1, line 21)	**1**	
	2　Net income (loss) from rental real estate activities *(attach Form 8825)*	**2**	
	3a　Gross income from other rental activities　**3a**		
	b　Less expenses *(attach schedule)*.　**3b**		
	c　Net income (loss) from other rental activities	**3c**	
	4　Portfolio income (loss):		
	a　Interest income	**4a**	
	b　Dividend income.	**4b**	
	c　Royalty income	**4c**	
	d　Net short-term capital gain (loss) *(attach Schedule D (Form 1120S))*	**4d**	
	e　Net long-term capital gain (loss) *(attach Schedule D (Form 1120S))*.	**4e**	
	f　Other portfolio income (loss) *(attach schedule)*	**4f**	
	5　Net gain (loss) under section 1231 (other than due to casualty or theft) *(attach Form 4797)*	**5**	
	6　Other income (loss) *(attach schedule)*	**6**	
Deductions	7　Charitable contributions (see instructions) *(attach list)*	**7**	
	8　Section 179 expense deduction *(attach Form 4562)*.	**8**	
	9　Deductions related to portfolio income (loss) (see instructions) (itemize)	**9**	
	10　Other deductions *(attach schedule)*.	**10**	
Investment Interest	11a　Interest expense on investment debts	**11a**	
	b (1)　Investment income included on lines 4a through 4f above	**11b(1)**	
	(2)　Investment expenses included on line 9 above	**11b(2)**	
Credits	12a　Credit for alcohol used as a fuel *(attach Form 6478)*	**12a**	
	b　Low-income housing credit (see instructions):		
	(1)　From partnerships to which section 42(j)(5) applies for property placed in service before 1990	**12b(1)**	
	(2)　Other than on line 12b(1) for property placed in service before 1990.	**12b(2)**	
	(3)　From partnerships to which section 42(j)(5) applies for property placed in service after 1989	**12b(3)**	
	(4)　Other than on line 12b(3) for property placed in service after 1989	**12b(4)**	
	c　Qualified rehabilitation expenditures related to rental real estate activities *(attach Form 3468)*.	**12c**	
	d　Credits (other than credits shown on lines 12b and 12c) related to rental real estate activities (see instructions).	**12d**	
	e　Credits related to other rental activities (see instructions)	**12e**	
	13　Other credits (see instructions)	**13**	
Adjustments and Tax Preference Items	14a　Accelerated depreciation of real property placed in service before 1987	**14a**	
	b　Accelerated depreciation of leased personal property placed in service before 1987	**14b**	
	c　Depreciation adjustment on property placed in service after 1986	**14c**	
	d　Depletion (other than oil and gas)	**14d**	
	e (1)　Gross income from oil, gas, or geothermal properties	**14e(1)**	
	(2)　Deductions allocable to oil, gas, or geothermal properties	**14e(2)**	
	f　Other adjustments and tax preference items *(attach schedule)*	**14f**	
Foreign Taxes	15a　Type of income ▶		
	b　Name of foreign country or U.S. possession ▶		
	c　Total gross income from sources outside the United States *(attach schedule)*	**15c**	
	d　Total applicable deductions and losses *(attach schedule)*.	**15d**	
	e　Total foreign taxes (check one): ▶ ☐ Paid ☐ Accrued	**15e**	
	f　Reduction in taxes available for credit *(attach schedule)*	**15f**	
	g　Other foreign tax information *(attach schedule)*	**15g**	
Other	16a　Total expenditures to which a section 59(e) election may apply	**16a**	
	b　Type of expenditures ▶		
	17　Total property distributions (including cash) other than dividends reported on line 19 below	**17**	
	18　Other items and amounts required to be reported separately to shareholders (see instructions) *(attach schedule)*		
	19　Total dividend distributions paid from accumulated earnings and profits	**19**	
	20　**Income (loss)** (Required only if Schedule M-1 must be completed.). Combine lines 1 through 6 in column (b). From the result, subtract the sum of lines 7 through 11a, 15e, and 16a.	**20**	

Schedule L — Balance Sheets

Assets	Beginning of tax year (a)	(b)	End of tax year (c)	(d)
1 Cash				
2a Trade notes and accounts receivable . .				
b Less allowance for bad debts				
3 Inventories				
4 U.S. Government obligations				
5 Tax-exempt securities				
6 Other current assets (attach schedule) .				
7 Loans to shareholders				
8 Mortgage and real estate loans . . .				
9 Other investments (attach schedule) . .				
10a Buildings and other depreciable assets				
b Less accumulated depreciation				
11a Depletable assets				
b Less accumulated depletion				
12 Land (net of any amortization) . . .				
13a Intangible assets (amortizable only) . .				
b Less accumulated amortization . . .				
14 Other assets (attach schedule) . . .				
15 Total assets				
Liabilities and Shareholders' Equity				
16 Accounts payable				
17 Mortgages, notes, bonds payable in less than 1 year				
18 Other current liabilities (attach schedule)				
19 Loans from shareholders				
20 Mortgages, notes, bonds payable in 1 year or more				
21 Other liabilities (attach schedule) . .				
22 Capital stock				
23 Paid-in or capital surplus				
24 Retained earnings				
25 Less cost of treasury stock		( )		( )
26 Total liabilities and shareholders' equity . .				

Schedule M-1 — Reconciliation of Income per Books With Income per Return (You are not required to complete this schedule if the total assets on line 15, column (d), of Schedule L are less than $25,000.)

1 Net income per books . . . . . .

2 Income included on Schedule K, lines 1 through 6, not recorded on books this year (itemize): ....
....

3 Expenses recorded on books this year not included on Schedule K, lines 1 through 11a, 15e, and 16a (itemize):

a Depreciation $ ....

b Travel and entertainment $ ....
....

4 Add lines 1 through 3 . . . .

5 Income recorded on books this year not included on Schedule K, lines 1 through 6 (itemize):

a Tax-exempt interest $ ....
....

6 Deductions included on Schedule K, lines 1 through 11a, 15e, and 16a, not charged against book income this year (itemize):

a Depreciation $ ....
....

7 Add lines 5 and 6 . . . .

8 Income (loss) (Schedule K, line 20). Line 4 less line 7

Schedule M-2 — Analysis of Accumulated Adjustments Account, Other Adjustments Account, and Shareholders' Undistributed Taxable Income Previously Taxed (See instructions.)

	(a) Accumulated adjustments account	(b) Other adjustments account	(c) Shareholders' undistributed taxable income previously taxed
1 Balance at beginning of tax year . . .			
2 Ordinary income from page 1, line 21 . .			
3 Other additions			
4 Loss from page 1, line 21	( )		
5 Other reductions	( )	( )	
6 Combine lines 1 through 5			
7 Distributions other than dividend distributions .			
8 Balance at end of tax year. Subtract line 7 from line 6			

★U.S. GPO:1991-285-273

Instructions for Form 4562

Depreciation and Amortization

(Section references are to the Internal Revenue Code, unless otherwise noted.)

General Instructions

Paperwork Reduction Act Notice

We ask for the information on this form to carry out the Internal Revenue laws of the United States. You are required to give us the information. We need it to ensure that taxpayers are complying with these laws and to allow us to figure and collect the right amount of tax.

The time needed to complete and file this form will vary depending on individual circumstances. The estimated average time is:

Recordkeeping . . . . 35 hrs., 17 min.

**Learning about the
law or the form** . . . . .3 hrs., 35 min.

**Preparing and sending
the form to the IRS** . . .4 hrs., 35 min.

If you have comments concerning the accuracy of these time estimates or suggestions for making this form more simple, we would be happy to hear from you. You can write to both the IRS and the Office of Management and Budget at the addresses listed in the instructions for the tax return with which this form is filed.

Purpose of Form

Use Form 4562 to claim your deduction for depreciation and amortization; to make the election to expense certain tangible property (section 179); and to provide information on the business/investment use of automobiles and other listed property.

Who Must File

You must complete and file Form 4562 if you are claiming:

● Depreciation for property placed in service during the 1991 tax year;

● A section 179 expense deduction (which may include a carryover from a previous year);

● Depreciation on any listed property (regardless of when it was placed in service);

● The standard mileage rate (unless **Form 2106**, Employee Business Expenses, is used for this purpose—see the Part V instructions); or

● Amortization of costs that begins during the 1991 tax year.

All corporations (other than S corporations) must also file Form 4562 for any depreciation claimed on assets acquired in previous tax years.

You should prepare and submit a separate Form 4562 for each business or activity on your return. If more space is needed, attach additional sheets. However, complete only one Part I in its entirety when computing your allowable section 179 expense deduction.

Definitions

Depreciation.—Depreciation is the annual deduction allowed to recover the cost or other basis of business or income-producing property with a determinable useful life of more than 1 year. However, land and goodwill are not depreciable.

Depreciation starts when you first use the property in your business or for the production of income. It ends when you take the property out of service, deduct all your depreciable cost or other basis, or no longer use the property in your business or for the production of income. For additional information, see **Pub. 534**, Depreciation, **Pub. 946**, How To Begin Depreciating Your Property, and **Pub. 917**, Business Use of a Car.

Amortization.—Amortization is similar to the straight line method of depreciation in that an annual deduction is allowed to recover certain costs over a fixed period of time. You can amortize such items as the costs of starting a business, reforestation, and pollution control facilities. For additional information, see **Pub. 535**, Business Expenses.

"Listed Property".—For a definition of "listed property" see the Part V instructions.

Recordkeeping

Except for Part V, relating to listed property, the IRS does not require you to submit detailed information with your return regarding the depreciation of assets placed in service in previous tax years. However, the information needed to compute your depreciation deduction (basis, method, etc.) must be part of your permanent records.

Because Form 4562 does not provide for permanent recordkeeping, you may use the depreciation worksheet on page 8 to assist you in maintaining depreciation records. However, the worksheet is designed only for Federal income tax purposes. You may need to keep additional records for accounting and state income tax purposes.

Certification of Business Use Requirement for Aircraft Exempt From Luxury Tax

If you purchased a new aircraft in 1991 with a sales price of more than $250,000, the 10% Federal luxury tax generally imposed on such a sale will not apply if at least 80% of your use of the aircraft (measured in hours of flight time) will be for business purposes. If you purchased an aircraft that was exempt from the luxury tax **solely** for this reason, you must attach a statement to your income tax return for each of the 2 tax years ending after the date the aircraft was placed in service. On this statement, you must certify that at least

80% of your use of the aircraft during the tax year was in a trade or business. If you fail to make this certification, you must pay a tax equal to the luxury tax that would have been imposed on the sale of the aircraft if the business use exemption had not applied. In addition, interest is imposed on the tax from the date of sale of the aircraft.

If you do not pay the tax when due because you failed to meet this requirement, no depreciation may be claimed on the aircraft for any tax year.

See the instructions for **Form 720**, Quarterly Federal Excise Tax Return, for more information on paying the tax and interest due.

Specific Instructions

Part I.—Election To Expense Certain Tangible Property (Section 179)

Note: *An estate or trust cannot make this election. If you are married filing separately, see section 179(b)(4) for special limitations.*

You may make an irrevocable election to expense part of the cost of certain tangible personal property used in your trade or business and certain other property described in Pub. 534. To do so, you must have purchased the property (as defined in section 179(d)(2)) and placed it in service during the 1991 tax year, or have a carryover of disallowed deduction from 1990. If you elect this deduction, the amount on which you figure your depreciation or amortization deduction must be reduced by the amount of the section 179 expense.

Section 179 property does **not** include: **(1)** property used 50% or less in your trade or business; or **(2)** property held for investment (section 212 property). If you are a noncorporate lessor, the property that you lease to others does not qualify as section 179 property unless:
(1) you manufactured or produced the property; or **(2)** the term of the lease is less than 50% of the property's class life, and for the first 12 months after the property is transferred to the lessee, the sum of the deductions related to the property that are allowed to you solely under section 162 (except rents and reimbursed amounts) is more than 15% of the rental income from the property.

The section 179 expense deduction is subject to two separate limitations, both of which are figured in Part I:

1. A dollar limitation; and

2. A taxable income limitation.

In the case of a partnership, these limitations apply to the partnership and each partner. In the case of an

Cat. No. 12907Y

S corporation, these limitations apply to the S corporation and each shareholder. In the case of a controlled group, all component members are treated as one taxpayer.

Line 1.—The maximum amount of section 179 deduction you can claim is $10,000. If you are married filing separately, your maximum deduction is $5,000, unless you and your spouse elect otherwise. However, the total deduction for both of you cannot be more than $10,000. If you are married filing separately, cross out the preprinted "$10,000" on line 1 and enter in the margin "$5,000" (or whatever other amount you elect, not to exceed $10,000 for both spouses).

Line 2.—Enter the cost of all section 179 property placed in service during the tax year. Be sure to include amounts from any listed property from Part V.

Line 5.—If you placed $210,000 or more of section 179 property in service during the 1991 tax year, you cannot elect to expense any property. If line 5 is -0-, skip lines 6 through 11, enter -0- on line 12, and enter the carryover of disallowed deduction from 1990, if any, on line 13.

Line 6.—

Column (a)—Enter a brief description of the property for which you are making the election (e.g., truck, office furniture, etc.).

Column (b)—Enter the cost of the property. If you acquired the property through a trade-in, do not include any undepreciated basis of the assets you traded in. See **Pub. 551**, Basis of Assets, for more information.

Column (c)—Enter the amount that you elect to expense. You do not have to elect to expense the entire cost of the property. Whatever amount is not elected to be expensed can be depreciated. See line 14 and line 15 instructions below.

To report your share of a section 179 expense deduction from a partnership or an S corporation, instead of completing columns (a) and (b), write "from Schedule K-1 (Form 1065)" or "from Schedule K-1 (Form 1120S)" across the columns.

Line 9.—The tentative deduction represents the amount you may expense in 1991 or carry over to 1992. If this amount is less than the taxable income limitation on line 11, you may expense the entire amount. If this amount is more than line 11, you may expense in 1991 only an amount equal to line 11. Any excess may be carried over to 1992.

Line 10.—The carryover of disallowed deduction from 1990 is the amount of section 179 property, if any, elected to be expensed in previous years, but not allowed as a deduction due to the taxable income limitation. If you filed Form 4562 for 1990, enter the amount from line 13 of your 1990 Form 4562. For additional information, see Pub. 534.

Line 11.—The section 179 expense deduction is further limited to the "taxable income" limitation under section 179(b)(3).

For an individual, enter the aggregate taxable income from any active trade or business computed without regard to any section 179 expense deduction or the deduction for one-half of self-employment taxes under section 164(f). Include in aggregate taxable income the wages,

salaries, tips, and other compensation you earned as an employee. If you are married filing a joint return, combine the aggregate taxable incomes for both you and your spouse. For all other entities, enter the taxable income computed without regard to any section 179 expense deduction. In any case, do not enter more than line 5.

Line 12.—The limitations on lines 5 and 11 apply to the taxpayer, and not to each separate business or activity. Therefore, if you have more than one business or activity, you may allocate your allowable section 179 expense deduction among them. To do so, write "Summary" at the top of Part I of the separate Form 4562 you are completing for the aggregate amounts from all businesses or activities. Do not complete the rest of that form. On line 12 of the Form 4562 you prepare for each separate business or activity, enter the amount allocated to the business or activity from the "Summary." No other entry is required in Part I of the separate Form 4562 prepared for each business or activity.

Part II.—MACRS Depreciation For Assets Placed in Service ONLY During Your 1991 Tax Year

Note: *The term "Modified Accelerated Cost Recovery System" (MACRS) includes the General Depreciation System and the Alternative Depreciation System. Generally, MACRS is used to depreciate any tangible property placed in service after 1986. However, MACRS does not apply to films, videotapes, and sound recordings. See section 168(f) for other exceptions.*

Depreciation may be an adjustment for alternative minimum tax (AMT) purposes. See the appropriate AMT form that you are required to file.

Lines 14a through 14h.—General Depreciation System (GDS).—
Note: *Use lines 14a through 14h only for assets placed in service during the tax year beginning in 1991 and depreciated under the General Depreciation System, except for automobiles and other listed property (which are reported in Part V).*

Determine which property you acquired and placed in service during the tax year beginning in 1991. Then, sort that property according to its classification (3-year property, 5-year property, etc.) as shown in column (a) of lines 14a through 14h. The classifications for some property are shown below. For property not shown, see **Determining the Classification** below.

● 3-year property includes: (1) a race horse that is more than 2 years old at the time it is placed in service; and (2) any horse (other than a race horse) that is more than 12 years old at the time it is placed in service.

● 5-year property includes:
(1) automobiles; (2) light general purpose trucks; (3) typewriters, calculators, copiers, and duplicating equipment; (4) any semi-conductor manufacturing equipment; (5) any computer or peripheral equipment; (6) any section 1245 property used in connection with research and experimentation; and (7) certain energy property specified in section 168(e)(3)(B)(vi).

● 7-year property includes: (1) office furniture and equipment; (2) appliances, carpets, furniture, etc. used in residential rental property; (3) railroad track; and
(4) any property that does not have a class life and is not otherwise classified.

● 10-year property includes: (1) vessels, barges, tugs, and similar water transportation equipment; (2) any single purpose agricultural or horticultural structure (see section 48(p)); and (3) any tree or vine bearing fruit or nuts.

● 15-year property includes: (1) any municipal wastewater treatment plant; and (2) any telephone distribution plant and comparable equipment used for 2-way exchange of voice and data communications.

● 20-year property includes any municipal sewers.

● Residential rental property is a building in which 80% or more of the total rent is from dwelling units.

● Nonresidential real property is any real property that is neither residential rental property nor property with a class life of less than 27.5 years.

● 50-year property includes any improvements necessary to construct or improve a roadbed or right-of-way for railroad track that qualifies as a railroad grading or tunnel bore under section 168(e)(4). There is no separate line to report 50-year property. Therefore, attach a statement showing the same information as required in columns (a) through (g). Include the deduction in the line 20 "Total" and write "See attachment" in the bottom margin of the form.

Determining the Classification.—If your depreciable property is **not** listed above, determine the classification as follows: First, find the property's class life. The class life of most property can be found in the Table of Class Lives and Recovery Periods in Pub. 534. Next, use the following table to find the classification in column (b) that corresponds to the class life of the property in column (a).

(a) Class life (in years) (See Pub. 534)	(b) Classification
4 or less	3-year property
More than 4 but less than 10	5-year property
10 or more but less than 16	7-year property
16 or more but less than 20	10-year property
20 or more but less than 25	15-year property
25 or more	20-year property

Column (b).—For lines 14g and 14h, enter the month and year the property was placed in service. If property held for personal use is converted to use in a trade or business or for the production of income, treat the property as being placed in service on the date of conversion.

Column (c).—To find the basis for depreciation, multiply the cost or other basis of the property by the percentage of business/investment use. From that result, subtract any section 179 expense deduction and the amount of any enhanced oil recovery credit (section 43). See section 50(c) to determine the basis adjustment for investment credit property.

Column (d).—See the "Note" in the line 14, column (f) instructions below, for an election you can make to use the 150% declining balance method of depreciation (for 3-, 5-, 7-, and 10-year property). If you do not elect to use the 150% method, determine the recovery period from the table below:

In the case of:	The applicable recovery period is:
3-year property	3 yrs.
5-year property	5 yrs.
7-year property	7 yrs.
10-year property	10 yrs.
15-year property	15 yrs.
20-year property	20 yrs.
Residential rental property	27.5 yrs.
Nonresidential real property	31.5 yrs.
Railroad gradings and tunnel bores . .	50 yrs.

If you elect the 150% declining balance method, you must use the recovery period under the Alternative Depreciation System discussed in the line 15 instructions below. You will not have an adjustment for alternative minimum tax purposes on the property for which you make this election.

Column (e).—The applicable convention determines the portion of the tax year for which depreciation is allowable during a year property is either placed in service or disposed of. There are three types of conventions (discussed below). To select the correct convention, you must know: **(a)** when you placed the property in service; and **(b)** the type of property.

Half-year convention (HY).—This convention applies to all property reported on lines 14a through 14f, unless the mid-quarter convention applies. It does not apply to residential rental property, nonresidential real property, and railroad gradings and tunnel bores. It treats all property placed in service (or disposed of) during any tax year as placed in service (or disposed of) on the mid-point of such tax year.

Mid-quarter convention (MQ).—This convention applies instead of the half-year convention if the aggregate bases of property subject to depreciation under section 168 that is placed in service during the last 3 months of your tax year exceeds 40% of the aggregate bases of property subject to depreciation under section 168 that is placed in service during the entire tax year.

The mid-quarter convention treats all property placed in service (or disposed of) during any quarter as placed in service (or disposed of) on the mid-point of such quarter.

In determining whether the mid-quarter convention applies, do not take into account:
- Property that is being depreciated under the pre-1987 rules;
- Any residential rental property, nonresidential real property, or railroad gradings and tunnel bores; and
- Property that is placed in service and disposed of within the same tax year.

Mid-month convention (MM).—This convention applies ONLY to residential rental property, nonresidential real property (lines 14g or 14h), and railroad gradings and tunnel bores. It treats all property placed in service (or disposed of) during any month as placed in service (or disposed of) on the mid-point of such month.

Enter "HY" for half-year; "MQ" for mid-quarter; or "MM" for mid-month convention.

Column (f).—Applicable depreciation methods are prescribed for each classification of property. For 3-, 5-, 7-, and 10-year property the applicable method is the 200% declining balance method, switching to the straight line method in the first tax year that maximizes the depreciation allowance.

Note: *You may make an irrevocable election to use the 150% declining balance method for one or more classes of property (except for residential rental property, nonresidential real property, any railroad grading or tunnel bore, or any tree or vine bearing fruit or nuts). If you make this election, see "Alternative Depreciation System" below for the recovery period.*

For 15- and 20-year property, and property used in a farming business, the applicable method is the 150% declining balance method, switching to the straight line method in the first tax year that maximizes the depreciation allowance.

For residential rental property, nonresidential real property, any railroad grading or tunnel bore, or any tree or vine bearing fruit or nuts, the only applicable method is the straight line method.

You may also make an irrevocable election to use the straight line method for all property within a classification that is placed in service during the tax year.

Enter "200 DB" for 200% declining balance; "150 DB" for 150% declining balance; or "S/L" for straight line.

Column (g).—To compute the depreciation deduction you may: **(a)** use the optional Tables A through D on page 7. Multiply the applicable rate from the appropriate table by the property's **unadjusted** basis (column (c)) (see Pub. 534 for complete tables); or **(b)** compute the deduction yourself. To compute the deduction yourself, complete the following steps:

Step 1.—Determine the depreciation rate as follows:

1. If you are using the 200% or 150% declining balance method in column (f), divide the declining balance rate (use 2.00 for 200 DB or 1.50 for 150 DB) by the number of years in the recovery period in column (d). For example, for property depreciated using the 200 DB method over a recovery period of 5 years, divide 2.00 by 5 for a rate of 40%.

2. If you are using the straight line method, divide 1.00 by the remaining number of years in the recovery period as of the beginning of the tax year (but not less than one). For example, if there are 6½ years remaining in the recovery period as of the beginning of the year, divide 1.00 by 6.5 for a rate of 15.38%.

Note: *If you are using the 200% or 150% DB method, be sure to switch to the straight line rate in the first year that the straight line rate exceeds the declining balance rate.*

Step 2.—Multiply the percentage rate determined in Step 1 by the property's unrecovered basis (cost or other basis reduced by any section 179 expense deduction and all prior years' depreciation).

Step 3.—For property placed in service or disposed of during the current tax year, multiply the result from Step 2 by the applicable decimal amount from the tables below (based on the convention shown in column (e)).

Half-year (HY) convention	0.5

Mid-quarter (MQ) convention

Placed in service (or disposed of) during the:	Placed in service	Disposed of
1st quarter	0.875	0.125
2nd quarter	0.625	0.375
3rd quarter	0.375	0.625
4th quarter	0.125	0.875

Mid-month (MM) convention

Placed in service (or disposed of) during the:	Placed in service	Disposed of
1st month.	0.9583	0.0417
2nd month	0.8750	0.1250
3rd month	0.7917	0.2083
4th month	0.7083	0.2917
5th month	0.6250	0.3750
6th month	0.5417	0.4583
7th month	0.4583	0.5417
8th month	0.3750	0.6250
9th month	0.2917	0.7083
10th month	0.2083	0.7917
11th month	0.1250	0.8750
12th month	0.0417	0.9583

Short Tax Years.—See Pub. 534 for rules on how to compute the depreciation deduction for property placed in service in a short tax year.

Line 15.—Alternative Depreciation System (ADS).—**Note:** *Lines 15a through 15c should be completed for assets, other than automobiles and other listed property, placed in service ONLY during the tax year beginning in 1991 and depreciated under the Alternative Depreciation System. Depreciation on assets placed in service in prior years is reported on line 16.*

Under ADS, depreciation is computed by using the applicable depreciation method, the applicable recovery period, and the applicable convention. The following types of property **must** be depreciated under ADS:

- Any tangible property used predominantly outside the U.S.;
- Any tax-exempt use property;
- Any tax-exempt bond financed property;
- Any imported property covered by an executive order of the President of the United States; and
- Any property used predominantly in a farming business and placed in service during any tax year in which you made an election under section 263A(d)(3).

Instead of depreciating property under GDS (line 14), you may make an irrevocable election with respect to any classification of property for any tax year to use ADS. For residential rental and nonresidential real property, you may make this election separately for each property.

Note: *See section 168(g)(3)(B) for a special rule for determining the class life for certain property.*

If the property does not have a class life, use line 15b.

Page 3

For residential rental and nonresidential real property, use line 15c.

For railroad gradings and tunnel bores, the recovery period is 50 years.

Column (b).—For 40-year property, enter the month and year it was placed in service, or converted to use in a trade or business, or for the production of income.

Column (c).—See the instructions for line 14, column (c).

Column (d).—Under ADS, the recovery period is generally the class life. However, when looking up the recovery period in Pub. 534, be sure to look under the heading "Alternate MACRS."

Column (e).—Under ADS, the applicable conventions are the same as those used under GDS. See the instructions for line 14, column (e).

Column (f).—Under ADS, the only applicable method is the straight line method.

Column (g).—The depreciation deduction is computed in the same manner as under GDS except you must apply the straight line method over the ADS recovery period and use the applicable convention.

Part III.—Other Depreciation

Note: *Do not use Part III for automobiles and other listed property. Instead, report this property in Part V on page 2 of Form 4562.*

Use Part III for

- ACRS property (pre-'87 rules);
- Property placed in service before 1981;
- Certain public utility property, which does not meet certain normalization requirements;
- Certain property acquired from related persons;
- Property acquired in certain nonrecognition transactions; and
- Certain sound recordings, movies, and videotapes.

Line 16.—GDS and ADS deduction for assets placed in service in tax years beginning before 1991.—For assets placed in service after 1986, and depreciated under post-'86 rules, enter the GDS and ADS deduction for the current year. To compute the deduction, see the instructions for column (g), line 14.

Line 17.—Property subject to section 168(f)(1) election.—Report property that you elect, under section 168(f)(1), to depreciate by the unit-of-production method or any other method not based on a term of years (other than the retirement-replacement-betterment method).

Attach a separate sheet, showing: **(a)** a description of the property and the depreciation method you elect that excludes the property from ACRS or MACRS; and **(b)** the depreciable basis (cost or other basis reduced, if applicable, by salvage value, enhanced oil recovery credit, and the section 179 expense deduction). See section 50(c) to determine the basis adjustment for investment credit property.

Line 18.—ACRS and other depreciation.— Enter the total depreciation attributable to assets, other than automobiles and other listed property, placed in service before 1981 (pre-ACRS), property subject to ACRS, or property that cannot otherwise be

depreciated under ACRS. For ACRS property, unless you use an alternate percentage, multiply the property's unadjusted basis by the applicable percentage as follows:

- *5-year property*—1st year (15%), 2nd year (22%), 3rd through 5th years (21%);
- *10-year property*—1st year (8%), 2nd year (14%), 3rd year (12%), 4th through 6th years (10%), 7th through 10th years (9%);
- *15-year public utility property*—1st year (5%), 2nd year (10%), 3rd year (9%), 4th year (8%), 5th and 6th years (7%), 7th through 15th years (6%);
- *15-year, 18-year, and 19-year real property and low-income housing*—Use the tables in Pub. 534.

If you elected an alternate percentage for any property listed above, use the straight line method over the recovery period you chose in the prior year. See Pub. 534 for more information and tables.

Include any amounts attributable to the Class Life Asset Depreciation Range (CLADR) system. If you previously elected the CLADR system, you must continue to use it to depreciate assets left in your vintage accounts. You must continue to meet recordkeeping requirements.

Prior years' depreciation, plus current year's depreciation, can never exceed the depreciable basis of the property.

The basis and amounts claimed for depreciation should be part of your permanent books and records. **No attachment is necessary.**

Line 20.—A partnership or S corporation does not include any section 179 expense deduction (line 12) on this line. Any section 179 expense deduction is passed through separately to the partners and shareholders on the appropriate line of their Schedules K-1.

Line 21—Section 263A Uniform Capitalization Rules.—If you are subject to the uniform capitalization rules of section 263A, enter the increase in basis from costs that are required to be capitalized. For a detailed discussion of who is subject to these rules, which costs must be capitalized, and allocation of costs among activities, see Temp. Regs. section 1.263A-1T.

Part V.—Automobiles and Other Listed Property

All taxpayers claiming any depreciation for automobiles and other listed property, regardless of the tax year such property was placed in service, must provide the information requested in Part V. However, employees claiming the standard mileage allowance or actual expenses (including depreciation) must use Form 2106 instead of Part V. Listed property includes, but is not limited to:

- Passenger automobiles weighing 6,000 pounds or less.
- Any other property used for transportation if the nature of the property lends itself to personal use, such as motorcycles, pick-up trucks, etc.
- Any property used for entertainment or recreational purposes (such as photographic, phonographic, communication, and video recording equipment).

- Cellular telephones (or other similar telecommunications equipment).
- Computers or peripheral equipment.

Listed property does not include: **(a)** photographic, phonographic, communication, or video equipment used exclusively in a taxpayer's trade or business or regular business establishment; **(b)** any computer or peripheral equipment used exclusively at a regular business establishment and owned or leased by the person operating the establishment; or **(c)** an ambulance, hearse, or vehicle used for transporting persons or property for hire.

Section A.—Depreciation

Lines 23 and 24.—

Qualified business use.—For purposes of determining whether to use line 23 or line 24 to report your listed property, you must first determine the percentage of qualified business use for each property. Generally, a qualified business use is any use in your trade or business. However, it does not include:

- Any investment use;
- Leasing the property to a 5% owner or related person;
- The use of the property as compensation for services performed by a 5% owner or related person; or
- The use of the property as compensation for services performed by any person (who is not a 5% owner or related person), unless an amount is included in that person's income for the use of the property and, if required, income tax was withheld on that amount.

As an exception to the general rule, if at least 25% of the total use of any aircraft during the tax year is for a qualified business use, the leasing or compensatory use of the aircraft by a 5% owner or related person is considered a qualified business use.

Determine your percentage of qualified business use in a manner similar to that used to figure the business/investment use percentage in column (c). Your percentage of qualified business use may be smaller than the business/investment use percentage.

For more information, see Pub. 534.

Column (a).—List on a property-by-property basis all of your listed property in the following order:

1. Automobiles and other vehicles; and

2. Other listed property (computers and peripheral equipment, etc.).

In column (a), list the make and model of automobiles, and give a general description of the listed property.

If you have more than five vehicles used 100% for business/investment purposes, you may group them by tax year. Otherwise, list each vehicle separately.

Column (b).—Enter the date the property was placed in service. If property held for personal use is converted to business/investment use, treat the property as placed in service on the date of conversion.

Column (c).—Enter the percentage of business/investment use. For automobiles and other "vehicles," this is determined by dividing the number of miles the vehicle is driven for trade or business purposes or for the production of income during the year (not to include any commuting mileage) by the total number of miles the vehicle is driven for any purpose. Treat vehicles used by employees as being used 100% for business/investment purposes if the value of personal use is included in the employees' gross income, or the employees reimburse the employer for the personal use.

Employers who report the amount of personal use of the vehicle in the employee's gross income, and withhold the appropriate taxes, should enter "100%" for the percentage of business/investment use. For more information, see Pub. 917. For listed property (such as computers or video equipment), allocate the use based on the most appropriate unit of time the property is actually used. See Temp. Regs. 1.280F-6T.

If you have property that is used solely for personal use that is converted to business/investment use during the tax year, figure the percentage of business/investment use only for the number of months the property is used in your business or for the production of income. Multiply that percentage by the number of months the property is used in your business or for the production of income, and divide the result by 12.

Column (e).—Multiply column (d) by the percentage in column (c). From that result, subtract any section 179 expense deduction and half of any investment credit taken before 1986 (unless you took the reduced credit). For automobiles and other listed property placed in service after 1985 (i.e., "transition property"), reduce the depreciable basis by the entire investment credit.

Column (f).—Enter the recovery period. For property placed in service after 1986 and used more than 50% in a qualified business use, use the table in the line 14, column (d) instructions. For property placed in service after 1986 and used 50% or less in a qualified business use, you must depreciate the property using the straight line method over its ADS recovery period. The ADS recovery period is 5 years for automobiles and computers.

. **Column (g).**—Enter the method and convention used to figure your depreciation deduction. See the instructions for line 14, columns (e) and (f). Write "200 DB," "150 DB," or "S/L," for the depreciation method, and "HY," "MM," or "MQ," for half-year, mid-month, or mid-quarter conventions, respectively. For property placed in service before 1987, write "PRE" if you used the prescribed percentages under ACRS. If you elected an alternate percentage, enter "S/L."

Column (h).—Caution: See "Limitations for automobiles" below before entering an amount in column (h).

If the property is used more than 50% in a qualified business use (line 23), and the property was placed in service after 1986, figure column (h) by following the instructions for line 14, column (g). If placed in service before 1987, multiply column (e) by the applicable percentages given in the line 18 instructions for ACRS property. If the recovery period for the property ended before your tax year beginning in 1991, enter your unrecovered basis, if any, in column (h).

If the property is used 50% or less in a qualified business use (line 24), and the

property was placed in service after 1986, figure column (h) by dividing column (e) by column (f) and using the same conventions as discussed in the instructions for line 14, column (e). For automobiles placed in service: (1) during your tax year beginning in 1986, multiply column (e) by 10%; or (2) after June 18, 1984, and before your tax year beginning in 1986, enter your unrecovered basis, if any, in column (h). For computers placed in service after June 18, 1984, and before 1987, multiply column (e) by 8.333%.

For property used 50% or less in a qualified business use, no section 179 expense deduction is allowed.

For property placed in service before 1987 that was disposed of during the year, enter zero.

Limitations for automobiles.—The depreciation deduction plus section 179 expense deduction for automobiles is limited for any tax year. The limitation depends on when you placed the property in service. Use Table E on page 7 to determine the limitation. For any automobile you list on line 23 or 24, the total of columns (h) and (i) for that automobile cannot exceed the limit shown in Table E.

Note: These limitations are further reduced when the business/investment use percentage (column (c)) is less than 100%. For example, if an automobile placed in service in 1991 is used 60% for business/investment purposes, then the first year depreciation plus section 179 expense deduction is limited to 60% of $2,660, which is $1,596.

Column (i).—Enter the amount you choose to expense for property used more than 50% in a qualified business use (subject to the limitations for automobiles noted above). Be sure to include the total cost of such property on line 2, page 1.

Recapture of depreciation and section 179 expense deduction.—If any listed property was used more than 50% in a qualified business use in the year it was placed in service, and used 50% or less in a later year, you may have to recapture in the later year part of the depreciation and section 179 expense deduction. Use **Form 4797**, Sales of Business Property, to figure the recapture amount.

Section B.—Information Regarding Use of Vehicles

The information requested in Questions 27 through 33 must be completed for each vehicle identified in Section A.

Employees must provide their employers with the information requested in Questions 27 through 33 for each automobile or vehicle provided for their use.

Employers providing more than five vehicles to their employees, who are not more than 5% owners or related persons, are not required to complete Questions 27 through 33 for such vehicles. Instead, they must obtain this information from their employees, check "Yes" to Question 37, and retain the information received as part of their permanent records.

Section C.—Questions for Employers Who Provide Vehicles for Use by Their Employees

For employers providing vehicles to their employees, a written policy statement regarding the use of such vehicles, if initiated and kept by the employer, will relieve the employee of keeping separate records for substantiation.

Two types of written policy statements will satisfy the employer's substantiation requirements under section 274(d): **(a)** a policy statement that prohibits personal use including commuting; and **(b)** a policy statement that prohibits personal use except for commuting.

Line 34.—Prohibits Personal Use (including commuting):

This policy must meet the following conditions:

● The vehicle is owned or leased by the employer and is provided to one or more employees for use in the employer's trade or business;

● When the vehicle is not used in the employer's trade or business, it is kept on the employer's business premises, unless it is temporarily located elsewhere, for example, for maintenance or because of a mechanical failure;

● No employee using the vehicle lives at the employer's business premises;

● No employee may use the vehicle for personal purposes, other than de minimis personal use (such as a stop for lunch between two business deliveries); and

● Except for de minimis use, the employer reasonably believes that no employee uses the vehicle for any personal purpose.

Line 35.—Prohibits Personal Use (except for commuting). This policy is NOT available if the commuting employee is an officer, director, or 1% or more owner.

This policy must meet the following conditions:

● The vehicle is owned or leased by the employer and is provided to one or more employees for use in the employer's trade or business and is used in the employer's trade or business;

● For bona fide noncompensatory business reasons, the employer requires the employee to commute to and/or from work in the vehicle;

● The employer establishes a written policy under which the employee may not use the vehicle for personal purposes, other than commuting or de minimis personal use (such as a stop for a personal errand between a business delivery and the employee's home);

● Except for de minimis use, the employer reasonably believes that the employee does not use the vehicle for any personal purpose other than commuting; and

● The employer accounts for the commuting use by including an appropriate amount in the employee's gross income.

For both written policy statements, there must be evidence that would enable the IRS to determine whether use of the vehicle meets the conditions stated above.

Line 38.—An automobile is considered to have qualified demonstration use if the employer maintains a written policy statement that:

- Prohibits its use by individuals other than full-time automobile salesmen;
- Prohibits its use for personal vacation trips;
- Prohibits storage of personal possessions in the automobile; and
- Limits the total mileage outside the salesmen's normal working hours.

Part VI.—Amortization

Each year you may elect to deduct part of certain capital costs over a fixed period. If you amortize property, the part you amortize does not qualify for the election to expense certain tangible property or depreciation.

For individuals reporting amortization of bond premium for bonds acquired before October 23, 1986, do not report the deduction here. See the instructions for Schedule A (Form 1040).

For taxpayers (other than corporations) claiming a deduction for amortization of bond premium for bonds acquired after October 22, 1986, but before January 1, 1988, the deduction is treated as interest expense and is subject to the investment interest limitations. Use **Form 4952,** Investment Interest Expense Deduction, to compute the allowable deduction.

For taxable bonds acquired after 1987, the amortization offsets the interest income. See **Pub. 550,** Investment Income and Expenses.

Line 39.—Complete line 39 only for those costs for which the amortization period begins during your tax year beginning in 1991.

Column (a).—Describe the costs you are amortizing. You may amortize—

- Pollution control facilities (section 169, limited by section 291 for corporations).
- Certain bond premiums (section 171).
- Research and experimental expenditures (section 174).
- Qualified forestation and reforestation costs (section 194).
- Business start-up expenditures (section 195).

- Organizational expenditures for a corporation (section 248) or partnership (section 709).
- Optional write off of certain tax preferences over the period specified in section 59(e).

Column (b).—Enter the date the amortization period begins under the applicable Code section.

Column (c).—Enter the total amount you are amortizing. See the applicable Code section for limits on the amortizable amount.

Column (d).—Enter the Code section under which you amortize the costs.

Column (f).—Compute the amortization deduction by: (1) dividing column (c) by the number of years over which the costs are to be amortized; or (2) multiplying column (c) by the percentage in column (e).

Attach any other information the Code and regulations may require to make a valid election. See Pub. 535 for more information.

Line 40.—Enter the amount of amortization attributable to those costs for which the amortization period began before 1991.

Table A.—General Depreciation System
Method: 200% declining balance switching to straight line
Convention: half-year

Year	If the recovery period is:			
	3 yrs.	5 yrs.	7 yrs.	10 yrs.
1	33.33%	20.00%	14.29%	10.00%
2	44.45%	32.00%	24.49%	18.00%
3	14.81%	19.20%	17.49%	14.40%
4	7.41%	11.52%	12.49%	11.52%
5		11.52%	8.93%	9.22%

Table B.—General and Alternative Depreciation System
Method: 150% declining balance switching to straight line
Convention: half-year

Year	If the recovery period is:					
	5 yrs.	7 yrs.	10 yrs.	12 yrs.	15 yrs.	20 yrs.
1	15.00%	10.71%	7.50%	6.25%	5.00%	3.750%
2	25.50%	19.13%	13.88%	11.72%	9.50%	7.219%
3	17.85%	15.03%	11.79%	10.25%	8.55%	6.677%
4	16.66%	12.25%	10.02%	8.97%	7.70%	6.177%
5	16.66%	12.25%	8.74%	7.85%	6.93%	5.713%

Table C.—General Depreciation System
Method: Straight line
Convention: Mid-month
Recovery period: 27.5 years

Year	The month in the 1st recovery year the property is placed in service:											
	1	2	3	4	5	6	7	8	9	10	11	12
1	3.485%	3.182%	2.879%	2.576%	2.273%	1.970%	1.667%	1.364%	1.061%	0.758%	0.455%	0.152%
2-8	3.636%	3.636%	3.636%	3.636%	3.636%	3.636%	3.636%	3.636%	3.636%	3.636%	3.636%	3.636%

Table D.—General Depreciation System
Method: Straight line
Convention: Mid-month
Recovery period: 31.5 years

Year	The month in the 1st recovery year the property is placed in service:											
	1	2	3	4	5	6	7	8	9	10	11	12
1	3.042%	2.778%	2.513%	2.249%	1.984%	1.720%	1.455%	1.190%	0.926%	0.661%	0.397%	0.132%
2-7	3.175%	3.175%	3.175%	3.175%	3.175%	3.175%	3.175%	3.175%	3.175%	3.175%	3.175%	3.175%

Table E.—Limitations for automobiles

Year of Deduction	after: / but before:	If placed in service—					
		6/18/84 1/1/85	12/31/84 4/3/85	4/2/85 1/1/87	12/31/86 1/1/89	12/31/88 1/1/91	12/31/90 1/1/92
1st tax year		4,000	4,100	3,200	2,560	2,660	2,660
2nd tax year		6,000	6,200	4,800	4,100	4,200	4,300
3rd tax year		6,000	6,200	4,800	2,450	2,550	2,550
each succeeding tax year		6,000	6,200	4,800	1,475	1,475	1,575

Depreciation Worksheet

Description of Property	Date Placed in Service	Cost or Other Basis	Business/ Investment Use %	Section 179 Deduction	Depreciation Prior Years	Basis for Depreciation	Method/ Convention	Recovery Period	Rate or Table %	Depreciation Deduction

☆ U.S. GOVERNMENT PRINTING OFFICE: 1992 312-732/54252

Form **4562**	**Depreciation and Amortization**	OMB No. 1545-0172
	(Including Information on Listed Property)	**1991**
Department of the Treasury Internal Revenue Service (o)	▶ **See separate instructions.** ▶ **Attach this form to your return.**	Attachment Sequence No. **67**

Name(s) shown on return		Identifying number

Business or activity to which this form relates

Part I — Election To Expense Certain Tangible Property (Section 179) (Note: *If you have any "Listed Property," complete Part V.*)

1	Maximum dollar limitation (see instructions)	**1**	$10,000
2	Total cost of section 179 property placed in service during the tax year (see instructions) . .	**2**	
3	Threshold cost of section 179 property before reduction in limitation	**3**	$200,000
4	Reduction in limitation—Subtract line 3 from line 2, but do not enter less than -0-	**4**	
5	Dollar limitation for tax year—Subtract line 4 from line 1, but do not enter less than -0- . .	**5**	

(a) Description of property	(b) Cost	(c) Elected cost	
6			

7	Listed property—Enter amount from line 26	**7**	
8	Total elected cost of section 179 property—Add amounts in column (c), lines 6 and 7 . . .	**8**	
9	Tentative deduction—Enter the lesser of line 5 or line 8	**9**	
10	Carryover of disallowed deduction from 1990 (see instructions).	**10**	
11	Taxable income limitation—Enter the lesser of taxable income or line 5 (see instructions) . .	**11**	
12	Section 179 expense deduction—Add lines 9 and 10, but do not enter more than line 11 . .	**12**	
13	Carryover of disallowed deduction to 1992—Add lines 9 and 10, less line 12 ▶	**13**	

Note: *Do not use Part II or Part III below for automobiles, certain other vehicles, cellular telephones, computers, or property used for entertainment, recreation, or amusement (listed property). Instead, use Part V for listed property.*

Part II — MACRS Depreciation For Assets Placed in Service ONLY During Your 1991 Tax Year (Do Not Include Listed Property)

(a) Classification of property	(b) Mo. and yr. placed in service	(c) Basis for depreciation (Business/investment use only—see instructions)	(d) Recovery period	(e) Convention	(f) Method	(g) Depreciation deduction
14 General Depreciation System (GDS) (see instructions):						
a 3-year property						
b 5-year property						
c 7-year property						
d 10-year property						
e 15-year property						
f 20-year property						
g Residential rental property			27.5 yrs.	MM	S/L	
			27.5 yrs.	MM	S/L	
h Nonresidential real property			31.5 yrs.	MM	S/L	
			31.5 yrs.	MM	S/L	
15 Alternative Depreciation System (ADS) (see instructions):						
a Class life					S/L	
b 12-year			12 yrs.		S/L	
c 40-year			40 yrs.	MM	S/L	

Part III — Other Depreciation (Do Not Include Listed Property)

16	GDS and ADS deductions for assets placed in service in tax years beginning before 1991 (see instructions)	**16**	
17	Property subject to section 168(f)(1) election (see instructions)	**17**	
18	ACRS and other depreciation (see instructions)	**18**	

Part IV — Summary

19	Listed property—Enter amount from line 25	**19**	
20	Total—Add deductions on line 12, lines 14 and 15 in column (g), and lines 16 through 19. Enter here and on the appropriate lines of your return. (Partnerships and S corporations—see instructions)	**20**	
21	For assets shown above and placed in service during the current year, enter the portion of the basis attributable to section 263A costs (see instructions)	**21**	

For Paperwork Reduction Act Notice, see page 1 of the separate instructions.　　Cat. No. 12906N　　Form **4562** (1991)

178

Part V **Listed Property.—Automobiles, Certain Other Vehicles, Cellular Telephones, Computers, and Property Used for Entertainment, Recreation, or Amusement**

If you are using the standard mileage rate or deducting vehicle lease expense, complete columns (a) through (c) of Section A, all of Section B, and Section C if applicable.

Section A.—Depreciation (Caution: *See instructions for limitations for automobiles.*)

22a Do you have evidence to support the business/investment use claimed? ☐ **Yes** ☐ **No** **22b** If "Yes," is the evidence written? ☐ **Yes** ☐ **No**

(a) Type of property (list vehicles first)	(b) Date placed in service	(c) Business/ investment use percentage	(d) Cost or other basis	(e) Basis for depreciation (business/investment use only)	(f) Recovery period	(g) Method/ Convention	(h) Depreciation deduction	(i) Elected section 179 cost
23 *Property used more than 50% in a qualified business use (see instructions):*								
		%						
		%						
		%						
24 *Property used 50% or less in a qualified business use (see instructions):*								
		%			S/L –			
		%			S/L –			
		%			S/L –			

25 Add amounts in column (h). Enter the total here and on line 19, page 1 . . . . | **25** |

26 Add amounts in column (i). Enter the total here and on line 7, page 1 . . . . | **26** |

Section B.—Information Regarding Use of Vehicles—*If you deduct expenses for vehicles:*
● *Always complete this section for vehicles used by a sole proprietor, partner, or other "more than 5% owner," or related person.*
● *If you provided vehicles to your employees, first answer the questions in Section C to see if you meet an exception to completing this section for those vehicles.*

		(a) Vehicle 1		(b) Vehicle 2		(c) Vehicle 3		(d) Vehicle 4		(e) Vehicle 5		(f) Vehicle 6	
27	Total business/investment miles driven during the year (DO NOT include commuting miles).												
28	Total commuting miles driven during the year												
29	Total other personal (noncommuting) miles driven												
30	Total miles driven during the year— Add lines 27 through 29												
		Yes	No	Yes	No	Yes	No	Yes	No	Yes	No	Yes	No
31	Was the vehicle available for personal use during off-duty hours?												
32	Was the vehicle used primarily by a more than 5% owner or related person? . .												
33	Is another vehicle available for personal use?												

Section C.—Questions for Employers Who Provide Vehicles for Use by Their Employees
(Answer these questions to determine if you meet an exception to completing Section B. Note: Section B must always be completed for vehicles used by sole proprietors, partners, or other more than 5% owners or related persons.)

	Yes	No
34 Do you maintain a written policy statement that prohibits all personal use of vehicles, including commuting, by your employees?		
35 Do you maintain a written policy statement that prohibits personal use of vehicles, except commuting, by your employees? (See instructions for vehicles used by corporate officers, directors, or 1% or more owners.)		
36 Do you treat all use of vehicles by employees as personal use?.		
37 Do you provide more than five vehicles to your employees and retain the information received from your employees concerning the use of the vehicles?		
38 Do you meet the requirements concerning qualified automobile demonstration use (see instructions)? . .		

Note: *If your answer to 34, 35, 36, 37, or 38 is "Yes," you need not complete Section B for the covered vehicles.*

Part VI **Amortization**

(a) Description of costs	(b) Date amortization begins	(c) Amortizable amount	(d) Code section	(e) Amortization period or percentage	(f) Amortization for this year
39 Amortization of costs that begins during your 1991 tax year:					
40 Amortization of costs that began before 1991				**40**	
41 Total. Enter here and on "Other Deductions" or "Other Expenses" line of your return				**41**	

Shareholder's Instructions for Schedule K-1 (Form 1120S)

Shareholder's Share of Income, Credits, Deductions, Etc.

(For Shareholder's Use Only)

(Section references are to the Internal Revenue Code unless otherwise noted.)

General Instructions

Purpose of Schedule K-1

The corporation uses Schedule K-1 (Form 1120S) to report your pro rata share of the corporation's income (reduced by any tax the corporation paid on the income), credits, deductions, etc. **Please keep it for your records. Do not file it with your tax return (unless you are required to file it with Form 8271**, Investor Reporting of Tax Shelter Registration Number). A copy has been filed with the IRS.

Although the corporation is subject to a capital gains tax (or built-in gains tax) and an excess net passive income tax, you, the shareholder, are liable for income tax on your share of the corporation's income, whether or not distributed, and you must include your share on your tax return if a return is required. **Your distributive share of S corporation income is not self-employment income and it is not subject to self-employment tax.**

You should use these instructions to help you report the items shown on Schedule K-1 on your tax return.

Where "(attach schedule)" appears next to a line on Schedule K-1, it means the information for these lines (if applicable) will be shown in the "Supplemental Information" space below line 20 of Schedule K-1. If additional space was needed, the corporation will have attached a statement to Schedule K-1 to show the information for the line item.

The notation "(see Instructions for Schedule K-1)" in items A and C at the top of Schedule K-1 is directed to the corporation. You, as a shareholder, should disregard these notations.

Schedule K-1 does not show the amount of actual **dividend** distributions the corporation paid to you. The corporation must report to you such amounts totaling $10 or more during the calendar year on **Form 1099-DIV,** Dividends and Distributions. You report actual dividend distributions on Schedule B (Form 1040).

Basis of Your Stock

You are responsible for maintaining records to show the computation of the basis of your stock in the corporation. Schedule K-1 provides you with information to help you make the computation at the end of each corporate tax year. The basis of your stock is adjusted as follows (this list is not all-inclusive).

Basis is increased by:

1. All income (including tax-exempt income) reported on Schedule K-1. **Note:** *Taxable income must be reported on your tax return (if a return is required) for it to increase your basis.*

2. The excess of the deduction for depletion over the basis of the property subject to depletion.

Basis is decreased by:

1. Property distributions made by the corporation (excluding dividend distributions reported on Form 1099-DIV and distributions in excess of basis) reported on Schedule K-1, line 17.

2. All losses and deductions (including nondeductible expenses) reported on Schedule K-1.

Inconsistent Treatment of Items

Generally, you must treat subchapter S items on your return consistent with the way the corporation treated the items on its filed return. This rule does not apply if your S corporation is within the "small S corporation exception" and does not elect to have the tax treatment of subchapter S items determined at the corporate level.

If the treatment on your original or amended return is inconsistent with the corporation's treatment, or if the corporation has not filed a return, you must file **Form 8082,** Notice of Inconsistent Treatment or Amended Return (Administrative Adjustment Request (AAR)), with your original or amended return to identify and explain the inconsistency (or noting that a corporate return has not been filed).

If you are required to file Form 8082 but fail to do so, you may be subject to the accuracy-related penalty. This penalty is in addition to any tax that results from making your amount or treatment of the item consistent with that shown on the corporation's return. Any deficiency that results from making the amounts consistent may be assessed immediately.

Errors

If you believe the corporation has made an error on your Schedule K-1, notify the corporation and ask for a corrected Schedule K-1. Do not change any items on your copy. Be sure that the corporation sends a copy of the corrected Schedule K-1 to the IRS. If your S corporation does not meet the small S corporation exception, and you are unable to reach agreement with the S corporation regarding the inconsistency, you must file Form 8082.

Tax Shelters

If you receive a copy of **Form 8271,** Investor Reporting of Tax Shelter Registration Number, or if your S corporation is involved in a tax shelter, see the instructions for Form 8271 for the information you are required to furnish the IRS. Attach the completed forms to your income tax return. You can find the tax shelter registration number on line C(1) at the top of your Schedule K-1.

International Boycotts

Every S corporation that had operations in, or related to, a boycotting country, company, or national of a country, must file **Form 5713,** International Boycott Report.

If the corporation cooperated with an international boycott, it must give you a copy of the Form 5713 that it filed. You also must file Form 5713 to report the activities of the corporation and any other boycott operations of your own. You may lose certain tax benefits if the corporation participated in, or cooperated with, an international

Cat. No. 11521O

boycott. Please see Form 5713 and the instructions for more information.

Elections

Generally, the corporation decides how to figure taxable income from its operations. For example, it chooses the accounting method and depreciation methods it will use.

However, certain elections are made by you separately on your income tax return and not by the corporation. These elections are made under:

● Section 59(e) (deduction of certain qualified expenditures ratably over the period of time specified in that section—see the instructions for lines 16a and 16b);

● Section 617 (deduction and recapture of certain mining exploration expenditures); and

● Section 901 (foreign tax credit).

Additional Information

For more information on the treatment of S corporation income, credits, deductions, etc., see **Pub. 589,** Tax Information on S Corporations; **Pub. 535,** Business Expenses; **Pub. 550,** Investment Income and Expenses; and **Pub. 925,** Passive Activity and At-Risk Rules.

The above publications and other publications referenced throughout these instructions may be obtained at most IRS offices. To order publications and forms, call our toll-free number, 1-800-TAX-FORM (829-3676).

Limitations on Losses, Deductions, and Credits

Aggregate Losses and Deductions Limited to Basis of Stock and Debt

Generally, the deduction for your share of aggregate losses and deductions reported on Schedule K-1 is limited to the basis of your stock and debt owed to you by the corporation. The basis of your stock is figured at year end. See **Basis of Your Stock** on page1. The basis of your loans made to the corporation is the balance the corporation now owes you, less any reduction for losses in a prior year. See the instructions for line 18. Any loss not allowed for the tax year because of this limitation is available for indefinite carryover, limited to the basis of your stock and debt, in each subsequent tax year. See section 1366(d) for details.

At-Risk Limitations

Generally, if you have:

1. A loss or other deduction from any activity carried on as a trade or business or for the production of income by the corporation, and

2. Amounts in the activity for which you are not at-risk, you will have to complete **Form 6198,** At-Risk Limitations, to figure the allowable loss to report on your return.

The at-risk rules generally limit the amount of loss (including loss on the disposition of assets) and other deductions (such as the section 179 expense deduction) that you can claim to the amount you could actually lose in the activity. However, if you acquired your stock before 1987, the at-risk rules do not apply to losses from an activity of holding real property placed in service before 1987 by the corporation. The activity of holding mineral property does not qualify for this exception.

Generally, you are not at risk for amounts such as the following:

● The basis of your stock in the corporation or basis of your loans made to the corporation if the cash or other property used to purchase the stock or make the loans was from a source covered by nonrecourse indebtedness (except for certain qualified nonrecourse financing, as defined in section 465(b)(6)) or protected against loss by a guarantee, stop-loss agreement, or other similar arrangement, or that is covered by indebtedness from a person who has an interest in the activity or from a related person to a person (except you) having such an interest, other than a creditor.

● Any cash or property contributed to a corporate activity, or your interest in the corporate activity, that is covered by nonrecourse indebtedness (except for certain qualified nonrecourse financing, as defined in section 465(b)(6)) or protected against loss by a guarantee, stop-loss agreement, or other similar arrangement, or that is covered by indebtedness from a person who has an interest in such activity or from a related person to a person (except you) having such an interest, other than a creditor.

Any loss from a section 465 activity not allowed for this tax year will be treated as a deduction allocable to the activity in the next tax year.

To help you complete Form 6198, if required, the corporation should tell you your share of the total pre-1976 losses from a section 465(c)(1) activity (i.e., films or video tapes, leasing section 1245 property, farm, or oil and gas property) for which there existed a corresponding amount of nonrecourse liability at the end of the year in which the losses occurred. Also, you should get a separate statement of income, expenses, etc., for each activity from the corporation.

Passive Activity Limitations

Section 469 provides rules that limit the deduction of certain losses and credits. The rules apply to shareholders who:

● Are individuals, estates, or trusts, and

● Have a passive activity loss or credit for the year.

Passive activities **include:**

1. Trade or business activities in which you do not materially participate, and

2. Activities that meet the definition of rental activities under Temporary Regulations section 1.469-1T(e)(3).

Passive activities **do not include:**

1. Trade or business activities in which you materially participate;

2. Qualifying low-income housing activities; and

3. An activity of trading personal property for the account of owners of interests in the activity.

The corporation will identify separately each activity that may be passive to you. If the corporation is conducting more than one activity, it will report information in the line 20 Supplemental Information space, or attach a statement if more space is needed, that: **(a).** identifies each activity (trade or business activity, rental real estate activity, rental activity other than rental real estate, etc.); **(b).** specifies the income (loss), deductions, and credits from each activity; **(c).** provides other details you may need to determine if an activity loss or credit is subject to the passive activity limitations.

If you determine that you have a passive activity loss or credit, get **Form 8582,** Passive Activity Loss Limitations, to figure your allowable passive loss, and **Form 8582-CR,** Passive Activity Credit Limitations, to figure your allowable passive credit. See the instructions for these forms for more information.

Material participation in trade or business activities.—You must determine whether you materially participated in each trade or business activity held through the corporation. All determinations of material participation are made with respect to participation during the corporation's tax year.

Material participation standards for shareholders who are individuals are listed below. Special rules apply to certain retired or disabled farmers and to the surviving spouses of farmers. See the Instructions for Form 8582 for details.

Individuals.—If you are an individual, you are considered to materially participate in a trade or business activity only if:

1. You participated in the activity for more than 500 hours during the tax year; or

2. Your participation in the activity for the tax year constituted substantially all of the participation in the activity of all individuals (including individuals who are not owners of interests in the activity); or

3. You participated in the activity for more than 100 hours during the tax year, and your participation in the activity for the tax year was not less than the participation in the activity of any other individual (including individuals who were not owners of interests in the activity) for the tax year; or

4. The activity was a significant participation activity for the tax year, and your aggregate participation in all significant participation activities (including those outside the corporation) during the tax year exceeded 500 hours. A significant participation activity is any trade or business activity in which you participated for more than 100 hours during the year and in which you did not materially participate under any of the material participation tests (other than this test 4); or

5. You materially participated in the activity for any five tax years (whether or not consecutive) during the 10 tax years that immediately precede the tax year; or

6. The activity was a personal service activity and you materially participated in the activity for any three tax years (whether or not consecutive) preceding the tax year. An activity is a personal service activity if it involves the performance of personal services in the fields of health, law, engineering, architecture, accounting, actuarial science, performing arts, consulting, or any other trade or business, in which capital is not a material income-producing factor; or

7. Based on all of the facts and circumstances, you participated in the activity on a regular, continuous, and substantial basis during the tax year.

Work counted toward material participation.—Generally, any work that you or your spouse does in connection with an activity held through an S corporation (in which you own stock at the time the work is done) is counted toward material participation. However, work in connection with an activity is not counted toward material participation if:

1. The work is not the sort of work that owners of the activity would usually do and one of the principal purposes of the work that you or your spouse does is to avoid the passive loss or credit limitations, or

2. You do the work in your capacity as an investor and you are not directly involved in the day-to-day operations of the activity. Examples of work done as an investor which would not count toward material participation include:

a. studying and reviewing financial statements or reports on operations of the activity;

b. preparing or compiling summaries or analyses of the finances or operations of the activity; and

c. monitoring the finances or operations of the activity in a non-managerial capacity.

Effect of determination.—If you determine that you materially participated in a trade or business activity of the corporation, report the income (loss), deductions, and credits from the Schedule K-1 as indicated in either column (c) of Schedule K-1 or the instructions for your tax return.

If you determine that you **did not** materially participate in a trade or business activity, or you have income (loss), deductions, or credits from a rental activity of the corporation, the amounts from that activity are passive. Report passive income (losses), deductions, and credits as follows:

1. If you have an overall gain (the excess of income over deductions and losses, including any prior year unallowed loss) from a passive activity, report the income, deductions, and losses from the activity as indicated on Schedule K-1 or in these instructions.

2. If you have an overall loss (the excess of deductions and losses, including any prior year unallowed loss, over income) or credits from a passive activity, you must report the income, deductions, losses, and credits from **all** passive activities following the Instructions for Form 8582 or Form 8582-CR, to see if your deductions, losses, and credits are limited under the passive activity rules.

Active participation in a rental real estate activity.—If you actively participated in a rental real estate activity, you may be able to deduct up to $25,000 of the loss from the activity from nonpassive income. This "special allowance" is an exception to the general rule disallowing losses in excess of income from passive activities. The special allowance is not available if you were married, file a separate return for the year, and did not live apart from your spouse at all times during the year.

Only individuals and qualifying estates can actively participate in a rental real estate activity. Estates (other than qualifying estates) and trusts cannot actively participate.

You are not considered to actively participate in a rental real estate activity if, at any time during the tax year, your interest (including your spouse's interest) in the activity was less than 10% (by value) of all interests in the activity.

Active participation is a less stringent requirement than material participation. You may be treated as actively participating if you participated, for example, in making management decisions or arranging for others to provide services (such as repairs) in a significant and bona fide sense. Management decisions that can count as active participation include approving new tenants, deciding on rental terms, approving capital or repair expenditures, and other similar decisions.

An estate is treated as actively participating for tax years ending less than 2 years after the date of the decedent's death if the decedent would have satisfied the active participation requirement for the activity for the tax year the decedent died. Such an estate is a "qualifying estate."

The maximum special allowance that single individuals and married individuals filing a joint return for the tax year can qualify for is $25,000. The maximum is $12,500 in the case of married individuals who file separate returns for the tax year and who lived apart at all times during the year. The maximum special allowance for which an estate can qualify is $25,000 reduced by the special allowance for which the surviving spouse qualifies.

If your modified adjusted gross income (defined below) is $100,000 or less ($50,000 or less in the case of married persons filing separately), your loss is deductible up to the amount of the maximum special allowance referred to in the preceding paragraph. If your modified adjusted gross income is more than $100,000 (more than $50,000 in the case of married persons filing separately), the special allowance is 50% of the difference between $150,000 ($75,000 in the case of married persons filing separately) and your modified adjusted gross income. When modified adjusted gross income is $150,000 or more ($75,000 or more in the case of married persons filing separately), there is no special allowance.

Modified adjusted gross income is your adjusted gross income figured without taking into account any passive activity loss, any taxable social security or equivalent railroad retirement benefits, any deductible contributions to an IRA or certain other qualified retirement plans under section 219, the deduction allowed under section 164(f) for one-half of self-employment taxes, or the exclusion from income of interest from Series EE U.S. Savings Bonds used to pay higher education expenses.

Special rule for low-income housing activities.—Transitional relief from the passive activity limitations is provided in the case of certain losses from qualified low-income housing projects. The corporation will identify losses from qualified low-income housing projects on an attachment to your Schedule K-1. See Pub. 925 for more information.

Specific Instructions

Name, Address, and Identifying Number

Your name, address, and identifying number, the corporation's name, address, and identifying number, and items A and B should have been completed. If the corporation is involved in a tax shelter, items C(1) and C(2) should also be completed.

If applicable, item D should be completed.

Lines 1 Through 20

The amounts on lines 1 through 20 show your pro rata share of ordinary income, loss, deductions, credits, and other information from all corporate activities. These amounts do not take into account limitations on losses, credits, or other items that may have to be adjusted because of:

1. The adjusted basis of your stock and debt in the corporation,

2. The at-risk limitations,

3. The passive activity limitations, or

4. Any other limitations that must be taken into account at the shareholder level in figuring taxable income (e.g., the section 179 expense limitation). The limitations of 1., 2., and 3. are discussed above, and the limitations for 4. are discussed throughout these instructions and in other referenced forms and instructions.

If you are an individual, and your pro rata share items are not affected by any of the limitations, report the amounts shown in column (b) of Schedule K-1 as indicated in column (c). If any of the limitations apply, adjust the column (b) amounts for the limitations before you enter the amounts on your return. When applicable, the passive activity limitations on losses are applied after the limitations on losses for a shareholder's basis in stock and debt and the shareholder's at-risk amount.

Note: *The line number references in column (c) are to forms in use for tax years beginning in 1991. If you are a calendar year shareholder in a fiscal year 1991–92 corporation, enter these amounts on the corresponding lines of the tax form in use for 1992.*

Caution: *If you have losses, deductions, credits, etc., from a prior year that were not deductible or usable because of certain limitations, such as the at-risk rules, they may be taken into account in determining your income, loss, etc., for this year. However, do not combine the prior-year amounts with any amounts shown on this Schedule K-1 to get a net figure to report on your return. Instead, report the amounts on your return on a year-by-year basis.*

Income

Line 1—Ordinary Income (Loss) From Trade or Business Activities

The amount reported on line 1 is your share of the ordinary income (loss) from trade or business activities of the corporation. Generally, where you report this amount on Form 1040 depends on whether the amount is from an activity that is a passive activity to you. If you are an individual shareholder, find your situation below and report your line 1 income (loss) as instructed after applying the basis and at-risk limitations on losses:

1. Report line 1 income (loss) from trade or business activities in which you materially participated on Schedule E (Form 1040), Part Ii, column (i) or (k).

2. Report line 1 income (loss) from trade or business activities in which you did not materially participate, as follows:

a. If income is reported on line 1, report the income on Schedule E, Part II, column (h).

b. If a loss is reported on line 1, report the loss following the Instructions for Form 8582 to determine how much of the loss can be reported on Schedule E, Part II, column (g).

Line 2—Net Income (Loss) From Rental Real Estate Activities

Generally, the income (loss) reported on line 2 is a passive activity amount for all shareholders. There is an exception, however, for losses from a qualified low-income housing project. The passive activity loss limitations do not apply to losses incurred by qualified investors in qualified low-income housing projects (see Pub. 925). The corporation will have attached a schedule for line 2 to identify any such amounts.

If you are filing a 1991 Form 1040, use the following instructions to determine where to enter a line 2 amount:

1. If you have a loss (other than from a qualified low-income housing project) on line 2 and you meet **all** of the following conditions, enter the loss on Schedule E (Form 1040), Part II, column (g):

a. You actively participated in the corporate rental real estate activities. (See **Active participation in a rental real estate activity,** on page 3.)

b. Rental real estate activities with active participation were your only passive activities.

c. You have no prior year unallowed losses from these activities.

d. Your total loss from the rental real estate activities was not more than $25,000 (not more than $12,500 if married filing separately and you lived apart from your spouse all year).

e. If you are a married person filing separately, you lived apart from your spouse all year.

f. You have no current or prior year unallowed credits from a passive activity.

g. Your modified adjusted gross income was not more than $100,000 (not more than $50,000 if married filing separately and you lived apart from your spouse all year).

2. If you have a loss (other than from a qualified low-income housing project) on line 2, and **you do not meet** all of the conditions in **1.** above, report the loss following the Instructions for Form 8582 to determine how much of the loss can be reported on Schedule E (Form 1040), Part II, column (g).

3. If you are a qualified investor reporting a qualified low-income housing project loss, report the loss on Schedule E, Part II, column (i).

4. If you have income on line 2, enter the income on Schedule E, Part II, column (h).

Line 3—Net Income (Loss) From Other Rental Activities

The amount on line 3 is a passive activity amount for all shareholders. Report the income or loss as follows:

1. If line 3 is a loss, report the loss following the Instructions for Form 8582.

2. If income is reported on line 3, report the income on Schedule E (Form 1040), Part II, column (h).

Line 4—Portfolio Income (Loss)

Portfolio income or loss is not subject to the passive activity limitations. Portfolio income includes interest, dividend, annuity and royalty income not derived in the ordinary course of a trade or business, and gain or loss on the sale of property that produces these types of income or is held for investment.

Column (c) of Schedule K-1 tells shareholders where to report this income on Form 1040 and related schedules. Line 4f of Schedule K-1 is used to report income other than that reported on lines 4a through 4e. The type and the amount of income reported on line 4f will be listed in the line 20 Supplemental Information space of Schedule K-1. An example of the type of income that is reported in line 4f is income from a Real Estate Mortgage Investment Company (REMIC) in which the corporation is a residual interest holder. Report your share of any REMIC income on Schedule E (Form 1040), Part IV.

Line 5—Net Gain (Loss) Under Section 1231 (Other Than Due to Casualty or Theft)

Section 1231 gain or loss is reported on line 5. The corporation will identify in the line 20 Supplemental Information space the activity to which the section 1231 gain (loss) relates.

If the amount on line 5 relates to a rental activity, the section 1231 gain (loss) is a passive activity amount. Likewise, if the amount relates to a trade or business activity and you do not materially participate in the activity, the section 1231 gain (loss) is a passive activity amount.

- If the amount is **not** a passive activity amount to you, report it on line 2, column (g) or (h), whichever is applicable, of **Form 4797,** Sales of Business Property. You do not have to complete the information called for in columns (b) through (f), Form 4797. Write "From Schedule K-1 (Form 1120S)" across these columns.
- If gain is reported on line 5 and it **is** a passive activity amount to you, report the gain on line 2, column (h) of Form 4797.
- If a loss is reported on line 5 and it **is** a passive activity amount to you, see **Passive Loss Limitations** in the Instructions for Form 4797. You will need to report the loss following the Instructions for Form 8582 to determine how much of the loss is allowed on Form 4797.

Line 6—Other Income (Loss)

Amounts on this line are other items of income, gain, or loss not included on lines 1 through 5. The corporation should give you a description and the amount of your share for each of these items.

Report loss items that are passive activity amounts to you following the Instructions for Form 8582.

Report income or gain items that are passive activity amounts to you as instructed below.

The instructions below tell you where to report line 6 items if such items are **not** passive activity amounts.

Line 6 items include the following:
- Income from recoveries of tax benefit items. A tax benefit item is an amount you deducted in a prior tax year that reduced your income tax. Report this amount on Form 1040, line 22, to the extent it reduced your tax.
- Gambling gains and losses.

1. If the corporation was not engaged in the trade or business of gambling:

a. Report gambling winnings on Form 1040, line 22.

b. Deduct gambling losses to the extent of winnings on Schedule A, line 25.

2. If the corporation was engaged in the trade or business of gambling:

a. Report gambling winnings in Part II of Schedule E.

b. Deduct gambling losses to the extent of winnings in Part II of Schedule E.
- Net gain (loss) from involuntary conversions due to casualty or theft. The corporation will give you a schedule that shows the amounts to be reported in Section B of **Form 4684,** Casualties and Thefts.
- Net short-term capital gain or loss and net long-term capital gain or loss from Schedule D (Form 1120S) that is **not**

portfolio income (e.g., gain or loss from the disposition of nondepreciable personal property used in a trade or business activity of the corporation). Report a net short-term capital gain or loss on Schedule D (Form 1040), line 4, column (f) or (g), and a net long-term capital gain or loss on Schedule D (Form 1040), line 11, column (f) or (g).
- Any net gain or loss from section 1256 contracts. Report this amount on line 1 of **Form 6781,** Gains and Losses From Section 1256 Contracts and Straddles.

Deductions

Line 7—Charitable Contributions

The corporation will give you a schedule that shows which contributions were subject to the 50%, 30%, and 20% limitations. For further information, see the Form 1040 instructions.

If property other than cash is contributed, and the claimed deduction for one item or group of similar items of property exceeds $5,000, the corporation is required to file **Form 8283,** Noncash Charitable Contributions, and give you a copy to attach to your tax return. Do not deduct the amount shown on Form 8283. It is the corporation's contribution. You should deduct the amount shown on line 7, Schedule K-1.

If the corporation provides you with information that the contribution was property other than cash and does not give you a Form 8283, see the Instructions for Form 8283 for filing requirements. A Form 8283 does not have to be filed unless the total claimed deduction of all contributed items of property exceeds $500.

Charitable contribution deductions are not taken into account in figuring your passive activity loss for the year. Do not enter them on Form 8582.

Line 8—Section 179 Expense Deduction

Use this amount, along with the total cost of section 179 property placed in service during the year from other sources, to complete Part I of **Form 4562,** Depreciation and Amortization. Part I of Form 4562 is used to figure your allowable section 179 expense deduction from all sources. Report the amount on line 12 of Form 4562 allocable to a passive activity from the corporation following the Instructions for Form 8582. If the amount is not a passive activity deduction, report it on Schedule E (Form 1040), Part II, column (j).

Line 9—Deductions Related to Portfolio Income

Amounts on line 9 are deductions that are clearly and directly allocable to portfolio income reported on lines 4a

through 4f (other than investment interest expense and section 212 expenses from a REMIC). Generally, you should enter line 9 amounts on Schedule A (Form 1040), line 20. See the instructions for Schedule A, lines 19 through 25, for more information.

These deductions are not taken into account in figuring your passive activity loss for the year. Do not enter them on Form 8582.

Line 10—Other Deductions

Amounts on this line are other deductions not included on lines 7, 8, 9, and 15e, such as:
- Itemized deductions that Form 1040 filers enter on Schedule A (Form 1040).

Note: *If there was a gain (loss) from a casualty or theft to property **not** used in a trade or business or for income-producing purposes, you will be notified by the corporation. You will have to complete your own Form 4684.*
- Any penalty on early withdrawal of savings.
- Soil and water conservation expenditures. See section 175 for limitations on the amount you are allowed to deduct.
- Expenditures for the removal of architectural and transportation barriers to the elderly and disabled that the corporation elected to treat as a current expense. The expenses are limited by section 190.
- Interest expense allocated to debt-financed distributions. The manner in which you report such interest expense depends on your use of the distributed debt proceeds. See Notice 89-35, 1989-1 C.B. 675, for details.

If the corporation has more than one corporate activity (line **1, 2,** or **3** of Schedule K-1), it will identify the activity to which the expenses relate.

The corporation should also give you a description and your share of each of the expense items. Associate any passive activity deduction included on line 10 with the line **1, 2,** or **3** activity to which it relates and report the deduction following the Instructions for Form 8582 (or only on Schedule E (Form 1040) if applicable).

Investment Interest

If the corporation paid or accrued interest on debts properly allocable to investment property, the amount of interest you are allowed to deduct may be limited.

For more information on the special provisions that apply to investment interest expense, see **Form 4952,** Investment Interest Expense Deduction, and **Pub. 550,** Investment Income and Expenses.

Line 11a—Interest Expense on Investment Debts

Enter this amount on Form 4952 along with investment interest expense from other sources to determine how much of your total investment interest is deductible.

Lines 11b(1) and (2)—Investment Income and Investment Expenses

Use the amounts on these lines to determine the amount to enter on Form 4952.

Caution: *The amounts shown on lines 11b(1) and 11b(2) include only investment income and expenses reported on lines 4 and 9 of Schedule K-1. If applicable, the corporation will have listed in the line 20 Supplemental Information space any other items of investment income and expenses reported elsewhere on Schedule K-1. Combine these items with lines 11b(1) and 11b(2) income and expenses to determine your total investment income and total investment expense from the corporation. Combine these totals with investment income and expenses from other sources to determine the amounts to enter on Form 4952.*

Credits

Caution: *If you have credits that are passive activity credits to you (i.e., the activity that generated the credit was a passive activity), you must complete Form 8582-CR in addition to the credit forms referenced below. See the Instructions for Form 8582-CR for more information.*

Also, if you are entitled to claim more than one general business credit (i.e., investment credit, jobs credit, credit for alcohol used as fuel, research credit, low-income housing credit, enhanced oil recovery credit, and disabled access credit), you must complete Form 3800, General Business Credit, in addition to the credit forms referenced below. If you have more than one credit, see the instructions for Form 3800 for more information.

Line 12a—Credit for Alcohol Used as Fuel

Your share of the corporation's credit for alcohol used as fuel that is related to all trade or business activities is reported on line 12a. Enter this credit on **Form 6478,** Credit for Alcohol Used as Fuel, to determine your allowed credit for the year.

Line 12b—Low-Income Housing Credit

Your share of the corporation's low-income housing credit is shown on lines 12b(1) through (4). Your allowable credit is entered on **Form 8586,** Low-Income Housing Credit, to

determine your allowed credit for the year.

If the corporation invested in a partnership to which the provisions of section 42(j)(5) apply, it will report separately on lines 12b(1) and 12b(3) your share of the credit it received from the partnership.

Your share of all other low-income housing credits of the corporation is reported on lines 12b(2) and 12b(4). You must keep a separate record of the amount of low-income housing credit from these lines so that you will be able to correctly compute any recapture of the credit that may result from the disposition of all or part of your stock in the corporation. For more information, see the instructions for **Form 8611,** Recapture of Low-Income Housing Credit.

Caution: *You cannot claim the low-income housing credit on any qualified low-income housing project if you, or any person, were allowed relief from the passive activity limitations on losses from the project (section 502 of the Tax Reform Act of 1986).*

Line 12c—Qualified Rehabilitation Expenditures Related to Rental Real Estate Activities

The corporation should identify your share of rehabilitation expenditures that are related to each rental real estate activity. The allowable investment credit for qualified rehabilitation expenditures is figured on **Form 3468,** Investment Credit.

Line 12d—Credits (Other Than Credits Shown on Lines 12b and 12c) Related to Rental Real Estate Activities

If applicable, your pro rata share of any other credit (other than on line 12b or 12c) related to rental real estate activities will be shown on line 12d. If more than one credit is involved, the credits will be shown and identified as line 12d credits in the line 20 Supplemental Information space. If the corporation has more than one rental real estate activity, each activity will be separately identified with any credits from the activity, and other information needed to figure the passive activity limitations.

Line 12e—Credits Related to Other Rental Activities

If applicable, your share of any credit related to other rental activities will be reported on line 12e. Income or loss for these activities is reported on line 3 of Schedule K-1. If more than one credit is involved, the credits will be listed separately, each credit identified as a line 12e credit, and the activity to which the credit relates will be identified. This information will be shown in the line 20

Supplemental Information space. The credit may be limited by the passive activity limitations.

Line 13—Other Credits

If applicable, your pro rata share of any other credit (other than on lines 12a through 12e) will be shown on line 13. If more than one credit is reported, the credits will be shown and identified in the line 20 Supplemental Information space. Expenditures qualifying for the **(a)** rehabilitation credit not related to rental real estate activities, **(b)** energy credit, or **(c)** reforestation credit will be reported to you on line 20.

Line 13 credits include the following:

● Nonconventional source fuel credit. Enter this credit on a schedule you prepare yourself to determine the allowed credit to take on your tax return. See section 29 for rules on how to figure the credit.

● Unused investment credit from cooperatives. Enter this credit on Form 3468 to figure your allowable investment credit.

● Credit for backup withholding on dividends, interest income, and other types of income. Include the amount the corporation reports to you in the total that you enter on line 54, page 2, Form 1040. Be sure to check the box on line 54 and write "From Schedule K-1".

● Credit for increasing research activities and orphan drug credit. Enter these credits on **Form 6765,** Credit for Increasing Research Activities.

● Jobs credit. Enter this credit on **Form 5884,** Jobs Credit.

● Disabled access credit. Enter this credit on **Form 8826,** Disabled Access Credit.

● Enhanced oil recovery credit. Enter this credit on **Form 8830,** Enhanced Oil Recovery Credit.

Adjustments and Tax Preference Items

Use the information reported on lines 14a through 14f (as well as adjustments and tax preference items from other sources) to prepare your **Form 6251,** Alternative Minimum Tax—Individuals, or **Form 8656,** Alternative Minimum Tax—Fiduciaries.

Lines 14e(1) and 14e(2)—Gross Income From, and Deductions Allocable to, Oil, Gas, and Geothermal Properties

The amounts reported on these lines include only the gross income from, and deductions allocable to, oil, gas, and geothermal properties that are included on line 1 of Schedule K-1. The corporation should have reported separately any income from or deductions allocable to such properties that are included on lines 2 through 10. This separate information is reported in the line 20 Supplemental Information space. Use the amounts reported on lines 14e(1) and 14e(2) and any amounts reported on a schedule to help you determine the net amount to enter on line 6g of Form 6251.

Line 14f—Other Adjustments and Tax Preference Items

Enter the line 14f adjustments and tax preference items that are shown in the line 20 Supplemental Information space, with other items from other sources, on the applicable lines of Form 6251.

Foreign Taxes

Use the information on lines 15a through 15g, and attached schedules, to figure your foreign tax credit. For more information, see **Form 1116,** Foreign Tax Credit—Individual, Fiduciary, or Nonresident Alien Individual, and the related instructions.

Other

Lines 16a and 16b

The corporation will show on line 16a the total qualified expenditures to which an election under section 59(e) may apply. It will identify the type of expenditures on line 16b. If there is more than one type of expenditure, the amount of each type will be listed on an attachment. Generally, section 59(e) allows each shareholder to elect to deduct certain expenses ratably over the number of years in the applicable period rather than deduct the full amount in the current year. Under the election, you may deduct ratably over a 3-year period circulation expenditures. Research and experimental expenditures and mining exploration and development costs qualify for a writeoff period of 10 years. Intangible drilling and development costs may be deducted over a 60-month period, beginning with the month in which such costs were paid or incurred. If you make this election, these items are not treated as adjustments or tax preference items for purposes of the alternative minimum tax. Make the election on Form 4562.

Because each shareholder decides whether to make the election under section 59(e), the corporation cannot provide you with the amount of the adjustment or tax preference item related to the expenses listed on line 16a. You must decide both how to claim the expenses on your return and how to compute the resulting adjustment or tax preference item.

Line 17

Reduce the basis of your stock in the corporation by the distributions on line 17. If these distributions exceed the

basis of your stock, the excess is treated as gain from the sale or exchange of property and is reported on Schedule D (Form 1040).

Line 18

If the line 18 payments are made on indebtedness with a reduced basis, the repayments result in income to you to the extent the repayments are more than the adjusted basis of the loan. See section 1367(b)(2) for information on reduction in basis of a loan and restoration in basis of a loan with a reduced basis. See Revenue Ruling 64-162, 1964-1 (Part 1) C.B. 304 and Revenue Ruling 68-537, 1968-2 C.B. 372, for other information.

Lines 19a and 19b—Recapture of Low-Income Housing Credit

The corporation will report separately on line 19a your share of any recapture of a low-income housing credit attributable to its investment in partnerships to which the provisions of section 42(j)(5) apply. All other recapture of low-income housing credits will be reported on line 19b. You must keep a separate record of recapture attributable to lines 19a and 19b so that you will be able to correctly figure any credit recapture that may result from the disposition of all or part of your corporate stock ownership. Use the lines 19a and 19b amounts to compute the low-income housing credit recapture on Form 8611. See the instructions for Form 8611 and section 42(j) for additional information.

Supplemental Information

Line 20

If applicable, the corporation should have listed in line 20, Supplemental Information, or if additional space was needed, on an attached statement to Schedule K-1, your distributive share of the following:

1. Information for lines 4f, 6, 7, 9, 10, 14f, 15c, 15d, 15f, and 15g of Schedule K-1.

2. Tax-exempt interest income realized by the corporation. Generally, this income increases your basis in stock of the corporation. Tax-exempt interest earned by the corporation is stated separately for the following reasons:

a. If applicable, use this amount to figure the taxable portion of your social security or railroad retirement benefits. See the Instructions for Form 1040 for details.

b. If you are required to file a tax return for 1991, you must report on your return as an item of information the amount of tax-exempt interest income received or accrued during the tax year. Individual shareholders should report this amount on line 8b of Form 1040.

3. Nondeductible expenses paid or incurred by the corporation. These expenses are not deducted on your tax return but decrease the basis of your stock.

4. Taxes paid on undistributed capital gains by a regulated investment company. (Form 1040 filers, enter your share of these taxes on line 59 of Form 1040, check the box for Form 2439, and add the words "Form 1120S". Also reduce the basis of your stock in the S corporation by this tax.)

5. Gross income from the property, share of production for the tax year, etc., needed to figure your depletion deduction for oil and gas wells. The corporation should also allocate to you a proportionate share of the adjusted basis of each corporate oil or gas property. The allocation of the basis of each property is made as specified in section 613A(c)(11). See Pub. 535 for how to figure your depletion deduction. Also reduce your basis in stock by this deduction (section 1367(a)(2)(E)).

6. Your share of the intangible drilling and development costs shown on line 16a that is attributable to qualified exploratory costs. Use this amount to compute the alternative minimum tax adjustment based on energy preferences. See section 56(h) for more details.

7. Recapture of the section 179 expense deduction. The corporation will tell you if the recapture was caused by a disposition of the property.

The recapture amount is limited to the amount you deducted in earlier years. See Form 4797 for additional information.

8. Recapture of certain mining exploration expenditures (section 617).

9. Any information or statements you need to comply with requirements under section 6111 (registration of tax shelters) or 6662(d)(2)(B)(ii) (regarding adequate disclosure of items that may cause an understatement of income tax).

10. Gross farming and fishing income. If you are an individual shareholder, enter this income on Schedule E (Form 1040), Part V, line 41. Do not report this income elsewhere on Form 1040.

For a shareholder that is an estate or trust, report this income to the beneficiaries on Schedule K-1 (Form 1041). Do not report it elsewhere on Form 1041.

11. Any information you need to compute the interest due under section 453A(c) with respect to certain installment sales of property. If you are an individual, report the interest on Form 1040, line 53. Write "453A(c)" and the amount of the interest on the dotted line to the left of line 53. See the instructions for **Form 6252,** Installment Sale Income, for more information. Also see section

453A(c) for details on making the computation.

12. Information you need to figure the interest due under section 453(l)(3). If the corporation elected to report the dispositions of certain timeshares and residential lots on the installment method, your tax liability must be increased by the interest on tax attributable to your pro rata share of the installment payments received by the corporation during its tax year. If applicable, use the information provided by the corporation to figure your interest. Include the interest on Form 1040, line 53. Also write "453(l)(3)" and the amount of the interest on the dotted line to the left of line 53.

13. Capitalization of interest under section 263A(f). To the extent that certain production or construction expenditures of the corporation are made from proceeds associated with debt that you incur as an owner-shareholder, you must capitalize the interest on this debt. If applicable, use the information on expenditures the corporation gives to you to determine the amount of interest you must capitalize. See Section XII of Notice 88-99, 1988-2 C.B. 422 for more information.

14. Any information you need to compute the interest due or to be refunded under the look-back method of section 460(b)(2) on certain long-term contracts. Use **Form 8697**, Interest Computation Under the Look-Back Method for Completed Long-Term Contracts, to report any such interest.

15. Your share of expenditures qualifying for the **(a)** rehabilitation credit not related to rental real estate activities, **(b)** energy credit, or **(c)** reforestation credit. Enter the expenditures on the appropriate line of Form 3468 to figure your allowable credit.

16. Investment credit properties subject to recapture. Any information you need to figure your recapture tax on **Form 4255**, Recapture of Investment Credit. See the Form 3468 on which you took the original credit for other information you need to complete Form 4255.

You may also need Form 4255 if you disposed of more than one-third of your stock in the corporation.

17. Preproductive period farm expenses. You may elect to deduct these expenses currently or capitalize them under section 263A. See **Pub. 225,** Farmer's Tax Guide, and Temporary Regulations section 1.263A-1T(c) for more information.

18. Any other information you may need to file with your individual tax return that is not shown elsewhere on Schedule K-1.

Shareholder's Share of Income, Credits, Deductions, etc.

► See separate instructions.

For calendar year 1991 or tax year
beginning   , 1991, and ending   , 19

OMB No. 1545-0130

1991

Shareholder's identifying number ► 458-00-0327	Corporation's identifying number ► 10-4487965
Shareholder's name, address, and ZIP code John H. Green 4340 Holmes Parkway Metro City, OH 43704	Corporation's name, address, and ZIP code StratoTech, Inc. 482 Winston Street Metro City, OH 43705

A Shareholder's percentage of stock ownership for tax year (see Instructions for Schedule K-1) . . . . . ► **45** %

B Internal Revenue service center where corporation filed its return ► **Cincinnati, OH**

C (1) Tax shelter registration number (see Instructions for Schedule K-1) . . . . ►

   (2) Type of tax shelter ►

D Check applicable boxes: (1) ☐ Final K-1   (2) ☐ Amended K-1

		(a) Pro rata share items		(b) Amount	(c) Form 1040 filers enter the amount in column (b) on:
Income (Loss)	1	Ordinary income (loss) from trade or business activities . .	1	53,550	See Shareholder's Instructions for Schedule K-1 (Form 1120S).
	2	Net income (loss) from rental real estate activities	2		
	3	Net income (loss) from other rental activities	3		
	4	Portfolio income (loss):			
	a	Interest	4a	1,800	Sch. B, Part I, line 1
	b	Dividends	4b	7,200	Sch. B, Part II, line 5
	c	Royalties	4c		Sch. E, Part I, line 4
	d	Net short-term capital gain (loss)	4d		Sch. D, line 4, col. (f) or (g)
	e	Net long-term capital gain (loss)	4e		Sch. D, line 11, col. (f) or (g)
	f	Other portfolio income (loss) (attach schedule)	4f		(Enter on applicable line of your return)
	5	Net gain (loss) under section 1231 (other than due to casualty or theft) .	5		See Shareholder's Instructions for Schedule K-1 (Form 1120S)
	6	Other income (loss) (attach schedule)	6		(Enter on applicable line of your return)
Deductions	7	Charitable contributions (see instructions) (attach schedule) .	7	10,800	Sch. A, line 13 or 14
	8	Section 179 expense deduction	8		See Shareholder's Instructions for Schedule K-1 (Form 1120S).
	9	Deductions related to portfolio income (loss) (attach schedule) .	9		
	10	Other deductions (attach schedule)	10		
Investment Interest	11a	Interest expense on investment debts	11a	1,350	Form 4952, line 1
	b	(1) Investment income included on lines 4a through 4f above	b(1)	9,000	See Shareholder's Instructions for Schedule K-1 (Form 1120S)
		(2) Investment expenses included on line 9 above	b(2)		
Credits	12a	Credit for alcohol used as fuel	12a		Form 6478, line 10
	b	Low-income housing credit:			
		(1) From section 42(j)(5) partnerships for property placed in service before 1990	b(1)		Form 8586, line 5
		(2) Other than on line 12b(1) for property placed in service before 1990	b(2)		
		(3) From section 42(j)(5) partnerships for property placed in service after 1989 .	b(3)		
		(4) Other than on line 12b(3) for property placed in service after 1989 . .	b(4)		
	c	Qualified rehabilitation expenditures related to rental real estate activities (see instructions)	12c		See Shareholder's Instructions for Schedule K-1 (Form 1120S).
	d	Credits (other than credits shown on lines 12b and 12c) related to rental real estate activities (see instructions) . . .	12d		
	e	Credits related to other rental activities (see instructions) .	12e		
	13	Other credits (see instructions). Jobs Credit . . .	13	2,700	
Adjustments and Tax Preference Items	14a	Accelerated depreciation of real property placed in service before 1987	14a		See Shareholder's Instructions for Schedule K-1 (Form 1120S) and Instructions for Form 6251
	b	Accelerated depreciation of leased personal property placed in service before 1987	14b		
	c	Depreciation adjustment on property placed in service after 1986	14c		
	d	Depletion (other than oil and gas)	14d		
	e	(1) Gross income from oil, gas, or geothermal properties .	e(1)		
		(2) Deductions allocable to oil, gas, or geothermal properties	e(2)		
	f	Other adjustments and tax preference items (attach schedule)	14f		

For Paperwork Reduction Act Notice, see page 1 of Instructions for Form 1120S.   Cat. No. 11520D   Schedule K-1 (Form 1120S) 1991

18

	(a) Pro rata share items		(b) Amount	(c) Form 1040 filers enter the amount in column (b) on:
Foreign Taxes	**15a** Type of income ▶			Form 1116, Check boxes
	b Name of foreign country or U.S. possession ▶			
	c Total gross income from sources outside the U.S. (attach schedule)	**15c**		Form 1116, Part I
	d Total applicable deductions and losses (attach schedule)	**15d**		
	e Total foreign taxes (check one): ▶ ☐ Paid ☐ Accrued	**15e**		Form 1116, Part II
	f Reduction in taxes available for credit (attach schedule)	**15f**		Form 1116, Part III
	g Other foreign tax information (attach schedule)	**15g**		See Instructions for Form 1116
Other	**16a** Total expenditures to which a section 59(e) election may apply	**16a**		See Shareholder's Instructions for Schedule K-1 (Form 1120S).
	b Type of expenditures ▶			
	17 Property distributions (including cash) other than dividend distributions reported to you on Form 1099-DIV	**17**	*29,250*	
	18 Amount of loan repayments for "Loans From Shareholders"	**18**		
	19 Recapture of low-income housing credit:			
	a From section 42(j)(5) partnerships	**19a**		Form 8611, line 8
	b Other than on line 19a	**19b**		

20 Supplemental information required to be reported separately to each shareholder (attach additional schedules if more space is needed):

Tax-exempt interest $ 2,250

Nondeductible salaries and wages due to jobs credit

$ 2,700

SCHEDULE K-1 (Form 1120S) Department of the Treasury Internal Revenue Service	Shareholder's Share of Income, Credits, Deductions, etc. ▶ See separate instructions. For calendar year 1991 or tax year beginning , 1991, and ending , 19	OMB No. 1545-0130 **1991**

Shareholder's identifying number ▶ | **Corporation's identifying number ▶**

Shareholder's name, address, and ZIP code | Corporation's name, address, and ZIP code

A Shareholder's percentage of stock ownership for tax year (see Instructions for Schedule K-1) . . . . . ▶ .... %

B Internal Revenue service center where corporation filed its return ▶ --

C (1) Tax shelter registration number (see Instructions for Schedule K-1) . . . . ▶ ----------------------

   (2) Type of tax shelter ▶ ---

D Check applicable boxes: **(1)** ☐ Final K-1   **(2)** ☐ Amended K-1

	(a) Pro rata share items		(b) Amount	(c) Form 1040 filers enter the amount in column (b) on:
Income (Loss)	**1** Ordinary income (loss) from trade or business activities . .	**1**		See Shareholder's Instructions for Schedule K-1 (Form 1120S).
	2 Net income (loss) from rental real estate activities	**2**		
	3 Net income (loss) from other rental activities	**3**		
	4 Portfolio income (loss):			
	a Interest.	**4a**		Sch. B, Part I, line 1
	b Dividends	**4b**		Sch. B, Part II, line 5
	c Royalties	**4c**		Sch. E, Part I, line 4
	d Net short-term capital gain (loss)	**4d**		Sch. D, line 4, col. (f) or (g)
	e Net long-term capital gain (loss)	**4e**		Sch. D, line 11, col. (f) or (g)
	f Other portfolio income (loss) (attach schedule).	**4f**		(Enter on applicable line of your return.)
	5 Net gain (loss) under section 1231 (other than due to casualty or theft).	**5**		See Shareholder's Instructions for Schedule K-1 (Form 1120S).
	6 Other income (loss) (attach schedule).	**6**		(Enter on applicable line of your return.)
Deductions	**7** Charitable contributions (see instructions) (attach schedule) .	**7**		Sch. A, line 13 or 14
	8 Section 179 expense deduction	**8**		See Shareholder's Instructions for Schedule K-1 (Form 1120S).
	9 Deductions related to portfolio income (loss) (attach schedule)	**9**		
	10 Other deductions (attach schedule)	**10**		
Investment Interest	**11a** Interest expense on investment debts	**11a**		Form 4952, line 1
	b (1) Investment income included on lines 4a through 4f above	**b(1)**		See Shareholder's Instructions for Schedule K-1 (Form 1120S).
	(2) Investment expenses included on line 9 above	**b(2)**		
Credits	**12a** Credit for alcohol used as fuel	**12a**		Form 6478, line 10
	b Low-income housing credit:			
	(1) From section 42(j)(5) partnerships for property placed in service before 1990	**b(1)**		
	(2) Other than on line 12b(1) for property placed in service before 1990 .	**b(2)**		Form 8586, line 5
	(3) From section 42(j)(5) partnerships for property placed in service after 1989 .	**b(3)**		
	(4) Other than on line 12b(3) for property placed in service after 1989 . .	**b(4)**		
	c Qualified rehabilitation expenditures related to rental real estate activities (see instructions)	**12c**		
	d Credits (other than credits shown on lines 12b and 12c) related to rental real estate activities (see instructions)	**12d**		See Shareholder's Instructions for Schedule K-1 (Form 1120S).
	e Credits related to other rental activities (see instructions) .	**12e**		
	13 Other credits (see instructions)	**13**		
Adjustments and Tax Preference Items	**14a** Accelerated depreciation of real property placed in service before 1987	**14a**		See Shareholder's Instructions for Schedule K-1 (Form 1120S) and Instructions for Form 6251
	b Accelerated depreciation of leased personal property placed in service before 1987	**14b**		
	c Depreciation adjustment on property placed in service after 1986	**14c**		
	d Depletion (other than oil and gas)	**14d**		
	e (1) Gross income from oil, gas, or geothermal properties . .	**e(1)**		
	(2) Deductions allocable to oil, gas, or geothermal properties	**e(2)**		
	f Other adjustments and tax preference items (attach schedule)	**14f**		

For Paperwork Reduction Act Notice, see page 1 of Instructions for Form 1120S.   Cat. No. 11520D   **Schedule K-1 (Form 1120S) 1991**

	(a) Pro rata share items	(b) Amount	(c) Form 1040 filers enter the amount in column (b) on:
Foreign Taxes	**15a** Type of income ▶		Form 1116, Check boxes
	b Name of foreign country or U.S. possession ▶		
	c Total gross income from sources outside the U.S. *(attach schedule)* .	**15c**	Form 1116, Part I
	d Total applicable deductions and losses *(attach schedule)* . .	**15d**	
	e Total foreign taxes (check one): ▶ ☐ Paid ☐ Accrued . .	**15e**	Form 1116, Part II
	f Reduction in taxes available for credit *(attach schedule)* . .	**15f**	Form 1116, Part III
	g Other foreign tax information *(attach schedule)*	**15g**	See Instructions for Form 1116
Other	**16a** Total expenditures to which a section 59(e) election may apply	**16a**	See Shareholder's Instructions for Schedule K-1 (Form 1120S).
	b Type of expenditures ▶		
	17 Property distributions (including cash) other than dividend distributions reported to you on Form 1099-DIV	**17**	
	18 Amount of loan repayments for "Loans From Shareholders" .	**18**	
	19 Recapture of low-income housing credit:		
	a From section 42(j)(5) partnerships	**19a**	Form 8611, line 8
	b Other than on line 19a	**19b**	

20 Supplemental information required to be reported separately to each shareholder *(attach additional schedules if more space is needed)*:

Supplemental Information

....

....

....

....

....

....

....

....

....

....

....

....

....

....

....

....

....

....

Instructions for Schedule D (Form 1120S)

Capital Gains and Losses and Built-In Gains

(Section references are to the Internal Revenue Code unless otherwise noted.)

Purpose of Schedule

Schedule D is used by all S corporations to report **(a)** sales or exchanges of capital assets, and **(b)** gains on distributions to shareholders of appreciated assets that are capital assets (hereinafter referred to as distributions). See definition of capital assets below.

If the corporation filed its election to be an S corporation before 1987 (or filed its election during 1987 or 1988 and qualifies for the transitional relief from the built-in gains tax described in Part IV below), and had net capital gain (line 9) of more than $25,000, it may be liable for a capital gains tax on the gain in excess of $25,000. The tax is figured in Part III of Schedule D.

Generally, if the corporation **(a)** filed an election to be an S corporation after 1986, **(b)** was a C corporation at the time it made the election, and **(c)** has net recognized built-in gain as defined in section 1374(d)(2), **it is liable** for the built-in gains tax. The tax is figured in Part IV of Schedule D.

Sales, exchanges, and distributions of property other than capital assets, including property used in a trade or business, involuntary conversions (other than casualties or thefts), and gain from the disposition of an interest in oil, gas, or geothermal property should be reported on **Form 4797,** Sales of Business Property.

If property is involuntarily converted because of a casualty or theft, use **Form 4684,** Casualties and Thefts.

Parts I and II

Generally, report sales or exchanges (including like-kind exchanges) even if there is no gain or loss. In Part I, report the sale, exchange, or distribution of capital assets held 1 year or less. In Part II, report the sale, exchange, or distribution of capital assets held more than 1 year. Use the trade dates for the dates of acquisition and sale of stocks and bonds on an exchange or over-the-counter market.

What Are Capital Assets?— Each item of property the corporation held (whether or not connected with its trade or business) is a capital asset **except:**

1. Assets that can be inventoried or property held mainly for sale to customers.

2. Depreciable or real property used in the trade or business.

3. Certain copyrights; literary, musical, or artistic compositions; letters or memorandums; or similar property.

4. Accounts or notes receivable acquired in the ordinary course of trade or business for services rendered or from the sale of property described in **1** above.

5. U.S. Government publications, including the Congressional Record, that the corporation received from the Government, other than by purchase at the normal sales price, or that the corporation got from another taxpayer who had received it in a similar way, if the corporation's basis is determined by reference to the previous owner.

Exchange of "Like-Kind" Property.— Use **Form 8824,** Like-Kind Exchanges, to report an exchange of like-kind property. Also report the exchange on Schedule D or on Form 4797, whichever applies. Complete and attach a Form 8824 to the corporation's return for each exchange. The corporation must report an exchange of business or investment property for "like-kind" property even if no gain or loss on the property is recognized.

If Schedule D is used to report a like-kind exchange, write **"From Form 8824"** on the appropriate line (line 1 or 4, column (a)). Skip columns (b) through (e) and enter the gain or loss, if any, from Form 8824 in column (f). If an exchange was made with a related party, write **"Related Party Like-Kind Exchange"** in the top margin of Schedule D. See Form 8824 and its instructions for details.

Special Rules for the Treatment of Certain Gains and Losses

Note: *For more information, get* **Pub. 544,** *Sales and Other Dispositions of Assets, and* **Pub. 589,** *Tax Information on S Corporations.*

● **Loss from a sale or exchange between the corporation and a related person.**—Except for distributions in complete liquidation of a corporation, no loss is allowed from the sale or exchange of property between the corporation and certain related persons. See section 267 for details.

● **Loss from a wash sale.**—The corporation cannot deduct a loss from a wash sale of stock or securities (including contracts or options to acquire or sell stock or securities) unless the corporation is a dealer in stock or securities and the loss was sustained in a transaction made in the ordinary course of the corporation's trade or business. A wash sale occurs if the corporation acquires (by purchase or exchange), or has a contract or option to acquire, substantially identical stock or securities within 30 days before or after the date of the sale or exchange. See section 1091 for more information.

● **Gain on distribution of appreciated property.**—Generally, gain (but not loss) is recognized on a nonliquidating distribution of appreciated property to the extent that the property's fair market value exceeds its adjusted basis. See section 311 for more information.

● **Gain or loss on distribution of property in complete liquidation.**— Generally, gain or loss is recognized by a corporation upon the liquidating distribution of property as if it had sold the property at its fair market value. See section 336 for details and exceptions.

● **Gains and losses on section 1256 contracts and straddles.**—Use **Form 6781,** Gains and Losses From Section 1256 Contracts and Straddles, to report gains and losses from section 1256 contracts and straddles.

● **Gain or loss on certain short-term Federal, state, and municipal obligations.**—Such obligations are treated as capital assets in determining gain or loss. On any gain realized, a portion is treated as ordinary income and the balance is considered as a short-term capital gain. See section 1271.

● **Gain from installment sales.**—If a corporation has a gain this year from the sale of real property or a casual sale of personal property other than inventory and is to receive any payment in a later year, it must use the installment method (unless it elects not to) and file **Form 6252,** Installment Sale Income. Also use

Cat. No. 64419L

Form 6252 if a payment is received this year from a sale made in an earlier year on the installment basis.

The corporation may elect out of the installment method by doing the following on a timely filed return (including extensions):

1. Report the full amount of the sale on Schedule D.

2. If the corporation received a note or other obligation and is reporting it at less than face value (including all contingent obligations), state that fact in the margin and give the percentage of valuation.

The installment method may not be used for sales of stock or securities (or certain other property described in the regulations) traded on an established securities market. See section 453(k).

● **Gain or loss on an option to buy or sell property.**—See sections 1032 and 1234 for the rules that apply to a purchaser or grantor of an option.

● **Gain or loss from a short sale of property.**—Report the gain or loss to the extent that the property used to close the short sale is considered a capital asset in the hands of the taxpayer.

● **Loss from securities that are capital assets that become worthless during the year.**—Except for securities held by a bank, treat the loss as a capital loss as of the last day of the tax year. (See section 582 for the rules on the treatment of securities held by a bank.)

● **Nonrecognition of gain on sale of stock to an ESOP.**—See section 1042 for rules under which a taxpayer may elect not to recognize gain from the sale of certain stock to an employee stock ownership plan (ESOP).

● **Disposition of market discount bonds.**—See section 1276 for rules on the disposition of any market discount bonds that were issued after July 18, 1984.

● **Capital gain distributions.**—Report capital gain distributions paid by mutual funds as long-term capital gain on line 4 regardless of how long the corporation owned stock in the fund.

How To Determine the Cost or Other Basis of the Property

In determining gain or loss, the basis of property will generally be its cost (see section 1012 and related regulations). The exceptions to the general rule are provided in sections contained in subchapters C, K, O, and P of the Code. For example, if the corporation acquired the property by dividend, liquidation of another corporation, transfer from a shareholder, reorganization, bequest, contribution or gift, tax-free exchange, involuntary conversion, certain asset acquisitions, or wash sale of stock, see sections 301 (or 1059), 334, 362 (or 358), 1014, 1015, 1031, 1033, 1060, and 1091, respectively. Attach an explanation

if you use a basis other than actual cash cost of the property.

If the corporation is allowed a charitable contribution deduction because it sold property to a charitable organization, figure the adjusted basis for determining gain from the sale by dividing the amount realized by the fair market value and multiplying that result by the adjusted basis.

See section 852(f) for the treatment of certain load charges incurred in acquiring stock in a mutual fund with a reinvestment right.

Part III—Capital Gains Tax

If the net long-term capital gain is more than the net short-term capital loss, there is a net capital gain. If this gain exceeds $25,000, and the corporation elected to be an S corporation before 1987 (or filed its election during 1987 or 1988 and qualifies for the transitional relief from the built-in gains tax described in Part IV below), the corporation may be liable for income tax on the gain.

By answering the following questions, it can be determined whether the corporation is liable for the tax. If answers to questions A, B, and C or A, B, and D are "Yes," the tax applies and Part III of Schedule D must be completed. Otherwise, the corporation is not liable for the tax.

If net capital gain is more than $25,000, and the corporation is not liable for the tax, attach the Part III instructions to Schedule D with questions A through D answered to show why the tax does not apply.

A. Is net capital gain (line 9, Schedule D) more than $25,000, and more than 50% of taxable income (see the instructions for line 13, Schedule D)? . . . . ☐ Yes ☐ No

B. Is taxable income (see the instructions for line 13, Schedule D) more than $25,000? . . . . . . ☐ Yes ☐ No

C. Has the corporation been other than an S corporation at any time during the 3 tax years just before this year, or since existence, if it has been in existence for less than 4 years? . . . . . . ☐ Yes ☐ No

D. If the answer to question C is "No," does any long-term capital gain (line 8, Schedule D) represent gain from property described in each of items 1, 2, and 3 that follow? . . ☐ Yes ☐ No

1. The property was acquired during the tax year or within 36 months before the beginning of the tax year;

2. The property was acquired, directly or indirectly, from a corporation that was not in existence as an S corporation during the tax year or within 36 months before the tax year up to the time of the acquisition; and

3. The property has a substituted basis to you. (A substituted basis is determined by reference to its basis in the hands of the transferor corporation.)

If the answer to question D is "Yes" and the tax applies, multiply the net capital gain from property described in question D (reduced by any excess net passive income attributable to this gain—see instruction for line 9) by 34%. If this amount is less than the tax figured on line 14, Part III, enter this amount on line 15, Part III, and write to the right of the amount, **"Substituted basis."** Attach the computation of the substituted basis amount to Schedule D. (See section 1374(c)(3) as in effect before the enactment of the Tax Reform Act of 1986 (1986 Act).)

Line 9.—If the corporation is liable for the tax on excess net passive income (line 22a, page 1, Form 1120S) or the built-in gains tax (see Part IV below), and capital gain or loss was included in the computation of either tax, figure the amount to enter on line 9 as follows:

Step 1—Refigure lines 1, 2, and 4 through 7 of Schedule D by:

1. Excluding the portion of any recognized built-in capital gain or loss that does not qualify for transitional relief, and

2. Reducing any capital gain taken into account in determining passive investment income (line 2 of the worksheet for line 22a, page 1 of Form 1120S) by the portion of excess net passive income attributable to such gain. The portion so attributable is figured by multiplying excess net passive income by a fraction, the numerator of which is the amount of the capital gain (less any expenses attributable to such gain), and the denominator of which is net passive income.

Step 2—Refigure lines 3, 8, and 9 of Schedule D using the amounts determined in step 1.

Line 13.—Figure taxable income by completing lines 1 through 28 of **Form 1120,** U.S. Corporation Income Tax Return. Enter the amount from line 28 of Form 1120 on line 13 of Schedule D. Attach to Schedule D the Form 1120 computation or other worksheet used to figure taxable income.

Line 14.—Figure the tax under section 11 on the taxable income shown on line 13 as if the corporation were not an S corporation. You may use Schedule J of Form 1120 to figure the tax. Attach your tax computation to Schedule D.

Part IV—Built-In Gains Tax

Section 1374 provides for a tax on built-in gains that applies to certain corporations that made the election to be an S corporation after 1986. This tax does not apply to any corporation that has been an S corporation for each of its tax years, unless the corporation acquired an asset with a basis determined by reference to its basis (or the basis of any other property) in the hands of a C corporation.

Transitional Relief From Built-in Gains Tax.—Section 633(d)(8) of the 1986 Act provides special transitional relief from the built-in gains tax for qualified corporations. A qualified corporation is any corporation that **(a)** on August 1, 1986, and all times thereafter before the corporation is completely liquidated, is more than 50% owned by a qualified group, and **(b)** has an applicable value of $10 million or less.

A qualified group is a group of 10 or fewer qualified persons. A qualified person is:

1. An individual,

2. An estate, or

3. A trust described in section 1361(c)(2)(A)(ii) or (iii).

The qualified group must have owned (or be treated as having owned) more than 50% (by value) of the corporation's stock at all times during the 5-year period ending on the date of adoption of a plan of complete liquidation (or, if shorter, the period of the corporation's existence). The 5-year requirement does not apply to any corporation that made an S election before March 31, 1988. The term "applicable value" means the fair market value of all of the stock of the corporation on the date a valid S election is made (or, if greater, on August 1, 1986).

The transitional relief rule applies to qualified corporations that elected to be S corporations during 1987 or 1988. However, the relief rule does **not** apply to the following items:

1. Ordinary gains or losses (determined without regard to section 1239),

2. Gains or losses from the disposition of capital assets held 6 months or less, and

3. Gains from the disposition of any asset acquired by the corporation with a substituted basis if a principal purpose for acquiring the asset was to secure transitional relief from the built-in gains tax.

Qualified corporations with an applicable value of between $5 million and $10 million are given only partial relief from the built-in gains tax. The portion of the built-in gain **not** eligible for relief is a fraction, the numerator of which is the amount by which the applicable value of the corporation exceeds $5 million and the denominator of which is $5 million.

Line 16.—Enter the amount that would be the taxable income of the corporation for the tax year if only recognized built-in gains (including any carryover of gain under section 1374(d)(2)(B)) and recognized built-in losses were taken into account.

Section 1374(d)(3) defines a **recognized built-in gain** as any gain recognized during the recognition period (the 10-year period beginning on the 1st day of the 1st tax year for which the corporation is an S corporation, or beginning the date the asset was acquired by the S corporation, for an asset with a basis determined by reference to its basis (or the basis of any other property) in the hands of a C corporation) on the sale or distribution (disposition) of any asset, except to the extent the corporation establishes that:

1. The asset was not held by the corporation as of the beginning of the 1st tax year the corporation was an S corporation (except that this does not apply to an asset acquired by the S corporation with a basis determined by reference to its basis (or the basis of any other property) in the hands of a C corporation), or

2. The gain exceeds the excess of the fair market value of such asset as of the beginning of the 1st tax year (or as of the date the asset was acquired by the S corporation, for an asset with a basis determined by reference to its basis (or the basis of any other property) in the hands of a C corporation) over the adjusted basis of the asset at that time.

Section 1374(d)(4) defines a **recognized built-in loss** as any loss recognized during the recognition period (stated above) on the disposition of any asset to the extent the corporation establishes that:

1. The asset was held by the corporation as of the beginning of the 1st tax year the corporation was an S corporation (except that this does not apply to an asset acquired by the S corporation with a basis determined by reference to its basis (or the basis of any other property) in the hands of a C corporation), and

2. The loss does not exceed the excess of the adjusted basis of the asset as of the beginning of the 1st tax year (or as of the date the asset was acquired by the S corporation, for an asset with a basis determined by reference to its basis (or the basis of any other property) in the hands of a C corporation), over the fair market value of the asset as of that time.

A qualified corporation must show on an attachment to Schedule D its total net recognized built-in gain and also list separately the gain or loss that is **(a)** gain or loss from capital assets held 6 months or less, and **(b)** gain or loss from assets for which the disposition results in ordinary income or loss. A nonqualified corporation must show on an attachment its total net recognized built-in gain and list separately any capital gain or loss and ordinary gain or loss.

Line 17.—Figure taxable income by completing lines 1 through 28 of Form 1120. Enter the amount from line 28 of Form 1120 on line 17. Attach to Schedule D the Form 1120 computation or other worksheet used to figure taxable income.

Line 18.—Do not enter on line 18 more than the excess (if any) of the net unrealized built-in gain over the net recognized built-in gain for prior years. This is the amount that should have been entered on line 9 of Schedule B on page 2 of Form 1120S. See section 1374(c)(2). If, for any tax year, the amount on line 16 exceeds the taxable income on line 17, the excess is treated as a recognized built-in gain in the succeeding tax year. This carryover provision applies only in the case of an S corporation that made its election to be an S corporation on or after March 31, 1988. See section 1374(d)(2)(B).

Line 19.—Enter the section 1374(b)(2) deduction. Generally, this is any net operating loss carryforward or capital loss carryforward (to the extent of net capital gain included in recognized built-in gain for the tax year) arising in tax years for which the corporation was a C corporation. See section 1374(b)(2) for details.

SCHEDULE D
(Form 1120S)

Department of the Treasury
Internal Revenue Service

Capital Gains and Losses and Built-In Gains

▶ Attach to Form 1120S.

▶ See separate instructions.

OMB No. 1545-0130

1991

Name	Employer identification number

Part I — Short-Term Capital Gains and Losses—Assets Held One Year or Less

(a) Kind of property and description (Example, 100 shares of "Z" Co.)	(b) Date acquired (mo., day, yr.)	(c) Date sold (mo., day, yr.)	(d) Gross sales price	(e) Cost or other basis, plus expense of sale	(f) Gain or (loss) ((d) less (e))
1					

2 Short-term capital gain from installment sales from Form 6252, line 22 or 30 . . . . | **2** |

3 **Net short-term capital gain or (loss).** Combine lines 1 and 2 and enter here. Also enter this amount on Form 1120S, Schedule K, line 4d or line 6 (but first reduce it by any tax on short-term gain included on line 23 below) . . . . | **3** |

Part II — Long-Term Capital Gains and Losses—Assets Held More Than One Year

4					

5 Long-term capital gain from installment sales from Form 6252, line 22 or 30 . . . . | **5** |

6 **Net long-term capital gain or (loss).** Combine lines 4 and 5 and enter here. Also enter this amount on Form 1120S, Schedule K, line 4e or line 6 (but first reduce it by any tax on long-term gain included on lines 15 and 23 below) . . . . | **6** |

Part III — Capital Gains Tax (See instructions before completing this part.)

7 Enter section 1231 gain from Form 4797, line 9 . . . . | **7** |

8 Net long-term capital gain or (loss)—Combine lines 6 and 7 . . . . | **8** |

Note: *If the corporation is liable for the excess net passive income tax (Form 1120S, page 1, line 22a) or the built-in gains tax (Part IV below), see the line 9 instructions before completing line 9.*

9 Net capital gain—Enter excess of net long-term capital gain (line 8) over net short-term capital loss (line 3) . . . . | **9** |

10 Statutory minimum . . . . | **10** | $25,000 |

11 Subtract line 10 from line 9 . . . . | **11** |

12 Enter 34% of line 11 . . . . | **12** |

13 Taxable income (see instructions and attach computation schedule) . . . . | **13** |

14 Enter tax on line 13 amount (see instructions and attach computation schedule) . . . . . | **14** |

15 **Tax.** Enter smaller of line 12 or line 14 here and on Form 1120S, page 1, line 22b . . . . | **15** |

Part IV — Built-In Gains Tax (See instructions before completing this part.)

16 Excess of recognized built-in gains over recognized built-in losses (see instructions and attach computation schedule) . . . . | **16** |

17 Taxable income (see instructions and attach computation schedule) . . . . | **17** |

18 Net recognized built-in gain. Enter smaller of line 16 or line 17 (see instructions) . . . . . | **18** |

19 Section 1374(b)(2) deduction . . . . | **19** |

20 Subtract line 19 from line 18. (If zero or less, enter zero here and on line 23.) . . . . . | **20** |

21 Enter 34% of line 20 . . . . | **21** |

22 Business credit and minimum tax credit carryforwards under section 1374(b)(3) from C corporation years | **22** |

23 **Tax.** Subtract line 22 from line 21 (if zero or less, enter -0-). Enter here and on Form 1120S, page 1, line 22b | **23** |

For Paperwork Reduction Act Notice, see page 1 of Instructions for Form 1120S.   Cat. No. 11516V   **Schedule D (Form 1120S) 1991**

★U.S.GPO:1991-0-285-275

Form **8716**
(Rev. November 1989)
Department of the Treasury
Internal Revenue Service

Election To Have a Tax Year Other Than a Required Tax Year

OMB No. 1545-1036
Expires 9-30-92

Please type or print

Name	Employer identification number

Number and street (P.O. box number if mail is not delivered to street address)

City or town, state, and ZIP code

1 Check applicable box to show type of taxpayer:
☐ Partnership
☐ S Corporation
☐ Personal Service Corporation (PSC)

2 Name and telephone number (including area code) of person who may be called for information:

3 Enter ending date of the tax year for the entity's last filed return. (A new entity should enter the ending date of the tax year it is adopting.) . . . .

Month	Day	Year

4 Enter ending date of required tax year determined under section 441(i), 706(b), or 1378 . . . . .

Month	Day

5 Section 444(a) Election—Check the applicable box and enter the ending date of the tax year the entity is (see instructions):
☐ Adopting   ☐ Retaining   ☐ Changing to

Month	Day	Year

Under penalties of perjury, I declare that the entity named above has authorized me to make this election under section 444(a), and that the statements made are, to the best of my knowledge and belief, true, correct, and complete.

▶ _____
Signature and title (see instruction G)

▶ _____
Date

Paperwork Reduction Act Notice.—We ask for this information to carry out the Internal Revenue laws of the United States. We need it to ensure that taxpayers are complying with these laws and to allow us to figure and collect the right amount of tax. You are required to give us this information.

The time needed to complete and file this form will vary depending on individual circumstances. The estimated average time is:

Form	Recordkeeping	Learning about the law or the form	Preparing and sending the form to IRS
8716	2 hrs., 23 min.	2 hrs., 35 min.	2 hrs., 44 min.
Schedule H	5 hrs., 59 min.	47 min.	56 min.

If you have comments concerning the accuracy of these time estimates or suggestions for making this form more simple, we would be happy to hear from you. You can write to the **Internal Revenue Service**, Washington, DC 20224, Attention: IRS Reports Clearance Officer, T:FP; or the **Office of Management and Budget**, Paperwork Reduction Project (1545-1036), Washington, DC 20503.

General Instructions

(Section references are to the Internal Revenue Code unless otherwise noted.)

A. Purpose of Form.—Form 8716 is filed by partnerships, S corporations, and personal service corporations (as defined in section 441(i)(2)) to elect to have a tax year other than a required tax year. The election is provided by section 444.

A copy of the Form 8716 you file must be attached to Form 1065 or a Form 1120 series form (1120, 1120A, 1120S, etc.), whichever is applicable, for the first tax year for which the election is made.

B. When To File.—Form 8716 must be filed by the earlier of:

(1) The 15th day of the 5th month following the month that includes the 1st day of the tax year for which the election will be effective, or

(2) The due date (without regard to extensions) of the income tax return for the tax year resulting from the section 444 election.

Items (1) and (2) relate to the tax year, or the return for the tax year, for which the ending date is entered on line 5 above.

See Temporary Regulations section 1.444-3T for more information.

C. Where To File.—File the election with the Internal Revenue Service Center where the entity will file its return. See the instructions for Form 1065 and the Form 1120 series form(s) for Service Center addresses. If the entity is a foreign entity, file Form 8716 with the Service Center in Philadelphia, PA 19255.

D. Effect of Section 444 Election.—If the section 444 election is made, electing partnerships and S corporations must make a required payment of tax as provided by section 7519. Willful failure of an entity to make the required payment may result in the cancellation of an entity's election. See Instruction H for more information on figuring and making the required payment.

Electing PSCs are subject to the limitations of section 280H. Willful failure of any PSC to comply with section 280H may result in the cancellation of the PSC's election. See Instruction I for more information on section 280H limitations.

E. Acceptance of Election.—After your election is received and accepted by the Service Center, the Center will stamp it "ACCEPTED" and return a copy to you. Be sure to keep a copy of the form marked "ACCEPTED" for your records.

F. End of Election.—Once the election is made, it remains in effect until the entity terminates its election. If the election is terminated, the entity may not make another section 444 election. See section 444(d)(2).

G. Signature.—Form 8716 is not considered an election unless it is signed. For partnerships, a general partner must sign and date the election. If a receiver, trustee in bankruptcy, or assignee controls the organization's property or business, that person must sign the election.

For corporations, the election must be signed and dated by the president, vice president, treasurer, assistant treasurer, chief accounting officer, or any other corporate officer (such as tax officer) authorized to sign its tax return. If a receiver, trustee in bankruptcy, or assignee controls the corporation's property or business, that person must sign the election.

H. Required Payment of Tax.—Partnerships and S corporations (entities) are required to make a payment for each tax year if: (1) an election under section 444 is in effect for the tax year (any tax year that a section 444 election is in effect, including the first year the section 444 election is made, is hereinafter called an applicable election year), and (2) the required payment for the applicable

Form **8716** (Rev. 11-89)

election year (or any preceding applicable election year) exceeds $500. Required payments for applicable election years beginning in 1989 are made on the first-quarter 1990 **Form 720**, Quarterly Federal Excise Tax Return. The instructions for the 1989 Form 1065 or Form 1120S contain a Computation Schedule for Required Payments Under Section 7519 for applicable election years beginning in 1989 (1989 required payments). Instructions for the section 7519 computation schedule give details on making the 1989 required payments, and how to obtain a refund or credit for prior year payments.

Note: *The Instructions for Form 1120S and Form 1065 for tax years beginning after 1989 will indicate how payments are made and refunds are obtained for applicable election years beginning after 1989.*

Also see section 7519 and related regulations for other details.

I. Minimum Distribution Requirements for a PSC.—An electing PSC is subject to the minimum distribution requirements of section 280H for its first applicable election year (and each subsequent applicable election year). If the PSC fails in any applicable election year to make the minimum distributions required by section 280H, the applicable amounts it may deduct for that applicable election year are limited to a maximum deductible amount.

The PSC may use **Schedule H (Form 8716)**, Section 280H Limitations for a Personal Service Corporation (PSC), to figure the required minimum distribution and the maximum deductible amount. If the PSC has not made the required minimum distribution, Schedule H must be attached to its income tax return. The PSC should figure its compliance with the provisions of section 280H at the end of each tax year that the section 444 election is in effect. See section 280H and related regulations for other details.

J. Members of Certain Tiered Structures May Not Make Election.—No election may be made under section 444(a) by an entity which is part of a tiered structure other than a tiered structure that consists entirely of partnerships or S corporations (or both) all of which have the same tax year. An election previously made shall be terminated if an entity later becomes part of a tiered structure that is not allowed to make the election. See section 444(d)(3) and related regulations for other details.

Specific Instructions

Line 1.—Check the applicable box in line 1 to show that you are a partnership, S corporation (or electing to be an S corporation), or a personal service corporation.

A corporation electing to be an S corporation that wants to make a section 444 election must make its section 444 election by the time specified in General Instruction B. The corporation is not required to attach a copy of Form 8716 to its **Form 2553**, Election by a Small Business Corporation. However, the corporation is required to state on Form 2553 its intention to make a section 444 election (or a backup section 444 election). If a corporation is making a backup section 444 election (provided for in item Q, Part II, of Form 2553 (Rev. October 1989)), it must type or legibly print the words "BACKUP ELECTION" at the top of the Form 8716 it files to make the backup election. See Temporary Regulations section 1.444-3T for additional information.

Line 2.—Enter the name and telephone number (including the area code) of a person that the Service may call for information that may be needed to complete the processing of the election.

Line 4.—See the Instructions for Form 1065 or a Form 1120 series form, whichever is applicable, and section 441(i), 706(b), or 1378 for a definition of a required tax year and other details.

Line 5.—Enter the ending date of the tax year the entity is electing under section 444. The following limitations and special rules apply in determining the tax year an entity may elect:

(a) New entity adopting a tax year.— An entity adopting a tax year may elect a tax year under section 444 only if the deferral period of the tax year is not longer than 3 months. For a definition of deferral period, see (d) below and section 444(b)(4).

(b) Existing entity retaining a tax year.—In certain cases, an entity may elect to retain its tax year if the deferral period is no longer than 3 months. If the entity does not want to elect to retain its tax year, it could elect to change its tax year under (c) below.

(c) Existing entity changing a tax year.—An existing entity may elect to change its tax year if the deferral period of the elected tax year is no longer than the shorter of: (1) three months, or (2) the deferral period of the tax year being changed.

For example, ABC, a C corporation that historically used a tax year ending October 31, elects S status and wants to make a section 444 election for its tax year beginning 11-1-89. ABC's required tax year under section 1378 is a calendar tax year. In this case, the deferral period of the tax year being changed is 2 months. Thus, ABC may elect to retain its tax year beginning 11-1-89 and ending 10-31-90, or change it to a short tax year beginning 11-1-89 and ending 11-30-89. However, it may not elect a short tax year beginning 11-1-89 and ending 9-30-90 because the deferral period for that elected tax year is 3 months (9-30 to 12-31), which is longer than the 2-month deferral period of the tax year being changed. After filing the short year return (11-1-89 to 11-30-89), and as long as the section 444 election remains in effect, the corporation's tax year will begin 12-1 and end 11-30.

(d) Deferral period.—If you are electing **to retain** your tax year, the term "DEFERRAL PERIOD" means the months that occur between the beginning of the elected tax year and the close of the 1st required tax year. For example, if you elected to retain a tax year beginning 10-1-89 and ending 9-30-90 and your required tax year was a calendar tax year, the deferral period would be 3 months (the number of months between 9-30-89 and 12-31-89).

If you are electing **to adopt or change** a tax year, the term "DEFERRAL PERIOD" means the months that occur after the end of the elected tax year and before the close of the 1st required tax year. For example, if you elect to adopt a tax year ending September 30, 1989, and your required tax year is a calendar tax year, the deferral period would be 3 months (the number of months between 9-30-89 and 12-31-89).

See section 444(b) and related Temporary Regulations for additional information on the above rules.

✩ U.S. Government Printing Office: 1989-245-415

Form **1128**

(Rev. June 1991)

Department of the Treasury
Internal Revenue Service

Application to Adopt, Change, or Retain a Tax Year

▶ **For Paperwork Reduction Act Notice, see page 1 of Separate Instructions.**

OMB No. 1545-0134
Expires 8-31-93

Before completing Form 1128, see Sections B and C of the General Instructions to determine if this form must be filed.

Form 1128 consists of three parts:

- **Part I** must be completed by all applicants.

- **Part II** must be completed only by applicants requesting approval on a change or retention of a tax year under an expeditious approval rule. See the "Expeditious Approval Rules" in the Specific Instructions to determine who qualifies.

- **Part III,** Section A must be completed by all applicants requesting a ruling from the IRS National Office on a change, adoption, or retention of their tax year. For this type of application, a user fee must be attached. In addition to completing Section A, corporations, S corporations, partnerships, controlled foreign corporations, tax-exempt organizations, estates, and passive foreign investment companies must also complete the specific section in Part III that applies to the particular entity.

Each applicant must check one of the boxes below:

- ☐ Individual
- ☐ Partnership
- ☐ Estate
- ☐ Corporation
- ☐ S Corporation
- ☐ Personal Service Corporation
- ☐ Cooperative (Sec. 1381(a))
- ☐ Tax-Exempt Organization
- ☐ Controlled Foreign Corporation (Sec. 957)
- ☐ Passive Foreign Investment Company (Sec. 1296)
- ☐ Foreign Personal Holding Company (Sec. 552)
- ☐ Other Foreign Corporation
- ☐ Other _____
  (Specify entity and applicable Code section)

Part I   **All Applicants (See page 4 for required signature(s)).**

Please Type or Print

Name of applicant (if joint return is filed, also show your spouse's name)	Identifying number (See Specific Instructions.)
Number, street, and room or suite no. (If a P.O. box, see specific Instructions.)	Service Center where tax return will be filed
City or town, state, and ZIP code	Applicant's telephone number ( )
Name of person to contact (See Specific Instructions.)	Telephone number of contact person ( )

1a Approval is requested to (check one):

☐ Adopt a tax year ending ▶ ....
(If filing to adopt a tax year, go to Part III after completing Part I.)

☐ Change to a tax year ending ▶ ....

☐ Retain a tax year ending ▶ ....

b If changing a tax year, indicate the date the present tax year ends ▶ ....

c If adopting or changing a tax year, indicate the short period return that will be required to be filed for the tax year
beginning ▶ _____ , 19____ , and ending ▶ _____ , 19____ .

2 Nature of business or principal source of income:

3 Indicate the applicant's overall method of accounting:

☐ Cash receipts and disbursements

☐ Accrual

☐ Other (explain) ▶

Form **1128** (Rev. 6-91)

Part II	Expeditious Approval Rules

(If Part II applies, file Form 1128 with the IRS Service Center where the applicant's tax return is filed.)

		Yes	No
1	Is this a corporation described in section 3 of Rev. Proc. 84-34, 1984-1 C.B. 508 that is requesting a change in a tax year under Rev. Proc. 84-34? . . . . ▶		
2a	Is this a partnership, an S corporation, or a personal service corporation that is requesting a tax year under the expeditious approval rules in section 4 of Rev. Proc. 87-32, 1987-2 C.B. 396, **and** that is not precluded from using the expeditious approval rules under section 3 of that revenue procedure? . . . . ▶		
b	Is this a partnership, an S corporation, or a personal service corporation that is retaining or changing to a tax year that coincides with its natural business year as defined in section 4.01(1) of Rev. Proc. 87-32, **and** such tax year results in no greater deferral of income to the partners or shareholders than the present tax year? ▶		
c	Is this an S corporation whose shareholders hold more than half of the shares of stock (as of the first day of the tax year to which the request relates) of the corporation **and** have the same tax year that the corporation is retaining or changing to? . . . . ▶		
d	Is this an S corporation whose shareholders hold more than half of the shares of stock (as of the first day of the tax year to which the request relates) of the corporation **and** have requested approval to concurrently change to the tax year that the corporation is retaining or changing to? . . . . ▶		
3	Are you an individual requesting a change from a fiscal year to a calendar year under Rev. Proc. 66-50, 1966-2 C.B. 1260? . . . . ▶		
4	Is this a tax-exempt organization requesting a change under Rev. Proc. 85-58, 1985-2 C.B. 740, or Rev. Proc. 76-10, 1976-1 C.B. 548? . . . . ▶		

If the answer to any of the above questions is "Yes," see the Instructions for the "Expeditious Approval Rules" and file this form with the Internal Revenue Service Center where the income tax return of the applicant is filed. **Do not** file Form 1128 with the National Office and do not include a user fee. See the Instructions for "Where To File" under Part II.

| Part III | Ruling Provisions (If Part III applies, file Form 1128 with the National Office and attach a user fee. See Specific Instructions.) |

SECTION A.—General Information

		Yes	No

1 In the last 6 years have you changed or requested approval to change your tax year? (See Part III in the Specific Instructions.) . . . . ▶

a If "Yes" and there was a ruling letter issued granting approval to make the change, attach a copy. If a copy of the ruling letter is not available, explain and give the date approval was granted. If a ruling letter was not issued, explain the facts and give the date the change was implemented.

b If a change in tax year was granted within the last 6 years, explain in detail why another change in tax year is necessary.

2 Do you have pending any accounting method, tax year, ruling, or technical advice request in the National Office? ▶
If "Yes," attach a statement explaining the type of request (method, tax year, etc.) and the specific issues involved in each request.

3 Enter the taxable income * or (loss) for the 3 tax years immediately before the short period and for the short period. If necessary, estimate the amount for the short period.
First preceding year $ ....   Second preceding year $ ....
Third preceding year $ ....   Short period $ ....
Individuals enter adjusted gross income. Partnerships and S corporations enter ordinary income. Section 501(c) organizations enter unrelated business taxable income. Corporations enter taxable income before net operating loss deduction and special deductions. Estates enter adjusted total income.

4 Are you a U.S. shareholder in a controlled foreign corporation (CFC)? . . . . ▶
If "Yes," attach a statement for each CFC stating the name, address, identifying number, tax year, your percentage of total combined voting power, and the amount of income included in your gross income under section 951 for the 3 tax years immediately before the short period and for the short period.

5a Are you a U.S. shareholder in a passive foreign investment company as defined in section 1296 of the Code? . ▶
If "Yes," attach a statement showing the name, address, identifying number and tax year of the passive foreign investment company, your percentage of interest owned, and the amount of ordinary earnings and net capital gain from the passive foreign investment company included in your income.
b Did you elect under section 1295 to treat the passive foreign investment company as a qualified electing fund? . ▶

6 Are you a member of a partnership, a beneficiary of a trust or estate, a shareholder of an S corporation, a shareholder of an Interest Charge Domestic International Sales Corporation (IC-DISC) or a shareholder in a Foreign Sales Corporation (FSC)? . . . . ▶
If "Yes," attach a statement showing the name, address, identifying number, tax year, percentage of interest in capital and profits, or percentage of interest of each IC-DISC and the amount of income received from each partnership, trust, estate, S corporation, IC-DISC, or FSC for the first preceding year and for the short period. Also indicate the percentage of your gross income represented by each amount.

7 State the reasons for requesting the change. (Attach a separate sheet if you need more space.) This is required by Regulations section 1.442-1(b)(1). If this information is not provided, the application will be denied.

SECTION B.—Corporations (other than S corporations and controlled foreign corporations)

		Yes	No

1 Date of incorporation ▶

2 Is the corporation a member of an affiliated group filing a consolidated return? . . . . ▶
If "Yes," attach a statement showing: (a) the name, address, identifying number used on the consolidated return, the tax year, and the Internal Revenue Service Center where the taxpayer files the return; (b) the name, address, and identifying number of each member of the affiliated group; (c) the taxable income (loss) of each member for the 3 years immediately before the short period and for the short period; and (d) the name of the parent corporation.

3 Did the corporation make any distributions to its shareholders during the short period? . . . . ▶
If "Yes," furnish the following information:
a Taxable dividends . . . . |$
b Nondividend distributions (explain how determined) . . . . |$

4 If this is a personal service corporation, attach a statement showing each shareholder's name, type of entity (e.g., individual, partnership, corporation, etc.), address, identifying number, tax year, and percentage of ownership.

SECTION C.—S Corporations

		Yes	No
1	Date of election ▶		
2	Is any shareholder applying for a corresponding change in tax year? . . . . ▶		
3	Attach a statement showing each shareholder's name, type of entity (e.g., individual, estate, trust, or qualified Subchapter S Trust as defined in section 1361(d)(3)), address, identifying number, tax year, and percentage of ownership.		

SECTION D.—Partnerships

		Yes	No
1	Date business began (See Specific Instructions.) ▶		
2	Is any partner applying for a corresponding change in tax year? . . . . ▶		
3	Attach a statement showing each partner's name, type of partner (e.g., individual, partnership, estate, trust, corporation, S corporation, IC-DISC, etc.), address, identifying number, tax year, and the percentage of interest in capital and profits.		
4	Is any partner of this partnership a shareholder of a personal service corporation as defined in Temporary Regulations section 1.441-4T(d)(1)? . . . . ▶		
	If "Yes," attach a separate sheet providing the name, address, identifying number, tax year, percentage of interest in capital and profits, and the amount of income received from each personal service corporation for the first preceding year and the short period.		

SECTION E.—Controlled Foreign Corporations

Attach a statement for each U.S. shareholder (as defined in section 951(b)) stating the name, address, identifying number, tax year, percentage of total combined voting power, and the amount of income included in gross income under section 951 for the 3 tax years immediately before the short period and for the short period.

SECTION F.—Tax-Exempt Organizations

		Yes	No
1	Form of organization: ☐ Corporation ☐ Trust ☐ Other (specify) ▶		
2	Date of organization ▶		
3	Code section under which the organization is exempt ▶		
4	Is the organization required to file an annual return on Form 990, 990-C, 990-PF, 990-T, 1120-H, or 1120-POL? . . . . ▶		
5	Date exemption was granted ▶........................... Attach a copy of the ruling letter granting exemption. If a copy of the letter is not available, attach explanation.		
6	If a private foundation, is the foundation terminating its status under section 507? . . . . ▶		

SECTION G.—Estates

1   Date estate established ▶

2   Attach a statement showing:

a   Name, identifying number, address, and tax year of each beneficiary and each person who is an owner or treated as an owner of any portion of the estate.

b   Based on the taxable income of the estate entered in Part III, Section A, line 3, show the distribution deduction and the taxable amounts distributed to each beneficiary for the 2 tax years immediately before the short period and for the short period.

SECTION H.—Passive Foreign Investment Company

Attach a statement showing each U.S. shareholder's name, address, identifying number, and the percentage of interest owned.

Signature—All Filers (See Specific Instructions.)

Under penalties of perjury, I declare that I have examined this application, including accompanying schedules and statements, and to the best of my knowledge and belief it is true, correct, and complete. Declaration of preparer (other than applicant) is based on all information of which preparer has any knowledge.

Applicant's name	**Date**
Signature (officer of parent corporation, if applicable)	**Title**
Signing official's name (print or type)	**Date**
Signature of individual or firm (other than applicant) preparing the application	**Date**
Firm or preparer's name	

● Has the authorized representative attached a power of attorney? (For information on a power of attorney, see "Preparer Other Than Applicant" in the Specific Instructions.) . . . . ▶ ☐ **Yes** ☐ **No**

*U.S. Government Printing Office: 1991 — 282-002/40043

Instructions for Form 940

Employer's Annual Federal Unemployment (FUTA) Tax Return

(Section references are to the Internal Revenue Code unless otherwise noted.)

Paperwork Reduction Act Notice.—We ask for the information on this form to carry out the Internal Revenue laws of the United States. You are required to give us the information. We need it to ensure that you are complying with these laws and to allow us to figure and collect the right amount of tax.

The time needed to complete and file this form will vary depending on individual circumstances. The estimated average time is:

Recordkeeping . . .14 hr., 21 min.

Learning about the law or the form . . . . . 12 min.

Preparing and sending the form to the IRS . . . 26 min.

If you have comments concerning the accuracy of these time estimates or suggestions for making this form more simple, we would be happy to hear from you. You can write to both the **Internal Revenue Service,** Washington, DC 20224, Attention: IRS Reports Clearance Officer, T:FP; and the **Office of Management and Budget,** Paperwork Reduction Project (1545-0028), Washington, DC 20503. Do not send the tax form to either of these offices. Instead, see the instructions for Where To File on page 2.

Items You Should Note

Credit Reduction State.—For 1991, Michigan is a credit reduction state. If you pay any wages that are subject to the unemployment compensation laws of the state of Michigan, you must file Form 940, instead of Form 940-EZ, described next.

Form 940-EZ.—You may be able to use Form 940-EZ. It is a simplified version of Form 940. Generally, employers who pay all unemployment contributions to only one state in a timely manner and do not have taxable FUTA wages that are exempt from state

unemployment tax, can use Form 940-EZ. For more details, get Form 940-EZ. Do not file Form 940 if you have already filed Form 940-EZ for 1991.

FUTA Tax Rate.—The FUTA tax rate is scheduled to remain at 6.2% for years 1991 through 1995.

Revised Part III.—The Computation of Tentative Credit, previously Part V, was combined with Part III and is labeled line 3.

Final and Amended Returns.— Checkboxes have been added for you to mark if this is your final return or an amended return.

General Instructions

Purpose of Form.—The Federal Unemployment Tax Act (FUTA), together with state unemployment systems, provides for payments of unemployment compensation to workers who have lost their jobs. Most employers pay both a Federal and state unemployment tax. Use this form for your annual FUTA tax report. **Only the employer pays this tax.**

Who Must File

In General.—You must file this form if you were not a household or agricultural employer during 1990 or 1991, and you: (a) paid wages of $1,500 or more in any calendar quarter or (b) had one or more employees for some part of a day in any 20 different weeks. Count all regular, temporary, and part-time employees. A partnership should not count its partners. If there is a change in ownership or other transfer of business during the year, each employer who meets test (a) or (b) must file. Neither should report wages paid by the other. Organizations described in section 501(c)(3) of the Internal Revenue Code do not have to file.

Household Employers.—You do not have to file this form unless you paid

cash wages of $1,000 or more in any calendar quarter in 1990 or 1991 for household work in a private home, local college club, or a local chapter of a college fraternity or sorority. **Note:** *See* **Pub. 926,** *Employment Taxes for Household Employers, for more information.*

Agricultural Employers.—You must file Form 940 if either of the following applies to you:

1. You paid cash wages of $20,000 or more to farmworkers during any calendar quarter in 1990 or 1991.

2. You employed 10 or more farmworkers during some part of a day (whether or not at the same time) for at least one day during any 20 different weeks in 1990 or 1991.

Count aliens admitted to the United States on a temporary basis to perform farmwork to determine if you meet either of the tests. However, wages paid to these aliens are not subject to FUTA tax before 1993.

Completing Form 940

Employers Who Are Not Required To Deposit FUTA Tax.—If your total FUTA tax for the year is $100 or less, you do not have to deposit the tax. Make your FUTA tax payment when you file Form 940. If you do not have to deposit FUTA tax and you:

(a) made all required payments to state unemployment funds by the due date of Form 940,

(b) are required to make payments to the unemployment fund of only one state, and

(c) paid wages subject to Federal unemployment tax that are also subject to state unemployment tax, complete Parts I and II. Otherwise, complete Parts I and III.

Employers Who Are Required To Deposit FUTA Tax.—If you meet tests (a), (b), and (c) above, complete Parts I, II, and IV.

Cat. No. 13660I

Otherwise, complete Parts I, III, and IV.

Not Liable for FUTA Tax.—If you receive Form 940 and are not liable for FUTA tax for 1991, write "Not Liable" across the front, sign the return, and return it to the IRS. If you will not have to file returns in the future, check the box above Part I indicating that you will not have to file Form 940 in the future. Then complete and sign the return.

Due Date.—Form 940 for 1991 is due by January 31, 1992. However, if you deposited all tax due on time, you have 10 more days to file.

Where To File.—

If your principal business, office or agency is located in:	File with the Internal Revenue Service Center at:
Florida. Georgia. South Carolina	Atlanta. GA 39901
New Jersey. New York (New York City and counties of Nassau. Rockland. Suffolk. and Westchester)	Holtsville. NY 00501
New York (all other counties). Connecticut. Maine, Massachusetts. New Hampshire. Rhode Island. Vermont	Andover. MA 05501
Illinois. Iowa, Minnesota. Missouri, Wisconsin	Kansas City. MO 64999
Delaware. District of Columbia. Maryland. Pennsylvania. Puerto Rico. Virginia, Virgin Islands	Philadelphia. PA 19255
Indiana, Kentucky. Michigan, Ohio. West Virginia	Cincinnati. OH 45999
Kansas. New Mexico. Oklahoma. Texas	Austin. TX 73301
Alaska, Arizona. California (counties of Alpine. Amador. Butte. Calaveras. Colusa. Contra Costa, Del Norte. El Dorado, Glenn, Humboldt, Lake, Lassen, Marin, Mendocino, Modoc. Napa, Nevada, Placer, Plumas, Sacramento, San Joaquin. Shasta, Sierra, Siskiyou, Solano, Sonoma, Sutter, Tehama, Trinity, Yolo. and Yuba), Colorado, Idaho, Montana, Nebraska, Nevada, North Dakota. Oregon, South Dakota. Utah, Washington. Wyoming	Ogden. UT 84201
California (all other counties), Hawaii	Fresno, CA 93888
Alabama, Arkansas, Louisiana, Mississippi, North Carolina, Tennessee	Memphis. TN 37501

If you have no legal residence or principal place of business in any IRS district, file with the Internal Revenue Service Center, Philadelphia, PA 19255.

Employer's Name, Address, and Identification Number.—Use the preaddressed Form 940 mailed to you. If you must use a form that is not preaddressed, type or print your name, trade name, address, and employer identification number on it.

See **Pub. 583,** Taxpayers Starting a Business, for details on how to make tax deposits, file a return, etc., if these are due before you receive your employer identification number.

Identifying Your Payments.—On balance due payments of $100 or less made to the IRS (Part II, line 5, and Part III, line 9) and Federal tax deposit payments, write your employer identification number, "Form 940," and the tax period to which the payment applies on your check or money order. This will help ensure proper crediting of your account.

Penalties and Interest.—Avoid penalties and interest by making tax deposits when due, filing a correct return, and paying the proper amount of tax when due. The law provides penalties for late deposits and late filing unless you show reasonable cause for the delay. If you file late, attach an explanation to the return. See **Circular E,** Employer's Tax Guide, for information on penalties.

There are also penalties for willful failure to pay tax, keep records, make returns, and filing false or fraudulent returns.

Credit for Contributions Paid Into State Funds.—You can claim credit for amounts you pay into a certified state (including Puerto Rico and the Virgin Islands) unemployment fund by the due date of Form 940. Your FUTA tax will be higher if you do not pay the state contributions timely.

Note: *Be sure to enter your state reporting number where required on Form 940. This number is needed for the IRS to verify your state contributions.*

"Contributions" are payments that state law requires you to make to an unemployment fund because you are an employer. These payments are "contributions" only to the extent that they are not deducted or deductible from the employees' pay.

Do not take credit for penalties, interest, or special administrative taxes which are not included in the contribution rate the state assigned to you. Also, do not take credit for voluntary contributions paid to obtain a lower assigned rate.

If you have been assigned an experience rate lower than 5.4% (.054) by a state for the whole or part of the year, you are entitled to an additional credit. This **additional** credit is equal to the difference between actual payments and the amount you would have been required to pay at 5.4%.

The total credit allowable may not be more than 5.4% of the total taxable FUTA wages eligible for credit.

Special Credit for Successor Employers.—If you are claiming special credit as a successor employer, see section 3302(e) or Circular E, for the conditions you must meet.

Amended Returns.—If you are amending a previously filed return, complete a new Form 940, using the amounts that should have been used on the original return, and sign the return. Attach a statement explaining why you are filing an amended return. Be sure to use a Form 940 for the year you are amending. If you are correcting a 1990 or prior year form, write "Amended Return" at the top of the form. To amend a 1991 Form 940, check the amended return box above Part I. File the amended return with the Internal Revenue Service Center where you filed the original return.

Specific Instructions

You must answer questions A and B (check the box in C only if it applies), complete Part I and the other Parts that apply, and sign the return.

Note: *If you have been assigned a 0% experience rate by your state so that there are no required contributions to the state unemployment fund, check the "Yes" box in question A and write "0% rate" on the dollar amount line.*

Use Part II only if you checked the "Yes" boxes in questions A and B and did not check the box in C. Otherwise, skip Part II and complete Part III.

Complete Part IV if your total tax for the year is more than $100.

Box C.—Check this box **ONLY** if you pay any wages that are taxable for FUTA tax but are exempt from your state's unemployment tax.

Part I.—Computation of Taxable Wages

Line 1—Total payments.—Enter the total payments you made to employees during the calendar year, even if they are not taxable. Include salaries, wages, commissions, fees, bonuses, vacation allowances, amounts paid to temporary or part-time employees, and the value of goods, lodging, food, clothing, and noncash fringe benefits. Include the amount of tips reported to you in writing by your employees. Also, include contributions to a 401(k) pension plan. Enter the amount before any deductions.

How the payments are made is not important in determining if they are wages. Thus, you may pay wages for piecework or as a percentage of profits, and you may pay wages hourly, daily, weekly, monthly, or yearly. You may pay wages in cash or some other way, such as goods, lodging, food, or clothing. For items other than cash, use the fair market value at the time of payment.

Line 2—Exempt payments.— "Wages" and "employment" as defined for FUTA purposes do not include every payment and every kind of service an employee may perform. In general, payments excluded from wages and payments for services excepted from employment are not subject to tax. You may deduct these exempt payments from total payments only if you explain them on line 2.

Enter payments for the following items:

(1) Agricultural labor, if you did not meet either of the tests in **Agricultural Employers** on page 1.

(2) Benefit payments for sickness or injury under a worker's compensation law.

(3) Household service if you did not pay cash wages of $1,000 or more in any calendar quarter in 1990 or 1991.

(4) Certain family employment.

(5) Certain fishing activities.

(6) Noncash payments for farmwork or household services in a private home that are included on line 1. Only cash wages to these workers are taxable.

(7) Value of certain meals and lodging.

(8) Cost of group-term life insurance.

(9) Payments attributable to the employee's contributions to a sick pay plan.

(10) Any other exempt service or pay.

For more information, see Circular E.

Line 3.—Enter the total amounts over $7,000 you paid each employee. For example, if you have 10 employees to whom you paid $8,000 each during the year, enter $80,000 on line 1 and $10,000 on line 3. Only the first $7,000 paid to your employee is subject to FUTA tax. Do not use the state wage limitation for this entry.

Line 5—Total taxable wages.—If any part of these wages is exempt from state unemployment taxes, you must fill out Part III. For example, if you pay wages to corporate officers in a state that exempts these wages from its unemployment taxes (these wages are taxable for FUTA tax), you would check the box in C on page 1 and complete Part III.

Line 6—Computation of credit reduction.—Enter the amount of wages included on line 5 subject to the unemployment compensation laws of the state of Michigan. The wages shown on line 6 cannot exceed the total taxable wages shown on line 5. If no wages are subject to these laws, enter "none" on line 6. Multiply the wages by the rate shown.

The amount of this adjustment increases the FUTA tax by reducing the credit otherwise allowable against the FUTA tax for contributions made to state unemployment funds. However, the increase cannot be more than the credit otherwise allowable.

Part II.—Tax Due or Refund

Use this part only if you checked "Yes" for both questions A and B on Form 940, and did not check the box in C. The tax rate of .008 gives you credit for your payments to your state's unemployment fund.

The amount on line 2 is the additional tax resulting from credit reduction attributable to wages paid that are subject to the unemployment tax laws of the state of Michigan.

Part III.—Tax Due or Refund

Use this part if you do not qualify for Part II. Failure to provide this information could increase your tax.

Line 3.—Complete this schedule if you checked the "No" box in either question A or B on Form 940, or if you checked the box in C. If you have been assigned an experience rate by your state of 0% or more, but less than 5.4% for all or part of the year, use columns (a) through (i). If you have not been assigned any experience rate by your state, use columns (a), (b), (c), and (i) only. If you have been assigned a rate of 5.4% or higher, use columns (a), (b), (c), (d), (e) and (i) only. If you were assigned an experience rate for only part of the year or the rate was changed during the year, complete a separate line for each rate period.

If you need additional lines, attach a separate statement with a similar format.

Column (a).—Enter the name of the state(s) that you were required to pay contributions to (including Puerto Rico and the Virgin Islands).

Column (b).—Enter the state reporting number that was assigned to you when you registered as an employer with each state.

Column (c).—Enter the taxable payroll on which you must pay taxes to the unemployment fund of each state in column (a). If your experience rate is 0%, enter the amount of wages that you would have had to pay on if the rate had not been granted.

Columns (d) and (e).—Your "state experience rate" is the rate at which the state taxes your payroll for state unemployment purposes. This rate may be adjusted from time to time based on your "experience" with the state tax fund, that is, unemployment compensation paid to your former employees and other factors. If you do not know your rate, contact your state unemployment insurance service. The state experience rate can be stated as a percent or a decimal.

Column (h).—Subtract column (g) from column (f). If zero or less, enter "0."

Column (i).—Enter the contributions actually paid into the state fund by the due date of Form 940. Do not include any special assessments, surtaxes, surcharges, etc., used by the state to pay interest on unpaid advances from the Federal Government.

Line 3a.—Enter the totals of columns (c), (h), and (i) on this line. The total of all amounts reported in column (i) should equal the amount entered under question A at the top of Form 940.

Line 3b.—Add line 3a, columns (h) and (i) only. If you file Form 940 after its due date and any contributions in column (i) were made after the due date, your credit for late contributions is limited to **90%** of their amount. For example, if $1,500 of state contributions was paid on time, and $1,000 was paid after the due date for filing Form 940, the total tentative credit on line 3b would be $2,400 ($1,500 + $900 (90% of $1,000)). This is assuming there is no additional credit in column (h).

Note: *If you are receiving additional credit (column (h)) because your state experience rate is less than 5.4%, the additional credit is not subject to the 90% limitation.*

Line 4.—Enter the smaller of Part III, line 3b, or Part III, line 2. This is the credit allowable for your payments to state unemployment funds. If you do not have to make payments to the state, enter "0" on this line.

Lines 5 and 6.—Enter the amount from Part I, line 6 on line 5. Subtract this amount from line 4. The result on line 6 is your allowable credit for payments to the state.

Part IV.—Record of Federal Tax Liability

Complete this part if your total tax (Part II, line 3, or Part III, line 7) is over $100. To figure your FUTA tax liability **for each of the first 3 quarters of 1991,** multiply by .008 that part of the first $7,000 of each employee's annual wages you paid during the quarter. Enter this amount under that quarter.

Your liability for the 4th quarter is the total tax (Part II, line 3 or Part III, line 7) minus your liability for the first 3 quarters of the year. The total liability must equal your total tax. Otherwise, you may be charged a failure to deposit penalty figured on your average liability.

Depositing FUTA tax.—Generally, FUTA taxes are deposited on a quarterly basis. If your liability for any of the first 3 quarters of 1991 (plus any undeposited amount of $100 or less from any earlier quarter) is over $100, deposit it by the last day of the first month following the close of the quarter. If it is $100 or less, you may carry it to the next quarter; a deposit is not required. If your liability for the 4th quarter (plus any undeposited amount from any earlier quarter) is over $100, deposit the entire amount by January 31, 1992. If it is $100 or less, you can either make a deposit or pay it with your Form 940 by January 31, 1992.

Note: *The total amount of all deposits must be shown in Part II, line 4 or Part III, line 8.*

If you deposited the correct amounts, following these rules, the balance due with Form 940 will never be more than $100.

Deposit FUTA tax in an authorized financial institution or the Federal Reserve bank for your area. To avoid a possible penalty, do not mail deposits directly to the IRS. Records of your deposits will be sent to the IRS for crediting to your business accounts. See **Identifying Your Payments** on page 2.

You must use **Form 8109,** Federal Tax Deposit Coupon, when making each tax deposit. The IRS will send you a book of deposit coupons when you apply for an employer identification number. Follow the instructions in the coupon book. If you do not have coupons, see Circular E.

★U.S.GPO:1991-0-285-489

Form **940**

Department of the Treasury
Internal Revenue Service

Employer's Annual Federal Unemployment (FUTA) Tax Return

▶ **For Paperwork Reduction Act Notice, see separate instructions.**

OMB No. 1545-0028

1991

T	
FF	
FD	
FP	
I	
T	

If incorrect, make any necessary change. ▶

Name (as distinguished from trade name)   Calendar year

Trade name, if any

Address and ZIP code   Employer identification number

–

A Did you pay all required contributions to state unemployment funds by the due date of Form 940? (If a 0% experience rate is granted, check "Yes" and see instructions.) . . . . ☐ **Yes** ☐ **No**

If you checked the "Yes" box, enter the amount of contributions paid to state unemployment funds · ▶ $ ....

B Are you required to pay contributions to only one state? . . . . ☐ **Yes** ☐ **No**

If you checked the "Yes" box: (1) Enter the name of the state where you have to pay contributions ▶ ....

(2) Enter your state reporting number(s) as shown on state unemployment tax return. ▶ ....

If you checked the "No" box, be sure to complete Part III and see the instructions.

C If any part of wages taxable for FUTA tax is exempt from state unemployment tax, check the box. (See the instructions.). . . . . ☐

If you will not have to file returns in the future, check here, complete, and sign the return . . . . ▶ ☐
If this is an Amended Return, check here . . . . ▶ ☐

Part I **Computation of Taxable Wages** *(to be completed by all taxpayers)*

1	Total payments (including exempt payments) during the calendar year for services of employees.	**1**		
2	Exempt payments. (Explain each exemption shown, attach additional sheets if necessary.) ▶	Amount paid **2**		
3	Payments of more than $7,000 for services. Enter only the amounts over the first $7,000 paid to each employee. Do not include payments from line 2. Do not use the state wage limitation	**3**		
4	Total exempt payments (add lines 2 and 3).	**4**		
5	**Total taxable wages** (subtract line 4 from line 1). . . . . ▶	**5**		
6	Additional tax resulting from credit reduction for unpaid advances to the state of Michigan. Enter the wages included on line 5 above for that state and multiply by the rate shown. (See the instructions.) Enter the credit reduction amount here and in Part II, line 2, or Part III, line 5: Michigan wages _____ × .008 = ... ▶	**6**		

Cat. No. 112340

Form **940** (1991)

Part II   **Tax Due or Refund** *(Complete if you checked the "Yes" boxes in both questions A and B and did not check the box in C.)*

1	**FUTA tax.** Multiply the wages in Part I, line 5, by .008 and enter here.	**1**
2	Enter amount from Part I, line 6	**2**
3	**Total FUTA tax** (add lines 1 and 2) . . . . ▶	**3**
4	Total FUTA tax deposited for the year, including any overpayment applied from a prior year . .	**4**
5	**Balance due** (subtract line 4 from line 3). This should be $100 or less. Pay to the Internal Revenue Service. . . . . ▶	**5**
6	**Overpayment** (subtract line 3 from line 4). Check if it is to be: ☐ **Applied to next return,** or ☐ **Refunded** . . . . ▶	**6**

Part III   **Tax Due or Refund** *(Complete if you checked the "No" box in either question A or B or you checked the box in C.)*

1	Gross FUTA tax. Multiply the wages in Part I, line 5, by .062	**1**
2	Maximum credit. Multiply the wages in Part I, line 5, by .054. . . . **2**	
3	Computation of tentative credit	

(a) Name of state	(b) State reporting number(s) as shown on employer's state contribution returns	(c) Taxable payroll (as defined in state act)	(d) State experience rate		(e) State experience rate	(f) Contributions if rate had been 5.4% (col. (c) x .054)	(g) Contributions payable at experience rate (col. (c) x col. (e))	(h) Additional credit (col. (f) minus col.(g)). If 0 or less, enter 0.	(i) Contributions actually paid to the state
			From	To					

3a Totals . . . ▶

3b **Total tentative credit** (add line 3a, columns (h) and (i) only—see instructions for limitations on late payments) ▶

4	**Credit:** Enter the smaller of the amount in Part III, line 2, or line 3b **4**	
5	Enter the amount from Part I, line 6	**5**
6	**Credit allowable** (subtract line 5 from line 4). (If zero or less, enter 0.)	**6**
7	**Total FUTA tax** (subtract line 6 from line 1)	**7**
8	Total FUTA tax deposited for the year, including any overpayment applied from a prior year . .	**8**
9	**Balance due** (subtract line 8 from line 7). This should be $100 or less. Pay to the Internal Revenue Service. . . . . ▶	**9**
10	**Overpayment** (subtract line 7 from line 8). Check if it is to be: ☐ **Applied to next return,** or ☐ **Refunded** . . . . ▶	**10**

Part IV   **Record of Quarterly Federal Tax Liability for Unemployment Tax** *(Do not include state liability)*

Quarter	First	Second	Third	Fourth	Total for year
Liability for quarter					

Under penalties of perjury, I declare that I have examined this return, including accompanying schedules and statements, and to the best of my knowledge and belief, it is true, correct, and complete, and that no part of any payment made to a state unemployment fund claimed as a credit was or is to be deducted from the payments to employees.

Signature ▶   Title (Owner, etc.) ▶   Date ▶

Employer's Annual Federal
Unemployment (FUTA) Tax Return

OMB No. 1545-1110

1991

T	
FF	
FD	
FP	
I	
T	

If incorrect,
make any
necessary
changes. ▶

```
DD  10-1234567  9112  S28  B
Peter Cone
362 Main Street
Anytown        VA  23000
```

Calendar year

I R S
r identification number
_____ – _____

Follow the chart under "Who Can Use Form 940-EZ" on page 2. If you cannot use Form 940-EZ, you must use Form 940 instead.

A Enter the amount of contributions paid to your state unemployment fund. (See instructions for line A on page 4.) ▶ $ *630.00*

B (1) Enter the name of the state where you have to pay contributions . . . . ▶ *Virginia* ....

   (2) Enter your state reporting number(s) as shown on state unemployment tax return. ▶ *987654.32* ....

If you will not have to file returns in the future, check here (see *Who Must File a Return* on page 2) **complete, and sign the return** . . . ▶ ☐

If this is an Amended Return check here . . . . ▶ ☐

Part I   Taxable Wages and FUTA Tax

1	Total payments (including payments shown on lines 2 and 3) during the calendar year for services of employees	**1**	*78,000*	*00*

2	Exempt payments. (Explain all exempt payments, attaching additional sheets if necessary.) ▶	**2** Amount paid		
3	Payments for services of more than $7,000. Enter only amounts over the first $7,000 paid to each employee. Do not include any exempt payments from line 2 . . .	**3**	*57,000*	*00*
4	Total exempt payments (add lines 2 and 3)	**4**	*57,000*	*00*
5	**Total taxable wages** (subtract line 4 from line 1) . . . . ▶	**5**	*21,000*	*00*
6	**FUTA tax.** Multiply the wages on line 5 by .008 and enter here. (If the result is over $100, also complete Part II.) .	**6**	*168*	*00*
7	Total FUTA tax deposited for the year, including any overpayment applied from a prior year (from your records)	**7**	*142*	*40*
8	**Amount you owe** (subtract line 7 from line 6). This should be $100 or less. Pay to "Internal Revenue Service" . ▶	**8**	*25*	*60*
9	**Overpayment** (subtract line 6 from line 7). Check if it is to be: ☐ **Applied to next return, or** ☐ Refunded ▶	**9**		

Part II   Record of Quarterly Federal Unemployment Tax Liability (Do not include state liability.) Complete only if line 6 is over $100.

Quarter	First (Jan. 1 – Mar. 31)	Second (Apr. 1 – June 30)	Third (July 1 – Sept. 30)	Fourth (Oct. 1 – Dec. 31)	Total for Year
Liability for quarter	*142.40*	*25.60*			*168.00*

Under penalties of perjury, I declare that I have examined this return, including accompanying schedules and statements, and, to the best of my knowledge and belief, it is true, correct, and complete, and that no part of any payment made to a state unemployment fund claimed as a credit was, or is to be, deducted from the payments to employees.

Signature ▶ *Peter Cone*   Title (Owner, etc.) ▶ *Owner*   Date ▶ *1-24-92*

Form **940-EZ**

Department of the Treasury
Internal Revenue Service

Employer's Annual Federal Unemployment (FUTA) Tax Return

OMB No. 1545-1110

1991

T	
FF	
FD	
FP	
I	
T	

If incorrect, make any necessary changes. ▶

Name (as distinguished from trade name)

Trade name, if any

Address and ZIP code

Calendar year

Employer identification number
—

Follow the chart under "Who Can Use Form 940-EZ" on page 2. If you cannot use Form 940-EZ, you must use Form 940 instead.

A Enter the amount of contributions paid to your state unemployment fund. (See instructions for line A on page 4.)▶ $ ....

B (1) Enter the name of the state where you have to pay contributions . . . . ▶ ....

  (2) Enter your state reporting number(s) as shown on state unemployment tax return. ▶ ....

If you will not have to file returns in the future, check here (see *Who Must File a Return* on page 2) **complete, and sign the return** · · · ▶ ☐

If this is an Amended Return check here . . . . ▶ ☐

Part I Taxable Wages and FUTA Tax

1	Total payments (including payments shown on lines 2 and 3) during the calendar year for services of employees	1	

			Amount paid	
2	Exempt payments. (Explain all exempt payments, attaching additional sheets if necessary.) ▶	2		
3	Payments for services of more than $7,000. Enter only amounts over the first $7,000 paid to each employee. Do not include any exempt payments from line 2 . . .	3		

4	Total exempt payments (add lines 2 and 3)	4	
5	**Total taxable wages** (subtract line 4 from line 1) . . . . ▶	5	
6	**FUTA tax.** Multiply the wages on line 5 by .008 and enter here. (If the result is over $100, also complete Part II.) .	6	
7	Total FUTA tax deposited for the year, including any overpayment applied from a prior year (from your records)	7	
8	**Amount you owe** (subtract line 7 from line 6). This should be $100 or less. Pay to "Internal Revenue Service". ▶	8	
9	**Overpayment** (subtract line 6 from line 7). Check if it is to be: ☐ **Applied to next return, or** ☐ **Refunded** ▶	9	

Part II Record of Quarterly Federal Unemployment Tax Liability (Do not include state liability.) Complete only if line 6 is over $100.

Quarter	First (Jan. 1 – Mar. 31)	Second (Apr. 1 – June 30)	Third (July 1 – Sept. 30)	Fourth (Oct. 1 – Dec. 31)	Total for Year
Liability for quarter					

Under penalties of perjury, I declare that I have examined this return, including accompanying schedules and statements, and, to the best of my knowledge and belief, it is true, correct, and complete, and that no part of any payment made to a state unemployment fund claimed as a credit was, or is to be, deducted from the payments to employees.

Signature ▶   Title (Owner, etc.) ▶   Date ▶

Cat. No. 10983G

Form **940-EZ** (1991)

★U.S.GPO:1991-0-285-102

Paperwork Reduction Act Notice.—We ask for the information on this form to carry out the Internal Revenue laws of the United States. You are required to give us the information. We need it to ensure that you are complying with these laws and to allow us to figure and collect the correct tax.

The time needed to complete and file this form will vary depending on individual circumstances. The estimated average time is:

Recordkeeping . . . . .5 hr., 20 min.

Learning about the law or the form . . . . 7 min.

Preparing and sending the form to IRS . . . . . 26 min.

If you have comments concerning the accuracy of these time estimates or suggestions for making this form more simple, we would be happy to hear from you. You can write to both the **Internal Revenue Service,** Washington, DC 20224, Attention: IRS Reports Clearance Officer, T:FP; and the **Office of Management and Budget,** Paperwork Reduction Project (1545-1110), Washington, DC 20503. **DO NOT** send the form to either of these offices. Instead, see **Where To File.**

Who May Not Use Form 940–EZ.—

If you pay any wages that are subject to the unemployment compensation laws of the state of Michigan, you must file **Form 940,** instead of Form 940-EZ.

Who May Use Form 940-EZ.—You may use Form 940-EZ if:

(1) You paid unemployment taxes ("contributions") to only one state;

(2) You paid these taxes by the due date of Form 940-EZ; and

(3) All wages that were taxable for FUTA tax were also taxable for your state's unemployment tax. Otherwise, use Form 940. For example, if you paid wages to corporate officers (these wages are taxable for FUTA tax) in a state that exempts these wages from its unemployment taxes, you cannot use Form 940-EZ.

The following chart will lead you to the right form to use.

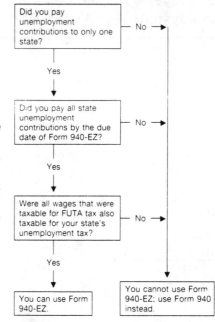

Note: *Do not file Form 940-EZ if you have already filed Form 940 for 1991.*

General Instructions

Purpose of Form.—The Federal Unemployment Tax Act (FUTA), together with state unemployment systems, provides for payments of unemployment compensation to workers who have lost their jobs. Most employers pay both Federal and state unemployment taxes. Use this form for your annual FUTA tax report. **Only the employer pays this tax.**

Who Must File

General Rule (household and agricultural employers see next column).—File a FUTA tax return if either of the following applies:

(1) You paid wages of $1,500 or more in any calendar quarter in 1990 or 1991; or

(2) You had at least one employee for some part of a day in any 20 different weeks in 1990 or 1991.

Count all regular, temporary, and part-time employees. A partnership should not count its partners. If a business changes hands during the year, each employer meeting test (1) or (2) above must file. Neither should report wages paid by the other.

Household Employers.—File a FUTA tax return **ONLY** if you paid cash wages of $1,000 or more in any calendar quarter in 1990 or 1991 for household work in a private home, local college club, or a local chapter of a college fraternity or sorority.

Note: *See Pub. 926, Employment Taxes for Household Employers, for more information.*

Agricultural Employers.—File a FUTA tax return if either of the following applies:

(1) You paid cash wages of $20,000 or more to farmworkers during any calendar quarter in 1990 or 1991; or

(2) You employed 10 or more farmworkers during some part of a day (whether or not at the same time) for at least 1 day during any 20 different weeks in 1990 or 1991.

Count aliens admitted to the United States temporarily to do farmwork to see if you met either of the above tests. However, wages paid to these aliens are not subject to FUTA tax before 1993.

Nonprofit Organizations.—Religious, educational, charitable, etc., organizations described in section 501(c)(3) of the Internal Revenue Code and exempt from tax under section 501(a) are not subject to FUTA tax and are not required to file.

Completing Form 940-EZ.—If your FUTA tax for 1991 (line 6) is $100 or less, complete only Part I of the form. If your FUTA tax is over $100, complete Parts I and II. See the instructions for Part II for information on FUTA tax deposits.

Filing Hint.—You can help avoid IRS contacts for missing information and delays in processing your return by making sure you fill in all the lines that apply to you. And, if you are not using a preaddressed Form 940-EZ, be sure you fill in the name lines exactly as they were shown on your **Form SS-4,** Application for Employer Identification Number.

(Instructions continued on next page.)

Where To File

If your principal business, office, or agency is located in:	File with the Internal Revenue Service Center at:
Florida, Georgia, South Carolina	Atlanta, GA 39901
New Jersey, New York (New York City and counties of Nassau, Rockland, Suffolk, and Westchester)	Holtsville, NY 00501
New York (all other counties). Connecticut, Maine, Massachusetts, New Hampshire, Rhode Island, Vermont	Andover, MA 05501
Illinois, Iowa, Minnesota. Missouri, Wisconsin	Kansas City, MO 64999
Delaware, District of Columbia, Maryland. Pennsylvania, Puerto Rico. Virginia, Virgin Islands	Philadelphia. PA 19255
Indiana, Kentucky. Michigan. Ohio, West Virginia	Cincinnati, OH 45999
Kansas. New Mexico. Oklahoma, Texas	Austin, TX 73301
Alaska, Arizona, California (counties of Alpine, Amador, Butte, Calaveras, Colusa, Contra Costa, Del Norte. El Dorado, Glenn, Humboldt, Lake, Lassen. Marin, Mendocino, Modoc, Napa. Nevada, Placer, Plumas. Sacramento. San Joaquin, Shasta, Sierra, Siskiyou, Solano, Sonoma, Sutter, Tehama, Trinity. Yolo, and Yuba), Colorado, Idaho. Montana, Nebraska, Nevada. North Dakota, Oregon, South Dakota, Utah, Washington, Wyoming	Ogden, UT 84201
California (all other counties), Hawaii	Fresno, CA 93888
Alabama, Arkansas. Louisiana, Mississippi, North Carolina, Tennessee	Memphis, TN 37501

If you have no legal residence or principal place of business in any IRS district, file with the Internal Revenue Service Center. Philadelphia. PA 19255.

Penalties and Interest.—Avoid penalties and interest by making tax deposits when due, filing a correct return, and paying all taxes when due. There are penalties for late deposits and late filing unless you can show reasonable cause. If you file late, attach an explanation to the return.

There are also penalties for willful failure to pay tax, keep records, make returns, and for filing false or fraudulent returns.

Credit for Contributions Paid Into State Funds.—You get a credit for amounts you pay to a state (including Puerto Rico and the Virgin Islands) unemployment fund by the due date of Form 940-EZ. This credit is reflected in the tax rate (.008) shown on line 6.

"Contributions" are payments that a state requires you, as an employer, to make to its unemployment fund for the payment of unemployment benefits. However, contributions do not include:

● Any payments you deducted or are deductible from your employees' pay.

● Penalties, interest, or special administrative taxes which are not included in the contribution rate the state assigned to you.

● Voluntary contributions you paid to get a lower assigned rate.

Note: *Be sure to enter your state reporting number(s) on line B(2) at the top of the form. We need this to verify your state contributions.*

Special Credit for Successor Employers.—If you are claiming special credit as a successor employer, you must use Form 940.

Amended Returns.—Use a new Form 940-EZ to amend a previously filed Form 940-EZ. Check the Amended Return box above Part I, enter the amounts that should have been on the original return, and sign the amended return. Explain why you are amending Form 940-EZ.

If you were required to file Form 940 but filed Form 940-EZ instead, file the amended return on Form 940. See Form 940 and the instructions for information.

Specific Instructions

You must complete lines A and B and Part I. If your FUTA tax (line 6) is over $100, you must also complete Part II. Please remember to sign the return.

Line A.—Enter the dollar amount of state unemployment contributions. However, if your state has given you a 0% experience rate, so that there are no required contributions, write "0% rate" in the space.

Part I. Taxable Wages and FUTA Tax

Line 1—Total payments.—Enter the total payments you made to employees during the calendar year, even if they are not taxable. Include salaries, wages, commissions, fees, bonuses, vacation allowances, amounts paid to temporary or part-time employees, and the value of goods, lodging, food, clothing, and noncash fringe benefits. Also include the amount of tips reported to you in writing by your employees. Enter the amount before any deductions.

How the payments are made is not important to determine if they are wages. Thus, you may pay wages for piecework or as a percentage of profits. You may pay wages hourly, daily, weekly, monthly, or yearly. You may pay wages in cash or some other way, such as goods, lodging, food, or clothing. For items other than cash, use the fair market value when paid.

Line 2—Exempt payments.—"Wages" and "employment" for FUTA purposes do not include every payment and every kind of service an employee may perform. In general, payments that are not wages and payments for services that are not employment are not subject to tax. You may deduct these payments from total payments only if you explain them on line 2.

Enter such items as the following:

(1) Agricultural labor, if you did not meet either of the tests in **Agricultural Employers** on page 2.

(2) Benefit payments for sickness or injury under a worker's compensation law.

(3) Household service if you did not pay cash wages of $1,000 or more in any calendar quarter in 1990 and 1991.

(4) Certain family employment.

(5) Certain fishing activities.

(6) Noncash payments for farmwork or household services in a private home that are included on line 1. Only cash wages to these workers are taxable.

(7) Value of certain meals and lodging.

(8) Cost of group-term life insurance.

(9) Payments attributable to the employee's contributions to a sick pay plan.

(10) Any other exempt service or pay.

For more information, see **Circular E,** Employer's Tax Guide.

Line 3—Enter the total amounts over $7,000 you paid each employee. For example, if you have 10 employees to whom you paid $8,000 each during the year, enter $80,000 on line 1 and $10,000 on line 3. Do not include any exempt payments from line 2 in figuring the $7,000.

Part II. Record of Quarterly Federal Unemployment Tax Liability

Complete this part only if your FUTA tax on line 6 is over $100. To figure your FUTA tax liability, multiply by .008 that part of the first $7,000 of each employee's annual wages you paid during the quarter. Enter the result in the space for that quarter.

Your total liability must equal your total tax. If not, you may be charged a failure to deposit penalty figured on your average liability.

Record your liability based on when you pay the wages, not on when you deposit the tax. For example, assume that you pay wages on March 29 and your FUTA tax liability on those wages is $200. You deposit the $200 by April 30. You would include that $200 in the first quarter, not the second.

Depositing FUTA Tax.—Generally, FUTA taxes are deposited quarterly. If your liability for any of the first 3 quarters of 1991 (plus any undeposited amount of $100 or less from any earlier quarter) is over $100, deposit it by the last day of the month after the end of the quarter. If it is $100 or less, carry it to the next quarter; a deposit is not required. If your liability for the 4th quarter (plus any undeposited amount from any earlier quarter) is over $100, deposit the entire amount by January 31, 1992. If it is $100 or less, you can either make a deposit or pay it with your Form 940-EZ by January 31.

Note: *The total amount of all deposits must be shown on line 7.*

If you deposited the right amounts, following these rules, the amount you owe with Form 940-EZ will never be over $100.

Deposit FUTA tax in an authorized financial institution or the Federal Reserve bank for your area. To avoid a possible penalty, do not mail deposits directly to the IRS. Records of your deposits will be sent to the IRS for crediting to your business accounts. See **Identifying Your Payments.**

You must use **Form 8109,** Federal Tax Deposit Coupon, when making tax deposits. IRS will send you a book of deposit coupons when you apply for an EIN. Follow the instructions in the coupon book. If you do not have coupons, see Circular E.

**Department of the Treasury
Internal Revenue Service**

Instructions for Form W-2

Wage and Tax Statement

Paperwork Reduction Act Notice.—
We ask for the information on this form to carry out the Internal Revenue laws of the United States. You are required to give us the information. We need it to ensure that you are complying with these laws and to allow us to figure and collect the right amount of tax.

The time needed to complete and file this form will vary depending on individual circumstances. The estimated average time is 30 minutes. If you have comments concerning the accuracy of this time estimate or suggestions for making this form more simple, we would be happy to hear from you. You can write to both the **Internal Revenue Service,** Washington, DC 20224, Attention: IRS Reports Clearance Officer T:FP; and the **Office of Management and Budget,** Paperwork Reduction Project (1545-0008), Washington, DC 20503. DO NOT send the tax form to either of these offices. Instead, see the instructions below for where to file it.

Changes You Should Note

Separate Reporting of Social Security Wages, Medicare Wages and Tips, Social Security Taxes, and Medicare Taxes.—
Beginning in 1991, the wage bases for the two parts of the social security tax (social security and Medicare) are different. Employers can no longer combine and report the withholding as a single amount. The **Form W-2,** Wage and Tax Statement, for 1991 will require employers to separately report the withholding for social security and Medicare.

The wage bases are $53,400 for social security (old age, survivors, and disability insurance) and $125,000 for Medicare (hospital insurance). For social security, the tax rate is 6.2% each for employers and employees. For Medicare, the rate is 1.45% each for employers and employees. In addition, there are changes to the codes for Box 17.

Obsolete Form W-2P.—Form W-2P, Statement for Recipients of Annuities, Pensions, Retired Pay, or IRA Payments, is obsolete. For 1991, payers must report distributions (periodic and total) from pensions, annuities, retirement pay, profit-sharing plans, IRAs, SEPs, and insurance contracts on **Form 1099-R,** Distributions From Pensions, Annuities, Retirement or Profit-Sharing Plans, IRAs, Insurance Contracts, etc. See the separate Instructions for Forms 1099, 1098, 5498, and W-2G, for more information.

Use **Form W-2c,** Statement of Corrected Income and Tax Amounts, to report corrections on Form W-2P for years ending before January 1, 1991.

State and Local Government Employees.—
State and local government employees who are not participants in a retirement program (with certain exceptions) will be subject to social security and Medicare taxes for services performed after July 1, 1991.

Reporting of Taxes for Group-Term Life Insurance Coverage.—Beginning in 1991, employers are required to report on Form W-2 any uncollected social security and Medicare taxes on group-term life insurance in excess of $50,000 provided to former employees (including retirees). (Information on reporting these taxes is included in items (g) and (h) in the instructions for Box 17).

General Instructions

(Section references are to the Internal Revenue Code unless otherwise noted.)

Who Must File Form W-2.—Form W-2 is filed by employers. (See **Circular A,** Agricultural Employer's Tax Guide, or **Circular E,** Employer's Tax Guide. Household employers, see **Form 942,** Employer's Quarterly Tax Return for Household Employees.) If you have 250 or more Forms W-2, see instructions for *Magnetic Media Reporting* on the next page.

When To File.—File Form W-2 with accompanying **Form W-3,** Transmittal of Income and Tax Statements, by March 2, 1992.

If you need an extension of time to file Form W-2, see *When To File* in the instructions for Form W-3.

Where To File.—See Form W-3 for instructions.

Calendar Year Basis.—The entries on Form W-2 must be based on a calendar year.

Taxpayer Identification Numbers.—We use these numbers to check the payments you report against the amounts shown on the employees' tax returns. **When you prepare Form W-2, be sure to show the correct social security number on the form or on magnetic media.**

Persons in a trade or business use an employer identification number (00-0000000). Individuals use a social security number (000-00-0000). When you list a number, please separate the nine digits properly to show the kind of number.

Sole proprietors who are payers should show their employer identification number on the statements they prepare. But if you prepare a statement showing payment to a sole proprietor, give the proprietor's social security number in Box 5 of Form W-2.

Please show the full name, address, and identification number of the payer and the recipient on the form. If you made payments to more than one individual, show on the first line **ONLY** the name of the recipient whose number is on the statement. Show the other names on the second line. If the recipient is **NOT** an individual and the name runs over the first line, you may continue on the second and following lines.

Note: *If your employee has been given a new social security card because of an adjustment to his or her alien residence status, which shows a different name or social security number, correct your records for 1991 and show the new information on the 1991 Form W-2. If you filed Form W-2 for the same employee in prior years under the old name and social security number, file Form W-2c, to correct the name and number. (See Corrections later.) In this case, one Form W-2c can be used to correct all prior years. Advise the employee to contact their local Social Security Administration (SSA) office to ensure their records have been updated.*

Statements to Employees.—Generally, give statements to employees by January 31, 1992. If employment ends before December 31, 1991, you may give copies any time after employment ends. If the employee asks for Form W-2, give him or her the completed copies within 30 days of the request or the final wage payment, whichever is later.

You may give statements to employees on government-printed official forms or on privately printed substitute forms.

Be sure that the statements you provide to employees are clear and legible (especially if using carbons).

A revenue procedure, titled "Specifications for Private Printing of Forms W-2 and W-3" reprinted as **Pub. 1141,** explains the format that must be used on all substitute paper forms. You can get a copy by calling 1-800-829-3676.

Corrections.—Use Form W-2c to correct errors on previously filed Form W-2. Use **Form W-3c,** Transmittal of Corrected Income and Tax Statements, to transmit the W-2c forms to the SSA. Instructions are on the forms.

If you are making an adjustment in 1991 to correct social security tax for a prior year, you must file **Form 941c,** Statement To Correct Information Previously Reported on the Employer's Federal Tax Return, with your **Form 941,** Employer's Quarterly Federal Tax Return, in the quarter you find the error and issue the employee a Form W-2c for the prior year.

Reissued Statement.—If an employee (or recipient) loses a statement, write "REISSUED STATEMENT" on the new copy, **but do not send Copy A of the reissued statement to SSA.**

Earned Income Credit Notification.— You must notify any employee not having income tax withheld that they may be eligible for an income tax refund because of the earned income credit. You can do this by using the official IRS Form W-2 which contains a statement on the back of Copy C concerning the earned income credit. If you use a substitute Form W-2, or you are not required to furnish Form W-2, or if you do not furnish a timely Form W-2 to your employee, you may have to give your employee **Notice 797,** Notice of a Possible Federal Tax Refund Due to the Earned Income Credit (EIC). Get **Pub. 1325** for more information.

Employee Business Expense Reimbursements.— Reimbursements for employee business expenses should be reported as follows:

● Generally, payments made under an accountable plan are excluded from the employee's gross income and are not required to be reported on Form W-2. However, if you pay a per diem or mileage allowance, and the amount paid exceeds the amount treated as substantiated under IRS rules, you must report as wages on Form W-2 the amount in excess of the amount treated as substantiated. The excess amount is subject to income tax withholding, social security tax, Medicare tax, and Federal unemployment tax. Report the amount treated as substantiated (*i.e.,* the nontaxable portion) in Box 17 using code "L."

- Payments made under a nonaccountable plan are reportable as wages on Form W-2 and are subject to income tax withholding, social security tax, Medicare tax, and Federal unemployment tax.

For more information on accountable plans, nonaccountable plans, and amounts treated as substantiated under a per diem or mileage allowance, see Regulations section 1.62-2, Revenue Procedure 89-66, 1989-2 C.B. 792, Revenue Procedure 89-67, 1989-2 C.B. 795, Revenue Procedure 90-15, 1990-1 C.B. 476, Revenue Procedure 90-34, 1990-1 C.B. 552, Revenue Procedure 90-38, 1990-28 I.R.B. 13, and Announcement 90-127, 1990-48 I.R.B. 8.

Sick Pay.—If you had employees who received sick pay in 1991 from an insurance company or other third-party payer, and the third party notified you of the amount of sick pay involved, you must report the following on the employees' Forms W-2:

(a) in Box 9, the amount (if any) of income tax withheld from the sick pay by the third-party payer;

(b) in Box 10, the amount the employee must include in income;

(c) in Box 11, the employee social security tax withheld (6.2%) by the third-party payer;

(d) in Box 12, the amount of sick pay that is subject to employee social security tax;

(e) in Box 14, the amount of sick pay that is subject to employee Medicare tax;

(f) in Box 15, the employee Medicare tax withheld (1.45%); and

(g) in Box 17, the amount (if any) not includible in income because the employee contributed to the sick pay plan. See the instructions for Box 17 for the correct code to use.

You can include these amounts on the Forms W-2 you issue the employees showing wages, or you can give the employees separate Forms W-2 and state that the amounts are for third-party sick pay. In either case, you must show in Box 25 of Form W-3 the total amount of income tax withheld by third-party payers, even though the amounts are includible in Box 9. Also, see the instructions for Form W-3 for more information on third-party sick pay.

Magnetic Media Reporting.—If you file 250 or more Forms W-2, you must report on magnetic media unless you have been granted a waiver by the IRS.

If you are filing Form W-2 using magnetic media, you will also need **Form 6559,** Transmitter Report of Magnetic Media Filing, and **Form 6560,** Employer Summary of Form W-2 Magnetic Media Wage Information.

You can get magnetic media reporting specifications at many Social Security Administration offices or you may write to the Social Security Administration, P.O. Box 2317, Baltimore, MD 21235, Attn: Magnetic Media Group.

Note: If you file on magnetic media, do not file the same returns on paper.

Penalties.—A penalty may be imposed if a person either fails to file an information return or files with incorrect information.

The amount of the penalty is based on when the correct information returns are filed. The penalty is as follows:

- $15 for each information return if the correct information is filed within 30 days after the due date with a maximum penalty of $75,000 per year ($25,000 for small businesses, defined later).

- $30 for each information return if the correct information is filed more than 30 days

after the due date but by August 1, with a maximum penalty of $150,000 per year ($50,000 for small businesses).

- $50 for each information return that is not filed at all or is not filed correctly by August 1, with a maximum penalty of $250,000 per year ($100,000 for small businesses).

Exceptions to the Penalty.—In general, the penalty will not apply to any failure that was due to reasonable cause.

In addition, the penalty will not apply to a de minimis number of failures. These failures are information returns that were filed timely but with incomplete or incorrect information and were corrected by August 1. The penalty will not apply to the greater of 10 information returns or 1/2 of 1% of the total number of information returns that are required to be filed for the year.

Definition of Small Business.—A small business is a firm with average annual gross receipts of $5,000,000 or less for the 3 most recent taxable years.

Failure To Provide Employee Statement or Providing Incorrect Employee Statement.—A penalty may be imposed if a person either fails to furnish a payee statement by the due date or fails to include correct information on a payee statement. The penalty is $50 for each failure. The maximum penalty for such failures is $100,000.

Penalties for Intentional Disregard.—Higher penalties of at least $100 per document may be imposed for intentional disregard of the filing, providing payee statements, and correct information return requirements.

How To Complete Form W-2

Copy A of Form W-2 is printed with two forms to an unperforated page. Send the whole page even if one of the forms is blank or void. If you are sending 42 or more Forms W-2, please show subtotals on every 42nd form for the preceding 41 forms to permit checking the transmittal totals.

Since this form is processed by optical scanning machines, please type the entries, if possible, using black ink. Please do not make any erasures, whiteouts, or strikeovers on Copy A. Also, do not use script type. **Make all dollar entries without the dollar sign and comma but with the decimal point (000.00).**

If possible, please file Forms W-2 either alphabetically by employees' last names or numerically by employees' SSNs. This will help SSA locate specific forms if there is a problem processing your submission.

The instructions below are for boxes on Form W-2. If an entry does not apply, leave it blank.

Box 1—Control number.—You may use this box to identify individual Forms W-2. *You do not have to use this box.*

Box 3—Employer's identification number.—Show the number assigned to you by IRS (00-0000000). This should be the same number that you used on your Federal employment tax returns (Forms 941, 942, 943). Do not use a prior owner's number.

Box 4—Employer's state I.D. number.—You do not have to complete this box, but you may want to use copies of this form for your state return. The number is assigned by the individual states.

This box is separated into two parts by a dotted line so that you may report two state I.D. numbers if you are reporting wages for two states. If you are only reporting for one state, enter the number above the dotted line.

Box 5—Employee's social security number.—Enter the number shown on the employee's social security card. If the employee does not have a card, he or she should apply for one at any SSA office.

Box 6—Check the boxes that apply.

Statutory employee.—Check this box for statutory employees whose earnings are subject to social security and Medicare taxes but **NOT** subject to Federal income tax withholding. (See Circular E for more information on statutory employees.)

Deceased.—Check this box if the employee is now deceased. If an employee is deceased, you must report wages or other compensation for services he or she performed and that were paid in the year of death to the estate or beneficiary. In addition, such wages received in a year after the year of death may be reportable on **Form 1099-MISC,** Miscellaneous Income. For information on how to report, see Rev. Rul. 86-109, 1986-2 C.B. 196.

Pension plan.—Check this box if the employee was an active participant (for any part of the year) in a retirement plan (including a 401(k) plan and a simplified employee pension (SEP) plan) maintained by you. Also check this box if the employee participates in a collectively bargained plan (*i.e.*, union plan). See IRS Notice 87-16, 1987-1 C.B. 446, for the definition of an active participant. Do not check this box if you are reporting contributions made to a nonqualified pension plan or a section 457 plan.

Legal representative.—Check this box when the employee's name is the only name shown but is shown as a trust account (*e.g.,* John Doe Trust), or another name is shown in addition to the employee's name and the other person or business is acting on behalf of the employee.

Representatives are identified by words such as "custodian," "parent," or "attorney"; sometimes the employee is identified as a minor, child, etc. Do **NOT** check this box if the address is simply in care of someone other than the employee (John Doe, c/o Jane Smith).

942 employee.—For household employers only. See Form 942 instructions for information on when to check this box.

Subtotal.—Do not subtotal if you are submitting 41 or less Forms W-2. If you are submitting **42 or more Forms W-2,** please give subtotal figures for every 41 individual forms. Check the "Subtotal" box on the form that shows the subtotal dollar amounts for the preceding 41 forms and for the last group of forms, even if less than 41 forms. Void statements are counted in order with good statements, **but do not include the money amounts from the void statements in the subtotal figures.** Subtotal statements should always be the last completed form on a page. The subtotal amounts to be shown are:

Boxes 7, 8, 9, 10, 11, 12, 13, 14, 15, 16, 17, and 22. However, in Box 17, subtotal only codes D, E, F, G, and H as one amount. See Box 17 instructions. Also, for Box 16, show one subtotal amount; that is, do not separate distributions from nonqualified plans (uncoded) and distributions from section 457 plans.

Example: *An employer with Forms W-2 for 86 employees should show a subtotal on the 42nd statement, the 84th statement (showing the subtotal for statements 43 through 83), and the 89th statement (showing the subtotal for statements 85 through 88).*

Deferred compensation.—Check this box if you made contributions on behalf of the employee to a section 401(k), 403(b), 408(k)(6), 457, or 501(c)(18)(D) retirement plan. See also instruction "(d)" under Box 17.

Void.—Put an X in this box when an error has been made. **(Be sure the amounts shown on void forms are NOT included in your subtotals.)**

Box 7—Allocated tips.—If you are a large food or beverage establishment, show the amount of tips allocated to the employee. (See the instructions for **Form 8027,** Employer's Annual Information Return of Tip Income and Allocated Tips.) **DO NOT** include this amount in Box 10 (Wages, tips, other compensation), Box 13 (Social security tips), or Box 14 (Medicare wages and tips).

Box 8—Advance EIC payment.—Show the total amount paid to the employee as advance earned income credit payments.

Box 10—Wages, tips, other compensation.—Show in Box 10 (excluding elective deferrals), before any payroll deductions, the following items:

(1) Total wages paid during the year. For example, if the employee worked from December 24, 1990, through January 4, 1991, and the wages for that period were paid on January 7, 1991, include those wages on the 1991 Form W-2;

(2) Total noncash payments (including fringe benefits);

(3) Total tips reported;

(4) Certain employee business expense reimbursements (See *Employee Business Expense Reimbursements* on page 1.); and

(5) All other compensation, including certain scholarships and fellowship grants and payments for moving expenses. Other compensation is amounts that you pay your employee from which Federal income tax is not withheld. If you prefer, you may show other compensation on a separate Form W-2.

Except for section 501(c)(18) contributions, contributions made to deferred compensation arrangements should not be included in Box 10. Also see instructions for Box 17, item "(d)."

Note: *Payments to statutory employees that are subject to social security and Medicare taxes but not subject to Federal income tax withholding must be shown in Box 10 as other compensation. (See Circular E for definition of a statutory employee.)*

Box 11—Employee social security tax withheld.—Show the total employee social security tax (not your share) withheld or paid by you for the employee. The amount shown should not exceed $3,310.80. Include only taxes withheld for 1991 wages.

Box 12—Social security wages.— Show the total wages paid (before payroll deductions) subject to employee social security tax but **NOT** including social security tips and allocated tips. Generally, noncash payments are considered wages. Include employee business expenses reported in Box 10. Also, include contributions to certain qualified cash or deferred compensation arrangements, even though the contributions are not includible in Box 10 as wages, tips, and other compensation. (See Circular E for more information.) Include any employee social security tax, Medicare tax, and employee state unemployment compensation tax you paid for your employee rather than deducting it from wages except for household or agricultural employees. (See Revenue Procedure 81-48, 1981-2 C.B. 623, for details.) **The total of Boxes 12 and 13 should not be more than $53,400** (the maximum social security wage base for 1991).

Box 13—Social security tips.—Show the amount the employee reported even if you did not have enough employee funds to collect the social security tax for the tips. The total of Boxes 12 and 13 should not be more than $53,400 (the maximum social security wage base for 1991). But report all tips in Box 10 along with wages and other compensation.

Box 14—Medicare wages and tips.—The wages and tips subject to Medicare tax are the same as those subject to social security tax (Boxes 12 and 13), except that the wage base for Medicare is $125,000. Enter the Medicare wages and tips in Box 14, but do not enter more than $125,000. Be sure to enter tips the employee reported even if you did not have enough employee funds to collect the Medicare tax for those tips.

If you are a Federal, state, or local agency with employees paying only the 1.45% Medicare tax, enter the Medicare wages in this box. File one Form W-3 for wages subject only to the Medicare tax, and a second Form W-3 for wages subject to both social security and Medicare taxes.

The following is an example of how to report social security and Medicare wages in Boxes 12 and 14. Assume you paid your employee $100,000 in wages. The amount shown in Box 12 (social security wages) should be 53400, but the amount shown in Box 14 (Medicare wages and tips) should be 100000. If the amount of wages paid was less than $53,400, the amounts entered in Boxes 12 and 14 would be the same.

Box 15—Medicare tax withheld.—Enter the total employee Medicare tax (not your share) withheld or paid by you for your employee. The amount shown should not exceed $1,812.50. Include only taxes withheld for 1991 wages. If you are a Federal, state, or local agency, with employees paying only the 1.45% Medicare tax, enter the Medicare tax in this box.

Box 16—Nonqualified plans.—Show the total amount of distributions to your employee from a nonqualified plan or a section 457 plan. This amount should be included as wages in Box 10.

State and local agencies should separately identify section 457 distributions in this box by using code "G" before the dollar amount. However, if you are reporting a distribution from both a nonqualified plan and a section 457 plan, report it as a single amount in this box and do not identify it by code "G."

Box 17—Complete and code this box for all items described in (a) through (i) below that apply. Do not report in Box 17 any items that are not listed in (a) through (i). Instead, use Box 18 for these items or for any other information you wish to give your employee. For example, union dues, moving expenses, etc., should be reported in Box 18. Also, any retirement plan contributions that are not listed in item (d) below should be reported in Box 18 (for example, section 414(h)(2) contributions).

Use the codes listed below along with the dollar amount. The code should be entered using capital letters. Leave one space blank after the code and enter the dollar amount on the same line. Use decimal points but do not use dollar signs or commas. For example, you are reporting $5,300.00 of contributions to a section 401(k) plan. The entry in Box 17 would be: D 5300.00.

(a) You did **not** collect employee social security tax on all the employee's tips. Show the amount of tax that you could not collect because the employee did not have enough funds from which to deduct it. Do not include this amount in Box 11. Use **code A** for uncollected social security tax on tips.

(b) You did **not** collect employee Medicare tax on tips because the employee did not have enough funds from which to deduct it. Enter the uncollected Medicare tax on tips. Do not include this amount in Box 15. Use **code B** for uncollected Medicare tax on tips.

(c) You provided your employee more than $50,000 of group-term life insurance. Show the cost of coverage over $50,000. Also include it in Boxes 10, 12, and 14. Use **code C** for cost of group-term life insurance coverage over $50,000.

(d) Employee contributions were made to a section 401(k) cash or deferred arrangement, to a section 403(b) salary reduction agreement to purchase an annuity contract, to a section 408(k)(6) salary reduction SEP, to a section 457 deferred compensation plan for state or local government employees, or to a section 501(c)(18)(D) tax-exempt organization plan. Check the "Deferred compensation" checkbox in Box 6, enter the total elective deferral (including any excess) in Box 17 Use the following codes for contributions made to the plans listed below.

    D—section 401(k)
    E—section 403(b)
    F—section 408(k)(6)
    G—section 457
    H—section 501(c)(18)(D)

Note: *The section 457 dollar limitation should be reduced by contributions made to certain other deferred compensation plans. See section 457(c)(2).*

(e) You made excess "golden parachute" payments to certain key corporate employees. Report in Box 17 the 20% excise tax on these payments. Use **code K** for the tax on excess golden parachute payments. If the excess payments are considered as wages, also report the 20% excise tax as income tax withholding and include it in Box 9.

(f) You reimbursed your employee for employee business expenses using a per diem or mileage allowance, and the amount you reimbursed exceeds the amount treated as substantiated under IRS rules. (See *Employee Business Expense Reimbursements* on page 1.) Report the amount treated as substantiated, *i.e.,* the nontaxable portion, in Box 17 using **code L.** In Box 10, show the portion of the reimbursement that is more than the amount treated as substantiated.

Do **NOT** include any per diem or mileage allowance reimbursements for employee business expenses in Box 17 if the total reimbursement is less than or equal to the amount treated as substantiated.

(g) You provided your former employees (including retirees) more than $50,000 of group-term life insurance coverage. Enter the amount of uncollected social security tax on the coverage in Box 17. Use **code M** for uncollected social security tax.

(h) You provided your former employees (including retirees) more than $50,000 of group-term life insurance coverage. Enter the amount of uncollected Medicare tax on the coverage in Box 17. Use **code N** for uncollected Medicare tax.

(i) You are reporting sick pay. Show the amount of any sick pay **NOT** includible in income because the employee contributed to the sick pay plan. If you issue a separate Form W-2 for sick pay, use Box 17 to code the Form W-2 as "Sick pay." Use **code J** for sick pay **NOT** includible as income.

Do **NOT** enter more than three codes in this box. If more than three items need to be reported in Box 17, use a separate Form W-2 or a substitute Form W-2 to report the

Page 3

additional items. If you issue multiple Forms W-2, do **NOT** report the same Federal tax data to the SSA on more than one Copy A. If you use a substitute Form W-2, the form must meet the requirements of Pub. 1141.

Box 18—Other.—You may use this box for any other information you want to give your employee. Please label each item. Examples are union dues, health insurance premiums deducted, moving expenses paid, or educational assistance payments.

Box 19a—Employee's name.—Enter the name as shown on the employee's social security card (first, middle initial, last). If the name has changed, have the employee get a corrected card from any SSA office. Use the name on the original card until you see the corrected one.

Box 19b—Employee's address and ZIP code.—This box has been combined with Box 19a (employee's name) on all copies except Copy A to allow employees' copies to be mailed in a window envelope or as a self-mailer.

Box 22—Dependent care benefits.—Show the total amount of dependent care benefits under section 129 paid or incurred by you for your employee including any amount in excess of the $5,000 exclusion. Also, include in Box 10 on Form W-2 any amount in excess of the $5,000 exclusion. For more information on the amount to report, see Notice 89-111, 1989-2 C.B. 449.

Box 23—Benefits included in Box 10.—Show the total value of the taxable fringe benefits included in Box 10 as other compensation. If you provided a vehicle and included 100% of its annual lease value in the employee's income, you must separately report this value to the employee in Box 23 or on a separate statement so the employee can compute the value of any business use of the vehicle.

Boxes 24 through 29—State or local income tax information.—You may use these to report state or local income tax information. You do not have to use them. But you may want to show the amounts on Copy A if you use copies of this form for your state or local tax returns or as recipients' statements. The state and local information boxes can be used to report wages and taxes on two states and two localities. Keep each state's and locality's information separated by the broken line.

Reducing Discrepancies Between Reports Filed with IRS and SSA

When there are discrepancies between reports filed with IRS and those filed with SSA, we must contact you to resolve the discrepancies. This costs time and money, both for the government and for you, the employer. To help reduce the number of these discrepancies, please:

(1) Reconcile the social security wages, social security tips, Medicare wages and tips, total compensation, advance earned income credit, income tax withheld, social security and Medicare taxes, on the four quarterly Forms 941 to your Form W-3. The amounts may not match for various reasons. If they do not match, you should determine that the reason is a valid one (such as some income tax withheld was reported on Form 1099, or adjustments were made on Form 941c). Please retain your reconciliation. This way, if there are inquiries in the future, you will know why the amounts did not match.

(2) Use Form W-2 for the current year.

(3) File all Forms W-2 with SSA.

(4) Report bonuses as social security and Medicare wages.

(5) Show social security taxes in the box for social security taxes withheld, not as social security wages.

(6) Make sure social security wage amounts for each employee do not exceed the annual social security wage base.

(7) Make sure Medicare wage amounts for each employee do not exceed the annual Medicare wage base.

(8) Do not include noncash wages not subject to social security or Medicare taxes as social security or Medicare wages.

1 Control number	22222	For Official Use Only ▶ OMB No. 1545-0008							

2 Employer's name, address, and ZIP code

6 Statutory employee ☐	Deceased ☐	Pension plan ☐	Legal rep. ☐	942 emp. ☐	Subtotal ☐	Deferred compensation ☐	Void ☐

7 Allocated tips	**8** Advance EIC payment
9 Federal income tax withheld	**10** Wages, tips, other compensation

3 Employer's identification number	**4** Employer's state I.D. number	**11** Social security tax withheld	**12** Social security wages
5 Employee's social security number		**13** Social security tips	**14** Medicare wages and tips
19a Employee's name (first, middle, last)		**15** Medicare tax withheld	**16** Nonqualified plans
		17 See Instrs. for Form W-2	**18** Other

19b Employee's address and ZIP code

20	**21**	**22** Dependent care benefits	**23** Benefits included in Box 10
24 State income tax	**25** State wages, tips, etc.	**26** Name of state	**27** Local income tax	**28** Local wages, tips, etc.	**29** Name of locality

Copy A For Social Security Administration   Department of the Treasury—Internal Revenue Service

Form **W-2 Wage and Tax Statement 1991**

For Paperwork Reduction Act Notice, see separate Instructions.

Do NOT Cut or Separate Forms on This Page

---

1 Control number	22222	For Official Use Only ▶ OMB No. 1545-0008							

2 Employer's name, address, and ZIP code

6 Statutory employee ☐	Deceased ☐	Pension plan ☐	Legal rep. ☐	942 emp. ☐	Subtotal ☐	Deferred compensation ☐	Void ☐

7 Allocated tips	**8** Advance EIC payment
9 Federal income tax withheld	**10** Wages, tips, other compensation

3 Employer's identification number	**4** Employer's state I.D. number	**11** Social security tax withheld	**12** Social security wages
5 Employee's social security number		**13** Social security tips	**14** Medicare wages and tips
19a Employee's name (first, middle, last)		**15** Medicare tax withheld	**16** Nonqualified plans
		17 See Instrs. for Form W-2	**18** Other

19b Employee's address and ZIP code

20	**21**	**22** Dependent care benefits	**23** Benefits included in Box 10
24 State income tax	**25** State wages, tips, etc.	**26** Name of state	**27** Local income tax	**28** Local wages, tips, etc.	**29** Name of locality

Copy A For Social Security Administration   Department of the Treasury—Internal Revenue Service

Form **W-2 Wage and Tax Statement 1991**

For Paperwork Reduction Act Notice, see separate Instructions.

Notice to Employee:

Getting a Refund.—Even if you do not have to file a tax return, you should file to get a refund if Box 9 shows Federal income tax withheld, or if you can take the earned income credit.

Earned Income Credit.—You must file a tax return if any amount is shown in Box 8.

For 1991, if your income is less than $21,245 and you have one qualifying child, you may qualify for an earned income credit (EIC) up to $1,192. If your income is less than $21,245 and you have two or more qualifying children, you may qualify for an earned income credit up to $1,235. Any EIC that is more than your tax liability is refunded to you, but ONLY if you file a tax return. For example, if you have no tax liability and qualify for a $300 EIC, you can get $300, but only if you file a tax return. The 1991 instructions for Forms 1040 and 1040A, and Pub. 596, explain the EIC in more detail. You can get the instructions and the publication by calling toll-free 1-800-829-3676.

Making Corrections.—If your name, social security number, or address is incorrect, correct Copies B, C, and 2. Ask your employer to correct your employment record. If your name and number are correct but are not the same as shown on your social security card, you should ask for a new card at any Social Security office.

If any of the dollar amounts are incorrect, ask your employer for a **Form W-2c**, Statement of Corrected Income and Tax Amounts. If you already filed a return and the information from this Form W-2 was not included, amend your income tax return by filing Form 1040X.

Credit for Excess Social Security Tax.—If more than one employer paid you wages during 1991 and more than the maximum

social security employee tax, Medicare tax, railroad retirement (RRTA) tax, or combined social security, Medicare, and RRTA tax was withheld, you may claim the excess as a credit against your Federal income tax. See your income tax return instructions.

Box 6.—If the "Pension plan" box is marked, special limits may apply to the amount of IRA contributions you may deduct on your return. If the "Deferred compensation" box is marked, the elective deferrals shown in Box 17 (for all employers, and for all such plans to which you belong) are generally limited to $7,979 ($9,500 for certain section 403(b) contracts and $7,500 for section 457 plans). Amounts over that must be included in income.

Caution: *The elective deferral dollar limitation of $7,979 is subject to change for 1991.*

Box 7.—For information on how to report tips on your tax return, see the instructions for Form 1040, 1040A, or 1040EZ. The amount of allocated tips is **not** included in Box 10.

Box 16.—Any amount in Box 16 is a distribution made to you from a nonqualified deferred compensation plan. This amount is also included in Box 10 and is taxable for Federal income tax purposes.

Box 17.—If there is an amount in Box 17, there should be a code (letter) next to it. You can find out what the code means from the list below. You may need this information to complete your tax return. The codes are:

A—Uncollected social security tax on tips (See your Form 1040 instructions for how to pay this tax.)

B—Uncollected Medicare tax on tips (See your Form 1040 instructions for how to pay this tax.)
C—Cost of group-term life insurance coverage over $50,000
D—Section 401(k) contributions
E—Section 403(b) contributions
F—Section 408(k)(6) contributions
G—Section 457 contributions
H—Section 501(c)(18)(D) contributions
J—Sick pay not includible as income
K—Tax on excess golden parachute payments
L—Nontaxable part of employee business expense reimbursements
M—Uncollected social security tax on cost of group-term life insurance coverage over $50,000 (former employees only) (See your Form 1040 instructions for how to pay this tax.)
N—Uncollected Medicare tax on cost of group-term life insurance coverage over $50,000 (former employees only) (See your Form 1040 instructions for how to pay this tax.)

Box 22.—The amount in this box is the total amount of dependent care benefits your employer paid to you (or incurred on your behalf). Any amount over $5,000 has been included in Box 10. Also, if you are claiming the credit for child and dependent care expenses, you must use this amount to determine the amount of credit you are able to claim. See the instructions for Form 1040 and 1040A.

Box 23.—This amount has already been included as wages in Box 10. Do not add this amount to Box 10. If there is an amount in Box 23, you may be able to deduct expenses that are related to fringe benefits; see the instructions for your income tax return.

Notice to Employee:

Getting a Refund.—Even if you do not have to file a tax return, you should file to get a refund if Box 9 shows Federal income tax withheld, or if you can take the earned income credit.

Earned Income Credit.—You must file a tax return if any amount is shown in Box 8.

For 1991, if your income is less than $21,245 and you have one qualifying child, you may qualify for an earned income credit (EIC) up to $1,192. If your income is less than $21,245 and you have two or more qualifying children, you may qualify for an earned income credit up to $1,235. Any EIC that is more than your tax liability is refunded to you, but ONLY if you file a tax return. For example, if you have no tax liability and qualify for a $300 EIC, you can get $300, but only if you file a tax return. The 1991 instructions for Forms 1040 and 1040A, and Pub. 596, explain the EIC in more detail. You can get the instructions and the publication by calling toll-free 1-800-829-3676.

Making Corrections.—If your name, social security number, or address is incorrect, correct Copies B, C, and 2. Ask your employer to correct your employment record. If your name and number are correct but are not the same as shown on your social security card, you should ask for a new card at any Social Security office.

If any of the dollar amounts are incorrect, ask your employer for a **Form W-2c**, Statement of Corrected Income and Tax Amounts. If you already filed a return and the information from this Form W-2 was not included, amend your income tax return by filing Form 1040X.

Credit for Excess Social Security Tax.—If more than one employer paid you wages during 1991 and more than the maximum

social security employee tax, Medicare tax, railroad retirement (RRTA) tax, or combined social security, Medicare, and RRTA tax was withheld, you may claim the excess as a credit against your Federal income tax. See your income tax return instructions.

Box 6.—If the "Pension plan" box is marked, special limits may apply to the amount of IRA contributions you may deduct on your return. If the "Deferred compensation" box is marked, the elective deferrals shown in Box 17 (for all employers, and for all such plans to which you belong) are generally limited to $7,979 ($9,500 for certain section 403(b) contracts and $7,500 for section 457 plans). Amounts over that must be included in income.

Caution: *The elective deferral dollar limitation of $7,979 is subject to change for 1991.*

Box 7.—For information on how to report tips on your tax return, see the instructions for Form 1040, 1040A, or 1040EZ. The amount of allocated tips is **not** included in Box 10.

Box 16.—Any amount in Box 16 is a distribution made to you from a nonqualified deferred compensation plan. This amount is also included in Box 10 and is taxable for Federal income tax purposes.

Box 17.—If there is an amount in Box 17, there should be a code (letter) next to it. You can find out what the code means from the list below. You may need this information to complete your tax return. The codes are:

A—Uncollected social security tax on tips (See your Form 1040 instructions for how to pay this tax.)

B—Uncollected Medicare tax on tips (See your Form 1040 instructions for how to pay this tax.)
C—Cost of group-term life insurance coverage over $50,000
D—Section 401(k) contributions
E—Section 403(b) contributions
F—Section 408(k)(6) contributions
G—Section 457 contributions
H—Section 501(c)(18)(D) contributions
J—Sick pay not includible as income
K—Tax on excess golden parachute payments
L—Nontaxable part of employee business expense reimbursements
M—Uncollected social security tax on cost of group-term life insurance coverage over $50,000 (former employees only) (See your Form 1040 instructions for how to pay this tax.)
N—Uncollected Medicare tax on cost of group-term life insurance coverage over $50,000 (former employees only) (See your Form 1040 instructions for how to pay this tax.)

Box 22.—The amount in this box is the total amount of dependent care benefits your employer paid to you (or incurred on your behalf). Any amount over $5,000 has been included in Box 10. Also, if you are claiming the credit for child and dependent care expenses, you must use this amount to determine the amount of credit you are able to claim. See the instructions for Form 1040 and 1040A.

Box 23.—This amount has already been included as wages in Box 10. Do not add this amount to Box 10. If there is an amount in Box 23, you may be able to deduct expenses that are related to fringe benefits; see the instructions for your income tax return.

9595 ☐ VOID   ☐ CORRECTED

Type or machine print PAYER'S name, street address, city, state, and ZIP code	1 Rents $	OMB No. 1545-0115	**Miscellaneous Income**
	2 Royalties $	**19**91	
	3 Prizes, awards, etc. $		

PAYER'S Federal identification number	RECIPIENT'S identification number	4 Federal income tax withheld $	5 Fishing boat proceeds $	**Copy A For Internal Revenue Service Center**
Type or machine print RECIPIENT'S name		6 Medical and health care payments $	7 Nonemployee compensation $	**File with Form 1096.**
		8 Substitute payments in lieu of dividends or interest $	9 Payer made direct sales of $5,000 or more of consumer products to a buyer (recipient) for resale ▶ ☐	For Paperwork Reduction Act Notice and instructions for completing this form, see Instructions for Forms 1099, 1098, 5498, and W-2G.
Street address (including apt. no.)				
City, state, and ZIP code		10 Crop insurance proceeds $	11 State income tax withheld $	
Account number (optional)	2nd TIN Not. ☐	12 State/Payer's state number		

Form **1099-MISC**   **Do NOT Cut or Separate Forms on This Page**   Department of the Treasury - Internal Revenue Service

---

9595 ☐ VOID   ☐ CORRECTED

Type or machine print PAYER'S name, street address, city, state, and ZIP code	1 Rents $	OMB No. 1545-0115	**Miscellaneous Income**
	2 Royalties $	**19**91	
	3 Prizes, awards, etc. $		

PAYER'S Federal identification number	RECIPIENT'S identification number	4 Federal income tax withheld $	5 Fishing boat proceeds $	**Copy A For Internal Revenue Service Center**
Type or machine print RECIPIENT'S name		6 Medical and health care payments $	7 Nonemployee compensation $	**File with Form 1096.**
		8 Substitute payments in lieu of dividends or interest $	9 Payer made direct sales of $5,000 or more of consumer products to a buyer (recipient) for resale ▶ ☐	For Paperwork Reduction Act Notice and instructions for completing this form, see Instructions for Forms 1099, 1098, 5498, and W-2G.
Street address (including apt. no.)				
City, state, and ZIP code		10 Crop insurance proceeds $	11 State income tax withheld $	
Account number (optional)	2nd TIN Not. ☐	12 State/Payer's state number		

Form **1099-MISC**   **Do NOT Cut or Separate Forms on This Page**   Department of the Treasury - Internal Revenue Service

---

9595 ☐ VOID   ☐ CORRECTED

Type or machine print PAYER'S name, street address, city, state, and ZIP code	1 Rents $	OMB No. 1545-0115	**Miscellaneous Income**
	2 Royalties $	**19**91	
	3 Prizes, awards, etc. $		

PAYER'S Federal identification number	RECIPIENT'S identification number	4 Federal income tax withheld $	5 Fishing boat proceeds $	**Copy A For Internal Revenue Service Center**
Type or machine print RECIPIENT'S name		6 Medical and health care payments $	7 Nonemployee compensation $	**File with Form 1096.**
		8 Substitute payments in lieu of dividends or interest $	9 Payer made direct sales of $5,000 or more of consumer products to a buyer (recipient) for resale ▶ ☐	For Paperwork Reduction Act Notice and instructions for completing this form, see Instructions for Forms 1099, 1098, 5498, and W-2G.
Street address (including apt. no.)				
City, state, and ZIP code		10 Crop insurance proceeds $	11 State income tax withheld $	
Account number (optional)	2nd TIN Not. ☐	12 State/Payer's state number		

Form **1099-MISC**   Department of the Treasury - Internal Revenue Service

Instructions for Recipient

If you are an individual, report the taxable amounts shown on this form on your tax return, as explained below. (Other taxpayers, such as fiduciaries or partnerships, report the amounts on the corresponding lines of your tax return.)

Boxes 1 and 2.—Report on Schedule E (Form 1040); or Schedule C (Form 1040) if you provided services that were primarily for your customer's convenience, such as regular cleaning, changing linen, or maid service. But for royalties on timber, coal, and iron ore, see **Pub. 544,** Sales and Other Dispositions of Assets.

Box 3.—Report on the line for "Other income" on Form 1040 and identify the payment. If it is trade or business income, report this amount on Schedule C or F (Form 1040).

Box 4.—Shows backup withholding. For example, persons not furnishing their taxpayer identification number to the payer become subject to backup withholding at a 20% rate on certain payments. See **Form W-9,** Request for Taxpayer Identification Number and Certification, for information on backup withholding. **Include this on your income tax return as tax withheld.**

Box 5.—An amount in this box means the fishing boat operator considers you self-employed. Report this amount on Schedule C (Form 1040). See **Publication 595,** Tax Guide for Commercial Fishermen.

Box 6.—Report on Schedule C (Form 1040).

Box 7.—Generally, this amount is considered income from self-employment. Report it as part of your trade or business income on Schedule C or F (Form 1040). If you are not self-employed, amounts paid to you for services rendered are generally reported on Form 1040 on the line for "Wages, salaries, tips, etc."

If there are two amounts shown in this box, one may be labeled "EPP." This represents excess golden parachute payments. You must pay a 20% excise tax on this amount. See your Form 1040 instructions under "Other Taxes." The unlabeled amount is your total compensation.

Box 8.—Report as "Other income" on your tax return. The amount shown is substitute payments in lieu of dividends or tax-exempt interest received by your broker on your behalf after transfer of your securities for use in a short sale.

Box 9.—An entry in the checkbox means sales to you of consumer products on a buy-sell, deposit-commission, or any other basis for resale have amounted to $5,000 or more. The person filing this return does not have to show a dollar amount in this box. Any income from your sale of these products should generally be reported on Schedule C (Form 1040).

Box 10.—Report on the line for "Crop insurance proceeds" on Schedule F (Form 1040).

Certain amounts shown on this form may be subject to self-employment (social security) tax computed on **Schedule SE (Form 1040).** See **Publication 533,** Self-Employment Tax, for more information on amounts considered self-employment income. Since no income or social security taxes are withheld by the payer, you may have to make estimated tax payments if you are still receiving these payments. See **Form 1040-ES,** Estimated Tax for Individuals.

Instructions for Recipient

If you are an individual, report the taxable amounts shown on this form on your tax return, as explained below. (Other taxpayers, such as fiduciaries or partnerships, report the amounts on the corresponding lines of your tax return.)

Boxes 1 and 2.—Report on Schedule E (Form 1040); or Schedule C (Form 1040) if you provided services that were primarily for your customer's convenience, such as regular cleaning, changing linen, or maid service. But for royalties on timber, coal, and iron ore, see **Pub. 544,** Sales and Other Dispositions of Assets.

Box 3.—Report on the line for "Other income" on Form 1040 and identify the payment. If it is trade or business income, report this amount on Schedule C or F (Form 1040).

Box 4.—Shows backup withholding. For example, persons not furnishing their taxpayer identification number to the payer become subject to backup withholding at a 20% rate on certain payments. See **Form W-9,** Request for Taxpayer Identification Number and Certification, for information on backup withholding. **Include this on your income tax return as tax withheld.**

Box 5.—An amount in this box means the fishing boat operator considers you self-employed. Report this amount on Schedule C (Form 1040). See **Publication 595,** Tax Guide for Commercial Fishermen.

Box 6.—Report on Schedule C (Form 1040).

Box 7.—Generally, this amount is considered income from self-employment. Report it as part of your trade or business income on Schedule C or F (Form 1040). If you are not self-employed, amounts paid to you for services rendered are generally reported on Form 1040 on the line for "Wages, salaries, tips, etc."

If there are two amounts shown in this box, one may be labeled "EPP." This represents excess golden parachute payments. You must pay a 20% excise tax on this amount. See your Form 1040 instructions under "Other Taxes." The unlabeled amount is your total compensation.

Box 8.—Report as "Other income" on your tax return. The amount shown is substitute payments in lieu of dividends or tax-exempt interest received by your broker on your behalf after transfer of your securities for use in a short sale.

Box 9.—An entry in the checkbox means sales to you of consumer products on a buy-sell, deposit-commission, or any other basis for resale have amounted to $5,000 or more. The person filing this return does not have to show a dollar amount in this box. Any income from your sale of these products should generally be reported on Schedule C (Form 1040).

Box 10.—Report on the line for "Crop insurance proceeds" on Schedule F (Form 1040).

Certain amounts shown on this form may be subject to self-employment (social security) tax computed on **Schedule SE (Form 1040).** See **Publication 533,** Self-Employment Tax, for more information on amounts considered self-employment income. Since no income or social security taxes are withheld by the payer, you may have to make estimated tax payments if you are still receiving these payments. See **Form 1040-ES,** Estimated Tax for Individuals.

Instructions for Recipient

If you are an individual, report the taxable amounts shown on this form on your tax return, as explained below. (Other taxpayers, such as fiduciaries or partnerships, report the amounts on the corresponding lines of your tax return.)

Boxes 1 and 2.—Report on Schedule E (Form 1040); or Schedule C (Form 1040) if you provided services that were primarily for your customer's convenience, such as regular cleaning, changing linen, or maid service. But for royalties on timber, coal, and iron ore, see **Pub. 544,** Sales and Other Dispositions of Assets.

Box 3.—Report on the line for "Other income" on Form 1040 and identify the payment. If it is trade or business income, report this amount on Schedule C or F (Form 1040).

Box 4.—Shows backup withholding. For example, persons not furnishing their taxpayer identification number to the payer become subject to backup withholding at a 20% rate on certain payments. See **Form W-9,** Request for Taxpayer Identification Number and Certification, for information on backup withholding. **Include this on your income tax return as tax withheld.**

Box 5.—An amount in this box means the fishing boat operator considers you self-employed. Report this amount on Schedule C (Form 1040). See **Publication 595,** Tax Guide for Commercial Fishermen.

Box 6.—Report on Schedule C (Form 1040).

Box 7.—Generally, this amount is considered income from self-employment. Report it as part of your trade or business income on Schedule C or F (Form 1040). If you are not self-employed, amounts paid to you for services rendered are generally reported on Form 1040 on the line for "Wages, salaries, tips, etc."

If there are two amounts shown in this box, one may be labeled "EPP." This represents excess golden parachute payments. You must pay a 20% excise tax on this amount. See your Form 1040 instructions under "Other Taxes." The unlabeled amount is your total compensation.

Box 8.—Report as "Other income" on your tax return. The amount shown is substitute payments in lieu of dividends or tax-exempt interest received by your broker on your behalf after transfer of your securities for use in a short sale.

Box 9.—An entry in the checkbox means sales to you of consumer products on a buy-sell, deposit-commission, or any other basis for resale have amounted to $5,000 or more. The person filing this return does not have to show a dollar amount in this box. Any income from your sale of these products should generally be reported on Schedule C (Form 1040).

Box 10.—Report on the line for "Crop insurance proceeds" on Schedule F (Form 1040).

Certain amounts shown on this form may be subject to self-employment (social security) tax computed on **Schedule SE (Form 1040).** See **Publication 533,** Self-Employment Tax, for more information on amounts considered self-employment income. Since no income or social security taxes are withheld by the payer, you may have to make estimated tax payments if you are still receiving these payments. See **Form 1040-ES,** Estimated Tax for Individuals.

APPENDIX 3
OTHER INFORMATION

THE LISTINGS IN THIS SECTION

1. *Helpful IRS Publications*
   Key publications from the IRS that can help you to understand and comply with the tax regulations that will affect your S Corporation and its operation.

2. *State Bar Associations*
   Where to go within your state for information about local attorney services that are available to you.

3. *State Government Contacts*
   Whom to contact within state government for information concerning incorporation, business regulations, registration and certification, and tax regulations.

4. *State "S Corporation" Statutes*
   A listing of states that recognize federal S Corporation tax regulations for state taxation purposes. Includes statute references for ease of reference.

HELPFUL IRS PUBLICATIONS

The Internal Revenue Service makes available a number of publications covering specific areas of tax law. These publications can be quite helpful for both the shareholders of an S Corporation and the officers operating the business. Page 222 lists the addresses from which to order these publications.

1: Your Rights as a Taxpayer

15: Employer's Tax Guide

463: Travel, Entertainment, and Gift Expenses

505: Tax Withholding and Estimated Tax

509: Tax Calendars

510: Excise Taxes

533: Self-Employment Tax

534: Depreciation

535: Business Expenses

536: Net Operating Losses

537: Installment Sales

538: Accounting Periods and Methods

539: Employment Taxes

542: Tax Information on Corporations

544: Sales and Other Dispositions of Assets

545: Interest Expense

548: Deductions for Bad Debts

549: Condemnations and Business Casualties and Thefts

550: Investment Income & Expenses

551: Basis of Assets

556: Examination of Returns, Appeal Rights, and Claims for Refund

560: Retirement Plans for the Self-Employed

583: Taxpayers Starting a Business

587: Business Use of Your Home

589: Tax Information on S Corporations

590: Individual Retirement Arrangements (IRAs)

910: Guide to Free Tax Services

911: Tax Information for Direct Sellers

916: Information Returns

917: Business Use of a Car

925: Passive Activity and At-Risk Rules

937: Business Reporting

How to Get IRS Forms and Publications

You can order tax forms and publications from the IRS Forms Distribution Center for your state at the address below. Or, if you prefer, you can photocopy tax forms from reproducible copies kept at many participating public libraries. In addition, many of these libraries have reference sets of IRS publications which you can read or copy.

If you are located in:

Send to "Forms Distribution Center" for your state

Alaska, Arizona, California, Colorado, Hawaii, Idaho, Montana, Nevada, New Mexico, Oregon, Utah, Washington, Wyoming — Rancho Cordova, Ca. 95743-0001

Alabama, Arkansas, Illinois, Indiana, Iowa, Kansas, Kentucky, Louisiana, Michigan, Minnesota, Mississippi, Missouri, Nebraska, North Dakota, Ohio, Oklahoma, South Dakota, Tennessee, Texas, Wisconsin — P.O. Box 9903, Bloomington, IL 61799

Connecticut, Delaware, District of Columbia, Florida, Georgia, Maine, Maryland, Massachusetts, New Hampshire, New Jersey, New York, North Carolina, Pennsylvania, Rhode Island, South Carolina, Vermont, Virginia, West Virginia — P.O. Box 25866, Richmond, VA 23289

Foreign Addresses—Taxpayers with mailing addresses in foreign countries should send their requests for forms and publications to: Forms Distribution Center, P.O. Box 25866, Richmond, VA 23289; Forms Distribution Center, Rancho Cordova, Ca. 95743-0001, whichever is closer.

Puerto Rico—Forms Distribution Center, P.O. Box 25866, Richmond, VA 23289

Virgin Islands—V.I. Bureau of Internal Revenue, Lockharts Garden, No. 1A, Charlotte Amalie, St. Thomas, VI 00802

☆U.S. GOVERNMENT PRINTING OFFICE: 1990-265-628

STATE BAR ASSOCIATIONS

If you need to find an attorney with specific background for the legal aspects of incorporation, and you are unable to determine which attorneys listed in the Yellow Pages to contact, you may be able to receive advice from your state bar association. The following list was adapted from the *1991 Directory of Bar Associations*, and is published by permission of the Division for Bar Services of the American Bar Association (ABA), 541 North Fairbanks Court, 14th Floor, Chicago, IL 60611-3314; telephone (312) 988-5352. It should be noted that the ABA directory also contains listings of county and selected major-city bar associations and lawyer's clubs.

Alabama **State Bar**
PO Box 671, Montgomery, AL 36101
Telephone: (205) 269-1515

Alaska **Bar Association**
PO Box 100279, Anchorage, AK 99510
Telephone: (907) 272-7469

State Bar of *Arizona*
363 North First Avenue, Phoenix, AZ 85003
Telephone: (602) 252-4804

State Bar of *California*
555 Franklin Street, San Francisco, CA 94102
Telephone: (415) 561-8200

The *Colorado* Bar Association
1900 Grant Street, #950, Denver, CO
  80203
Telephone: (303) 860–1115

***Connecticut* Bar Association**
101 Corporate Place, Rocky Hill, CT
  06067
Telephone: (203) 721–0025

***Delaware* State Bar Association**
PO Box 1709, Wilmington, DE 19899
Telephone: (302) 658–5278

The *District of Columbia* Bar
1707 L Street NW, 6th Floor,
  Washington, DC 20036
Telephone: (202) 331–3883

The *Florida* Bar
650 Apalachee Parkway, Tallahassee,
  FL 32399-2300
Telephone: (904) 561–5600

State Bar of *Georgia*
800 The Hurt Building, 50 Hurt Plaza,
  Atlanta, GA 30303
Telephone: (404) 527–8700

***Hawaii* State Bar Association**
PO Box 26, Honolulu, HI 96810
Telephone: (808) 537–1868

***Idaho* State Bar**
PO Box 895, Boise, ID 83701
Telephone: (208) 342–8958

***Illinois* State Bar Association**
424 South Second Street, Springfield,
  IL 62701
Telephone: (217) 525–1760

***Indiana* State Bar Association**
230 East Ohio, 6th Floor, Indianapolis,
  IN 46204
Telephone: (317) 639–5465

***Iowa* State Bar Association**
1101 Fleming Building, Des Moines, IA
  50309
Telephone: (515) 243–3179

***Kansas* Bar Association**
PO Box 1037, Topeka, KS 66601
Telephone: (913) 234–5696

***Kentucky* Bar Association**
West Main at Kentucky River,
  Frankfort, KY 40601
Telephone: (502) 564–3795

***Louisiana* State Bar Association**
601 St. Charles Avenue,
  New Orleans, LA 70130
Telephone: (504) 566–1600

***Maine* State Bar Association**
PO Box 788, Augusta, ME 04332-0788
Telephone: (207) 622–7523

***Maryland* State Bar Association**
520 West Fayette Street, Baltimore, MD
  21201
Telephone: (301) 685–7878

***Massachusetts* Bar Association**
20 West Street, Boston, MA 02111
Telephone: (617) 542-3602

State Bar of *Michigan*
306 Townsend Street, Lansing, MI
  48933-2083
Telephone: (517) 372–9030

***Minnesota* State Bar Association**
430 Marquette Avenue, Suite 403,
  Minneapolis, MN 55401
Telephone: (612) 333–1183

***Mississippi* State Bar**
PO Box 2168, Jackson, MS 39225-2168
Telephone: (601) 948–4471

The *Missouri* Bar
PO Box 119, Jefferson City, MO 65102
Telephone: (314) 635–4128

State Bar of *Montana*
PO Box 577, Helena, MT 59624
Telephone: (406) 442–7660

***Nebraska* State Bar Association**
PO Box 81809, Lincoln, NE 68501
Telephone: (402) 475–7091

State Bar of _Nevada_
500 South Third Street, Suite 2, Las
Vegas, NV 89101
Telephone: (702) 382–0502

New Hampshire Bar Association
112 Pleasant Street, Concord, NH
03301
Telephone: (603) 224–6942

New Jersey State Bar Association
New Jersey Law Center
One Constitution Square, New
Brunswick, NJ 08901-1500
Telephone: (908) 249–5000

State Bar of _New Mexico_
PO Box 25883, Albuquerque, NM
87125
Telephone: (505) 842–6132

New York State Bar Association
One Elk Street, Albany, NY 12207
Telephone: (518) 463–3200

North Carolina State Bar
PO Box 25908, Raleigh, NC 27611
Telephone: (919) 828–4620

State Bar Association of _North Dakota_
515-1/2 East Broadway, Suite 101,
Bismark, ND 58502
Telephone: (701) 255–1404

Ohio State Bar Association
33 West Eleventh Avenue, Columbus,
OH 43201
Telephone: (614) 421–2121

Oklahoma Bar Association
PO Box 53036, Oklahoma City, OK
73152
Telephone: (405) 524–2365

Oregon State Bar
PO Box 1689, Lake Oswego, OR 97035
Telephone: (503) 620–0222

Pennsylvania Bar Association
PO Box 186, Harrisburg, PA 17108
Telephone: (717) 238–6715

Puerto Rico Bar Association
PO Box 1900, San Juan, PR 00903
Telephone: (809) 721–3358

Rhode Island Bar Association
115 Cedar Street, Providence, RI 02903
Telephone: (401) 421–5740

South Carolina Bar
950 Taylor Street, Columbia, SC 29202
Telephone: (803) 799–6653

State Bar of _South Dakota_
222 East Capitol, Pierre, SD 57501
Telephone: (605) 224–7554

Tennessee Bar Association
3622 West End Avenue, Nashville, TN
37205
Telephone: (615) 383–7421

State Bar of _Texas_
PO Box 12487, Austin, TX 78711
Telephone: (512) 463–1463

Utah State Bar
645 South 200 East, Salt Lake City, UT
84111
Telephone: (801) 531–9077

Vermont Bar Association
PO Box 100, Montpelier, VT 05601
Telephone: (802) 223–2020

Virginia State Bar
801 East Main Street, Suite 1000,
Richmond, VA 23219-2900
Telephone: (804) 786–2061

Virgin Islands Bar Association
PO Box 4108, Christiansted, VI 00822
Telephone: (809) 778–7497

Washington State Bar
  AssociationDepartment of
  Corporation
500 Westin Building, 2001 Sixth
  Avenue, Seattle, WA 98121-2599
Telephone: (206) 448–0441

West Virginia State Bar
State Capitol, Charleston, WV 25305
Telephone: (304) 348–2456

State Bar of *Wisconsin*
402 West Wilson, Madison, WI 53703
Telephone: (608) 257–3838

Wyoming State Bar
PO Box 109, Cheyenne, WY 82003-0109
Telephone: (307) 632–9061

DEPARTMENT OF CORPORATION
(BY STATE)

Alabama

Secretary of State
State Capitol, Montgomery, AL 36130
Telephone: (205) 242–7210

Alaska

State of Alaska
Department of Commerce and
  Economic Development
  Corporations
Juneau, AK 99811
Telephone: (907) 465–2500

Arizona

Arizona Corporation Commission
Incorporating Division
1200 West Washington, Room 102,
  Phoenix, AZ 85009
Telephone: (602) 542–3135

Arkansas

Secretary of State
State Capitol, Little Rock, AR 72201
Telephone: (501) 682–1010

California

Secretary of State
1230 J Street, Sacramento, CA 95814
Telephone: (916) 445–6371

Colorado

Secretary of State
1560 Broadway, Denver, CO 80202
Telephone: (303) 984–2200

Connecticut

Office of the Secretary of State, State of
  Connecticut
30 Trinity Street, Hartford, CT 06106
Telephone: (203) 566–2739

Delaware

Department of State, State of Delaware
Division of Incorporations
Townsend Building, PO Box 898,
  Dover, DE 19901
Telephone: (302) 739–4711

District of Columbia

Recorder of Deeds
Washington, DC 20001
Telephone: (202) 727–5374

Florida

Secretary of State
The Capitol, Tallahassee, FL 32399
Telephone: (904) 488–3680

Georgia

Secretary of State
Corporations Department
2 Martin Luther King Dr., West Tower,
  Room 315, Atlanta, GA 30334
Telephone: (404) 656–2817

Hawaii

Director of the Department of
  Commerce and Consumers Affairs
State Capitol, Honolulu, HI 96813
Telephone: (808) 586–2850

Idaho

Secretary of State, State of Idaho
State Capitol, Boise, ID 83720
Telephone: (208) 334–2300

Illinois

Secretary of State
213 State Capitol, Springfield, IL 62706
Telephone: (217) 782–2201

Indiana

Secretary of State
201 State House, Indiana, IN 46204
Telephone: (317) 232–6531

Iowa

Secretary of State
State House, Des Moines, IA 50319
Telephone: (515) 281–5864

Kansas

Secretary of State, State of Kansas
The State House, 2nd Floor, Topeka,
  KS 66612
Telephone: (913) 296–2236

Kentucky

Secretary of State
State Capitol, Frankfort, KY 40601
Telephone: (502) 564–3490

Louisiana

Secretary of State
PO Box 94125, Baton Rouge, LA 70804
Telephone: (504) 342–5710

Maine

Secretary of State
State House
Station 148, Augusta, ME 04333
Telephone: (207) 626–8400

Maryland

State Department of Assessments and
  Taxation
300 West Lexington Street, Baltimore,
  MD 21201
Telephone: (410) 333–4630

Massachusetts

Secretary of State
Corporations Division
1 Ashburton Place, 17th Floor, Boston,
  MA 02108
Telephone: (617) 727–7030

Michigan

State of Michigan
Department of Commerce
Corporation Division
PO Box 30054, Lansing, MI 48909
Telephone: (517) 373–1820

Minnesota

Secretary of State
180 State Office Building, St. Paul, MN
  55155
Telephone: (612) 296–2079

Mississippi

Secretary of State
401 Mississippi Street, Jackson, MS
  39201
Telephone: (601) 359–1350

Missouri

Secretary of State
210 State Capitol, PO Box 778,
　Jefferson City, MO 65102
Telephone: (314) 751–2379

Montana

Secretary of State
State Capitol, Helena, MT 59620
Telephone: (406) 444–2034

Nebraska

Secretary of State
State Capitol, Lincoln, NE 68509
Telephone: (402) 471–2554

Nevada

Secretary of State
Capitol Complex, Carson City, NV
　89710
Telephone: (702) 687–5203

New Hampshire

Department of Revenue
　Administration
Returns Processing Division
PO Box 637, Concord, NH 03301
Telephone: (603) 271–3244

New Jersey

Department of State, State of New
　Jersey
CN-300, Trenton, NJ 08625
Telephone: (609) 984–1900

New Mexico

State Corporation Commission
PERA Building, 4th Floor, Old Santa
　Fe Trail, Santa Fe, NM 87501
Telephone: (505) 827–4500

New York

Department of State, State of New
　York
162 Washington Avenue, Albany, NY
　12231
Telephone: (518) 474–4750

North Carolina

Secretary of State
300 N. Salisbury Street, Raleigh, NC
　27603
Telephone: (919) 733–4161

North Dakota

Secretary of State
State Capitol, 600 East Boulevard,
　Bismark, ND 58505
Telephone: (701) 224–2900

Ohio

Secretary of State
30 East Broad Street, 14th Floor,
　Columbus, OH 43266
Telephone: (614) 466–4981

Oklahoma

Secretary of State
101 State Capitol, Oklahoma City, OK
　73105
Telephone: (405) 521–3911

Oregon

State of Oregon
Corporation Division
Commerce Building, Salem, OR 97310
Telephone: (503) 378–4166

Pennsylvania

Department of State, Commonwealth
　of Pennsylvania
302 North Office Building, Harrisburg,
　PA 17120
Telephone: (717) 787–7630

Rhode Island

Secretary of State
State House, Providence, RI 02903
Telephone: (401) 277–2357

South Carolina

Secretary of State
PO Box 11350, Columbia, SC 29211
Telephone: (803) 734–2155

South Dakota

Secretary of State
State Capitol, 500 East Capitol, Pierre, SD 57501
Telephone: (605) 773–3537

Tennessee

Secretary of State
Corporations Division C1-101
Central Services Building, Nashville, TN 37219
Telephone: (615) 741–2286

Texas

Secretary of State
PO Box 12697, Austin, TX 78711
Telephone: (512) 463–5701

Utah

Secretary of State
203 State Capitol Building, Salt Lake City, UT 84114
Telephone: (801) 538–1040

Vermont

Secretary of State
26 Terrace Street, Montpelier, VT 05602
Telephone: (802) 828–2464

Virginia

Commonwealth of Virginia
State Corporation Commission
Richmond, VA 23209
Telephone: (804) 786–3672

Washington

Secretary of State
PO Box 9000, Olympia, WA 98504
Telephone: (206) 753–7121

West Virginia

Secretary of State
State Capitol, Charleston, WV 25305
Telephone: (304) 345–4000

Wisconsin

Secretary of State
30 West Mifflin Street, Madison, WI 53703
Telephone: (608) 266–8888

Wyoming

Secretary of State
State Capitol, Cheyenne, WY 82002
Telephone: (305) 777–7378

STATES WITH S CORPORATION STATUTES

The states listed below have laws relating to S Corporations, their formation and taxation. This list is *advisory* only, as every session of every state legislature results in new or changed laws. As recently as 1984, for example, California, Connecticut, Louisiana, Massachusetts, Michigan, and North Carolina had no laws relating to S Corporations.

Alabama

Definitions; exemption from tax imposed by §40-18-31; Ala. Code §40-14-90 through 40-14-103

Definitions; exemption from tax imposed by §40-18-31; Ala. Code §40-18-160

Determination of taxable income; Ala. Code §40-18-161

Determination of tax of shareholder; Ala. Code §40-18-162

Adjustments for services rendered or capital furnished by spouse, and so forth of shareholder or beneficiary; Ala. Code §40-18-163

Increase or decrease in basis of shareholder's stock; special rules; Ala. Code §40-18-164

Distribution of property generally; Ala. Code §40-18-165

"Accumulated adjustments account" defined; application generally; "S period" defined; applicability of subdivision (c)(1) of §40-18-165 to certain distributions; "affected shareholder" defined; Ala. Code §40-18-166

Applicability of Chapter 18, Title 40; corporation may be considered an individual; Ala. Code §40-18-167

"Carryforward" and "carryback" provisions; Ala. Code §40-18-168

Adjustments to earnings and profits; Ala. Code §40-18-169

Circumstances under which corporation treated as partnership; "two-percent shareholder" defined; Ala. Code §40-18-170

Determination of shareholder's pro rata share; Ala. Code §40-18-171

"Post-termination transition period" and "determination" defined; Ala. Code §40-18-172

Interpretation of Article generally; Ala. Code §40-18-173

Tax imposed on certain built-in gains; Ala. Code §40-18-174

Tax imposed when passive investment income of corporation having Subchapter C earnings and profits exceeds 25 percent of gross receipts; Ala. Code §40-18-175

Nonresident shareholder composite returns; Ala. Code §40-18-176

Alaska

S Corporation; Alaska Stat. §43.20.021

Arizona

Small business corporation; election as to taxable status; return; termination; Ariz. Rev. Stat. Ann. §43-1126

Arkansas

S Corporation; Ark. Stat. Ann. §84-2004.1

California

S Corporation shareholder income; Cal. Rev. & T. Code §17087.5 State, local, foreign income, war profits, excess profits taxes, limited partnership taxes, and S Corporation and shareholder taxes; Cal. Rev. & T. Code §17220

Election by partner or corporate shareholder to be treated as S Corporation; taxes paid to another state; determination of credit; Cal. Rev. & T. Code §18006

Imposition; inapplicability to corporation electing to be treated as S Corporation; Cal. Rev. & T. Code §23400

Determination in accordance with Internal Revenue Code; extensions of time for implementation of chapter; Cal. Rev. & T. Code §23800

Election by Corporation to be treated as "S Corporation;" conditions; nonresident shareholder; determination of tax on "C Corporation;" termination of "S Corporation;" Cal. Rev. & T. Code §23801

Inapplicability of provisions of Internal Revenue Code; tax treatment of S Corporations; Cal. Rev. & T. Code §23802

Credits allowed to reduce taxes; limitation; carry forward; minimum taxes; S Corporation credits; modifications; Cal. Rev. & T. Code §23803

Adjustments to basis of stock of shareholders; Cal. Rev. & T. Code §23804

Inapplicability of provisions of Internal Revenue Code on investment credit recapture; Cal. Rev. & T. Code §23806

Application of partnership rules for fringe benefit purposes; Cal. Rev. & T. Code §23807

Inapplicability of provisions of Internal Revenue Code on foreign income and transitional rules on enactment; Cal. Rev. & T. Code §23808

Modification of amount of tax imposed on certain built-in gains; Cal. Rev. & T. Code §23809

Election by "S Corporation" shareholders to apply provisions relating to group return; Cal. Rev. & T. Code §23810

Passive investment income; imposition of taxes; modifications; S Corporation; Cal. Rev. & T. Code §23811

Change in S Corporation or Personal Service Corporation accounting period necessitated by federal tax reform law; Cal. Rev. & T. Code §24633.5

Corporation electing to be treated as S Corporation; application to transfer overpayment of estimated taxes to shareholders' accounts; contents; Cal. Rev. & T. Code §26083

Colorado

Subchapter S Corporations; Colo. Rev. Stat. Ann. §39-22-302

Connecticut

Exemption for gains subject to tax as income of a Subchapter S Corporation; Ct. Gen. Stat. Ann. 224, 12-50g

Delaware

Imposition of tax on corporations; exemptions; Del. Code Ann. Title 30, §1902

Florida

S Corporation; Fla. Stat. Ann. §220.13(2)(i)

Georgia

S Corporation; Ga. Code Ann. §91A-3602(2)(8)(B)

Hawaii

Hawaii S Corporation income tax act; Hawaii Rev. Stat. Chap. 235

Title; definitions; federal conformity; construction; Hawaii Rev. Stat. §235-121

Taxation of an S Corporation and its shareholders; Hawaii Rev. Stat. §235-122

Modification and characterization of income; Hawaii Rev. Stat. §235-123

Basis and adjustments; Hawaii Rev. Stat. §235-124

Carryforwards and carrybacks; loss limitation; Hawaii Rev. Stat. §235-125

Part-year residence; Hawaii Rev. Stat. §235-126

Distributions; Hawaii Rev. Stat. §235-127

Returns; shareholder agreements; mandatory payments; Hawaii Rev. Stat. §235-128

Tax credits; Hawaii Rev. Stat. §235-129

LIFO recapture; Hawaii Rev. Stat. §235-130

S Corporation; Hawaii Rev. Stat. §239-94.5

Idaho

S Corporation; Id. Code §§63-3022(k), 63-3030(a)(3)

Illinois

S Corporation; Ill. Ann. Stat. Chap. 120, §2-205(c)

Allocation of Subchapter S Corporation income by Subchapter S Corporations and shareholders other than residents; Ill. Ann. Stat. Chap. 120; §3-308

Indiana

S Corporation; Ind. Code Ann. §6-3-2.28(b)

Subchapter S Corporations withholding tax from payments to nonresident shareholders; Ind. Code Ann. §6-3-4-13

Iowa

S Corporation; Ia. Code Ann. §422.36 (5)

Kansas

S Corporation; Kan. Stat. Ann. §79-32,139

Kentucky

S Corporation; Ky. Rev. Stat. §§141.010 (25), 141.040

Filing of returns by, and liability of, partnerships and S Corporations; Ky. Rev. Stat. §141.206

Louisiana

S Corporation; La. Stat. Ann. Title 47 §287.732

Maine

S Corporation; Me. Rev. Stat. Ann. Title 36 §§5102(6), 5102(8)

Partnership and S Corporation returns; Me. Rev. Stat. Ann. Title 36 §5241

Maryland

S Corporation; Md. Ann. Code Art. 81 §288(d)(9)

Massachusetts

Taxation of S Corporations; Mass. Gen. Law. Ann. Chap. 62

Taxation of shareholders of S Corporations; Mass. Gen. Law Ann. Chap. 62, §17A

S Corporations; net income measure; Mass. Gen. Law Ann. Chap. 63, §32D

Michigan

Deduction; S Corporation income, definitions; Mich. Comp. Laws Ann. §205.133a

Minnesota

S Corporation; Minn. Stat. Ann. §290-9725

Mississippi

S Corporation; Miss. Code Ann. §27-7-29(b)

Missouri

S Corporation; Mo. Rev. Stat. §143.471

Montana

S Corporation; Mont. Code Ann §§15-31-201 through 15-31-209

Nebraska

Small business corporations; shareholders; determination of income; credit; Tax Commissioner; powers; return; when required; Neb. Rev. Stat. §77-2734.01

New Mexico

S Corporation; N.M. Stat. Ann. §7-2A-2.M

New York

New York adjusted gross income of a resident individual; McKinney's Tax Law §612

New York itemized deduction of a resident individual; McKinney's Tax Law §615

Resident partners and shareholders of S Corporations; McKinney's Tax Law §617

New York minimum taxable income of resident individual; McKinney's Tax Law §622

New York Source income of a nonresident individual; McKinney's Tax Law §631

Nonresident partners and electing shareholders of S Corporations; McKinney's Tax Law §632

Requirements concerning returns, notices, records, and statements; McKinney's Tax Law §658

Election by shareholders of S Corporation; McKinney's Tax Law §660

Additions to tax and civil penalties; McKinney's Tax Law §685

North Carolina

Title; definitions; interpretation; G.S of N.C. §105-131

Taxation of an S Corporation and its shareholders; G.S of N.C. §105-131.1

Adjustment and characterization of income; G.S of N.C. §105-131.2

Basis and adjustments; G.S of N.C. §105-131.3

Carryforwards; carrybacks; loss limitation; G.S of N.C. §105-131.4

Part-year resident shareholder; G.S of N.C. §105-131.5

Distributions; G.S of N.C. §105-131.6

Returns; shareholder agreements; mandatory withholding; G.S of N.C. §105-131.7

Tax credits; G.S of N.C. §105-131.8

North Dakota

S Corporation; N.D. Cent. Code §57-38-01.4

Oklahoma

Subchapter S Corporations; Okla. Stat. Ann. Title 68 §2365

Oregon

"C Corporation" and "S Corporation" defined for this chapter and ORS chapters 316, 317, and 318; Ore. Rev. Stat. §314.730

Taxation of S Corporation; application of Internal Revenue Code; carryforwards and carrybacks; Ore. Rev. Stat. §314.732

Taxation of shareholder's income; computation; character of income, gain, loss, or deduction; Ore. Rev. Stat. §314.734

Treatment of distributions by S corporations; Ore. Rev. Stat. §314.736

Employee fringe benefits; foreign income; Ore. Rev. Stat. §314.738

Tax on built-in gains; Ore. Rev. Stat. §314.740

Tax on excess net passive income; Ore. Rev. Stat. §314.742

S Corporation or shareholder elections; Ore. Rev. Stat. §314.744

Application of Sections 1377 and 1379 of Internal Revenue Code; Ore. Rev. Stat. §314.746

Tax treatment of item determined at corporate level; Ore. Rev. Stat. §314.748

Recapture of LIFO benefits; Ore. Rev. Stat. §314.750

Shareholder or partner may join in filing nonresident return; Ore. Rev. Stat. §314.760

Pro rata share of S Corporation income of nonresident shareholder; Ore. Rev. Stat. §316.118

S Corporation; Ore. Rev. Stat. §317.281

Pennsylvania

S Corporation; Pa. Stat. Ann. Title 72 §7301

[S Corporation] Election by small corporation; Pa. Stat. Ann. Title 72 §7307

Manner of making election; Pa. Stat. Ann. Title 72 §7307.1

Effective years of election; Pa. Stat. Ann. Title 72 §7307.2

Revocation of election; Pa. Stat. Ann. Title 72 §7307.3

Termination by corporation ceasing to be a small corporation; Pa. Stat. Ann. Title 72 §7307.4

Revocation or termination year; Pa. Stat. Ann. Title 72 §7307.5

Election after revocation or termination; Pa. Stat. Ann. Title 72 §7307.6

Taxable year of a Pennsylvania S Corporation; Pa. Stat. Ann. Title 72 §7307.7

Income of a Pennsylvania S Corporation; Pa. Stat. Ann. Title 72 §7307.8

Income of Pennsylvania S Corporations taxed to shareholders; Pa. Stat. Ann. Title 72 §7307.9

Limitation on pass-through of losses to shareholders; Pa. Stat. Ann. Title 72 §7307.10

Adjustments to the basis of the stock of shareholders; Pa. Stat. Ann. Title 72 §7307.11

Distributions; Pa. Stat. Ann. Title 72 §7307.12

Return of Pennsylvania S Corporations; Pa. Stat. Ann. Title 72 §7330.1

Rhode Island

S Corporation; R.I. Gen. Laws §44-11-2(3)

Utah

S Corporation; Utah Code Ann. §59-13-4(17)

Vermont

S Corporation; Vt. Stat. Ann. Title 32 §5811(18)

Virginia

S Corporation; Va. Code §58.1-401(4)

West Virginia: Chapter 11

Resident shareholders of S Corporations; W.Va. Code §11-21-17a

Nonresident S Corporation shareholders; W.Va. Code §11-21-37a

Composite returns; W.Va. Code §11-21-51a

Meaning of terms; specific terms defined; W.Va. Code §11-23-3

S Corporation; W.Va. Code §11-24-5(e)

Information return for corporations electing to be taxed under Subchapter S; W.Va. Code §11-24-13b

Wisconsin

S Corporation; Wis. Stat. Ann. §§71.02(1)(f), 71.042

INDEX